THE NEW
JUVENILE
JUSTICE

THE NEW JUVENILE JUSTICE

Martin L. Forst

SONOMA STATE UNIVERSITY

Nelson-Hall Publishers
Chicago

Project Editor: Dorothy J. Anderson
Typesetter: Precision Typographers, Inc.
Printer: Capital City Press
Cover Painting: No. 6 in the series, *Beyond the Door* by Chris Rose

Library of Congress Cataloging-in-Publication Data

Forst, Martin Lyle.
   The new juvenile justice / Martin L. Forst.
      p.   cm.
   Includes index.
   ISBN 0-8304-1386-3
    1. Juvenile justice, Administration of—United States.
   2. Juvenile corrections—United States. I. Title.
HV9104.F655   1995
364.3′6′0973—dc20   94-25212
                               CIP

Manufactured in the United States of America

10 9 8 7 6 5 4 3 2 1

 TM The paper used in this book meets the
minimum requirements of American
National Standard for Information
Sciences—Permanence of Paper for
Printed Library Materials, ANSI
Z39.48-1984.

Contents

Section I

Introduction

Nothing in the U.S. Constitution guarantees a separate court or system of justice for juvenile offenders. Juvenile courts throughout the country were created by statute by the fifty state legislatures, many around the start of this century. Because the juvenile justice system was created by statute, it can be changed—or even abolished—by statute.

And that is just what has been happening throughout the United States. Juvenile justice policymakers have embarked on a precarious course. They have been changing in fundamental ways the system's philosophy, structure, and procedures. These changes, followed to their logical conclusions, have serious implications for the continued existence of a separate system for juvenile offenders.

A separate juvenile justice system was originally created for a multiplicity of complex, sometimes conflicting reasons. Some people felt the punishment of juveniles in the adult criminal justice system was too harsh. Others thought the legal formalities of the criminal justice system were inappropriate for juvenile offenders. And still others wanted to "save" children from a life of crime and degradation in a decaying society. These reformers are often called—somewhat pejoratively—the "child savers."

The traditional juvenile justice system was based on the longstanding legal concept of *parens patriae*, which is loosely translated as the responsibility of government to care for persons who are unable to care for

1

themselves or whose family members are unable to care for them. The original idea of juvenile justice was not to punish delinquent children but to help them. The purpose clauses of many statutes stated that the juvenile court was to do whatever was in the "best interests of the *child*."

The juvenile court attempted to "individualize" justice to help the child address his or her problems—whatever they might be. The court was supposed to act *in loco parentis*, that is, to take the place of the parents if the parents were not doing a proper job raising their children, as evidenced by delinquent activity.

The basic structure and procedures of the early juvenile court corresponded to its philosophical underpinnings. Under the traditional juvenile justice system, founded on the philosophy of rehabilitation and individualized justice, due process rights for juvenile offenders were not considered essential. Children involved in the juvenile justice system did not need procedural protections, it was assumed, because the state was attempting to help or treat them. A parent does not have to provide a lawyer to discipline his or her child and neither should the juvenile court, according to this logic.

Sentencing structure also followed the underlying philosophy. For most of this century, the indeterminate sentence has been the hallmark of the juvenile justice system. The juvenile court and juvenile correctional administrators (for example, parole board members) have been given wide latitude regarding the disposition of any particular case. The nature of the sanction imposed bore no particular relation to the crime at hand. After all, the philosophy of the juvenile court was *not* to "make the punishment fit the crime," because children were not supposed to be punished for their misbehavior. Rather, the disposition of a case—including length of stay in a juvenile training school—was to be based on the offender's individual needs and prospects for rehabilitation.

Within the past decade or two, however, an assault has been launched against the traditional juvenile justice system, with calls for change coming from diverse groups throughout the country. The traditional system has been challenged on several separate but related grounds.

The first criticism centers on the apparent inability of the juvenile justice system to fulfill its intended mission of rehabilitating juvenile offenders. Many reasons have been cited for the failure of the treatment approach. One argument holds simply that rehabilitation has never been given a fair chance to succeed. "Penny-pinching" legislatures have meant inadequate facilities, low staff salaries, and personnel shortages, with the result that youths have not been provided with the services and programs needed for rehabilitation to take place.

Other sources believe the informal procedures of the juvenile justice system, contrary to original expectation, have themselves constituted a further obstacle to the effective treatment of delinquents. This theory holds that informal procedures engender in the child a sense of injustice provoked by seemingly all-powerful judges and other juvenile justice officials.

Second, critics decry the abuses of the juvenile justice system. Many observers believe that injustices are perpetrated daily under the guise of "helping youth." For example, youths may spend inordinately long periods of time locked up in prisonlike institutions under the guise of treatment or rehabilitation. Some authorities stress the punitive nature of the juvenile justice system, notwithstanding the rehabilitative rhetoric. Locking people up and restricting their liberty is punitive, critics contend, no matter how benevolent the motivation.

Some sources contend that the juvenile justice system functions primarily as a form of social control. The argument goes that the "child savers" were actually trying to control an unruly underclass of youths to protect middle class interests. Based on historical analysis, some critics believe that the juvenile justice system should more aptly be called "the juvenile social control system."

Several studies have also shown the discriminatory aspects (both race and gender) of juvenile corrections. In either case—punishment or control—the ability to harm youths in the name of doing good has been a central theme in the literature. In the name of *parens patriae*, the American system of juvenile justice has denied youths the due process of law that is deemed necessary to protect adult defendants, and then incarcerated adjudicated delinquents in substandard institutions.

The third prong of the attack has been advanced by "law and order" advocates concerned about rising crime rates and particularly about violent crime committed by juveniles. Critics claim that juveniles are not held properly accountable for the crimes they commit and that chronic offenders and youths who commit crimes against the person are not incarcerated for long enough periods of time. Their rationale for changing the current juvenile justice policy is usually one of social protection. As some people point out, the victim of a fifteen-year-old rapist is just as raped as the victim of a thirty-five-year-old rapist. The need for social defense or protection is the same in either case.

These multifaceted, broad-based attacks have encouraged a reexamination of the structure and functioning of the traditional juvenile justice system. It is now much more clear that the juvenile justice system has conflicting goals, specifically for juvenile justice officials to do what is in the best interests of both the child *and* the society. Increasingly, critics have come to believe that these two interests can be incompatible. Some contend that the conflicting interests are most often resolved at the expense of the youth, while others claim that it is society that usually suffers. The fact that it is often impossible to satisfactorily balance these competing interests has become readily apparent. People are taking sides—for children or for society.

Based on these criticisms, several interrelated proposals for change in the field of juvenile justice have been advanced, and some trends are now discernible. First, there has been a growing interest in *procedural justice* for youths. Until the late 1960s, the courts held that most due process rights were not constitutionally required. Critics of that view, however, contended that the abuses in the juvenile justice system, mentioned above, have their roots in the inadequate procedural safeguards accorded alleged juvenile offenders. The courts have therefore provided greater procedural protections, a trend one authority has called a "legal renaissance" in juvenile justice. Now, many of the procedural protections accorded adults in the criminal justice system are also provided in the juvenile justice system.

Second, some authorities have advocated providing more *substantive justice* for children who come under juvenile court jurisdiction. The call for substantive justice was advanced originally by those who were concerned that, in the name of treatment, minor offenders were being incarcerated, often for extraordinarily long periods of time. These concerns intensified when compelling evidence showed that treatment either was not provided, for one reason or another, or failed to achieve the desired results. Ultimately, these critics sought the deinstitutionalization of minor offenders and the removal of status offenders from the jurisdiction of the juvenile court. These efforts were consistent with the notion that the sanction a youth receives in the juvenile justice system should be proportionate to the seriousness of his or her conduct.

Many authorities now also endorse a shift in the philosophy of juvenile justice from treatment and rehabilitation to punishment, justice, accountability, and public protection. Some argue that children have a right to be punished for the offenses they have committed as opposed to being treated for what others perceive to be wrong with them. This justice model, it is claimed, is more likely to prevent the disproportionately long periods of incarceration so frequently in evidence in the past. Punishment clearly implies limits whereas treatment does not. Under the new approach, a youth should not be incarcerated for longer than is justified by the nature of his or her delinquent conduct. The nature of the sanction should be in accordance with the harmfulness of the youth's behavior rather than based on his or her personal or social needs.

Some of the more recent conservative commentators, like the liberal critics before them, have suggested a wide variety of changes pertaining to the commitment and release of adjudicated delinquents. Some conservatives ally themselves with liberals to promote determinate sentencing for adjudicated delinquents, stressing harsher, fixed terms for serious or repeat offenders. If justice demands that minor offenders not be incarcerated for too long, then justice also demands that serious juvenile offenders not be let back into society too soon.

Various interest groups have continued to propose more restrictive policies for controlling and sanctioning juvenile crime. Many lobbying groups want to crack down on juvenile crime—and juvenile offenders—the way the criminal justice system has for adults. A variety of general strategies to get tough with juvenile offenders have been advanced. These include:

- changing the philosophy of juvenile justice away from the child and in favor of innocent victims and society in general;
- making the sanctions imposed by the juvenile justice system more punitive;
- removing serious offenders from the juvenile justice system through waiver or transfer for prosecution in criminal court; and
- making greater use of the death penalty for the most serious juvenile offenders.

The goal of these strategies is to make the juvenile justice system more like the criminal justice system. These approaches have resulted in "criminalizing" the juvenile justice system.

This book explores all of these areas in a unique way, combining a variety of sources that include:

- original state statutes, which indicate legislative intent;
- appellate court decisions, which indicate the reasoning of the judiciary;
- government documents, which show standards for juvenile justice and statistics; and
- articles on relevant topics by experts in the field.

Through an integration of all these materials, the student should be able to obtain a better appreciation for current trends in the juvenile justice system and engage in the debate about the future of juvenile justice.

SECTION II

THE TRADITIONAL MODEL OF JUVENILE JUSTICE

Introduction

Since the late nineteenth century, the juvenile justice system in this country has rested on a philosophy of rehabilitation and individualized justice. Under the rehabilitative or treatment model, the state's mission was to act in the best interests of the child, no matter why the youth was appearing before the juvenile court.

The juvenile justice system was the product of efforts by "progressive" reformers at the turn of the century to change the way children were treated by the legal system. Specifically, the social reformers, sometimes called child savers, envisioned a separate system of justice that assumed juveniles were different from adults and needed special protection and treatment, rather than being held responsible and punished for their actions. Underlying the reforms was the assumption that minors were not fully developed, either physically or mentally, and needed to complete their intellectual, social, and moral maturation before being expected to bear the responsibilities of adulthood. It was the state's responsibility—through the enactment of child labor laws, compulsory education, and the juvenile court—to ensure that juveniles completed this development. Furthermore, their socialization process was to be supervised by professional educators and, when necessary, by social workers and treatment experts.

By invoking the doctrine of *parens patriae*, juvenile court judges were given the authority to assume guardianship over youthful offenders. Rather than subjecting juveniles to the rigors of the criminal trial or the harsh conditions of prisons and jails used to house adult offenders, juvenile court judges were to act benevolently and protectively toward the minor.

Because youths, almost by definition, were impulsive yet malleable, progressive reformers asserted they were not completely responsible for their wrongful acts. They should not be liable in the way the criminal law holds adults liable, because they had not yet achieved the cognitive or moral maturity associated with adulthood. Moreover, the reformers believed that the causes of crime did not lie within the ill will of the individual—especially not within an individual whose moral beliefs were not fully formed. Rather, they believed that the causes of crime came from the broader social environment—the neighborhood, the family, and the specific child-rearing practices of parents. Delinquency was viewed as an illness brought on by the social diseases of poverty, parental neglect, ignorance, and urban decay.

The sentencing structure proposed for the newly created juvenile justice system was a logical extension of the underlying philosophy that delinquency was an illness that could be cured by providing individualized treatment to the unique problems each delinquent youth faced. To take account of variations in the causes and cures of delinquency, state juvenile codes gave juvenile justice personnel—judges, probation officers, training school officials, and parole boards—broad discretion in the control they could exercise over a juvenile offender. Minors could be wards of the court or the juvenile correctional system for an indeterminate period up to the age of majority, which was typically eighteen years. Whether under supervision of probation officers in the community or confined in a state-level institution, each youth's "progress" in receiving treatment and training would be carefully monitored to determine, on an individual basis, whether he or she was ready for release into the community or discharge from juvenile supervision. The focus was clearly on the offender rather than on the offense.

The four selections for this section describe this early juvenile justice system. To begin, Judge Julian W. Mack writes about the early period of the juvenile court. His article, published in the *Harvard Law Review* in 1909, shows the attitude of a practicing juvenile court judge at the turn of the century. This article was published ten years after the formation of the first juvenile court in Chicago, Illinois, in 1899. As Judge Mack states, "The past decade marks a revolution in the attitude of the state toward its offending children. . . ."

The revolution Judge Mack describes was in the way the state, and specifically the courts, would look at children who broke the law. No more was it a matter of punishing children for their wrongful behavior. Judge Macks asks:

> Why is it not just and proper to treat these juvenile offenders, as we deal with the neglected children, as a wise and merciful father handles his own child whose errors are not discovered by the authorities? Why is it not the duty of the state, instead of asking merely whether a boy or a girl has committed a specific offense, to find out what he is, physically, mentally, and then if it learns that he is treading the path that leads to criminality, to take him in charge, not so much to punish as to reform, not to degrade but to uplift, not to crush but to develop, not to make him a criminal but a worthy citizen.

These sentiments form the basis of the juvenile court's informal treatment-oriented approach. Judge Mack then reviews the legislation and the appellate court decisions regarding the new juvenile court movement.

The second selection is an early juvenile court statute enacted by the California legislature in 1915. This section to the juvenile court law specifies the jurisdiction of the California juvenile court at that time. This statute demonstrates the wide range of jurisdiction enjoyed by the early juvenile court. The court could assume wardship, for example, over youths for "begging, receiving or gathering alms." At the other end of the spectrum, the juvenile court could assume wardship over any youth "who violates any law of this state." This California statute, like most other states' statutes, in the country, was all encompassing. The juvenile court could act *in loco parentis*, assuming the role of the parent when the natural parents exhibited an inability to raise their child properly.

The case of *Childress v. State*, the third selection, is an example of how the appellate courts upheld the newly created juvenile court statutes. This case, decided by the Supreme Court of Tennessee in 1915, is but one of many examples of appellate courts upholding the philosophy and structure of the juvenile court.

In this decision, the Tennessee Supreme Court reaffirms the basic rehabilitative philosophy of the juvenile court.

> The [Juvenile] Court . . . does not undertake to punish the child for the crime committed, but undertakes to remove him from bad influences and to make such disposition of the child as to eradicate evil propensities by education, wholesome training and moral instruction.

This case also emphasizes that the juvenile court is not a criminal court, which means that the proceedings are deemed to be civil in nature. Thus, a juvenile found to be "delinquent" because he committed, for example, a robbery, is not to be considered a criminal.

Finally, F. R. Aumann describes the juvenile court movement in Ohio as of 1931. Aumann first reviews the historical origins of the juvenile court in general, and then outlines the early juvenile court of Ohio. The article points out the structure of the juvenile court, its basic provisions, and its shortcomings. Aumann ends the article with a note of optimism. That is, when policymakers learn of the great value of the juvenile court, it will grow and prosper as a judicial institution—comparable to the criminal courts.

1

The Juvenile Court

Julian W. Mack

The past decade marks a revolution in the attitude of the state toward its offending children, not only in nearly every American commonwealth, but also throughout Europe, Australia, and some of the other lands. The problem of the delinquent child, though juristically comparatively simple, is, in its social significance, of the greatest importance, for upon its wise solution depends the future of many of the rising generation. The legal questions, while not complicated, have, nevertheless, given rise to some discussion and to some slight dissent from the standpoint of constitutional law.

The first thought which suggests itself in connection with the juvenile court is, What is there distinctively new about it? We are familiar with the conception that the state is the higher or the ultimate parent of all of the dependents within its borders. We know that, whatever may have been the historical origin of the practice, for over two centuries, as evidenced by judgments both of the House of Lords and of the Chancellors, the courts of chancery in England have exercised jurisdiction for the protection of the unfortunate child.

The proposition that the court of chancery could not act unless the infant had property, was declared by North, J., in *Re* McGrath, to be wholly unsupported by either principle or authority. He added:

Source: *Harvard Law Review*, 23 (1909): 109–122.

In *In re* Spence, 2 Ph. 247, Lord Chancellor Cottenham said: "I have no doubt about the jurisdiction. The cases in which the court interferes on behalf of infants are not confined to those in which there is property. . . . This court interferes for the protection of infants, *qua* infants, by virtue of the prerogative which belongs to the crown as *parens patriae* and the exercise of which is delegated to the great seal.

In the early case of Cowles v. Cowles Caton, J., said:

The power of the court of chancery to interfere with and control not only the estates but the persons of all minors within the limits of its jurisdiction, is of very ancient origin and cannot now be questioned. This is a power which must necessarily exist somewhere in every well-regulated society, and more especially in a republican government. A jurisdiction thus extensive and liable, as we have seen, to enter into the domestic relations of every family in the community, is necessarily of a very delicate and even of a very embarrassing nature; and yet its exercise is indispensable in every well-governed society; it is indispensably necessary to protect the persons and preserve the property of those who are unable to protect and take care of themselves;

and shortly thereafter in the case of Miner v. Miner he enunciated the practically unanimous American doctrine that the parents' rights are always

subject to control by the court of chancery when the best interests of the child demand it.

Support was found for the contention that a property interest is essential to jurisdiction in the fact that, until comparatively recent times, the aid of the court in England was seldom sought, except when the child had an independent fortune; but, as was said by Lord Eldon, whose decree in the Wellesley case was affirmed by the House of Lords,

It is not from any want of jurisdiction that it does not act, but from a want of means to exercise its jurisdiction, because the court cannot take upon itself the maintenance of all the children in the kingdom. It can exercise this jurisdiction fully and practically only where it has the means of applying property for the maintenance of the infant.

This want has now been met both through the extension of the parental obligations and through public grants of money or institutions for the support, maintenance, and education of the children. The judges of the juvenile court, in exercising jurisdiction, have, in accordance with the most advanced philanthropic thought, recognized that the lack of proper home care can best be supplied by the true foster parent. Though the orphan asylums of the civilized world have ever been valuable and their recent improvement is marked, nevertheless, following the splendid lead of Massachusetts, greater effort is being put forth everywhere to solve the problem of the permanently dependent or neglected child by finding for it a foster home where it shall receive that individualized love and care that a true father gives to and would always desire for his own little ones.

While in most jurisdictions the juvenile-court laws make provision for the dependent as well as the neglected, the truant and the delinquent child, some of the best workers in this field have objected to a court's having anything to do with the strictly dependent child, the child whose parents must ask assistance, merely because of poverty or misfortune. If friends or the church fail to supply the necessary help, and the aid of the state is to be sought, it should be granted through poor law or relief commissioners. The court should be called upon to act only in the case of a persistent truant, or a victim of neglect or wrongdoing, either on the part of others or of itself. It is particularly in dealing with those children who have broken the law or who are leading the kind of life which will inevitably result in such breach, that the new and distinctive features of the juvenile-court legislation appear.

Our common criminal law did not differentiate between the adult and the minor who had reached the age of criminal responsibility, seven at common law and in some of our states, ten in others, with a chance of escape up to twelve, if lacking in mental and moral maturity. The majesty and dignity of the state demanded vindication for infractions from both alike. The fundamental thought in our criminal jurisprudence was not, and in most jurisdictions is not, reformation of the criminal, but punishment; punishment as expiation for the wrong, punishment as a warning to other possible wrongdoers. The child was arrested, put into prison, indicted by the grand jury, tried by a petit jury, under all the forms and technicalities of our criminal law, with the aim of ascertaining whether it had done the specific act—nothing else—and if it had, then of visiting the punishment of the state upon it.

It is true that during the last century ameliorating influences mitigated the severity of the old régime; in the last fifty years our reformatories have played a great and very beneficent part in dealing with juvenile offenders. They supplanted the penitentiary. In them the endeavor was made, while punishing, to reform, to build up, to educate the prisoner so that when his time should have expired he could go out into the world capable at least of making an honest living. And in course of time, in some jurisdictions, the youths were separated from the older offenders even in stations, jails, and workhouses; but, nevertheless, generally in this country, the two classes were huddled together. The result of it all was that instead of the state's training its bad boys so as to make them decent citizens, it permitted them to become the outlaws and outcasts of society; it criminalized them by the very methods that it used in dealing with them. It did not aim to find out what the accused's history was, what his heredity, his environments, his associations; it did not ask how he had come to do the particular act which had brought him before the court. It put but one question, "Has he committed this crime?" It did not inquire, "What is the best thing to do for this lad?" It did not even punish him in a manner that would tend to improve him; the punishment was visited in proportion to the degree of wrongdoing evidenced by the single act; not by the needs of the boy, not by the needs of the state.

To-day, however, the thinking public is putting another sort of question. Why is it not just and proper to treat these juvenile offenders, as we deal with the neglected children, as a wise and merciful father handles his own child whose errors are not discovered by the authorities? Why is it not the duty of the state, instead of asking merely whether a boy or a girl has committed a specific offense, to find out what he is, physically, mentally, morally, and then if it learns that he is treading the path that leads to criminality, to take him in charge, not so much to punish as to reform, not to degrade but to uplift, not to crush but to develop, not to make him a criminal but a worthy citizen.

And it is this thought—the thought that the child who has begun to go wrong, who is incorrigible, who has broken a law or an ordinance, is to be taken in hand by the state, not as an enemy but as a protector, as the ultimate guardian, because either the unwillingness or inability of the natural parents to guide it toward good citizenship has compelled the intervention of the public authorities; it is this principle, which, to some extent theretofore applied in Australia and a few American states, was first fully and clearly declared, in the Act under which the Juvenile Court of Cook County, Illinois, was opened in Chicago, on July 1, 1899, the Hon. R. S. Tuthill presiding. Colorado followed soon after, and since that time similar legislation has been adopted in over thirty American jurisdictions, as well as in Great Britain and Ireland, Canada, and the Australian colonies. In continental Europe and also in Asia, the American juvenile courts have been the object of most careful study, and either by parliamentary or administrative measures similar courts have been established, or at least some of their guiding principles have been enforced.

The Lord Advocate of Scotland, in the course of the debates last year on the Children's Bill, stated that

> There was a time in the history of this House when a Bill of this kind would have been treated as a most revolutionary measure, and half a century ago, if such a measure had been introduced it would have been said that the British constitution was being undermined.

That era has passed away forever.

Juvenile-court legislation has assumed two aspects. In Great Britain, in New York, and in a few other jurisdictions the protection is accomplished by suspending sentence and releasing the child under probation, or, in case of removal from the home, sending it to a school instead of to a jail or penitentiary. The criminal proceeding remains, however. The child is charged with the commission of a definite offense, of which it must be found either guilty or not guilty. If not guilty of the one certain act, it is discharged, however much it may need care or supervision. If guilty, it is then dealt with, but as a criminal. And this would seem to be true even under the New York statute of May 25, 1909, which provides that

> A child of more than seven and less than sixteen years of age, who shall commit any act or omission, which, if committed by an adult, would be a crime not punishable by death or life imprisonment, shall not be deemed guilty of any crime, but of juvenile delinquency only. . . . Any child charged with any act or omission which may render him guilty of juvenile delinquency shall be dealt with in the same manner as now is or may hereafter be provided in the case of adults charged with the same act or omission except as specially provided heretofore in the case of children under the age of sixteen years.

This would seem to effectuate merely a change in the name of every crime or offense from that by which it was theretofore known to that of juvenile delinquency. Beyond question, much good may be accomplished under such legislation, dependent upon the spirit in which it is carried out, particularly if, as the English law provides, the conviction should not be regarded as a conviction of felony for the purposes of any of the disqualifications attached to felony.

But in Illinois, and following the lead of Illinois, in most jurisdictions, the form of procedure is totally different and wisely so. It would seem to be obvious that, if the common law could fix the age of criminal responsibility at seven, and if the legislature could advance that age to ten or twelve, it can also raise it to sixteen or seventeen or eighteen, and that is what, in some measure, has been done. Under most of the juvenile-court laws a child under the designated age is to be proceeded against as a criminal only when in the judgment of the judge of the juvenile court, either as to any child, or in some states as to one over fourteen or over sixteen years of age, the interests of the state and of the child require that this be done. It is to be observed that the language of the law should be explicit in order to negative the jurisdiction of the criminal courts in the first instance. In the absence of such express provision the Supreme Court of New Hampshire in State v. Burt recently upheld a criminal conviction. On the other hand, the Supreme Court of Louisiana has decided in the case of State v. Reed that a criminal proceeding against one within the age limit must be quashed and the case transferred to the juvenile court.

To get away from the notion that the child is to be dealt with as a criminal; to save it from the brand of criminality, the brand that sticks to it for life; to take it in hand and instead of first stigmatizing and then reforming it, to protect it from the stigma,—this is the work which is now being accomplished by dealing even with most of the delinquent children through the court that represents the *parens patriae* power of the state, the court of chancery. Proceedings are brought to have a guardian or representative of the state appointed to look after the child, to have the state intervene between the natural parent and the child because the child needs it, as evidenced by some of its acts, and because the parent is either unwilling or unable to train the child properly.

Objection has been made from time to time that this is nevertheless a criminal proceeding, and that therefore the child is entitled to a trial by jury and to all the constitutional rights that hedge about the criminal.

The Supreme Courts of several states have well answered this objection. In Commonwealth v. Fisher the court says:

> To save a child from becoming a criminal, or from continuing in a career of crime, to end in maturer years in public punishment and disgrace, the legislature surely may provide for the salvation of such a child, if its parents or guardian be unable or unwilling to do so, by bringing it into one of the courts of the state without any process at all, for the purpose of subjecting it to the state's guardianship and protection.
>
> The action is not for the trial of a child charged with a crime, but is mercifully to save it from such an ordeal, with the prison or penitentiary in its wake, if the child's own good and the best interests of the state justify such salvation. Whether the child deserves to be saved by the state is no more question for a jury than whether the father, if able to save it, ought to save it. The act is but an exercise by the state of its supreme power over the welfare of its children, a power under which it can take a child from its father, and let it go where it will, without committing it to any guardianship or any institution, if the welfare of the child, taking its age into consideration, can be thus best promoted.
>
> The design is not punishment, nor the restraint imprisonment, any more than is the wholesome restraint which a parent exercises over his child. The severity in either case must necessarily be tempered to meet the necessities of the particular situation. There is no probability, in the proper administration of the law, of the child's liberty being unduly invaded. Every statute which is designed to give protection, care, and training to children, as a needed substitute for parental authority, and performance of parental duty, is but a recognition of the duty of the state, as the legitimate guardian and protector of children where other guardianship fails. No constitutional right is violated.

In one of the most recent decisions the Supreme Court of Idaho thus refers to the juvenile court:

> Its object is to confer a benefit both upon the child and the community in the way of surrounding the child with better and more elevating influences,

and of educating and training him in the direction of good citizenship and thereby saving him to society and adding a good and useful citizen to the community. This, too, is done for the minor at a time when he is not entitled, either by natural law or the laws of the land, to his absolute freedom, but rather at a time when he is subject to the restraint and custody of either a natural guardian or a legally constituted and appointed guardian to whom he owes obedience and subjection. Under this law the state, for the time being, assumes to discharge the parental duty and to direct his custody and assume his restraint.

It would be carrying the protection of "inalienable rights," guaranteed by the Constitution, a long ways to say that that guaranty extends to a free and unlimited exercise of the whims, caprices, or proclivities of either a child or its parents or guardians for idleness, ignorance, crime, indigence, or any kindred dispositions or inclinations.

Years ago, in considering the power of the court to send a child to the House of Refuge, Chief Justice Gibson said:

> May not the natural parents, when unequal to the task of education, or unworthy of it, be superseded by the *parens patriae*, or common guardian of the community? It is to be remembered that the public has a paramount interest in the virtue and knowledge of its members, and that of strict right the business of education belongs to it. That parents are ordinarily entrusted with it, is because it can seldom be put in better hands; but where they are incompetent or corrupt, what is there to prevent the public from withdrawing their faculties, held as they obviously are, at its sufferance? The right of parental control is a natural, but not an inalienable one. It is not excepted by the declaration of rights out of the subject of ordinary legislation.

Care must, however, be taken not to provide for dealing with the child as a criminal. The city of Detroit lacked, for a time, a juvenile court, as the result of the decision in Robinson v. Wayne Circuit Judges. The Supreme Court of Michigan, following the cases cited and numerous others, overruled many objections urged against the constitutionality of the Detroit Juvenile Court Act, but nevertheless held it invalid, saying:

> The statute, it is true, declares that the proceedings shall not be taken to be criminal proceedings in any sense; and yet by section 14 it is provided that if the child be adjudged a delinquent child, the court may place the case on trial, and impose a fine not to exceed $25.00, with costs, etc. This can have no other purpose than punishment for a delinquency, which means nothing less, or at least includes one who violates any law of this state or any city ordinance.
>
> In the present case, however, this statute is a state law, providing for a penalty. A complaint, an arrest, and trial are authorized, and, upon a determination, the imposition of a fine. It is difficult to conceive of any element of a criminal prosecution which may be said to be lacking. And, as section 28 of

article 6 of the Constitution very plainly provides for a jury of twelve men in all courts of record in every criminal prosecution, the provision for a jury of six for the trial of delinquents is in violation of this section.

Further legislation has now corrected this defect.

In answer to the objection that the act has the effect of depriving a parent of the custody of his child, in violation of his constitutional rights, the Supreme Court of Idaho, in *Ex parte* Sharpe, says:

> If the parent objects to the child's being taken care of by the state in the manner provided for by the act, he may appear and present his objections. If, on the other hand, he is not made a party to the hearing and proceeding, under all the recognized rules of legal procedure, he is clearly not bound by the judgment and none of his rights are precluded.
>
> The parent or guardian cannot be bound by the order or judgment of the Probate Court in adjudging a child delinquent and sending him to the Industrial Training School unless he has appeared or been brought into the proceeding in the Probate Court.

The Supreme Court of Utah, in Mill v. Brown, emphasized this requirement when it said:

> Before the state can be substituted to the right of the parent, it must affirmatively be made to appear that the parent has forfeited his natural and legal right to the custody and control of the child by reason of his failure, inability, neglect, or incompetency to discharge the duty and thus to enjoy the right.
>
> Unless, therefore, both the delinquency of the child and the incompetency, for any reason, of the parent concur and are so found, the court exceeds its power when committing a child to any of the institutions contemplated by the act.

It is, therefore, important to provide, as has been done in the most recent statutes, but as was not done in the earlier acts, that the parents be made parties to the proceedings, and that they be given an opportunity to be heard therein in defense of their parental rights.

The Supreme Court of Illinois, however, in the case of People *ex rel.* Schwartz v. McLain, struck a discordant note in a decision releasing a child from the State Training School for Boys. Subsequently, it granted a rehearing, and because of the discontinuance thereafter of the *habeas corpus* proceedings, rendered no final judgment in the cause. In the original opinion, which we may, in view of the rehearing, regard as retracted, the court, while upholding the constitutionality of the juvenile-court law in the case of a child whose parents actively contributed to its wrongdoing, said:

If this enactment is effective and capable of being enforced as against the relator, father of the boy, it must be upon the theory that it is within the power of the state to seize any child under the age of sixteen years who has committed a misdemeanor, though the father may have always provided a comfortable, quiet, orderly, and moral home for him, and have supplied him with school facilities, had not neglected his moral training, and had been and was still ready to render him all the duties of a parent. We do not think it is within the power of the General Assembly to thus infringe upon parental rights.

The answer to this, made by counsel in the argument on rehearing, would seem to be conclusive. They said:

> The boy incorrigible at home must be corrected by the state. Whether this correction be by fine, imprisonment, or commitment to school, is a matter which does belong to the legislature and not to this court to determine.
> This law applies, with equal force, to the son of the pauper and the millionaire, to the minister's son (who is sometimes the wolf among the flock) as well as to the son of the convict and the criminal. The circumstances and disposition of the parents are not the test by which the state measures its power over the child; the right of the parent to retain the society and the services of the child is rightfully suspended when the parent is unsuccessful in keeping the child in a state of obedience to the criminal law of the state; he cannot keep his child and allow him to continue to violate the law of the state without successful check or barrier thereon, just because he has a comfortable and moral home.
> The manner in which the power of the state shall be exercised, and the extent to which the deprivation of the parent shall go, is a matter for the determination of the legislature, and the legislature by this Act has confided it to a court of chancery, where the parental power of the state has been lodged and exercised from time immemorial.

They quote, too, the passage heretofore cited from the decision of Chief Justice Gibson in *Ex parte* Crouse, with this addition:

> The right of parental control is a natural but not an inalienable one. It is not excepted by the Declaration of Rights out of the subjects of ordinary legislation, and it consequently remains subject to the ordinary legislative power, which, if wantonly or inconveniently used, would soon be constitutionally restricted, but the competency of which, as the government is constituted, cannot be doubted.

One more legal question remains. In a decision, characterized by the Supreme Court of Michigan in the Robinson case as "now chiefly notable as an example of the vigor with which that which is not the law may be stated," the Supreme Court of Illinois, in People *ex rel.* v. Turner, released a child from the reformatory on the ground that the reformatory was a prison; that incarceration therein was necessarily punishment for a crime, and that such a punishment could be inflicted only after criminal proceedings conducted with due regard to the constitutional rights of the defendant. Whether the criticism be just or not, the case suggests a real truth, and one which, in the enthusiastic progress of the juvenile-court movement, is in danger of being overlooked. If a child must be taken away from its home, if for the natural parental care that of the state is to be substituted, a real school, not a prison in disguise, must be provided. Whether the institutional life be only temporary until a foster home can be found, or for a longer period until the child can be restored to its own home or be given its complete freedom, the state must, both to avoid the constitutional objections suggested by the Turner case, and in fulfilment of its moral obligation to the child, furnish the proper care. This cannot be done in one great building, with a single dormitory for all of the two or three or four hundred or more children, in which there will be no possibility of classification along the lines of age or degrees of delinquency, in which there will be no individualized attention. What is needed is a large area, preferably in the country,—because these children require the fresh air and contact with the soil even more than does the normal child,—laid out on the cottage plan, giving opportunity for family life, and in each cottage some good man and woman who will live with and for the children. Locks and bars and other indicia of prisons must be avoided; human love, supplemented by human interest and vigilance, must replace them. In such schools there must be opportunity for agricultural and industrial training, so that when the boys and girls come out, they will be fitted to do a man's or woman's work in the world, and not be merely a helpless lot, drifting aimlessly about.

Some states have begun to supply this need. But despite the great ultimate financial saving to the state through this method of dealing with children, a saving represented by the value of a decent citizen as against a criminal, the public authorities are nowhere fully alive to the new obligations that the spirit as well as the letter of this legislation imposes upon them. It has, however, been specifically provided in Canada that before the Dominion Act shall be put into force in any province, the governor in council must be satisfied, among other things, that an industrial school, as defined by the Act, exists, to which juvenile delinquents may be committed.

Private philanthropy has supplemented, and doubtless in the future will supplement the work of the state in providing for the delinquents. To a large extent it is denominational, though many organizations are non-sectarian. None have accomplished more good or give promise of greater continued usefulness than the George Junior Republics and similar organizations that stand for self-government, self-reliance, and redemption through honest labor.

Some of the main principles involved in juvenile-court legislation were pointed out by Mr. Herbert Samuels, in introducing into the House of Commons his excellent Children's Bill. In reference to that part of the bill which has to do with juvenile offenders, he said that it is based on three main principles:

> *The first* is that the child offender ought to be kept separate from the adult criminal, and should receive at the hands of the law a treatment differentiated

to suit his special needs; that the courts should be agencies for the rescue as well as the punishment of children. We require the establishment through the country of juvenile courts—that is to say, children's cases shall be heard in a court held in a separate room or at a separate time from the courts which are held for adult cases, and that the public who are not concerned in the cases shall be excluded from admission.

In London we propose to appoint by administrative action a special children's magistrate to visit in turn a circuit of courts. Further, we require police authorities throughout the whole of the country to establish places of detention to which children shall be committed on arrest, if they are not bailed, and on remand or commitment for trial, instead of being committed to prison.

The second principle on which this bill is based is that the parent of the child offender must be made to feel more responsible for the wrongdoing of his child. He cannot be allowed to neglect the up-bringing of his children, and having committed the grave offense of throwing on society a child criminal, wash his hands of the consequences and escape scot free. We require the attendance in court of the parent in all cases where the child is charged, where there is no valid reason to the contrary, and we considerably enlarge the powers, already conferred upon the magistrates by the Youthful Offenders Act of 1901, to require the parent, where it is just to do so, to pay the fines inflicted for the offense which his child has committed.

The third principle which we had in view in framing this part of the bill is that the commitment of children in the common gaols, no matter what the offense may be that is committed, is an unsuitable penalty to impose. The government has come to the conclusion that the time has now arrived when Parliament can be asked to abolish the imprisonment of children altogether, and we extend this proposal to the age of sixteen with a few carefully defined and necessary exceptions.

To these, however, should be added, as the fourth principle, that taking a child away from its parents and sending it even to an industrial school is, as far as possible, to be avoided; and as the fifth and most important principle, that when it is allowed to return home, it must be under probation, subject to the guidance and friendly interest of the probation officer, the representative of the court. To raise the age of criminal responsibility from seven or ten to sixteen or eighteen, without providing for an efficient system of probation, would indeed be disastrous. Probation is, in fact, the keynote of juvenile-court legislation.

But even in this there is nothing radically new. Massachusetts has had probation, not only in the case of minors, but even in the case of adults, for nearly forty years, and several other states now have provisions for the suspension of a criminal sentence in the case of adults, permitting the defendant to go free, but subject to the control of a probation officer. Wherever juvenile courts have been established, a system of probation has been provided for, and even where as yet the juvenile-court system has not been fully developed, some steps have been taken to substitute probation for imprisonment of juvenile offenders.

Most of the children who come before the court are, naturally, the children of the poor. In many cases the parents are foreigners, frequently unable to speak English, and without an understanding of American methods and views. What they need, more than anything else, is kindly assistance; and the aim of the court, in appointing a probation officer for the child, is to have the child and the parents feel, not so much the power, as the friendly interest of the state; to show them that the object of the court is to help them to train the child right; and therefore the probation officers must be men and women fitted for these tasks.

Their duties are oftentimes of the most delicate nature. Tact, forbearance, and sympathy with the child, as well as a full appreciation of the difficulties that the poorer classes, and especially the immigrants, are confronted with in our large cities, are indispensable. The New York Probation Commission say, in their second annual report for the year 1908, p. 32:

> In courts where the probation system is most effectively conducted there is great variety in the work done by probation officers. The most successful workers regard the receiving of reports from probationers as much less important than the visiting and other work done by the probation officers. The probation officers obtaining the best results enter into intimate friendly relations with their probationers, and bring into play as many factors as possible, such as, for instance, securing employment for their probationers, readjusting family difficulties, securing medical treatment or charity if necessary, interesting helpful friends and relatives, getting the coöperation of churches, social settlements and various other organizations, encouraging probationers to start bank accounts, to keep better hours, to associate with better companions, and so forth.

The procedure and practice of the juvenile court is simple. In the first place the number of arrests is greatly decreased. The child and the parents are notified to appear in court, and unless the danger of escape is great, or the offense very serious, or the home totally unfit for the child, detention before hearing is unnecessary. Children are permitted to go on their own recognizance or that of their parents, or on giving bail. Probation officers should be and often are authorized to act in this respect. If, however, it becomes necessary to detain the children either before a hearing or pending a continuance, or even after the adjudication, before they can be admitted into the home or institution to which they are to be sent, they are no longer kept in prisons or jails, but in detention homes. In some states, the laws are mandatory that the local authorities provide such homes managed in accordance with the spirit of this legislation. These are feasible even in the smallest communities, inasmuch as the simplest kind of a building best meets the need.

The jurisdiction to hear the cases is generally granted to an existing court having full equity powers. In some cities, however, special courts have been provided, with judges devoting their entire time to this work. If these special courts can constitutionally be vested with full and complete chancery and criminal jurisdiction, much is to be said in favor of their establishment. In the large cities particularly the entire time of one judge may well be needed. It has been suggested from time to time that all of the judges of the municipal or special sessions courts be empowered to act in these cases, but while it would be valuable in metropolitan communities to have more than one detention home and court house, nevertheless it would seem to be even more important to have a single juvenile court judge. The British government has adopted this policy for London.

By the Colorado Act of 1909 provision is made for hearings before masters in chancery, designated as masters of discipline, to be appointed by the juvenile court judge and to act under his directions. This may prove to be the best solution of a difficult problem, combining as it does the possibility of a quick disposition of the simpler cases in many sections of a large city or county, with a unity of administration through the supervisory power of a single judge.

The personality of the judge is an all-important matter. The Supreme Court of Utah, in the case of Mill v. Brown, commenting upon the choice of a layman, a man genuinely interested in children, pointed out that,

> To administer juvenile laws in accordance with their true spirit and intent requires a man of broad mind, of almost infinite patience, and one who is the possessor of great faith in humanity and thoroughly imbued with that spirit.
>
> The judge of any court, and especially a judge of a juvenile court, should be willing at all times, not only to respect, but to maintain and preserve, the legal and natural rights of men and children alike. . . . The fact that the American system of government is controlled and directed by laws, not men, cannot be too often or too strongly impressed upon those who administer any branch or part of the government. Where a proper spirit and good judgment are followed as a guide, oppression can and will be avoided. . . .
>
> The juvenile-court law is of such vast importance to the state and society that it seems to us it should be administered by those who are learned in the law and versed in the rules of procedure, to the end that the beneficent purposes of the law may be made effective and individual rights respected. Care must be exercised both in the selection of a judge and in the administration of the law.

The decision but emphasizes the dangers which beset the path of the judge of the juvenile court. The public at large, sympathetic to the work, and even the probation officers who are not lawyers, regard him as one having almost autocratic power. Because of the extent of his jurisdiction and the tremendous responsibility that it entails, it is, in the judgment of the writer, absolutely essential that he be a trained lawyer thoroughly imbued with the doctrine that ours is a "government of laws and not of men."

He must, however, be more than this. He must be a student of and deeply interested in the problems of philanthropy and child life, as well as a lover of children. He must be able to understand the boys' point of view and ideas of justice; he must be willing and patient enough to search out the underlying causes of the trouble and to formulate the plan by which, through the coöperation, ofttimes, of many agencies, the cure may be effected.

In some very important jurisdictions the vicious practice is indulged in of assigning a different judge to the juvenile-court work every month or every three months. It is impossible for these judges to gain the necessary experience or to devote the necessary time to the study of new problems. The service should under no circumstances be for less than one year, and preferably for a longer period. In some of our cities, notably in Denver, the judge has discharged not only the judicial functions, but also those of the most efficient probation officer. Judge Lindsey's love for the work and his personality has enabled him to exert a powerful influence on the boys and girls that are brought before him. While doubtless the best results can be obtained in such a court, lack of time would prevent a judge in the largest cities from adding this work to his strictly judicial duties, even were it not extremely difficult to find the necessary combination of elements in one man.

The problem for determination by the judge is not, Has this boy or girl committed a specific wrong, but, What is he, how has he become what he is, and what had best be done in his interest and in the interest of the state to save him from a downward career. It is apparent at once that the ordinary legal evidence in a criminal court is not the sort of evidence to be heard in such a proceeding. A thorough investigation, usually made by the probation officer, will give the court much information bearing on the heredity and environment of the child. This, of course, will be supplemented in every possible way; but this alone is not enough. The physical and mental condition of the child must be known, for the relation between physical defects and criminality is very close. It is, therefore, of the utmost importance that there be attached to the court, as has been done in a few cities, a child study department, where every child, before hearing, shall be subjected to a thorough psycho-physical examination. In hundreds of cases the discovery and remedy of defective eyesight or hearing or some slight surgical operation will effectuate a complete change in the character of the lad.

The child who must be brought into court should, of course, be made to know that he is face to face with the power of the state, but he should at the same time, and more emphatically, be made to feel that he is the object of its care and solicitude. The ordinary trappings of the court-room are out of place in such hearings. The judge on a bench, looking down upon the boy standing at the bar, can never evoke a proper sympathetic spirit. Seated at a desk, with the child at his side, where he can on occasion put his arm around his shoulder and draw the lad to him, the judge, while losing none of his judicial dignity, will gain immensely in the effectiveness of his work.

The object of the juvenile court and of the intervention of the state is, of course, in no case to lessen or to weaken the sense of responsibility either of the child or of the parent. On the contrary, the aim is to develop and to enforce it. Therefore it is wisely provided in most of the recent acts that the child may be compelled when on probation, if of working age, to make restitution for any damage done by it. Moreover, the parents may not only be compelled to contribute to the support even of the children who are taken away from them and sent to institutions, but following Colorado, in many states, they, as well as any other adults, may be made criminally liable for their acts or neglect contributing to a child's dependency or delinquency. In most of the jurisdictions which have established separate juvenile courts, as well as in some of the others, all criminal cases affecting children are tried by the juvenile-court judge. In drafting legislation of this kind, however, it must not be overlooked that if the proceedings against the adult are criminal, his constitutional rights must be carefully safeguarded. Following general principles, such penal acts are strictly construed, and therefore in the recent case of Gibson v. People the Colorado Supreme Court limited the application of the Act of 1903 to the parents and those standing in a parental relation to the child. Colorado, in 1907, however, as well as other states, expressly extended the scope of such statutes so as to include any person, whether standing in loco parentis or not. The Supreme Court of Oregon in State v. Dunn construed such legislation to refer only to misconduct not otherwise punishable.

Kentucky in 1908, followed by Colorado in 1909, has enacted a statute providing for the enforcement of parental obligations, not in the criminal but in the chancery branch of the juvenile court. A decree not merely for the payment of support money, but for the performance or omission of such acts, as under the circumstances of the case are found necessary, may be enforced by contempt proceedings.

Valuable, however, as the introduction of the juvenile court into our system of jurisprudence, valuable both in its effect upon the child, the parents, and the community at large, and in the great material saving to the state which the substitution of probation for imprisonment has brought about, nevertheless it is in no sense a cure-all. Failures will result from probation, just as they have resulted from imprisonment. As Judge Lindsey has said:

> It does not pretend to do all the work necessary to correct children or to prevent crime. It is offered as a method far superior to that of the old criminal court system of dealing with the thing rather than the child. That method was more or less brutal. The juvenile court system has a danger in becoming one of leniency, but as between this method and that of the criminal court, it is

much to be preferred. But the dangers of leniency as well as those of brutality can be avoided in most cases. Juvenile-court workers must not be sentimentalists any more than brutalists. In short, the idea is a system of probation work, which contemplates coöperation with the child, the home, the school, the neighborhood, the church, and the business man in its interests and that of the state. Its purpose is to help all it can, and to hurt as little as it can; it seeks to build character—to make good citizens rather than useless criminals. The state is thus helping itself as well as the child, for the good of the child is the good of the state.

But more than this, the work of the juvenile court is, at the best, palliative, curative. The more important, indeed the vital thing, is to prevent the children from reaching that condition in which they have to be dealt with in any court, and we are not doing our duty to the children of to-day, the men and women of to-morrow, when we neglect to destroy the evils that are leading them into careers of delinquency, when we fail not merely to uproot the wrong, but to implant in place of it the positive good. It is to a study of the underlying causes of juvenile delinquency and to a realization of these preventive and positive measures that the trained professional men of the United States, following the splendid lead of many of their European brethren, should give some thought and some care. The work demands the united and aroused efforts of the whole community, bent on keeping children from becoming criminals, determined that those who are treading the downward path shall be halted and led back.

In a word, as was well said in the course of the debates on the Children's Bill in the House of Commons:

> We want to say to the child that if the world or the world's law has not been his friend in the past, it shall be now. We say that it is the duty of this Parliament and that this Parliament is determined to lift, if possible and rescue him, to shut the prison door, and to open the door of hope.

2

California Juvenile Court Jurisdiction Statute–1915

The people of the State of California do enact as follows:

SECTION I.   This act shall be known as the "juvenile court law" and shall apply to any person under the age of twenty-one years:

1. Who is found begging, receiving or gathering alms, or who is found in any street, road or public place for the purpose of so doing, whether actually begging or doing so under the pretext of selling or offering for sale any article or articles, or of singing or playing on any musical instrument, or of giving any public entertainment or accompanying or being used in aid of any person so doing; or

2. Who has no parent or guardian; or who has no parent or guardian willing to exercise or capable of exercising proper parental control; or who has no parent or guardian actually exercising such proper parental control and who is in need of such control; or

3. Who, being a minor, is destitute, or whose father, said person being a minor, does not or can not provide for said person the necessities of life, and who has no other means, through his mother or otherwise, of obtaining said necessities.

4. Whose home, said person being a minor, by reason of neglect, cruelty or depravity on the part of his parents or either of them, or on the part of his

Source: Statutes and Amendments to the Codes of California, chapter 631, pp. 1225–1229 (1915).

guardian, or on the part of the person in whose custody or care he may be, is an unfit place for said person; or

5. Who is found wandering and either has no home or no settled place of abode or no visible means of subsistence or no proper guardianship; or

6. Who is a vagrant or who frequents the company of criminals, vagrants or prostitutes, or persons so reputed; or who is in any house of prostitution or assignation; or

7. Who habitually visits without parent or guardian any public billiard room or public pool room, or any saloon or any place where any spirituous, vinous or malt liquors are sold, bartered, exchanged or given away; or

8. Who habitually uses intoxicating liquors or habitually smokes cigarettes, or habitually uses opium, cocaine, morphine or other similar drug without the direction of a competent physician; or

9. Who, being a minor, persistently or habitually refuses to obey the reasonable and proper orders or directions of, or who is beyond the control of, his parent, parents, guardian or custodian; or

10. Who is an habitual truant from school within the meaning of any law of this state; or

11. Who is leading, or from any cause is in danger of leading, an idle, dissolute, lewd or immoral life; or

12. Who is insane, or feeble-minded, or so far mentally deficient that the parents or guardian are unable to exercise proper parental control over said person, or whose mind is so far deranged or impaired as to endanger the health, person, or property of himself or others.

13. Who violates any law of this state or any ordinance of any town, city, county, or city and county of this state defining crime.

14. Who shall be declared free from the custody and control of his parents, as more fully defined in section fifteen of this act.

. . . .

SEC. 5.   In no case shall an order adjudging a person to be a ward of the juvenile court be deemed to be a conviction of crime.

3

Childress v. State

Supreme Court of Tennessee. Nov. 6, 1915.

GREEN, J. In this case John Childress, a minor under sixteen years of age, was committed as a delinquent child to the state reformatory for a period of twelve months, after due proceedings under chapter 58, Public Acts of 1911. It appeared that he was guilty of the crime of larceny, and was properly found to be a delinquent child on a hearing before the county judge of Anderson county sitting as a juvenile court under the said statute.

The case has been brought to this court, and Childress seeks to escape the judgment below by attacking the validity of chapter 58, Public Acts of 1911. It is insisted that said act violates section 14, of art. 1 of the Constitution, to the effect:

"That no person shall be put to answer any criminal charge but by presentment, indictment or impeachment."

The statute mentioned outlines certain proceedings to be had before the juvenile courts thereby established with reference to dependent, neglected, and delinquent children, and provides for the disposition, care, education, protection, etc., of such children. Any child under the age of sixteen years who violates any law of the state is declared to be a delinquent child, and the juvenile courts are authorized to commit such a child to the state reformatory or otherwise dispose of the child as set forth in said act.

Source: 179 *Southwestern Reporter*, 642 (1915).

Such proceedings before a juvenile court do not amount to a trial of the child for any criminal offense. If it be found that the child has violated a law of the state, then he may be adjudged a delinquent child within the meaning of the act. The court, however, does not undertake to punish the child for the crime committed, but undertakes to remove him from bad influences and to make such disposition of the child as to eradicate evil propensities by education, wholesome training, and moral instruction.

As pointed out by the court in Ex parte Januszewski (C. C.) 196 Fed. 123, the commission of a crime by a child may set the juvenile court in motion, but the court does not try the delinquent minor for the crime. The crime being evidence of delinquency, the court undertakes to remedy the delinquency.

Our statute provides that a child who shall have committed a misdemeanor or felony and has been adjudged to be a delinquent child, if thereafter found by the court to be incorrigible and incapable of reformation, or dangerous to the community, is then to be remanded to the proper courts for the trial of criminal offenses. So the proceedings in a juvenile court are entirely distinct from proceedings in the courts ordained to try persons for crime.

Statutes like chapter 58 of the Public Acts of 1911 have been enacted in many of the states, and have been uniformly upheld.

This court, speaking of the commitment of children to the state reformatory under a previous statute has said:

> Such statutes are not penal, and commitment is not in the nature of punishment. Such an institution is a house of refuge, a school—not a prison. The object is the upbuilding of the inmate by industrial training, by education and instilling principles of morality and religion, and, above all, by separating them from the corrupting influences of improper associates. State ex rel. v. Kilvington, 100 Tenn. 227, 45 S. W. 433, 41 L. R. A. 284.
>
> The commitment of infants to industrial schools, reformatories, or houses of refuge by a judge or justice without a trial is not in violation of the constitutional provisions relating to trial by jury. Such institutions are not prisons, and the proceeding is not a criminal prosecution. The object of the commitment is not punishment, but reformation and education of the infant. . . . 24 Cyc. 147.

To the effect that these statutes do not interfere with constitutional rights to trial by jury, or immunity from trial except upon presentment or indictment, or with other constitutional rights, see Rooks v. Tindall, 138 Ga. 863, 76 S. E. 878; Ex parte Januszewski (C. C.) 196 Fed. 123; Marlowe, v. Commonwealth, 142 Ky. 106, 133 S. W. 1137; Mill v. Brown, 31 Utah, 473, 88 Pac. 609, 120 Am. St. Rep. 935; Lindsay v. Lindsay, 257 Ill. 328, 100 N. E. 892, 45 L. R. A. (N. S.) 908, Ann. Cas. 1914A, 1222. See, also, cases collected in notes to 45 L. R. A. (N. S.) 908, and 18 L. R. A. (N. S.) 886.

The judgment of the juvenile court is affirmed.

4

The Juvenile Court Movement in Ohio

F. R. Aumann

Although the juvenile court is a comparatively new addition to the judicial system of this country, the forces which gave rise to it may be traced to the period of the industrial revolution and the humanitarian movement which followed. In that period of ferment there was a demand for factory legislation favorable to women and children; a movement to abolish slavery; the beginnings of the movement against strong drink and for the reform of the adult criminal. In this bewildering array of competing interests, the cause of the juvenile offender was lost sight of. Consequently, the problem was not given the serious consideration it merited for a long time.

In 1869, Massachusetts[1] broke new ground in this field in a law providing for the presence of a visiting agent or officer of the state board of charity at the trial of juvenile cases.[2] This officer was to be notified of every criminal action against a child under sixteen and was to have an opportunity to investigate their cases, attend their trials, protect their interests, and make such recommendations to the judge as might seem best.

In 1870, a law was passed requiring separate hearings for the trial of juvenile offenders in Suffolk County. (Boston.) In 1872, this requirement was extended to the police, district and municipal courts of the state. The governor was also authorized to commission as "trial justices of juvenile offenders,"

Source: *American Institute of Criminal Law*, 22 (1931–32): 556–565.

such number of justices of the peace as the public interest and convenience might require. In 1877, a law was passed which not only authorized separate trial of children's cases, but also used the term ''session for juvenile offenders'' of which session a separate docket and record was kept.[3] In 1877, New York passed a somewhat similar law.[4]

Similar measures for the special handling of juvenile cases in criminal courts were adopted in a number of states. It was not until 1899, however, that a juvenile court as we now know it, was set up. In that year statutes were exacted in Illinois and Colorado providing for juvenile courts.[5] In July, 1899, under the authority of the Illinois law, the Chicago Juvenile Court technically called the Juvenile Court of Cook County, was established. While the Illinois law was chiefly a codification of the existing law of the state plus some additional provisions from the laws of other states, it introduced one idea of outstanding importance. The gist of this idea was, that the child who broke the law was not to be regarded as a criminal, but as a ward of the state, subject to the care, guardianship, and control of the juvenile courts.[6]

In granting a special treatment to the child, a decisive departure was made from the traditional point of view towards criminal justice which was characterized by the theories of retribution, of determent, and of law as an inflexible body of rules.[7] Common law theory contemplated the offender as a free moral agent, who having before him the choice to do right or wrong, chose to do wrong. Justice was rendered by imposing upon this willful offender a penalty exactly corresponding to his crime. The crime was classified but the criminal was not.[8]

The spirit of social justice which gave rise to the juvenile court would have none of these things.[9] A correct treatment of crime and delinquency from the new approach supplements the orthodox criminal law and procedure with help from scientific sources, particularly from medical sciences, and those sources which deal with human behaviour, such as biology, sociology, and psychology.[10]

Consequently much of the evidence used in the Juvenile Court is taken from outside of the court by court officials, and is based in great part on these sciences of human behaviour plus the observations of a trained worker.[11] This is quite different from the orthodox method, where evidence is presented and arguments are made by opposing attorneys before a judge who decides each case according to established principles on the legally admissible evidence of the witnesses. The tendency in the juvenile court is towards a more human emphasis and requires a more liberal procedure in transacting the business of the courts.[12] In the course of time, this procedure may affect other courts as well.[13]

This possibility is increased by the activities of the proponents of the new sociological jurisprudence and by the new point of view which has been developed by this group as to the nature and purposes of law.[14] The old approach to these problems had been from the angle of history or legal analysis. This approach which was set forth in the writings of Sir Henry Maine and John Austin[15] has been definitely discarded by such legal thinkers as Holmes, Cardozo, and Pound, who are impressed with the idea of orienting law to life.[16]

Since the establishment of the Chicago court the juvenile court movement has extended throughout the country and to most parts of the world.[17] Its rapid spread is one of the most remarkable developments of the American judicial system. Juvenile courts have now been established in most states although not always as independent bodies.[18] As a matter of fact, no uniformity exists in the provisions made for juvenile courts in the several states, or in the same state for that matter.[19]

Generally speaking, certain features are considered essential for the organization of a juvenile court. These features might be outlined as follows: (1) Separate hearings for children's cases; (2) Informal or chancery procedure, including the use of petition or summons; (3) Regular probation service, both for supervisory care and investigation; (4) Detention separate from adults; (5) Special courts and probation records both legal and social; (6) Provision for mental and physical examination.[20]

The Ohio law strives for these essentials, but has not secured all of them as yet. In Ohio as in most states a judge of some other court is designated as judge of the juvenile court.[21] Courts of common pleas, probate courts, insolvency courts, superior courts, all have jurisdiction in this field.[22] This jurisdiction extends to all delinquent, neglected and dependent minors;[23] and to their parents and guardians, or any person or corporation who in any way contributes to their delinquency, neglect, or dependency.[24] Accordingly, these courts may hear and determine any charge against such persons for any misdemeanor involving the care, protection, education, or comfort of a minor. In several counties, however, juvenile jurisdiction is conferred upon the common pleas judge who is elected to the division of domestic relations.[25]

Under the Ohio law the juvenile judge and no one else, may hear children's cases. When a minor under eighteen is arrested he must be taken directly before that judge. If by chance, the child is brought before a justice of the peace, or a police court judge, he must be transferred immediately to the juvenile court.[26] Whenever possible the county commissioners are required to provide a special room for these cases.[27] An especial attempt is made to hold them in a different place than where the usual criminal cases are held.

In arresting children under eighteen years, officers are required to avoid incarceration if possible. In such cases, they are required to accept the written promise of some reputable person, usually the child's parent or guardian to be responsible for the presence of the child in court at the proper time.[28] In passing on the future of the child at the trial, probation is made a very important factor.[29]

Not only does the Ohio law safeguard the trial of children but it makes special provision for their detention.[30] Accordingly, the county commissioners are required to provide a suitable place as a "detention home" for delinquent, or neglected minors.[31] In counties which have a population exceeding forty thousand, the juvenile judge may appoint a superintendent and matron to take care of the home and the children detained there. These officials are required to meet certain standards of fitness for the position. They must be particularly qualified as teachers of children. In administering the affairs of the home, the delinquent children are kept separate from the dependent children insofar as it is possible.[32]

Wide powers are given the juvenile court to treat dependent, or neglected children as well as delinquent children. Such children may be committed to any one of a number of suitable institutions or persons.[33] Strict rules govern the practice of committing children to the care and custody of an institution, association, or to the state.[34] For the purpose of information and cooperative supervision, the juvenile court is required to report monthly to a division of the state welfare department the names of children committed to institutions and individuals. This report does not include children coming under the supervision and custody of the court but permitted to remain with their parents or guardians.[35]

At the present time, the work of the Juvenile Court in Ohio is greatly aided by other agencies. For instance sixty-three of the eighty-eight counties of the state have a county organization for the care of dependent children.[36] Eight counties out of the sixty-three that have some form of public child-care organization aside from the juvenile court, have a non-institutional plan, each with a social worker or placing agent in charge of the case work and child placing, some operating with, others without, a receiving home. In each case foster homes free or boarding, are the medium for child-care and adjustment.[37]

Another agency which cooperates with the various Juvenile Courts of Ohio is the Bureau of Juvenile Research of the State Department of Welfare, which is maintained for the purpose of studying the problem child. The Ohio law as noted provides that all minors who in the judgment of the juvenile court require institutional care and guardianship shall be wards of the state, and shall be committed to the care and custody of the State Department of Welfare.[38] The Bureau of Juvenile Research was established primarily in the terms of the law ''for the purpose of mental, physical, and other examination inquiry, or treatment'' of children admitted to the guardianship of the state. The law also authorized the receipt for observation from ''any public institution other than a state institution, or from a private charitable institution having legal custody'' of the child.[39]

The Bureau receives its cases from three sources: The Department of Welfare may assign to the Bureau any child committed to its guardianship; Juvenile Courts may commit directly to the Bureau any cases upon which expert diagnosis is desired; children of county homes, orphanages, hospitals, schools, or private homes may be brought to the Bureau of examination and advice concerning their care, education and medical status. Up to date, it would seem that the Bureau has not realized its fullest possibilities; neither have Juvenile Courts used it to the best advantage.[40] There are other psychiatric clinics in Ohio, however, which the Juvenile Courts may and do use to some extent.[41]

In addition to their judicial duties, juvenile courts in Ohio have certain duties of a strictly administrative character to perform as well. Their principal duties in this connection are the administration of the mother's pension law. In 1913, Ohio enacted a Mother's Pension Law and provided that it should be administered by the juvenile court.[42] This law made it possible for the court upon application to give aid for the support of children to women whose husbands are dead, permanently disabled, prisoners, or deserters. In the case of deserters, the desertion must be for a period of three years. The family in all cases, must have a two years' residence in the county granting assistance. The maximum allowance is $35 for the first child and $10 for each child not eligible for age and schooling certificates. Vesting this function in the Juvenile Court has not proved altogether satisfactory.[43]

Up to date, the juvenile court in Ohio has not realized its fullest possibilities. Although the ideas underlying the juvenile court movement have been adopted quite generally throughout the state, that does not mean that they have been put into effective operation. Many rural communities and small towns throughout the state have no facilities for dealing with children in need of the protection that a juvenile court can give. Even in many of the larger cities, the juvenile court lacks an adequate staff and the means for a careful, systematic study of the child. Results are obtained through the method of trial and error instead of through scientific study followed by treatment adapted to the needs discovered.

As the fundamental relationship between juvenile delinquency and crime in general becomes more apparent, more attention will necessarily have to be directed to this still neglected field. More of the money and energy now expended in maintaining and perfecting the costly apparatus for dealing with the adult criminal will be increasingly devoted to getting at the roots of criminal behavior as the public finds itself blocked in dealing successfully with such behavior. When that time comes, the necessity for organizing our juvenile court system on an effective basis will be realized, and we may then expect to find it given the same consideration and attention as are the other courts, with regards to organization, personnel, and working facilities in general.

Notes

1. In 1825, the so-called House of Refuge was established in New York, based on the principle that a child guilty of an offense should be kept apart from the adult criminal. In 1828, Pennsylvania established a similar institution and in 1847 Massachusetts followed suit.

2. Although the systematic development of the idea of the juvenile court has taken place in this country, various European countries early recognized the desirability of differentiating the trials of adult criminals and youthful offenders. See H. H. Lou, *Juvenile Courts in the United States,* pp. 14–15. For the present situation in European countries see p. 23, ibid.

3. Laws of Massachusetts (1869), ch. 143; (1870), ch. 359; (1872), ch. 358; (1877), ch. 210; (1878), ch. 198; (1880), ch. 129.

4. Laws of New York (1877), ch. 248.

5. Laws of Illinois (1899), p. 131; Laws of Colorado (1899), ch. 136.

6. That proceedings constituted under juvenile court acts and other statutes, are not criminal, has been frequently asserted by the courts. The Illinois Supreme Court in discussing this point said: ''Our statute and those of a similar character, treat children coming within their provisions as wards of the state to be protected, rather than as criminals to be punished and their purpose is to save them from the possible effects of delinquency and neglect liable to result in their leading a criminal career.'' *Lindsay* v. *Lindsay,* 257 Ill. 328, 333. See also *Mill* v. *Brown,* 31 Utah 473, 481; *Commonwealth* v. *Fisher,* 213 Pa. St. 48, 54. A good discussion of the nature of the juvenile court is found in the case of Januszewski (196 Fed. 123).

7. Bernard Flexner in discussing this point asserts that the juvenile courts represent a growth in legal theory, rather than a departure from it, although their methods in dealing with children are for the most part unknown to common-law procedure or to chancery procedure. See *Legal Aspects of the Juvenile Court* by Bernard Flexner and Reuben Oppenheimer, p. 21, U.S. Children's Bureau Publications, No. 99 (1922).

8. The classification of the criminal, that is the juvenile offender, which came in the wake of the juvenile court movement was prompted not only by motives looking toward ''social justice'' but by expediency as well. Studies made of the criminal brought out several important facts which had been previously ignored. They were: (1) the fact that criminals in many cases enter upon their career of crime at an early age; (2) the fact that imprisonment of youthful offenders in the general penal institution served no good purpose. Instead of deterring them from future criminal acts, it had the effect of encouraging them by placing them in close contact with the hardened criminal in a virtual ''school of crime.'' To successfully cope with crime, the youthful offenders must be intelligently dealt with. An intelligent treatment would provide at once for a different method of punishment than incarceration with hardened adult prisoners. The youthful offender presenting a special problem, required a special solution.

9. Roscoe Pound speaking in connection with this said: ''The fundamental theory of our orthodox criminal law has gone down before modern psychology and psychopathology. The results are beginning to be felt,'' p. 588, *Criminal Justice in Cleveland,* The Cleveland Foundation (1922).

10. ''Scientific diagnostic study as a regular science for delinquents and for a court began in the juvenile court in Chicago in 1909. This work which was started and continued under the name of the Juvenile Psychopathic Institute, was soon perceived to have much wider bearing and usefulness than study of merely psychopathic cases; the cases of quite normal offenders often justify as much, if not more attention given them for the sake of effective understandings.'' William Healey, *The Practical Value of Scientific Study of Juvenile Delinquents,* United States Children's Bureau Publication, No. 96 (1922), p. 7.

For further discussion on the subject see A. L. Jacoby, *The Psychopathic Clinic in a Criminal Court: Its Use and Possibilities*, Am. Jud. Soc. Journ., Vol. 7, June, 1923, p. 21, 25; Harry Olson, *Crime and Heredity*, Am. Jud. Soc. Journ., Vol. 7, Aug., 1923, pp. 33–77.

11. The probation officer assumes an important role in this process. Thomas D. Elliot, *The Juvenile Court and the Educational System*, JOURNAL OF CRIMINAL LAW AND CRIMINOLOGY.

12. "When a court is acting, not as an arbiter of private strife but as the medium of the state's performance of its sovereign duties as parens patriae and promoter of the general welfare, it is natural that some of the safeguards of judicial contests should be laid aside." Edward F. Waite, *How Far Can Court Procedure Be Socialized Without Impairing Individual Rights?* p. 55, U.S. Children's Bureau Publication, No. 97 (1922). See further in this connection, Miriam Van Waters, *The Socialization of Juvenile Court Procedure*, U.S. Children's Bureau Publication, No. 97 (1922). For further comments on this subject see p. 62, ibid.

13. "Today the vanguard of thought is recognizing that many of the principles of socialized treatment—such as a study of the characteristics of the individual and the environment in which he lives and constructive probation—are applicable and should be extended gradually to the whole field of criminal justice," p. 13, *The Child, the Family, and the Court*, U.S. Children's Bureau Publication, No. 193 (1929).

14. "The main problem to which sociological jurists are addressing themselves today," Dean Pound says, "is to enable and to compel lawmaking and also interpretation and application of legal rules, to take more account, and more intelligent account, of the social facts upon which law must proceed and to which it is applied." Roscoe Pound, *Scope and Purpose of Sociological Jurisprudence*, Harvard Law Review, Vol. 25, April 1912, pp. 512–513.

15. See John Austin (1790–1859), *Lectures on Jurisprudence* and Sir Henry Maine (1812–1888), *Ancient Law: Its Connections with Early History of Society and Its Relations to Modern Ideas*.

16. These men believe that the methods of jurisprudence can be improved by studying the methods of the other social sciences. The test of the law would seem to be coming more and more to be, not the theoretical accuracy of its philosophy but its actual results. "Our philosophy," says Benjamin Cardozo, "will tell us the proper function of the law in telling us the ends the law should endeavor to attain; but closely related to such a study is the inquiry whether law, as it has developed in this subject or that, does in truth fulfill its function—is functioning well or ill. The latter branch is perhaps a branch of social science calling for a survey of social facts rather than a branch of philosophy itself, yet the two subjects converge, and one will seldom be fruitful unless supplemented by the other." "Consequences can not alter statutes but may help to fix their meaning." "We test the rule by its results." B. N. Cardozo, *The Growth of the Law*, p. 112 (1924); see also O. W. Holmes, *The Path of the Law*, Harvard Law Review, vol. 10, No. 8 (March, 1897), pp. 467, 468.

17. See Sophonisba P. Breckenridge and Helen R. Jeter, *Summary of Juvenile Court Legislation in the United States*, U.S. Children's Bureau Publications, No. 70 (1920); Katherine F. Lenroot and Emma O. Lundberg, *Juvenile Courts of Work*, U.S. Children's Bureau Publications, No. 141 (1925).

18. Every state but Wyoming has made special provisions for juvenile courts. For a list of the states which have adopted such courts see H. H. Lou, *Juvenile Courts in the United States,* p. 24.

19. In 1918 a survey was made of the courts which have authority to hear children's cases involving delinquency or neglect. Of the 2,034 courts reporting only 321 were effectively organized for juvenile work. Specially organized courts served all cities of over 100,000 population, and 70 per cent of the population in cities of 25,000 to 100,000; but only 29 per cent of the population in cities of 5,000 to 25,000. In the rural areas, moreover, only 16 per cent of the population was served. In half of the 48 states less than a fourth of the population was within reach of the courts equipped for children's cases, and in several states no courts with special organization was reported. See pp. 10, 11, 12, Evelina Belden, *Courts in the United States Hearing Children's Cases,* U.S. Children's Bureau Publication, No. 65 (1920).

20. Evelina Belden, *Courts in the United States Hearing Children's Cases,* U.S. Children's Bureau Publications, No. 65 (1920), p. 10.

21. The usual practice has been to make juvenile work a specialized part of the work of an existing court. It is only in the larger cities that district agencies for trying children's cases are found. Jurisdiction over juvenile cases is usually made a part of the county court. However, the probate court in Arkansas, Michigan, Wisconsin, Missouri, and Kansas; the superior court in Arizona, California, and North Carolina; and the district court in Iowa, Minnesota, and New Mexico, exercise jurisdiction in juvenile cases. See Katherine F. Lenroot, *The Evolution of the Juvenile Court,* 105 Annals of the Amer. Acad. of Pol. and Soc. Sci. pp. 213–23 (1923).

22. See O. G. C. sec. 1639.

23. The Juvenile Court age throughout the United States varies from 16 to 18 years. In Ohio the age is 18 years.

24. Providing they are not inmates of a state institution or any institution incorporated under the laws of the state for the care and correction of delinquent, neglected, and dependent children.

25. O. G. C. sec. 1639.

26. O. G. C. sec. 1659.

27. O. G. C. sec. 1649.

28. O. G. C. sec. 1648.

29. O. G. C. sec. 1652.

30. A child under eighteen years of age coming under the custody of the court continues to be the ward of the state until twenty-one years old unless committed to the care of the Department of Welfare, or some institution certified by it, with permission to place the child in a foster home for adoption purposes. O. G. C. sec. 1643; Opinions of the Atty. Gen. (1920), 1009.

31. Consideration of the use of boarding homes for children as places of detention is just beginning in Ohio. In one populous county of the state, many of the delinquent juvenile and court children pass from the detention home into boarding homes, or go directly to boarding homes after the court hearing. They are tried out in normal home environments with considerable sympathy and patience before industrial school sentences are imposed, if environment has seemed to be their chief difficulty. In Canton, the Juvenile Court has selected an experienced and well known foster home that has boarded boys for years. With this family the court is placing their problem boys for observation and a chance to make good before conferring a court sentence. P. 69,

Esther McClain, *Child Placing in Ohio,* Division of Charities, Departments of Public
Welfare, Columbus, Ohio, March, 1928.

    32. O. G. C. sec. 1670.

    33. Eighteen counties in the state have no public or private institution or organi-
zation to do this work. Consequently it remains for the Juvenile Court to do it. Miss
McClain of the State Department of Welfare in discussing this feature said: "The
greatest need today in child placing in the state is the need for standardization of this
work by the juvenile courts. Further developments of county child welfare boards with
a competent social worker in charge, is anticipated in these counties to which the courts
may turn for placing service. Being continuous boards, the child is not affected or
lost sight of through political changes as has often happened when his welfare and
control rested completely with the court." Esther McClain, *Child Placing in Ohio,*
Division of Charities, State Department of Welfare, Columbus, Ohio, March, 1928,
p. 47.

    34. Children may be committed to (1) a suitable state or county institution; (2)
to a reputable citizen or training or industrial school; (3) to a duly authorized association
for caring for dependent, neglected or dependent children; or (4) to a private or public
hospital. A child committed to an institution for permanent care becomes a ward,
subject to the sole and exclusive guardianship of such institution. Such agency may
place the child in a family home and it must be made party to any proceeding for the
adoption of a child and may assent to the adoption. The individual to whose care the
child is committed, may not consent to adoption, however, without further order of
the court. All associations receiving children under the juvenile court act are subject
to supervision by the State Department of Welfare. There are some ninety-five child-
caring organizations in the State of Ohio. These organizations not only undertake to
find and investigate boarding houses and recommend them to the state for license
approval or disapproval but tend to function more broadly as community support is
given and case working methods are employed. See O. G. C. sec. 1653. Also Esther
McClain, *Child Placing in Ohio,* Division of Charities, Department of Public Welfare,
Dec., 1928, p. 49.

    35. O. G. C. sec. 1672. For a good discussion of this whole topic, see Mary
M. Leete, *The Children's Bureau of Cleveland, A Study of the Care of Dependent
Children in Cleveland,* U.S. Children's Bureau Publication, No. 177 (1927).

    36. Fifty-three have an institution known as the "County Children's Home"
and three, Hancock, Hocking and Lawrence counties, carry that name but operate
without an institution; using instead a receiving home and foster homes (free and
boarding) with a placing agent to engineer the admissions of children, home finding,
and placements. Five others, Lake, Brown, Ross, Morgan and Mercer counties, have
county Child Welfare Boards as made legally possible by the law of 1921 (O. G. C.
sec. 3092), providing for the abandonment of children's homes in counties so desiring
and setting up a county child welfare board in any county not operating a Children's
Home. Of these five counties, Brown and Morgan abandoned their Children's Homes
in 1922 and 1923 to adopt the Child Welfare Board plan with a placing agent in charge
and a number of boarding and free foster homes in which to place the children, using
a special boarding home for receiving purposes. The three counties of Lake, Ross,
and Mercer had no county system of child-care prior to the creation of Child Welfare
Boards. P. 18. Esther McClain, *Child Placing in Ohio,* Division of Charities, Department of Public Welfare, Columbus, Ohio, March, 1928.

37. Of the sixty-three counties having a children's home or a county board, twenty-three (35 per cent of them) have the services of a placing agent or agents, some of them over a period of years, although nineteen of the twenty-three have been secured since 1920. Esther McClain, *Child Placing in Ohio*, Division of Charities, Department of Public Welfare, Columbus, Ohio, March, 1928, p. 19.

38. O. G. C. secs. 1841-1, 1841-6.

39. The Bureau receives numerous calls from public school systems, special schools, children's homes, welfare organizations, courts and the like. In commenting on this phase of the Bureau's work, the chief neuro-psychiatrist in his annual report for 1926 said: "It is probable that these latter agencies, particularly the courts, will make a much greater demand for our field service when it is more generally known, that an adequate study can be made of many of the problem cases without the necessity of an extended commitment to the Bureau itself." P. 407, *Fifth Annual Report of the Department of Public Welfare*, Columbus, Ohio (1926).

40. For criticism of the work of the Bureau of Juvenile Research and recommendations, see *Report of the Joint Committee on Economy in Public Service*, Part V, pp. 18–24. This report is the result of the study of state administrative agencies made by a joint legislative committee of the Ohio General Assembly during 1927–28–29.

41. Besides the Bureau of Juvenile Research which maintains both traveling and stationary clinics, there are psychiatric clinics at Canton, Cincinnati, Cleveland, Hamilton, Massilon and Toledo, of a public and private character, available for the examination of children. In Canton there is a city clinic. In Cincinnati there is the clinic of the Hamilton County Court of Domestic Relations; the Neuro-psychiatric Clinic at the Medical Dispensary of the United Jewish Social Agencies; the Psychopathic Institute of the Jewish Hospital; and the Central Clinic. In Cleveland, there is the Behaviour Clinic of the Day Nursery, and Free Kindergarten Association; the Child Guidance Clinic; the Mental Hygiene Department of Mt. Sinai Hospital; the Neuro-psychiatric Clinic of the Red Cross; the Neuro-psychiatric Department of Lakeside Hospital; and the Psychiatric Clinic of St. Luke's Hospital. In Hamilton, there is a Mental Hygiene Clinic; in Massilon, the Mental Hygiene Clinic of the Massilon State Hospital; and in Toledo, there is the Mental Hygiene Clinic in conjunction with the Toledo District Nurses' Association. See pp. 21–22, *List of Psychiatric Clinics for Children in the United States*, U.S. Children's Bureau Publication, No. 191 (1929).

42. See Ohio Laws (1913), vol. 103, p. 864; Ohio Laws (1915), vol. 104, p. 436; Ohio Laws (1919), vol. 108, p. 624; Ohio Laws (1921), vol. 109, p. 70.

43. For example the Akron Bureau of Municipal Research in a study made of the public welfare activities of Summit County in 1920 recommended that this function be transferred from the Juvenile Court to a proposed County Welfare Department. See *Public Welfare Activities of Summit County*, Bureau of Municipal Research, Akron, Dec., 1920 (Manuscript).

DISCUSSION QUESTIONS

1. What are Judge Mack's most significant reasons for the establishment of the juvenile court? Do you agree with these justifications?

2. How broad was the jurisdiction of the early juvenile court? Use California's statute to describe the types of youths or behaviors that fell within the jurisdiction of the juvenile court.

3. What line of reasoning does the court use in *Childress v. State?* Are you persuaded by the court's logic? Why or why not?

4. To what extent did Ohio achieve the ideal juvenile court described by Judge Mack?

5. Can you anticipate any problems that might arise in a system that allows unbridled discretion to juvenile court judges while offering minimal procedural safeguards to the youths processed through it? What problems might arise?

SECTION III

DUE PROCESS AND PROCEDURAL PROTECTIONS

Introduction

The initial criticisms of the juvenile justice system, beginning in the 1960s and extending into the 1970s, focused largely on the system's procedural inadequacies. At that time, studies on the juvenile system's operations raised questions about injustices resulting from the informality of court hearings. The broad discretionary authority given to juvenile justice officials was specifically challenged. Because the juvenile court had been founded on a theory of benevolent state intervention, due process rights were not considered important. Unlike the situation of the adult defendant facing trial and punishment for his or her criminal acts, the youth's relation with the government in a hearing before the juvenile court judge was considered to be nonadversarial. The doctrine of *parens patriae* assumed that the interests of the child were the same as the interests of society in general. Children entangled in the juvenile justice system did not need procedural protections, the theory held, because the proceedings were civil in nature and the state was attempting to help or rehabilitate them.

In part, the move for more procedural protections came from people concerned about the injustices that followed from the broad discretion given to officials in the commitment and release of juvenile offenders. Empirical studies had demonstrated that this broad discretion resulted in gross inequalities in the duration and type of sanction ordered by juvenile authorities. Critics of this discretion argued that even if it could be adequately demonstrated that the system rehabilitated juvenile delinquents, the traditional model of "individualized justice" should be abandoned simply because of the injustices that resulted from it.

Concerns for the constitutional rights of juveniles and for the negative labeling inherent in delinquency proceedings also called attention to the inadequacies of juvenile court procedures. Under the "best interests of the child" theory, the interests of the youth, the family, and society were considered to be synonymous. But critics began to point out the conflicting goals of the juvenile justice system and to ask whether the system could do simultaneously what was in the best interests of the child *and* the best interests of the state. Increasingly, observers of the juvenile justice system said *no*—that these two interests frequently conflict.

Some authorities began to question the major assumptions underlying the legal doctrines of the juvenile court. They also began to acknowledge the punitive characteristics of the juvenile court's sanctions. The concern for procedural protections in juvenile court grew, therefore, in part as it became more apparent that the functions of the juvenile justice system closely resembled those of the criminal justice system—punishment, deterrence, and incapacitation. To the extent that the aims of the juvenile justice system increasingly approximated those of the criminal justice system, critics argued that juvenile offenders should be accorded the procedural safeguards granted to adults.

Child rights advocates began to assert that juveniles, like their adult counterparts in criminal court, had liberty interests that deserved protection when threatened by prosecution, regardless of whether the state was trying to help a juvenile offender or to protect the public. The goal of the legal reforms was to provide greater *procedural justice* for youths in juvenile court.

The reforms devised to address these problems largely involved the extension of procedural safeguards to juveniles whenever they were charged with wrongdoing and adjudicated in the juvenile court. One of the first cases in the procedural revolution was *In re Gault*, decided by the U.S. Supreme Court in 1967. Since then, a multitude of procedural protections have been accorded juveniles in delinquency proceedings.

In the first selection in this section, Sol Rubin briefly traces the history of providing due process rights to youths in juvenile court. Based on his earlier writings, he then makes the case that the *parens patriae* concept requires due process rights for children. The traditional juvenile justice system is based on the notion of protecting the welfare of the child. Rubin argues compellingly that looking after the welfare of the child would include treating the child as a person—specifically a person with rights. If a juvenile is a person with rights to be protected, due process safeguards would be appropriate in juvenile court proceedings. If an adult must be protected by the law, why shouldn't a juvenile?

The next selection consists of excerpts from the eighty-one pages of the revolutionary decision *In re Gault*. Gerald Gault was a fifteen-year-old boy living in Arizona. He was taken into custody as a result of a complaint that he made lewd telephone calls. Pursuant to the existing Arizona Juvenile Code, Gault was denied most due process safeguards, such as a right to a lawyer and to confront and cross examine witnesses against him. He was sent to the State Industrial School for an indeterminate period, not to exceed his twenty-first birthday—or up to six years. He appealed, claiming his due process rights were violated. The Supreme Court agreed and set forth minimum procedural protections for youths in juvenile proceedings.

Following the *Gault* decision, many state legislatures revised and codified various due process rights in the state juvenile court statutes. The third selection is but one of many examples of this state codification. Indiana's Family Law sets forth specific procedural rights for youths coming before the juvenile court. These rights, generally speaking, are those found in the U.S. Constitution's Bill of Rights, originally applicable to adults in criminal proceedings.

With a few exceptions, most of the procedural safeguards given adults—as defendants, prisoners, probationers, or parolees—are now also accorded to juveniles. One of the remaining issues is how far the juvenile justice system should go in extending procedural rights to juveniles.

The *Gault* case did not require *all* adult procedural rights to be accorded juveniles. For instance, the U.S. Supreme Court decided in *Schall v. Martin* (1984) that juveniles do not have a constitutional right to bail, notwithstanding the provisions of the Eighth Amendment.

What about the right to a trial by jury, one of the most basic procedural protections accorded adults? That issue is addressed in the next selection in this section—excerpts from the case of *McKeiver v. Pennsylvania*, decided by the U.S. Supreme Court in 1971. In the *McKeiver* case, the Supreme Court was confronted with the issue of going beyond the *Gault* case and granting juveniles the right to a jury trial. But the court could not take that major step, and held that the U.S. Constitution does not require a trial in the adjudicatory phase of a state's juvenile court proceedings.

If the juvenile justice system provides almost all of the procedural protections accorded to adults, should there be a separate juvenile court? This is the issue discussed in the final selection by Robert O. Dawson. He first examines the trend toward making juvenile court proceedings similar to adult proceedings and then gets to the central issue of retaining a separate juvenile court. After carefully considering the arguments on both sides of the issue, he concludes that the juvenile justice system should be retained.

5

The Juvenile Court
Needs a New Turn

Sol Rubin

The by now "old" juvenile court system has in its history been subject to considerable criticism and attack. The criticism, not much noticed when an occasional article or state court decision complained that neither the child nor the parent received even a semblance of due process before the court or other elements of the juvenile justice system,[1] startled the juvenile court judges when the Supreme Court of the United States rendered decisions in the same vein. The first decision, in 1962, condemned confessions obtained by "secret inquisitorial processes" as suspect, especially so when applied to a 14-year-old boy.[2] This did not touch the juvenile court directly, but presently others did.

In 1966, in *Kent* v. *United States*,[3] the Court reversed a conviction in a case transferred from juvenile to criminal court in accordance with the statute. It held that required elements of due process and fairness had not been met; it required a hearing, effective assistance of counsel, and a statement of reasons. The storm came over the following language in the decision: "There is much evidence that some juvenile courts, including that of the District of Columbia, lack the personnel, facilities, and techniques to perform adequately as representatives of the State in a *parens patriae* capacity, at least with respect to children charged with law violation. There is evidence, in fact, that there may be grounds for concern that the child received the worst of both worlds;

Source: *Federal Probation*, 45(2) (1981): 48–53.

that he gets neither the protections accorded to adults nor the solicitous care and regenerative treatment postulated for children.'' The next case, *In re Gault*,[4] generated even more excitement, yet its holding broke no new ground, and any other decision—once the Supreme Court took the case for review— could hardly have been expected.

The case is really of significance for its bringing to attention the still prevalent paternalistic (autocratic) pattern of the juvenile courts, what Roscoe Pound called ''star chamber.'' The Arizona Supreme Court upheld a commitment, to age 21, of a 15-year-old boy who was alleged to have made a lewd telephone call to a neighbor. The complainant was not present at the meeting; the adjudication was based on the judge's statement that the boy had admitted making some of the remarks, although Gault denied the charge. The parents never received a copy of the petition and they were not informed of their right to subpoena or cross-examine witnesses. One must blink at the crassness of the procedure, upheld by the Arizona Supreme Court on the ground that the juvenile court is noncriminal, hence the child was not being punished (despite the fact that he was committed to a training school for a potentially 6-year term), and, no punishment being involved, no due process was required. The United States Supreme Court reversed, only on procedural grounds, saying nothing about the 6-year commitment on a charge for which an adult could have been punished at most by a commitment of 2 months. We shall have more to say about this omission, and about the concept of ''noncriminal.''

The attack on the court (as distinguished from what we have called legalistic criticism) was of a different order. It was a reproach that the juvenile court was not stemming the tide of delinquency. It resulted at first in such statutes (of dubious constitutionality) as contributing to delinquency, sometimes requiring no fault on the part of the parent or other adult, and curfew and other restrictions on children. It included reducing juvenile court jurisdiction over serious offenses, giving jurisdiction to criminal courts concurrently with juvenile courts, or exclusively. More recently it has included demands, which legislatures initiated or to which they acceded, to expand these exceptions, so that more severe terms could be imposed on young people, and to reduce or eliminate such typical juvenile court provisions as protection against fingerprinting and dissemination of juvenile records.

In general, juvenile court judges were less agitated at the latter encroachments on juvenile court jurisdiction than they were at the due process requirements. Yet their complaint that the decisions threatened to make the juvenile court a ''junior criminal court'' could much more legitimately be directed to the legislative reductions in the privacy and confidentiality protections.

But such resistance as there was on the part of the old juvenile court system was principally based on proprietary values—due process additions were seen as taking prerogatives away from the judges, and the legislation was taking jurisdiction away from the courts. In fact, children were not necessarily dealt with more harshly in criminal court than in juvenile court, and the old charge that children were being overdetained and overcommitted by juvenile courts was demonstrated repeatedly with little or no correction. It is this circumstance, and other substantive protections that are needed, that point the way to the basic failure of the court—the failure to protect children.

Doesn't "Welfare" Include Rights?

All juvenile court statutes include the criterion of the *welfare of the child* in guiding the action of judges or other personnel dealing with the child or his parents. One would think that the "welfare" of the child included the notion that the child was a *person*, with *rights*. This is hardly the case. A juvenile court judge slated for the presidency of the National Council of Juvenile Court Judges wrote, in an article entitled "Should Children Be as Equal as People?"—"should children be as equal as people? Certainly not. They should not have equal liberty; they should have less."[5] When the National Juvenile Law Center issued a statement on the rights of children, this was its key sentence: "Youth or juveniles of today are the most discriminated-against class in the world."[6]

These statements of partisans might be of minor significance if not for what the Supreme Court of the United States has and has not done. In the Gault case the Court said: "The right of the state, as *parens patriae*, to deny to the child procedural rights available to his elders was elaborated by the assertion that a child, unlike an adult, has a right 'not to liberty but to custody.' He can be made to attorn to his parents, to go to school, etc. If his parents default in effectively performing their custodial functions—that is, if the child is 'delinquent'—the state may intervene. In doing so, it does not deprive the child of any rights, because he has none." The Supreme Court having said that, it did nothing to improve the situation, either in the Gault case or in any other case.

The phrase, a right "not to liberty but to custody" is confusing. It is the parents, not the state, who have the basic right to the child's custody. The child has a right to liberty, subject to that custody. To deny that right is still another way of asserting that the child is property.

The Court even recognized (again, in Gault) that "the constitutional and theoretical basis for this peculiar system is—to say the least—debatable. And in practice, as we remarked in the *Kent Case*, . . . the results have not been entirely satisfactory." Yet recognizing all that, the Court treats the child as property, not as a person, when it holds that a child may be beaten by its custodian.[7]

It would appear that a turn is needed in this "peculiar system." Since the needed change does not appear to be forthcoming in the courts, and since the juvenile court system is entirely statutory, the needed change ought to come through legislation. What is needed? As I see it—to truly protect the child (the *parens patriae* concept), the child must be treated as, must be, a person, with rights, not merely procedural rights in the court, but substantive rights without which he is not a person.[8]

In a book published in 1976[9] I include a model juvenile court act that proposes this turn, setting forth statutory language to effectuate it. So far as I know, it is the only model statute (or existing statute) to undertake this path. Section 1, Construction and Purpose, reads: "This act shall be liberally construed to assure children their specially needed services, human rights, dignity, and freedom as individuals and as functioning responsible members of the community. Each child is an individual, entitled in his own right to appropriate elements of due process of law, substantive and procedural."

To support this concept, I begin in the jurisdiction section (section 5), giving the juvenile court jurisdiction

> Where it is alleged that the child's rights are improperly denied or infringed. Such rights shall include:
> (a) Rights specifically granted to children, or which inhere in responsibilities imposed on parents or others on behalf of children;
> (b) Any complaint by a child, his parents or next friend, that an agency, public or private, which provides services or care to children, has discriminatorily denied such service or care, whether based on race, religion, nationality, or a child's or a family's social or economic status.

The concept of a child as a person with rights is also supported by *not* giving the court jurisdiction over "incorrigible" children, children beyond the control of their parents, and other such language, and certainly not the newest, vaguest, language in the statutes—"person in need of supervision." The evidence is that more harm than good is done by the court taking jurisdiction in these cases.[10] Instead, the neglect section (§5 (2)) gives the court jurisdiction "Concerning any child who is in a situation subjecting him to serious physical harm, or who is in clear and present danger of suffering lasting or permanent damage."

The neglect section differs from current neglect provisions in being applicable only in serious cases. Early cases declared that courts did not have neglect jurisdiction unless the parents were totally unfit. One case says: "Before any abridgement of the right (to custody) gross misconduct or almost total unfitness on the part of the parent, should be clearly proved." The author of an article tracing neglect law writes: "Certainly it cannot be questioned that where the child has been subjected to or threatened with serious physical harm, such as a brutal beating or starvation, the right of a parent to deal with his child as he sees fit must give way to the state's fundamental interest in protecting the lives of children. Short of some such severe and fairly objective danger, however, the state's interest becomes much more speculative."[10a]

The same subdivision gives the court jurisdiction "Concerning any child who requires emergency medical treatment in order to preserve his life, prevent permanent physical impairment or deformity, or alleviate prolonged agonizing pain." Such a provision is needed because current acts are no better—no more protective of children—than the 1959 Standard Juvenile Court Act, which allows a judge to order a medical examination of any child, without criteria, concerning whom a petition has been filed; and it can order treatment, without limitation or restraint stated in the statute, of a child who has been adjudicated. It can order examination of parents with only the vague restraint that the parent's ability to care for the child be at issue, and require a hearing.

I cite, in support of the provision, a publication of the Council of Judges of the National Council on Crime and Delinquency,[11] whose suggested language I have adopted. Section 20 in my model act provides for procedural requirements, attempting in it to provide due process protections in both emergency and nonemergency situations.

In contrast to the foregoing approach, existing juvenile court laws are like the Standard Juvenile Court Act provision, declaring that each child within the jurisdiction of the court "shall receive . . . the care, guidance and control that will conduce to his welfare and the best interests of the state." "The best interests of the state"—this is the kind of language that enables courts to take control over almost any child they want to, at the request of parents, schools, police, neighbors. The state should have no interest except seeing to it that the child's rights are given to him, the same responsibility it has to other citizens.

The *parens patriae* basis on which the juvenile court system rests is caring for incompetent persons. But some courts find children, at least in their teens, to be pretty competent. A United States Court of Appeals, in a case upholding the right of students not to participate in flag pledge ceremonies, stated that "neither students nor teachers 'shed their constitutional rights to freedom of speech or expression at the schoolhouse gates'; and it said, of the 14- to 16-year-old students, that they were not fresh out of their cradles. . . . Young men and women at this age of development are approaching an age when they form their own judgments. They readily perceive the existence of conflicts in the world around them; indeed, unless we are to screen them from all newspapers and television, it will be only a rather isolated teenager who does not have some understanding of the political divisions that exist and have existed in this country. Nor is this knowledge to be dreaded."[12]

The Supreme Court, on the other hand, does not speak in this vein. A Queens, New York, school board barred children from borrowing Piri Thomas' book *Down These Mean Streets* from the school library. A principal, a librarian, parents and child sued to assert their right to know; but they lost, and the Supreme Court refused to review it,[13] but there was a dissenting opinion by Justice Douglas who said, "Are we sending children to school to be educated by the norms of one School Board or are we educating our youth to shed the prejudices of the past, to explore all forms of thought, and to find solutions to the world's problems?'' The majority view is consistent with what is deemed ''the welfare of the state,'' which equates with great control over children, through truant officers, police—but principally the juvenile courts and their personnel and detention homes. And of course it is through the juvenile court and other special statutes restricting children that it is possible to conclude that this is a most discriminated against group.

As for the attack on the court for its failure to prevent delinquency (the cover for more punitive treatment), the Supreme Court in the Gault case says, ''The high crime rate among juveniles . . . could not lead us to conclude that the absence of constitutional protections reduces crime, or that the juvenile system, functioning free of constitutional inhibitions as it has largely done, is effective to reduce crime or rehabilitate offenders.''

But if I share the sense of some courts regarding the competency of teenagers, then I also place on them a corresponding responsibility. Accordingly, my model act would give the court jurisdiction over children only under 16 years of age, whereas most juvenile court statutes give some jurisdiction to children under 18.

Substantive Protections Are Also Needed

If the requirements of the *parens patriae* concept are to be fulfilled, more than procedural due process must be provided. Substantive protections are also needed. In the Gault case the Supreme Court made no reference to the provision in the Arizona juvenile court law permitting commitment of a juvenile until he reaches majority, in that case, 6 years. This provision, common to almost all juvenile court laws, has not been held to be unconstitutional, although the violence they do to the 14th amendment requirement of equal protection is obvious.[14] Accordingly, in my model act I provide that if a child is committed, ''in no case may the commitment or order exceed the term of commitment, authorized for an adult committing the same violation of law'' [§22].

More than this provision is needed. Considerable data attest to the general overcommitment of children.[15] The same section reads: ''Provided the act which the child is found to have committed was a violent act seriously endangering another person, and the child has a history of violent behavior, commit the minor'' etc. Senator Birch Bayh, when chairman of the Subcommittee to Investigate Juvenile Delinquency of the Senate Judiciary Committee, wrote, ''The incarceration of youthful offenders should be reserved for those dangerous youths who cannot be handled by other alternatives.''[16] This result has been substantially achieved in Massachusetts, by administrative action.[17] That is, such a provision is feasible.

There is another, perhaps even more basic protection that must be realized. Every juvenile court statute declares the proceeding to be noncriminal, and spells out some protections to the child that do not prevail in a criminal proceeding. Among these are confidentiality of records, and the declaration that a juvenile court record shall not be used against the interest of the person with the record. I doubt that there is a single jurisdiction in which these provisions are not violated. Violations are routine, even, and perhaps especially, where another government agency requests juvenile court information.[17a] Yet *without the noncriminality of the proceeding the juvenile court special procedure constitutionally fails.* And so long as in *practice* the noncriminality is violated, the proceedings are skating on thin ice.

Accordingly I have in my model act sections that attempt to make real the noncriminal effect of an adjudication. Section 23 reads as follows:

> No adjudication by the court of the status of any child shall be deemed a conviction; no adjudication shall impose any civil disability ordinarily resulting from conviction; no child shall be deemed guilty or be deemed a criminal by reason of adjudication; and no child shall be charged with crime or be convicted in any court. The disposition made of a child, or any evidence given in the court, shall not operate to disqualify or prejudice the person in any civil service or military application or appointment or in any employment, license, or service. On any application or in any proceeding a person may state that he has not been arrested or taken into custody if such arrest or custody occurred when he was under 16 years of age. On any application or in any proceeding a person may not be asked questions to elicit information of juvenile court proceedings, or adjudication, or apprehension when a child.

Section 27 on records and publication contains much that is found in the model acts and existing statutes, but attempts to strengthen them. Section 28 provides for erasure of arrest and court records, a procedure that has some precedent even in models and statutes relating to adults in criminal court.

Above I cited Senator Bayh who spoke of "other alternatives" to avoid commitment of most juveniles. My model act authorizes a fine as a disposition. Few juvenile court laws authorize fines as a disposition, but fines are an alternative disposition as important as any other. The Supreme Court in one case has encouraged the use of fines, to avoid commitment wherever possible,[17b] a view that supports the least restrictive alternative in sentencing.[18] I see no reason why this alternative should not be available for juveniles.

In the model act I have attempted to provide substantive due process ingredients again to avoid overcommitment. This is done in section 14, authorizing use of citation in place of taking a child into custody, and prompt attention to deciding on release if a child is taken into custody; section 17 authorizing trial by jury where an adult would be entitled to a jury trial for the underlying offense. The Supreme Court has upheld the almost universal provision in juvenile court statutes that deny children a right to trial by jury,[19] but several states do provide for trial by jury in children's cases, and the dissenters in the Supreme Court's decision cite the satisfactory experience in those states. In addition, some state courts have decided (as they can) that a jury trial is a right of juveniles in their jurisdiction.[20]

In all of the foregoing I have stressed the provisions in the model act that would turn the court around from one enforcing controls on children to one recognizing children with rights, the juvenile court enforcing those rights. But most of the act is a reaffirmation of the basic concept of a juvenile court—a noncriminal procedure, with informal hearings, and an intake process, fairly typical detention and shelter provisions, and so on. My view is that the current juvenile court statutes are in great danger of invalidation. As already cited above, the Supreme Court has said that "the constitutional and theoretical basis for this peculiar system is—to say the least—debatable." The doubts about the constitutionality of the system can be overcome only by making its noncriminality a truth rather than a fiction; and the *parens patriae* foundation also must be based on factual caring for the child, not a fictional pretense covering a quite punitive system. It is these fictions that I have tried to revise, so that the juvenile court can survive against constitutional doubts that now exist.

The concern of judges is that such a model reduces the jurisdiction of the court, particularly taking away status offenses, and reducing the age limit; but this model also *adds* jurisdiction—the bundle of children's rights that are included. As for the age level, the provision in the model is that the jurisdiction over children under 16 is *exclusive*, whereas most juvenile court statutes have a variety of exceptions under which children not only under 18 but under 16 can be—or must be—tried in criminal court.

The model act that I have proposed is only a beginning, but I hope it *is* a beginning toward not only a constitutional court but a system affording to children their rightful status as people with rights. I do not view *parens patriae* as contradicting that status, especially in the light of the comments of the Supreme Court in the Gault case, calling the concept of "murky" meaning. It is also only a beginning only in the sense that numerous other statutes, outside the juvenile court act itself, affect or govern the status of children. Certainly in a code on children I would prohibit corporal punishment of children. We worry about violence in our society. All the rationalization by the Supreme Court upholding corporal punishment of children, amounts to a justification of violence against children. But this violence at an early age must surely contribute to the general atmosphere of violence. Denmark has very little violent crime. When asked about it, a Danish criminologist said, "It is a cultural phenomenon, something you have in the culture of the United States that we don't have here. . . . We have never had this concept of fighting and competition in the Danish culture that you have in the States."[21]

It is quite clear that our system of compulsory education must be reexamined; that our child labor laws need modernization. Many states now permit children access to contraceptives and abortion without the approval of their parents. Most states have brought their age of majority down from 21 to 18. California has a freedom of the press statute applying to high school papers. Treating the child as a person and not the property of his parents would require a new look at the modes and ingredients of emancipation, perhaps not returning to an age level of 10, 11, or 12, as once prevailed, but not delaying until a child is out of his teens, either.[22] A code of children's laws, based on the concept of the child as a person and not property, a person to whom the Constitution applies, is badly needed.

Notes

1. H. N. Lou, *Juvenile Court Laws in the United States (1927).*
2. Gallegos v. Colorado, (370 U.S. 49 (1962).
3. Kent v. United States, 383 U.S. 541 (1966).
4. In re Gault, 387 U.S. 1 (1967).
5. Lindsay G. Arthur, "Should Children Be as Equal as People?" 43 North Dakota L. Rev. 204 (1969).
6. National Juvenile Law Center, St. Louis University, St. Louis, Mo., July 6, 1970, mimeo.
7. *Ingraham v. Wright,* 97 S. Ct. 1401 (1977). Outside the school systems the decision has generally been criticized; e.g., Joan Clark Olsen, "Physical Punishment in Public Schools," 61 Marquette L. Rev. 199 (1977); Nancy K. Splain, "The Ingraham Decision, Protecting the Rod," *Trial,* October 1977.
8. The idea of children having rights is quite *frightening* to some; Grace C. Hefen, "Puberty, Privacy, and Protection: The Risks of Children's 'Rights,' American Bar Association Journal, October 1977. But see: *The Children's Rights Movement: Overcoming the Oppression of Young People,* ed. Beatrice and Ronald Gross (1977); Henry H. Foster, *A 'Bill of Rights' for Children* (1974).
9. *Law of Juvenile Justice, With a New Model Juvenile Court Act* (Ocean Publications, 1976).
10. One California study found this: "Section 601 in effect permits irresponsible parents, overworked or ineffective school personnel and agencies unable to effectively collect evidence to establish parental neglect, to 'put a record' on a youngster who, in most cases, is not the one primarily responsible for the activity involved. It is a section ofttimes used against dependent and neglected children who are difficult to handle in company with other dependent and neglected children. It is also used as a 'dealing' section to encourage a plea where a delinquency conviction could not be sustained. The experience of Juvenile court judges has been that the intrusion of the juvenile court accentuates and perpetuates the family schism that is "characteristic of the 601 cases.' "—Report to the Governor and legislature of the Special Judicial Reform Committee of the Superior Court of Los Angeles County, February 22, 1971. That community agencies can do better in these cases is supported by another California study, "Preventing Delinquency Through Diversion—The Sacramento County Proba-

tion Department,'' noted in 3 Crim. Justice Newsletter 151, Sept. 25, 1972. See also Jill K. McNulty, ''The Right to Be Left Alone,'' 11 American Criminal Rev. 141 (1972); Sol Rubin, ''Legal Definition of Offenses by Children and Youth,'' 1980 III. L. Forum 512 (1960).

10a. Note, ''Child Neglect: Due Process for the Parent,'' 70 Columbia L. Rev. 465 (1970).

11. Council of Judges, NCCD. ''Guides to the Judge in Medical Orders Affecting Children'' (reprinted from *Crime and Delinquency*, April 1968).

12. *Russo v. Central School District*, 469 F.2d 623 (2nd Cir. 1972).

13. *President's Council, District 25 et al. v. Community School Board No. 25 et al.*, 93 S. Ct. 308 (1972). But the Court did uphold the first amendment right of public school pupils to wear black armbands in protest against the Vietnam War, *Tinker v. Des Moines Independent Community School District*, 393 U.S. 503 (1969). See Mike Wiener, ''Free Press in the High Schools,'' *The Nation*, January 28, 1978.

14. Sol Rubin, *The Law of Criminal Correction* ch. 12 §§ 10–12 (1973).

15. Sol Rubin, ''Children as Victims of Overinstitutionalization,'' *Child Welfare*. No. 1, 1972.

16. Birch Bayh, ''New Directions for Juvenile Justice,'' *Trial Magazine*, February 1977.

17. Task Force on Secure Facilities, Division of Youth Services, Massachusetts. ''The Issue of Security in a Community-Based System of Juvenile Corrections'' (1978).

17a. Edward V. Sparer, ''Employability and the Juvenile 'Arrest' Record,'' N.Y.U. Graduate School of Social Work, Center for the Study of Unemployed Youth, June 1966; John C. Coffee, ''Privacy Versus *parens patriae*: The Role of Police Records in the Sentencing and Surveillance of Juveniles,'' 57 Cornell L. Rev. 571 (1972). Sol Rubin, ''The Juvenile Court System in Evolution,'' 2 Valparaiso U. L. Rev. 1 (1967) relates the effort—that failed—by a Council of Judges committee to convince the Job Corps not to reject applicants because of a juvenile court record.

17b. *Tate v. Short*, 401 U.S. 395, 91 S. Ct. 668 (1971).

18. Sol Rubin, ''Probation or Prison: Applying the Principle of the Least Restrictive Alternative'' (*Crime and Delinquency*, October 1975).

19. *McKeiver v. Pennsylvania*. In re Burrus, 403 U.S. 528 (1971).

20. In the Matter of McCloud, Family Court of Providence, R.1., January 15, 1971: *R.I.R. v. State,* 487 P.2d 27 (Alaska, 1971).

21. Quoted in Michael S. Serrill, ''Profile/Denmark,'' *Corrections Magazine*, March 1977, p. 23 at 34.

22. See letter of Peter Bull, *American Bar Association Journal*, January 1978, at 12.

6

Excerpts from
In re Gault

Appeal from the Supreme Court of Arizona . . .
Decided May 15, 1967.

MR. JUSTICE FORTAS delivered the opinion of the Court.

This is an appeal under 28 U.S.C. § 1257 (2) from a judgment of the Supreme Court of Arizona affirming the dismissal of a petition for a writ of habeas corpus. 99 Ariz. 181, 407 P.2d 760 (1965). The petition sought the release of Gerald Francis Gault, appellants' 15-year-old son, who had been committed as a juvenile delinquent to the State Industrial School by the Juvenile Court of Gila County, Arizona. The Supreme Court of Arizona affirmed dismissal of the writ against various arguments which included an attack upon the constitutionality of the Arizona Juvenile Code because of its alleged denial of procedural due process to juveniles charged with being "delinquents." The court agreed that the constitutional guarantee of due process of law is applicable in such proceedings. It held that Arizona's Juvenile Code is to be read as "impliedly" implementing the "due process concept." It then proceeded to identify and describe "the particular elements which constitute due process in a juvenile hearing." It concluded that the proceedings ending in commitment of Gerald Gault did not offend those requirements. We do not agree, and we reverse. We begin with a statement of the facts.

Source: *In re Gault*, 387 U.S. 1 (1967).

On Monday, June 8, 1964, at about 10 a.m., Gerald Francis Gault and a friend, Ronald Lewis, were taken into custody by the Sheriff of Gila County. Gerald was then still subject to a six months' probation order which had been entered on February 25, 1964, as a result of his having been in the company of another boy who had stolen a wallet from a lady's purse. The police action on June 8 was taken as the result of a verbal complaint by a neighbor of the boys, Mrs. Cook, about a telephone call made to her in which the caller or callers made lewd or indecent remarks. It will suffice for purposes of this opinion to say that the remarks or questions put to her were of the irritatingly offensive, adolescent, sex variety.

At the time Gerald was picked up, his mother and father were both at work. No notice that Gerald was being taken into custody was left at the home. No other steps were taken to advise them that their son had, in effect, been arrested. Gerald was taken to the Children's Detention Home. When his mother arrived home at about 6 o'clock, Gerald was not there. Gerald's older brother was sent to look for him at the trailer home of the Lewis family. He apparently learned then that Gerald was in custody. He so informed his mother. The two of them went to the Detention Home. The deputy probation officer, Flagg, who was also superintendent of the Detention Home, told Mrs. Gault "why Jerry was there" and said that a hearing would be held in Juvenile Court at 3 o'clock the following day, June 9.

Officer Flagg filed a petition with the court on the hearing day, June 9, 1964. It was not served on the Gaults. Indeed, none of them saw this petition until the habeas corpus hearing on August 17, 1964. The petition was entirely formal. It made no reference to any factual basis for the judicial action which it initiated. It recited only that "said minor is under the age of eighteen years, and is in need of the protection of this Honorable Court; [and that] said minor is a delinquent minor." It prayed for a hearing and an order regarding "the care and custody of said minor." Officer Flagg executed a formal affidavit in support of the petition.

On June 9, Gerald, his mother, his older brother, and Probation Officers Flagg and Henderson appeared before the Juvenile Judge in chambers. Gerald's father was not there. He was at work out of the city. Mrs. Cook, the complainant, was not there. No one was sworn at this hearing. No transcript or recording was made. No memorandum or record of the substance of the proceedings was prepared. Our information about the proceedings and the subsequent hearing on June 15, derives entirely from the testimony of the Juvenile Court Judge,[1] Mr. and Mrs. Gault and Officer Flagg at the habeas corpus proceeding conducted two months later. From this, it appears that at the June 9 hearing Gerald was questioned by the judge about the telephone call. There was conflict as to what he said. His mother recalled that Gerald said he only dialed Mrs. Cook's number and handed the telephone to his friend, Ronald. Officer Flagg recalled that Gerald had admitted making the lewd remarks. Judge McGhee testified that Gerald "admitted making one of these [lewd] statements." At the conclusion of the hearing, the judge said he would "think about it." Gerald was taken back to the Detention Home. He was not sent to his own home with his parents. On June 11 or 12, after having been detained since June 8, Gerald was released and driven home.[2] There is no explanation in the record as to why he was kept in the Detention Home or why he was released. At 5 p.m. on the day of Gerald's release, Mrs. Gault received a note signed by Officer Flagg. It was on plain paper, not letterhead: Its entire text was as follows:

> Mrs. Gault:
>   Judge McGHEE has set Monday June 15, 1964 at 11:00 A.M. as the date and time for further Hearings on Gerald's delinquency
>
> /s/Flagg

At the appointed time on Monday, June 15, Gerald, his father and mother, Ronald Lewis and his father, and Officers Flagg and Henderson were present before Judge McGhee. Witnesses at the habeas corpus proceeding differed in their recollections of Gerald's testimony at the June 15 hearing. Mr. and Mrs. Gault recalled that Gerald again testified that he had only dialed the number and that the other boy had made the remarks. Officer Flagg agreed that at this hearing Gerald did not admit making the lewd remarks.[3] But Judge McGhee recalled that "there was some admission again of some of the lewd statements. He—he didn't admit any of the more serious lewd statements."[6] Again, the complainant, Mrs. Cook, was not present. Mrs. Gault asked that Mrs. Cook be present "so she could see which boy that done the talking, the dirty talking over the phone." The Juvenile Judge said "she didn't have to be present at that hearing." The judge did not speak to Mrs. Cook or communicate with her at any time. Probation Officer Flagg had talked to her once—over the telephone on June 9.

At this June 15 hearing a "referral report" made by the probation officers was filed with the court, although not disclosed to Gerald or his parents. This listed the charge as "Lewd Phone Calls." At the conclusion of the hearing, the judge committed Gerald as a juvenile delinquent to the State Industrial School "for the period of his minority [that is, until twenty-one], unless sooner discharged by due process of law." An order to that effect was entered. It recites that "after a full hearing and due deliberation the Court finds that said minor is a delinquent child, and that said minor is of the age of fifteen years."

No appeal is permitted by Arizona law in juvenile cases. On August 3, 1964, a petition for a writ of habeas corpus was filed with the Supreme Court of Arizona and referred by it to the Superior Court for hearing.

At the habeas corpus hearing on August 17, Judge McGhee was vigorously cross-examined as to the basis for his actions. He testified that he had taken into account the fact that Gerald was on probation. He was asked "under what section of . . . the code you found the boy delinquent?"

His answer is set forth in the end notes.[5] In substance, he concluded that Gerald came within ARS § 8-201-6(a), which specifies that a "delinquent child" includes one "who has violated a law of the state or an ordinance or regulation of a political subdivision thereof." The law which Gerald was found to have violated is ARS § 13-377. This section of the Arizona Criminal Code provides that a person who "in the presence or hearing of any woman or child . . . uses vulgar, abusive or obscene language, is guilty of a misdemeanor. . . ." The penalty specified in the Criminal Code, which would apply to an adult, is $5 to $50, or imprisonment for not more than two months. The judge also testified that he acted under ARS § 8-201-6(d) which includes in the definition of a "delinquent child" one who, as the judge phrased it, is "habitually involved in immoral matters."[6]

Asked about the basis for his conclusion that Gerald was "habitually involved in immoral matters," the judge testified, somewhat vaguely, that two years earlier, on July 2, 1962, a "referral" was made concerning Gerald, "where the boy had stolen a baseball glove from another boy and lied to the Police Department about it." The judge said there was "no hearing," and "no accusation" relating to this incident, "because of lack of material foundation." But it seems to have remained in his mind as a relevant factor. The judge also testified that Gerald had admitted making other nuisance phone calls in the past which, as the judge recalled the boy's testimony, were "silly calls, or funny calls, or something like that."

The Superior Court dismissed the writ, and appellants sought review in the Arizona Supreme Court. That court stated that it considered appellants' assignments of error as urging (1) that the Juvenile Code, ARS § 8-201 to § 8-239, is unconstitutional because it does not require that parents and children be apprised of the specific charges, does not require proper notice of a hearing, and does not provide for an appeal; and (2) that the proceedings and order relating to Gerald constituted a denial of due process of law because of the absence of adequate notice of the charge and the hearing; failure to notify appellants of certain constitutional rights including the rights to counsel and to confrontation, and the privilege against self-incrimination; the use of unsworn hearsay testimony; and the failure to make a record of the proceedings. Appellants further asserted that it was error for the Juvenile Court to remove Gerald from the custody of his parents without a showing and finding of their unsuitability, and alleged a miscellany of other errors under state law.

The Supreme Court handed down an elaborate and wide-ranging opinion affirming dismissal of the writ and stating the court's conclusions as to the issues raised by appellants and other aspects of the juvenile process.

. . . .

From the inception of the juvenile court system, wide differences have been tolerated—indeed insisted upon—between the procedural rights accorded to adults and those of juveniles. In practically all jurisdictions, there are rights granted to adults which are withheld from juveniles. In addition to the specific problems involved in the present case, for example, it has been held that the juvenile is not entitled to bail, to indictment by grand jury, to a public trial or to trial by jury.[7] It is frequent practice that rules governing the arrest and interrogation of adults by the police are not observed in the case of juveniles.

The history and theory underlying this development are well-known, but a recapitulation is necessary for purposes of this opinion. The Juvenile Court movement began in this country at the end of the last century. From the juvenile court statute adopted in Illinois in 1899, the system has spread to every State in the Union, the District of Columbia, and Puerto Rico.[8] The constitutionality of Juvenile Court laws has been sustained in over 40 jurisdictions against a variety of attacks.[9]

The early reformers were appalled by adult procedures and penalties, and by the fact that children could be given long prison sentences and mixed in jails with hardened criminals. They were profoundly convinced that society's duty to the child could not be confined by the concept of justice alone. They believed that society's role was not to ascertain whether the child was "guilty" or "innocent," but "What is he, how has he become what he is, and what had best be done in his interest and in the interest of the state to save him from a downward career."[10] The child—essentially good, as they saw it—was to be made "to feel that he is the object of [the state's] care and solicitude,"[11] not that he was under arrest or on trial. The rules of criminal procedure were therefore altogether inapplicable. The apparent rigidities, technicalities, and harshness which they observed in both substantive and procedural criminal law were therefore to be discarded. The idea of crime and punishment was to be abandoned. The child was to be "treated" and "rehabilitated" and the procedures, from apprehension through institutionalization, were to be "clinical" rather than punitive.

These results were to be achieved, without coming to conceptual and constitutional grief, by insisting that the proceedings were not adversary, but that the state was proceeding as *parens patriae*.[12] The Latin phrase proved to be a great help to those who sought to rationalize the exclusion of juveniles from the constitutional scheme; but its meaning is murky and its historic credentials are of dubious relevance. The phrase was taken from chancery practice, where, however, it was used to describe the power of the state to act in *loco parentis* for the purpose of protecting the property interests and the person of the child.[13] But there is no trace of the doctrine in the history of criminal jurisprudence. At common law, children under seven were considered incapable of possessing criminal intent. Beyond that age, they were subjected to arrest, trial, and in theory to punishment like adult offenders.[14] In these old days, the state was not deemed to have authority to accord them fewer procedural rights than adults.

The right of the state, as *parens patriae,* to deny to the child procedural rights available to his elders was elaborated by the assertion that a child, unlike an adult, has a right "not to liberty but to custody." He can be made to attorn to his parents, to go to school, etc. If his parents default in effectively performing their custodial functions—that is, if the child is "delinquent"— the state may intervene. In doing so, it does not deprive the child of any rights, because he has none. It merely provides the "custody" to which the child is entitled.[15] On this basis, proceedings involving juveniles were described as "civil" not "criminal" and therefore not subject to the requirements which restrict the state when it seeks to deprive a person of his liberty.[16]. . .

Failure to observe the fundamental requirements of due process has resulted in instances, which might have been avoided, of unfairness to individuals and inadequate or inaccurate findings of fact and unfortunate prescriptions of remedy. Due process of law is the primary and indispensable foundation of individual freedom. It is the basic and essential term in the social compact which defines the rights of the individual and delimits the powers which the state may exercise.[17] As Mr. Justice Frankfurter has said: "The history of American freedom is, in no small measure, the history of procedure."[18] But in addition, the procedural rules which have been fashioned from the generality of due process are our best instruments for the distillation and evaluation of essential facts from the conflicting welter of data that life and our adversary methods present. It is these instruments of due process which enhance the possibilities that truth will emerge from the confrontation of opposing versions and conflicting data. "Procedure is to law what 'scientific method' is to science."[19]

. . . .

Ultimately, however, we confront the reality of that portion of the Juvenile Court process with which we deal in this case. A boy is charged with misconduct. The boy is committed to an institution where he may be restrained of liberty for years. It is of no constitutional consequence—and of limited practical meaning—that the institution to which he is committed is called an Industrial School. The fact of the matter is that, however euphemistic the title, a "receiving home" or an "industrial school" for juveniles is an institution of confinement in which the child is incarcerated for a greater or lesser time. His world becomes "a building with whitewashed walls, regimented routine and institutional hours. . . ."[20] Instead of mother and father and sisters and brothers and friends and classmates, his world is peopled by guards, custodians, state employees, and "delinquents" confined with him for anything from waywardness[21] to rape and homicide.

In view of this, it would be extraordinary if our Constitution did not require the procedural regularity and the exercise of care implied in the phrase "due process." Under our Constitution, the condition of being a boy does not justify a kangaroo court. The traditional ideas of Juvenile Court procedure, indeed, contemplated that time would be available and care would be used to establish precisely what the juvenile did and why he did it—was it a prank of adolescence or a brutal act theatening serious consequences to himself or society unless corrected?[22] Under traditional notions, one would assume that in a case like that of

Gerald Gault, where the juvenile appears to have a home, a working mother and father, and an older brother, the Juvenile Judge would have made a careful inquiry and judgment as to the possibility that the boy could be disciplined and dealt with at home, despite his previous transgressions.[23] Indeed, so far as appears in the record before us, except for some conversation with Gerald about his school work and his "wanting to go to . . . Grand Canyon with his father," the points to which the judge directed his attention were little different from those that would be involved in determining any charge of violation of a penal statute.[24] The essential difference between Gerald's case and a normal criminal case is that safeguards available to adults were discarded in Gerald's case. The summary procedure as well as the long commitment was possible because Gerald was 15 years of age instead of over 18. . . .

We now turn to the specific issues which are presented to us in the present case.

Notice of Charges

. . . Notice, to comply with due process requirements, must be given sufficiently in advance of scheduled court proceedings so that reasonable opportunity to prepare will be afforded, and it must "set forth the alleged misconduct with particularity."[25] It is obvious, as we have discussed above, that no purpose of shielding the child from the public stigma of knowledge of his having been taken into custody and scheduled for hearing is served by the procedure approved by the court below. The "initial hearing" in the present case was a hearing on the merits. Notice at that time is not timely; and even if there were a conceivable purpose served by the deferral proposed by the court below, it would have to yield to the requirements that the child and his parents or guardian be notified, in writing, of the specific charge or factual allegations to be considered at the hearing, and that such written notice be given at the earliest practicable time, and in any event sufficiently in advance of the hearing to permit preparation. Due process of law requires notice of the sort we have described—that is, notice which would be deemed constitutionally adequate in a civil or criminal proceeding.[26] It does not allow a hearing to be held in which a youth's freedom and his parents' right to his custody are at stake without giving them timely notice, in advance of the hearing, of the specific issues that they must meet. Nor, in the circumstances of this case, can it reasonably be said that the requirement of notice was waived.[27]

Right to Counsel

. . . .

We conclude that the Due Process Clause of the Fourteenth Amendment requires that in respect of proceedings to determine delinquency which may result in commitment to an institution in which the juvenile's freedom is curtailed, the child and his parents must be notified of the child's right to be represented by counsel retained by them, or if they are unable to afford counsel, that counsel will be appointed to represent the child.

At the habeas corpus proceeding, Mrs. Gault testified that she knew that she could have appeared with counsel at the juvenile hearing. This knowledge is not a waiver of the right to counsel which she and her juvenile son had, as we have defined it. They had a right expressly to be advised that they might retain counsel and to be confronted with the need for specific consideration of whether they did or did not choose to waive the right. If they were unable to afford to employ counsel, they were entitled in view of the seriousness of the charge and the potential commitment, to appointed counsel, unless they chose waiver. Mrs. Gault's knowledge that she could employ counsel was not an "intentional relinquishment or abandonment" of a fully known right.[28]

Confrontation, Self-Incrimination, Cross-Examination

. . . .

We conclude that the constitutional privilege against self-incrimination is applicable in the case of juveniles as it is with respect to adults. We appreciate that special problems may arise with respect to waiver of the privilege by or on behalf of children, and that there may well be some differences in technique—but not in principle—depending upon the age of the child and the presence and competence of parents. The participation of counsel will, of course, assist the police, Juvenile Courts and appellate tribunals in administering the privilege. If counsel was not present for some permissible reason when an admission was obtained, the greatest care must be taken to assure that the admission was voluntary, in the sense not only that it was not coerced or suggested, but also that it was not the product of ignorance of rights or of adolescent fantasy, fright or despair.[29]

The "confession" of Gerald Gault was first obtained by Officer Flagg, out of the presence of Gerald's parents, without counsel and without advising him of his right to silence, as far as appears. The judgment of the Juvenile Court was stated by the judge to be based on Gerald's admissions in court. Neither "admission" was reduced to writing, and, to say the least, the process by which the "admissions" were obtained and received must be characterized as lacking the certainty and order which are required of proceedings of such formidable consequences.[30] Apart from the "admissions," there was nothing upon which a judgment or finding might be based. There was no sworn testimony. Mrs. Cook, the complainant, was not present. The Arizona Supreme Court held that "sworn testimony must be required of all witnesses including police officers, probation officers and others who are part of or officially related to the juvenile court structure." We hold that this is not enough. No reason is suggested or appears for a different rule in respect of sworn testimony in juvenile courts than in adult tribunals. Absent a valid confession adequate to support the determination of the Juvenile Court, confrontation and sworn testimony by witnesses available for cross-examination were essential for a finding of "delinquency" and an order committing Gerald to a state institution for a maximum of six years.

The recommendations in the Children's Bureau's "Standards for Juvenile and Family Courts" are in general accord with our conclusions. They state that testimony should be under oath and that only competent, material and relevant evidence under rules applicable to civil cases should be admitted in evidence.[31] The New York Family Court Act contains a similar provision.[32]

As we said in *Kent v. United States,* 383 U.S. 541, 554 (1966), with respect to waiver proceedings, "there is no place in our system of law for reaching a result of such tremendous consequences without ceremony. . . ." We now hold that, absent a valid confession, a determination of delinquency and an order of commitment to a state institution cannot be sustained in the absence of sworn testimony subjected to the opportunity for cross-examination in accordance with our law and constitutional requirements.

Appellate Review and Transcript of Proceedings

. . . This Court has not held that a State is required by the Federal Constitution "to provide appellate courts or a right to appellate review at all."[33] In view of the fact that we must reverse the Supreme Court of Arizona's affirmance of the dismissal of the writ of habeas corpus for other reasons, we need not rule on this question in the present case or upon the failure to provide a transcript or recording of the hearings—or, indeed, the failure of the Juvenile Judge to state the grounds for his conclusion. Cf. *Kent v. United States, supra,* at 561, where we said, in the context of a decision of the juvenile court waiving jurisdiction to the adult court, which by local law, was permissible: ". . . it is incumbent upon the Juvenile Court to accompany its waiver order with a statement of the reasons or considerations therefor." As the present case illustrates, the consequences of failure to provide an appeal, to record the proceedings, or to make findings or state the grounds for the juvenile court's conclusion may be to throw a burden upon the machinery for habeas corpus, to saddle the reviewing process with the burden of attempting to reconstruct a record, and to impose upon the Juvenile Judge the unseemly duty of testifying under cross-examination as to the events that transpired in the hearings before him.[34]

For the reasons stated, the judgment of the Supreme Court of Arizona is reversed and the cause remanded for further proceedings not inconsistent with this opinion.

It is so ordered.

Notes

1. Under Arizona law, juvenile hearings are conducted by a judge of the Superior Court, designated by his colleagues on the Superior Court to serve as Juvenile Court

Judge. Arizona Const., Art. 6, § 15; Arizona Revised Statutes (hereinafter ARS) §§ 8-201, 8-202.

2. There is a conflict between the recollection of Mrs. Gault and that of Officer Flagg. Mrs. Gault testified that Gerald was released on Friday, June 12, Officer Flagg that it had been on Thursday, June 11. This was from memory; he had no record, and the note hereafter referred to was undated.

3. Officer Flagg also testified that Gerald had not, when questioned at the Detention Home, admitted having made any of the lewd statements, but that each boy had sought to put the blame on the other. There was conflicting testimony as to whether Ronald had accused Gerald of making the lewd statements during the June 15 hearing.

4. Judge McGhee also testified that Gerald had not denied "certain statements" made to him at the hearing by Officer Henderson.

5. "Q. All right. Now, Judge, would you tell me under what section of the law or tell me under what section of—of the code you found the boy delinquent?

"A. Well, there is a—I think it amounts to disturbing the peace. I can't give you the section, but I can tell you the law, that when one person uses lewd language in the presence of another person, that it can amount to—and I consider that when a person makes it over the phone, that it is considered in the presence, I might be wrong, that is one section. The other section upon which I consider the boy delinquent is Section 8-201, Subsection (d), habitually involved in immoral matters."

6. ARS § 8-201-6, the section of the Arizona Juvenile Code which defines a delinquent child, reads:

" 'Delinquent child' includes:

"(a) A child who has violated a law of the state or an ordinance or regulation of a political subdivision thereof.

"(b) A child who, by reason of being incorrigible, wayward or habitually disobedient, is uncontrolled by his parent, guardian or custodian.

"(c) A child who is habitually truant from school or home.

"(d) A child who habitually so deports himself as to injure or endanger the morals or health of himself or others."

7. See *Kent v. United States,* 383 U.S. 541, 555 and n. 22 (1966).

8. See National Council of Juvenile Court Judges, Directory and Manual (1964), p. 1. The number of Juvenile Judges as of 1964 is listed as 2,987, of whom 213 are full-time Juvenile Court Judges. *Id.*, at 305. The Nat'l Crime Comm'n Report indicates that half of these judges have no undergraduate degree, a fifth have no college education at all, a fifth are not members of the bar, and three-quarters devote less than one-quarter of their time to juvenile matters. See also McCune, Profile of the Nation's Juvenile Court Judges (monograph, George Washington University, Center for the Behavioral Sciences, 1965), which is a detailed statistical study of Juvenile Court Judges, and indicates additionally that about a quarter of these judges have no law school training at all. About one-third of all judges have no probation and social work staff available to them; between eighty and ninety percent have no available psychologist or psychiatrist. *Ibid.* It has been observed that while "good will, compassion, and similar virtues are . . . admirably prevalent throughout the system . . . expertise, the keystone of the whole venture, is lacking." Harvard Law Review Note, p. 809. In 1965, over 697,000 delinquency cases (excluding traffic) were disposed of in these courts, involving some 601,000 children, or 2% of all children between 10 and 17. Juvenile Court Statistics—1965, Children's Bureau Statistical Series No. 85 (1966), p. 2.

9. See Paulsen, Kent v. United States: The Constitutional Context of Juvenile Cases, 1966 Sup. Ct. Review 167, 174.

10. Julian Mack, The Juvenile Court, 23 Harv. L. Rev. 104, 119–120 (1909).

11. *Id.*, at 120.

12. There seems to have been little early constitutional objection to the special procedures of juvenile courts. But see Waite, How Far Can Court Procedure Be Socialized Without Impairing Individual Rights, 12 J. Crim. L. & Criminology 339, 340 (1922): "The court which must direct its procedure even apparently to do something to a child because of what he *has done*, is parted from the court which is avowedly concerned only with doing something *for* a child because of what he *is* and *needs*, by a gulf too wide to be bridged by any humanity which the judge may introduce into his hearings, or by the habitual use of corrective rather than punitive methods after conviction."

13. Hurley, Origin of the Illinois Juvenile Court Law, in The Child, The Clinic, and the Court (1925), pp. 320, 328.

14. Julian Mack, The Chancery Procedure in the Juvenile Court, in The Child, The Clinic, and the Court (1925), p. 310.

15. See, *e.g.,* Shears, Legal Problems Peculiar to Children's Courts, 48 A. B. A. J. 719, 720 (1962) ("The basic right of a juvenile is not to liberty but to custody. He has the right to have someone take care of him, and if his parents do not afford him this custodial privilege, the law must do so."); *Ex parte Crouse,* 4 Whart. 9, 11 (Sup. Ct. Pa. 1839); *Petition of Ferrier,* 103 Ill. 367, 371–373 (1882).

16. The Appendix to the opinion of Judge Prettyman in *Pee v. United States,* 107 U.S. App. D.C. 47, 274 F. 2d 556 (1959), lists authority in 51 jurisdictions to this effect. Even rules required by due process in civil proceedings, however, have not generally been deemed compulsory as to proceedings affecting juveniles. For example, constitutional requirements as to notice of issues, which would commonly apply in civil cases, are commonly disregarded in juvenile proceedings, as this case illustrates.

17. The impact of denying fundamental procedural due process to juveniles involved in "delinquency" charges is dramatized by the following considerations: (1) In 1965, persons under 18 accounted for about one-fifth of all arrests for serious crimes (Nat'l Crime Comm'n Report, p. 55) and over half of all arrests for serious property offenses (*id.*, at 56), and in the same year some 601,000 children under 18, or 2% of all children between 10 and 17, came before juvenile courts (Juvenile Court Statistics—1965, Children's Bureau Statistical Series No. 85 (1966) p. 2). About one out of nine youths will be referred to juvenile court in connection with a delinquent act (excluding traffic offenses) before he is 18 (Nat'l Crime Comm'n Report, p. 55). Cf. also Wheeler & Cottrell, Juvenile Delinquency—Its Prevention and Control (Russell Sage Foundation, 1965), p. 2; Report of the President's Commission on Crime in the District of Columbia (1966) (hereinafter cited as D.C. Crime Comm'n Report), p. 773. Furthermore, most juvenile crime apparently goes undetected or not formally punished. Wheeler & Cottrell, *supra,* observe that "[A]lmost all youngsters have committed at least one of the petty forms of theft and vandalism in the course of their adolescence." *Id.*, at 28–29. See also Nat'l Crime Comm'n Report, p. 55, where it is stated that "self-report studies reveal that perhaps 90 percent of all young people have committed at least one act for which they could have been brought to juvenile court." It seems that the rate of juvenile delinquency is also steadily rising. See Nat'l

Crime Comm'n Report, p. 56; Juvenile Court Statistics, *supra,* pp. 2–3. (2) In New York, where most juveniles are represented by counsel (see n. 69, *infra*) and substantial procedural rights are afforded (see, *e.g.,* nn. 80, 81, 99, *infra*), out of a fiscal year 1965–1966 total of 10,755 juvenile proceedings involving boys, 2,242 were dismissed for failure of proof at the fact-finding hearing; for girls, the figures were 306 out of a total of 1,051. New York Judicial Conference, Twelfth Annual Report, pp. 314, 316 (1967). (3) In about one-half of the States, a juvenile may be transferred to an adult penal institution after a juvenile court has found him "delinquent" (Delinquent Children in Penal Institutions, Children's Bureau Pub. No. 415–1964, p. 1). (4) In some jurisdictions a juvenile may be subjected to criminal prosecution for the same offense for which he has served under a juvenile court commitment. However, the Texas procedure to this effect has recently been held unconstitutional by a federal district court judge, in a habeas corpus action. *Sawyer v. Hauck,* 245 F. Supp. 55 (D.C.W.D. Tex. 1965). (5) In most of the States the juvenile may end in criminal court through waiver (Harvard Law Review Note, p. 793).

18. *Malinski v. New York,* 324 U.S. 401, 414 (1945) (separate opinion).

19. Foster, Social Work, the Law, and Social Action, in Social Casework, July 1964, pp. 383, 386.

20. *Holmes' Appeal,* 379 Pa. 599, 616, 109 A. 2d 523, 530 (1954) (Musmanno, J., dissenting). See also *The State (Sheerin) v. Governor,* [1966] I. R. 379 (Supreme Court of Ireland); *Trimble v. Stone,* 187 F. Supp. 483, 485–486 (D.C.D.C. 1960); Allen, The Borderland of Criminal Justice (1964), pp. 18, 52–56.

21. Cf. the Juvenile Code of Arizona, ARS § 8-201-6.

22. Cf., however, the conclusions of the D.C. Crime Comm'n Report, pp. 692–693, concerning the inadequacy of the "social study records" upon which the Juvenile Court Judge must make this determination and decide on appropriate treatment.

23. The Juvenile Judge's testimony at the habeas corpus proceeding is devoid of any meaningful discussion of this. He appears to have centered his attention upon whether Gerald made the phone call and used lewd words. He was impressed by the fact that Gerald was on six months' probation because he was with another boy who allegedly stole a purse—a different sort of offense, sharing the feature that Gerald was "along." And he even referred to a report which he said was not investigated because "there was no accusation" "because of lack of material foundation."

With respect to the possible duty of a trial court to explore alternatives to involuntary commitment in a civil proceeding, cf. *Lake v. Cameron,* 124 U.S. App. D.C. 264, 364 F. 2d 657 (1966), which arose under statutes relating to treatment of the mentally ill.

24. While appellee's brief suggests that the probation officer made some investigation of Gerald's home life, etc., there is not even a claim that the judge went beyond the point stated in the text.

25. Nat'l Crime Comm'n Report, p. 87. The Commission observed that "The unfairness of too much informality is . . . reflected in the inadequacy of notice to parents and juveniles about charges and hearings." *Ibid.*

26. For application of the due process requirement of adequate notice in a criminal context, see, *e.g., Cole v. Arkansas,* 333 U.S. 196 (1948); *In re Oliver,* 333 U.S. 257, 273–278 (1948). For application in a civil context, see, *e.g., Armstrong v. Manzo,* 380 U.S. 545 (1965); *Mullane v. Central Hanover Tr. Co.,* 339 U.S. 306 (1950). Cf. also *Chalomer v. Sherman,* 242 U.S. 455 (1917). The Court's discussion

in these cases of the right to timely and adequate notice forecloses any contention that the notice approved by the Arizona Supreme Court, or the notice actually given the Gaults, was constitutionally adequate. See also Antieau, Constitutional Rights in Juvenile Courts, 46 Cornell L. Q. 387, 395 (1961); Paulsen, Fairness to the Juvenile Offender, 41 Minn. L. Rev. 547, 557 (1957). Cf. Standards, pp. 63–65; Procedures and Evidence in the Juvenile Court, A Guidebook for Judges, prepared by the Advisory Council of Judges of the National Council on Crime and Delinquency (1962), pp. 9–23 (and see cases discussed therein).

27. Mrs. Gault's "knowledge" of the charge against Gerald, and/or the asserted failure to object, does not excuse the lack of adequate notice. Indeed, one of the purposes of notice is to clarify the issues to be considered, and as our discussion of the facts, *supra,* shows, even the Juvenile Court Judge was uncertain as to the precise issues determined at the two "hearings." Since the Gaults had no counsel and were not told of their right to counsel, we cannot consider their failure to object to the lack of constitutionally adequate notice as a waiver of their rights. Because of our conclusion that notice given only at the first hearing is inadequate, we need not reach the question whether the Gaults ever received adequately specific notice even at the June 9 hearing, in light of the fact they were never apprised of the charge of being habitually involved in immoral matters.

28. *Johnson v. Zerbat,* 304 U.S. 458, 464 (1938); *Carnley v. Cochran,* 369 U.S. 506 (1962); *United States ex rel. Brown v. Fay,* 242 F. Supp. 273 (D.C.S.D.N.Y. 1965).

29. The N.Y. Family Court Act § 744(b) provides that "an uncorroborated confession made out of court by a respondent is not sufficient" to constitute the required "preponderance of the evidence." See *United States v. Morales,* 233 F. Supp. 160 (D. C. Mont. 1964), holding a confession inadmissible in proceedings under the Federal Juvenile Delinquency Act (18 U. S. C. § 5031 *et seq.*) because, in the circumstances in which it was made, the District Court could not conclude that it "was freely made while Morales was afforded all of the requisites of due process required in the case of a sixteen year old boy of his experience." *Id.,* at 170.

30. Cf. *Jackson v. Denno,* 378 U.S. 368 (1964); *Miranda v. Arizona,* 384 U.S. 436 (1966).

31. Standards, pp. 72–73. The Nat'l Crime Comm'n Report concludes that "the evidence admissible at the adjudicatory hearing should be so limited that findings are not dependent upon or unduly influenced by hearsay, gossip, rumor, and other unreliable types of information. To minimize the danger that adjudication will be affected by inappropriate considerations, social investigation reports should not be made known to the judge in advance of adjudication." *Id.,* at 87 (bold face eliminated). See also Note, Rights and Rehabilitation in the Juvenile Courts, 67 Col. L. Rev. 281, 336 (1967): "At the adjudication stage, the use of clearly incompetent evidence in order to prove the youth's involvement in the alleged misconduct . . . is not justifiable. Particularly in delinquency cases, where the issue of fact is the commission of a crime, the introduction of hearsay—such as the report of a policeman who did not witness the events—contravenes the purposes underlying the sixth amendment right of confrontation." (Footnote omitted.)

32. N.Y. Family Court Act § 744(a). See also Harvard Law Review Note, p. 795. Cf. *Willner v. Committee on Character,* 373 U.S. 96 (1963).

33. *Griffin v. Illinois,* 351 U.S. 12, 18 (1956).

34. "Standards for Juvenile and Family Courts" recommends "written findings of fact, some form of record of the hearing" "and the right to appeal." Standards, p. 8. It recommends verbatim recording of the hearing by stenotypist or mechanical recording (p. 76) and urges that the judge make clear to the child and family their right to appeal (p. 78). See also, Standard Family Court Act §§ 19, 24, 28; Standard Juvenile Court Act §§ 19, 24, 28. The Harvard Law Review Note, p. 799, states that "The result [of the infrequency of appeals due to absence of record, indigency, etc.] is that juvenile court proceedings are largely unsupervised." The Nat'l Crime Comm'n Report observes, p. 86, that "records make possible appeals which, even if they do not occur, impart by their possibility a healthy atmosphere of accountability."

7

Indiana Juvenile Statutes— Procedural Protections

31-6-4-13 Delinquent Child

Sec. 13. (a) This section applies only to a child alleged to be a delinquent child.

(b) The juvenile court shall hold an initial hearing on each petition.

(c) The juvenile court shall first determine whether counsel has been waived under IC 31-6-7-3 or whether counsel has been previously obtained. If not waived or previously obtained, counsel shall be appointed under IC 31-6-7-2.

(d) The court shall next determine whether the prosecutor intends to seek a waiver of jurisdiction under IC 31-6-2-4. If waiver is sought, the court may not accept an admission or denial of the allegations from the child under subsection (i) and shall schedule a waiver hearing and advise the child according to subsection (e).

(e) The juvenile court shall inform the child and his parent, guardian, or custodian, if that person is present, of:

    (1) the nature of the allegations against the child;

    (2) the child's right to:

        (A) be represented by counsel

        (B) have a speedy trial;

Source: Indiana Juvenile Statutes, 31-6-4-13.

(C) confront witnesses against him;

(D) cross-examine witnesses against him;

(E) obtain witnesses or tangible evidence by compulsory process;

(F) introduce evidence on his own behalf;

(G) refrain from testifying against himself; and

(H) have the state prove that he committed the delinquent act charged beyond a reasonable doubt;

(3) the possibility of waiver to a court having criminal jurisdiction; and

(4) the dispositional alternatives available to the juvenile court if the child is adjudicated a delinquent child.

(f) The juvenile court shall inform the parent or guardian of the estate that if the child is adjudicated a delinquent child:

(1) he or the custodian of the child may be required to participate in a program of care, treatment, or rehabilitation for the child;

(2) he may be held financially responsible for any services provided for the child or himself; and

(3) he or the custodian of the child may controvert many allegations made at the dispositional or other hearing concerning his participation or he may controvert any allegations concerning his financial responsibility for any services that would be provided.

(g) If the prosecutor has not requested that the juvenile court waive its jurisdiction, or if waiver has been requested and denied, the juvenile court shall then determine whether the child admits or denies the allegations of the petition. A failure to respond constitutes a denial.

(h) If the child admits the allegations of the petition, the juvenile court shall enter judgment accordingly and schedule a dispositional hearing.

(i) If the child has admitted the allegations of the petition, the juvenile court may hold the dispositional hearing immediately after the initial hearing. If the child denies the allegations, the juvenile court may hold the factfinding hearing immediately after the initial hearing. In each case:

(1) the child;

(2) the child's counsel, guardian ad litem, parent, guardian, or custodian; and

(3) the person representing the interests of the state; must first give their consent. *As added by Acts 1978, P.L.136, SEC.1. Amended by Acts 1979, P.L.276, SEC.24.*

8

Excerpts from
McKeiver v. Pennsylvania

MR. JUSTICE BLACKMUN announced the judgments of the Court and an opinion in which THE CHIEF JUSTICE, MR. JUSTICE STEWART, and MR. JUSTICE WHITE join.

These cases present the narrow but precise issue whether the Due Process Clause of the Fourteenth Amendment assures the right to trial by jury in the adjudicative phase of a state juvenile court delinquency proceeding.

The issue arises understandably, for the Court in a series of cases already has emphasized due process factors protective of the juvenile:

1. *Haley* v. *Ohio,* 332 U.S. 596 (1948), concerned the admissibility of a confession taken from a 15-year-old boy on trial for first-degree murder. It was held that, upon the facts there developed, the Due Process Clause barred the use of the confession. MR. JUSTICE DOUGLAS, in an opinion in which three other Justices joined, said, "Neither man nor child can be allowed to stand condemned by methods which flout constitutional requirements of due process of law." 332 U.S., at 601.

2. *Gallegos* v. *Colorado,* 370 U.S. 49 (1962), where a 14-year-old was on trial, is to the same effect.

Source: *McKeiver v. Pennsylvania,* 403 U.S. 528 (1971).

3. *Kent* v. *United States,* 383 U.S. 541 (1966), concerned a 16-year-old charged with housebreaking, robbery, and rape in the District of Columbia. The issue was the propriety of the juvenile court's waiver of jurisdiction "after full investigation," as permitted by the applicable statute. It was emphasized that the latitude the court possessed within which to determine whether it should retain or waive jurisdiction "assumes procedural regularity sufficient in the particular circumstances to satisfy the basic requirements of due process and fairness, as well as compliance with the statutory requirement of a 'full investigation.' " 383 U.S., at 553.

4. *In re Gault,* 387 U.S. 1 (1967), concerned a 15-year-old, already on probation, committed in Arizona as a delinquent after being apprehended upon a complaint of lewd remarks by telephone. Mr. Justice Fortas, in writing for the Court, reviewed the cases just cited and observed,

> Accordingly, while these cases relate only to restricted aspects of the subject, they unmistakably indicate that, whatever may be their precise impact, neither the Fourteenth Amendment nor the Bill of Rights is for adults alone. 387 U.S., at 13.

The Court focused on "the proceedings by which a determination is made as to whether a juvenile is a 'delinquent' as a result of alleged misconduct on his part, with the consequence that he may be committed to a state institution" and, as to this, said that "there appears to be little current dissent from the proposition that the Due Process Clause has a role to play." *Ibid. Kent* was adhered to: "We reiterate this view, here in connection with a juvenile court adjudication of 'delinquency,' as a requirement which is part of the Due Process Clause of the Fourteenth Amendment of our Constitution." *Id.*, at 30–31. Due process, in that proceeding, was held to embrace adequate written notice; advice as to the right to counsel, retained or appointed; confrontation; and cross-examination. The privilege against self-incrimination was also held available to the juvenile. The Court refrained from deciding whether a State must provide appellate review in juvenile cases or a transcript or recording of the hearings.

5. *DeBacker* v. *Brainard,* 396 U.S. 28 (1969), presented, by state habeas corpus, a challenge to a Nebraska statute providing that juvenile court hearings "shall be conducted by the judge without a jury in an informal manner." However, because that appellant's hearing had antedated the decisions in *Duncan* v. *Louisiana,* 391 U.S. 145 (1968), and *Bloom* v. *Illinois,* 391 U.S. 194 (1968), and because *Duncan* and *Bloom* had been given only prospective application by *DeStefano* v. *Woods,* 392 U.S. 631 (1968), DeBacker's case was deemed an inappropriate one for resolution of the jury trial issue. His appeal was therefore dismissed. MR. JUSTICE BLACK and MR. JUSTICE DOUGLAS, in separate dissents, took the position that a juvenile is entitled to a jury

trial at the adjudicative stage. MR. JUSTICE BLACK described this as "a right which is surely one of the fundamental aspects of criminal justice in the English-speaking world," 396 U.S., at 34, and MR. JUSTICE DOUGLAS described it as a right required by the Sixth and Fourteenth Amendments "where the delinquency charged is an offense that, if the person were an adult, would be a crime triable by jury." 396 U.S., at 35.

6. *In re Winship*, 397 U.S. 358 (1970), concerned a 12-year-old charged with delinquency for having taken money from a woman's purse. The Court held that "the Due Process Clause protects the accused against conviction except upon proof beyond a reasonable doubt of every fact necessary to constitute the crime with which he is charged," 397 U.S., at 364, and then went on to hold, at 368, that this standard was applicable, too, "during the adjudicatory stage of a delinquency proceeding."

From these six cases—*Haley, Gallegos, Kent, Gault, DeBacker,* and *Winship*—it is apparent that:

1. Some of the constitutional requirements attendant upon the state criminal trial have equal application to that part of the state juvenile proceeding that is adjudicative in nature. Among these are the rights to appropriate notice, to counsel, to confrontation and to cross-examination, and the privilege against self-incrimination. Included, also, is the standard of proof beyond a reasonable doubt.

2. The Court, however, has not yet said that all rights constitutionally assured to an adult accused of crime also are to be enforced or made available to the juvenile in his delinquency proceeding. Indeed, the Court specifically has refrained from going that far:

> We do not mean by this to indicate that the hearing to be held must conform with all of the requirements of a criminal trial or even of the usual administrative hearing; but we do hold that the hearing must measure up to the essentials of due process and fair treatment. *Kent*, 383 U.S., at 562; *Gault*, 387 U.S., at 30.

3. The Court, although recognizing the high hopes and aspirations of Judge Julian Mack, the leaders of the Jane Addams School[1] and the other supporters of the juvenile court concept, has also noted the disappointments of the system's performance and experience and the resulting widespread disaffection. *Kent*, 383 U.S., at 555–556; *Gault*, 387 U.S., at 17–19. There have been, at one and the same time, both an appreciation for the juvenile court judge who is devoted, sympathetic, and conscientious, and a disturbed concern about the judge who is untrained and less than fully imbued with an understanding approach to the complex problems of childhood and adolescence. There has been praise for the system and its purposes, and there has been alarm over its defects.

4. The Court has insisted that these successive decisions do not spell the doom of the juvenile court system or even deprive it of its "informality, flexibility, or speed." *Winship,* 397 U.S., at 366. On the other hand, a concern precisely to the opposite effect was expressed by two dissenters in *Winship, Id.*, at 375–376.

With this substantial background already developed, we turn to the facts of the present cases:

No. 322. Joseph McKeiver, then age 16, in May 1968 was charged with robbery, larceny, and receiving stolen goods (felonies under Pennsylvania law, Pa. Stat. Ann., Tit. 18, §§ 4704, 4807, and 4817 (1963)) as acts of juvenile delinquency. At the time of the adjudication hearing he was represented by counsel.[2] His request for a jury trial was denied and his case was heard by Judge Theodore S. Gutowicz of the Court of Common Pleas, Family Division, Juvenile Branch, of Philadelphia County, Pennsylvania. McKeiver was adjudged a delinquent upon findings that he had violated a law of the Commonwealth. Pa. Stat. Ann., Tit. 11, § 243 (4) (a) (1965). He was placed on probation. On appeal, the Superior Court affirmed without opinion. *In re McKeiver,* 215 Pa. Super. 760, 255 A. 2d 921 (1969).

Edward Terry, then age 15, in January 1969 was charged with assault and battery on a police officer and conspiracy (misdemeanors under Pennsylvania law, Pa. Stat. Ann., Tit. 18, §§ 4708 and 4302 (1963)) as acts of juvenile delinquency. His counsel's request for a jury trial was denied and his case was heard by Judge Joseph C. Bruno of the same Juvenile Branch of the Court of Common Pleas of Philadelphia County. Terry was adjudged a delinquent on the charges. This followed an adjudication and commitment in the preceding week for an assault on a teacher. He was committed, as he had been on the earlier charge, to the Youth Development Center at Cornwells Heights. On appeal, the Superior Court affirmed without opinion. *In re Terry,* 215 Pa. Super. 762, 255 A. 2d 922 (1969).

The Supreme Court of Pennsylvania granted leave to appeal in both cases and consolidated them. The single question considered, as phrased by the court, was "whether there is a constitutional right to a jury trial in juvenile court." The answer, one justice dissenting, was in the negative. *In re Terry,* 438 Pa. 339, 265 A. 2d 350 (1970). We noted probable jurisdiction. 399 U.S. 925 (1970).

The details of the McKeiver and Terry offenses are set forth in Justice Roberts' opinion for the Pennsylvania court, 438 Pa., at 341–342, nn. 1 and 2, 265 A. 2d, at 351 nn. 1 and 2, and need not be repeated at any length here. It suffices to say that McKeiver's offense was his participating with 20 or 30 youths who pursued three young teenagers and took 25 cents from them; that McKeiver never before had been arrested and had a record of gainful employment; that the testimony of two of the victims was described by the court as somewhat inconsistent and as "weak"; and that Terry's offense consisted of hitting a police officer with his fists and with a stick when the officer broke up a boys' fight Terry and others were watching.

· ·

The right to an impartial jury "[i]n all criminal prosecutions" under federal law is guaranteed by the Sixth Amendment. Through the Fourteenth Amendment that requirement has now been imposed upon the States "in all criminal cases which—were they to be tried in a federal court—would come within the Sixth Amendment's guarantee." This is because the Court has said it believes "that trial by jury in criminal cases is fundamental to the American scheme of justice." *Duncan* v. *Louisiana,* 391 U.S. 145, 149 (1968); *Bloom* v. *Illinois,* 391 U.S. 194, 210–211 (1968).

This, of course, does not automatically provide the answer to the present jury trial issue, if for no other reason than that the juvenile court proceeding has not yet been held to be a "criminal prosecution," within the meaning and reach of the Sixth Amendment, and also has not yet been regarded as devoid of criminal aspects merely because it usually has been given the civil label. *Kent,* 383 U.S., at 554; *Gault,* U.S., at 17, 49–50; *Winship,* 397 U.S., at 365–366.

Little, indeed, is to be gained by any attempt simplistically to call the juvenile court proceeding either "civil" or "criminal." The Court carefully has avoided this wooden approach. Before *Gault* was decided in 1967, the Fifth Amendment's guarantee against self-incrimination had been imposed upon the state criminal trial. *Malloy* v. *Hogan,* 378 U.S. 1 (1964). So, too, had the Sixth Amendment's rights of confrontation and cross-examination. *Pointer* v. *Texas,* 380 U.S. 400 (1965), and *Douglas* v. *Alabama,* 380 U.S. 415 (1965). Yet the Court did not automatically and peremptorily apply those rights to the juvenile proceeding. A reading of *Gault* reveals the opposite. And the same separate approach to the standard-of-proof issue is evident from the carefully separated application of the standard, first to the criminal trial, and then to the juvenile proceeding, displayed in *Winship.* 397 U.S., at 361 and 365.

Thus, accepting "the proposition that the Due Process Clause has a role to play," *Gault,* 387 U.S., at 13, our task here with respect to trial by jury, as it was in *Gault* with respect to other claimed rights, "is to ascertain the precise impact of the due process requirement." *Id.,* at 13–14.

· ·

. . . [W]e conclude that trial by jury in the juvenile court's adjudicative stage is not a constitutional requirement. We so conclude for a number of reasons:

1. The Court has refrained, in the cases heretofore decided, from taking the easy way with a flat holding that all rights constitutionally assured for the

adult accused are to be imposed upon the state juvenile proceeding. What was done in *Gault* and in *Winship* is aptly described in *Commonwealth* v. *Johnson*, 211 Pa. Super. 62, 74, 234 A. 2d 9, 15 (1967):

> It is clear to us that the Supreme Court has properly attempted to strike a judicious balance by injecting procedural orderliness into the juvenile court system. It is seeking to reverse the trend [pointed out in *Kent*, 383 U.S., at 556] whereby "the child receives the worst of both worlds. . . ."

2. There is a possibility, at least, that the jury trial, if required as a matter of constitutional precept, will remake the juvenile proceeding into a fully adversary process and will put an effective end to what has been the idealistic prospect of an intimate, informal protective proceeding.

. . . .

5. The imposition of the jury trial on the juvenile court system would not strengthen greatly, if at all, the factfinding function, and would, contrarily, provide an attrition of the juvenile court's assumed ability to function in a unique manner. It would not remedy the defects of the system. Meager as has been the hoped-for advance in the juvenile field, the alternative would be regressive, would lose what has been gained, and would tend once again to place the juvenile squarely in the routine of the criminal process.

6. The juvenile concept held high promise. We are reluctant to say that, despite disappointments of grave dimensions, it still does not hold promise, and we are particularly reluctant to say, as do the Pennsylvania appellants here, that the system cannot accomplish its rehabilitative goals. So much depends on the availability of resources, on the interest and commitment of the public, on willingness to learn, and on understanding as to cause and effect and cure. In this field, as in so many others, one perhaps learns best by doing. We are reluctant to disallow the States to experiment further and to seek in new and different ways the elusive answers to the problems of the young, and we feel that we would be impeding that experimentation by imposing the jury trial. The States, indeed, must go forward. If, in its wisdom, any State feels the jury trial is desirable in all cases, or in certain kinds, there appears to be no impediment to its installing a system embracing that feature. That, however, is the State's privilege and not its obligation.

. . . .

12. If the jury trial were to be injected into the juvenile court system as a matter of right, it would bring with it into that system the traditional delay, the formality, and the clamor of the adversary system and, possibly, the public trial. It is of interest that these very factors were stressed by the District Committee of the Senate when, through Senator Tydings, it recommended, and Congress then approved, as a provision in the District of Columbia Crime Bill, the abolition of the jury trial in the juvenile court. S. Rep. No. 91-620, pp. 13–14 (1969).

13. Finally, the arguments advanced by the juveniles here are, of course, the identical arguments that underlie the demand for the jury trial for criminal proceedings. The arguments necessarily equate the juvenile proceeding—or at least the adjudicative phase of it—with the criminal trial. Whether they should be so equated is our issue. Concern about the inapplicability of exclusionary and other rules of evidence, about the juvenile court judge's possible awareness of the juvenile's prior record and of the contents of the social file; about repeated appearances of the same familiar witnesses in the persons of juvenile and probation officers and social workers—all to the effect that this will create the likelihood of pre-judgment—chooses to ignore, it seems to us, every aspect of fairness, of concern, of sympathy, and of paternal attention that the juvenile court system contemplates.

If the formalities of the criminal adjudicative process are to be superimposed upon the juvenile court system, there is little need for its separate existence. Perhaps that ultimate disillusionment will come one day, but for the moment we are disinclined to give impetus to it.

Affirmed.

Notes

1. See Mr. Justice Fortas' article, Equal Rights—For Whom?, 42 N. Y. U. L. Rev. 401, 406 (1967).

2. At McKeiver's hearing his counsel advised the court that he had never seen McKeiver before and "was just in the middle of interviewing" him. The court allowed him five minutes for the interview. Counsel's office, Community Legal Services, however, had been appointed to represent McKeiver five months earlier. App. 2.

9

The Future of Juvenile Justice: Is It Time to Abolish the System?

Robert O. Dawson

I. Introduction

The juvenile justice system in the United States is approximately ninety years old. That age is old for a person and maybe also for a social-legal institution. There are signs it may be time to begin thinking about whether that system has served its purpose and should be abolished.

Initially, it is necessary to define what I mean by the juvenile justice system. I have in mind only that aspect of the jurisdiction of a juvenile court that includes criminal conduct and certain non-criminal conduct. Modern juvenile statutes normally label the former "delinquency" and the latter—often called status offenses—by various names, such as "Persons (or Children, or Juveniles, or Minors) in Need of Supervision." Usually included in the latter are running away from home, truancy, and (less often) incorrigibility or ungovernability. I exclude from consideration other elements of the possible jurisdiction of a juvenile court, such as adoption, termination of parental rights, child abuse and neglect, paternity, custody, and support.

I include within my definition of the juvenile justice system not only court proceedings but the entire legal process, beginning with law enforcement,

Source: *Journal of Criminal Law and Criminology*, 81 (1990): 136–155. Reprinted by permission of Robert O. Dawson.

through court intake and detention, informal and formal probation, and ending with the juvenile correctional process.

It is also necessary to state what I mean by abolition. I have in mind abolishing the juvenile justice system as a system separate from the criminal justice system. The result of abolition would be a merger of the two systems or, perhaps more accurately, an acquisition of the juvenile justice system by the larger criminal justice system. Abolition would not mean that all distinctions based on age would be obliterated; there would still be differences in how the criminal justice system treats defendants based on their ages. There would, for example, still be separation of youthful from older persons in pretrial and post-trial detention, treatment, and correctional facilities. The separations would not, however, be as rigid as they now are.

II. Why the Time May Be Right to Consider This Question

If one were to do an analysis over time of legal rights and legal structure, comparing the juvenile justice to the criminal justice system, with a view to determining the legal differences between the two systems, the results would not be uniform. Were it possible to conduct such an analysis with some precision, one would probably find relatively little difference between the two systems initially, say in the beginning of this century. Legal structures establishing juvenile justice as a separate system were just being established, but resources were slower in coming. The system initially existed more in name than in reality. It was not until about 1925 that virtually every American state had enacted legislation establishing a juvenile justice system separate from the criminal system.[1] There was initially more overlap in personnel operating the two systems. However, as the treatment philosophy underlying the juvenile justice system gained wider acceptance, the differences in legal rights and structure grew. Those differences were probably greatest in the late 1950s and early 1960s when the driving legal philosophy of the juvenile justice system was to entrust maximum discretion to the court and treatment staff with the absolute minimum of legal control.

But, beginning in the early 1960s, voices of dissent from the dominant legal philosophy grew.[2] There was increasing skepticism about the ability of the system to perform on its promises and increasing concerns about whether the abuses of power that occurred[3] were really aberrations or whether they were the norm.

This criticism of the system culminated in famous opinions of the United States Supreme Court in *Kent v. United States*[4] in 1966 and *In re Gault*[5] in 1967. The immediate reaction to these decisions was often to declare the juvenile system dead, but that pronouncement proved premature. The system survived that round of constitutional domestication, but did not remain unchanged. The major legacy of *Kent* and *Gault*—and, later, *In re Winship*[6]—was the development and enactment of modern juvenile justice statutes.

That legislation reflected a different philosophy from the original statutes. The emphasis shifted from entrusting maximum power and discretion to system officials to limiting and controlling those powers. Room was made in the system for lawyers—as defenders, prosecutors, and judges. And, with the presence of lawyers, the system changed even more in the direction of a law-driven system and away from a treatment-driven system. To that extent, the juvenile system came increasingly to resemble the criminal system. The differences had narrowed as a consequence of those landmark Supreme Court decisions and the legislation they spawned.

Since the time of the ''reform'' legislation, there have been further developments that have narrowed the differences. We have lost even more of our faith in treatment and have replaced it with shadows of the criminal system philosophies of individual responsibility and punishment. We have increasingly embraced restitution, community service, and even fines in the juvenile system[7]—concepts that would have been anathema only a few years earlier. We have become increasingly concerned with the violent juvenile offender and have responded to that person by adopting even more of the characteristics of the criminal system.[8] In a few jurisdictions, we have even replaced the traditional, broad dispositional discretion of the juvenile court judge with a system of determinate sentences much like those now in vogue in the criminal system.[9]

In summary, the *legal differences* between the juvenile and criminal systems are now narrower than they have been at any point in our history since the juvenile system was created. We have, in a sense, returned full cycle to the beginning. To be sure, both the criminal and juvenile systems have undergone many changes in the past ninety years; but looking only at the legal differences between the two systems, we do appear now to be very close to the beginning.

I have included an impressionistic chart of the differences in the extent of departure of the legal rights and structure of the juvenile system from the criminal over the past ninety years. Landmark events are noted on the chart. Of course, the chart lacks quantitative validity; it is instead intended merely to suggest visually the magnitude of differences I have observed.

One now encounters juvenile court judges who state (with disgust) when an appellate court requires adherence to a rule of procedure normally associated with the criminal system, ''We might as well give up and abolish the juvenile system.'' One also encounters prosecutors and defense attorneys who articulate the same thought, some with disgust and some with relish. To the juvenile justice traditionalist, the system seems to have changed far beyond any recognition.

Figure 9.1.   Aggregate Differences in Legal Rights and Structure

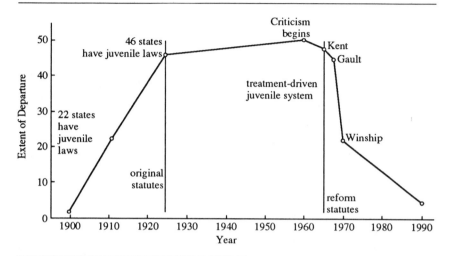

Taking a "legal snapshot" of the two systems at this time shows differences that are more nominal than substantial. We apply similar rules for both arrests of adults and for taking children into custody and for custodial interrogation. Identical rules for searches and pretrial identification apply. There is pervasive plea bargaining in both systems, only we are more likely to acknowledge it openly in the criminal system than the juvenile. The government is required to prove its case beyond a reasonable doubt in both systems and exclusionary rules apply with equal force. The guilt/innocence phase of court proceedings are separated from the sentencing phase in both systems, with the broad judicial discretion historically associated with the juvenile system now largely confined to the sentencing phase, as has long been true in the criminal system.

A cynic would examine the legal structure of the juvenile justice and criminal justice systems and conclude that one is an exact parallel of the other. The cynic might add that the only difference is in terminology and that such a difference exists only fraudulently to mask the underlying sameness. Thus, adults are "arrested" but juveniles are "taken into custody" even when the same law enforcement officer exercises the power and takes the person to the same police station. Adults are "booked" into custody, while juveniles are "processed." Adults are "jailed" awaiting trial or release pending trial, while juveniles are "detained." Adults plead "guilty" or "not guilty" to the "charge" in the "indictment" or "information," while juveniles plead "true" or "not true" to the "allegation" in the "petition" or "complaint."

Adults "plea bargain" most of their cases, while juveniles "stipulate" most of theirs. Adults have "trials" while juveniles have "adjudication hearings." Adults are found "guilty" or "not guilty" while juveniles are found to be "within the jurisdiction of the court" or "not within the jurisdiction of the court." An adult case proceeds to "sentencing" if the "defendant" is found guilty, while a juvenile case proceeds to "disposition" if the "respondent" is adjudicated. While both can be placed on probation, an adult who does not receive probation is likely "sentenced" to "prison" while a juvenile is "committed" to a "training school." An adult in prison is an "inmate" while a juvenile in a training school is a "resident" or a "student." An adult frequently is released from prison conditionally on "parole," while a juvenile often is released from training school conditionally on "aftercare."

An adult who is found guilty of having committed a crime is a "criminal"; a juvenile who is found to have committed the same crime is a "delinquent" or simply "within the jurisdiction of the court." The law specifically and in no uncertain terms declares that the juvenile adjudication is not a conviction of crime and carries none of the legal disabilities associated with such a conviction. In certain circumstances, we find even the term "delinquent" too harsh a judgment to place on the shoulders of a juvenile; instead, he or she is called a "Person in Need of Supervision" or some such similar euphemism. So ingrained is the difference in terminology, yet so self-consciously maintained, that when a judge or attorney is speaking about a juvenile case and accidently says the child was "convicted," he or she is likely immediately to correct the error, with a slight smile, by saying, "I mean adjudicated, or whatever you want to call it."

If the only justification for maintaining a separate juvenile justice system were the advantages that accrue from a distinct legal structure, a compelling case for abolition might be made. And, as will be shown later, there are substantial advantages that could accrue from "folding" the juvenile system back into the criminal. But there are considerations, some of which have little to do with different legal structures, that might give us pause in such an undertaking. Here, we are going to look at the advantages and the disadvantages of abolition. As in most such matters, conclusions depend upon the balance that can be struck between the two.

III. The Case for Abolition

There are two major clusters of arguments for abolition, which will be discussed in order: resource savings and eliminating frictional costs.

A. Resource Savings

Initially, it is important to observe that the wall that separates the systems is more complete in some jurisdictions than others, and in some places in the same jurisdiction than in other places. This fact has an important bearing on the resource savings that may be expected from the proposed merger. In some states, the same administrative structure, both line and staff, services both juvenile and criminal courts. In most, however, there is either a different structure from top to bottom or parallel divisions of the same state-wide department. In any event, in many jurisdictions there are adult probation officers and juvenile probation officers who are different people and work out of different offices with different support staff. In other jurisdictions, a probation officer's caseload may include some juveniles and some adults.

Similar distinctions may be found in the judiciary. In rural areas, the only judge available will be both the juvenile and the criminal court judge (and would also hear probate, divorce, general civil, and other types of cases). In urban areas, there are likely to be separate judges for the juvenile and criminal courts. In any event, the central point is that we already have in some parts of the country a substantial integration of resources between the systems. Abolition would not save resources in those places.

However, in jurisdictions without resource integration, the savings could be substantial. Duplication of many staff positions and functions could be eliminated—from computer systems to personnel officers to auditors to receptionists. Whether such duplication would be eliminated is, of course, another question. Merger would also permit more efficient use of courtroom space and personnel, such as bailiffs and court reporters. It should be observed, however, that in many localities such a savings would be difficult to achieve because the juvenile courtroom is located in a juvenile or family justice center several miles from the courthouse.

It would be possible, with relative ease, to combine juvenile and adult field probation officers and parole officers. Substantial savings might result from such a merger, especially in the elimination of duplicated staff positions and functions. However, juvenile probation officers perform many functions for which there are no counterparts in adult probation work. Juvenile officers frequently serve as intake and screening officers for the court system and also work directly with juveniles in pretrial detention facilities.

Merger might make some resource savings possible in detention and correctional facilities. It would at least create some opportunities for greater flexibility, both in assigning inmates (residents) to facilities and in transferring them from one facility to another. An old juvenile facility might be converted into a minimum security adult facility. One wing of an adult facility might be converted into a facility for youthful offenders. Of course, there would emerge a substantial turf battle between the county sheriff, who operates the local adult detention facilities, and the (former) juvenile probation department, which operates the local juvenile detention facility. Probably, the sheriff would win and would take over the juvenile detention facility.

In summary, the extent of resource savings resulting from merger would vary widely from place to place. It would depend upon the extent of pre-merger administrative integration, the configuration of physical facilities, and the extent to which officials wish to effect a resource savings or to maintain their own turfdoms after merger. The savings could range from great to almost none at all.

B. Frictional Costs

The juvenile justice and criminal justice systems are not totally separate from each other. There are bridges over which cases can and do pass from one system to the other. However, the fact that the systems are legally distinct makes those passages more difficult and more costly than if the systems were merged together.

1. Eliminating Transfer Costs Almost all juvenile systems have some mechanism for dealing with the case or the respondent that is beyond the capability of the system. Typical is the "*Kent* style"[10] transfer procedure. A case is filed in juvenile court against a respondent in the upper juvenile court age range. A prosecutor has discretion whether to handle that case as an ordinary delinquency case or to seek transfer of the case to criminal court for prosecution as an adult. Typically, a petition or motion for transfer must be filed, social and psychological studies conducted, and an extended, adversarial hearing held before the question of whether to retain the respondent in the juvenile system or to transfer him or her to the criminal system can be presented to a juvenile court judge.

Although transfer hearings undoubtedly occur in substantially fewer than one percent of the eligible cases that flow through the juvenile courts, they occupy a disproportionate amount of the time and energy of juvenile officials. Because transfer is extremely serious and the stakes are great for the respondent and society, the process is protracted and the hearing extremely adversarial. A transfer hearing is to the juvenile court what a capital murder case is to the criminal court.

The result of a transfer decision is merely to place the case in criminal court. It is not a trial. All of the trial and pretrial steps in the criminal court remain yet to be taken. A merger of the systems would totally eliminate the need for a transfer mechanism of any kind. The resource savings could be substantial.

2. Avoiding Frictional Miscarriages The separation of the juvenile justice from the criminal justice system is ordinarily based on the age of the offender at the time the offense is believed to have been committed. Thus, in many jurisdictions, if the offense is committed a day before the actor's seventeenth (or eighteenth) birthday, he or she must be treated as a juvenile and can be treated as an adult only if a transfer mechanism is invoked successfully. However, if the offense is committed on or after the seventeenth (or eighteenth) birthday, the case is a criminal case from the very beginning and the juvenile court has no involvement.

The difficulty with the system is that it assumes the appropriate officials will know the actor's true age. It happens that sometimes the arrested person will misrepresent his or her age in order to be handled in one or the other of the systems. Also, it is not uncommon for there to be official uncertainty about the age of the person arrested because of the lack of reliable documentation. When this occurs, it can cause substantial problems. In some systems, if the ruse is carried out long enough, it can mean that the actor goes free.[11]

Certainly, merger of the systems would eliminate any problems that occur because of the misrepresentation of the age of the accused or even official uncertainty as to age. While one cannot assert that such events occur often, they do occur, and when they do, the results are quite disruptive.

3. Providing for Continuity of Services   One of the abiding ironies of our handling of the chronic offender is that, although upon each pass through the juvenile system he or she is dealt with more harshly, upon becoming an adult, he or she is given a fresh start. A hardened juvenile offender a few days ago, he or she is now a first offender in adult court.

To some extent, this effect results from the confidentiality of records in the juvenile system that impedes the easy flow of information to criminal system officials. But, even when full information about juvenile involvement has been disclosed, there is an undeniable tendency on the part of criminal justice officials to discount that information substantially in making adult dispositional decisions. The person is treated as a first offender because he or she is a first offender in the system that is making the decision.

The ''fresh start'' phenomenon reflects more than anything else the attitudes of criminal justice officials toward the juvenile justice system. They view themselves as the real legal control system and the juvenile system as a ''kiddie court'' that only plays at legal control. This macho attitude ironically leads criminal justice officials to adopt a fresh start approach when a juvenile violator graduates to the criminal system.

That attitude is one reason why a surprising number of juveniles transferred to adult court for prosecution end up on adult probation supervision and why at least some persons of juvenile age and with prior juvenile system experiences who are arrested without identification misrepresent themselves as adults. A merger of the two systems would probably eliminate this totally inappropriate notion of a fresh start on crime when adult age is reached.

IV. The Case Against Abolition

The case against abolition is based on the same reasons the system was established in the first place. To a degree, then, it is an examination of the extent to which those initial reasons still have validity. The case against abolition is based on three clusters of arguments: (1) the notion that minors have less responsibility for their misconduct than do adults; (2) the greater rehabilitation potential of minors, justifying greater devotion of resources; and (3) the avoidance of inappropriate legal rules.

A. Lessened Responsibility

One reason for having a separate juvenile justice system is a belief that it is inappropriate to hold children to the same standards of responsibility as adults. Based on this same belief, the common law recognized a defense of infancy to a charge of crime. The matter of where to draw a line between childhood and adulthood is subject to different views and is ultimately arbitrary, but most people would agree that a line must be established and maintained. We simply react differently to misconduct by a twelve year old than to the same misconduct by a twenty year old.

We attach severe legal consequences to misconduct by the twenty year old. We label it a crime and the offender a criminal. We say that person has chosen to act badly. While we may recognize social and other restrictions on his or her freedom to choose, we believe that a choice was made and that one can be made by others in similar circumstances. We attach severe legal consequences in part to influence the choices others will make. We feel free to select the worst of adult malefactors for punishment, sometimes quite severe punishment. We save those we can and punish those we cannot.

With children, we are more likely to look outside the actor to understand the misbehavior. We are likely to look at parents, school, neighborhood, and companions. We view the education and development of the child as incomplete and, therefore, do not hold him or her to adult standards of conduct. We find it much easier to forgive the misconduct of a child than an adult. After all, the adult should know better.

So, for children we seek to avoid the imposition of the same severe sanctions that we affirmatively desire to impose on adults. We avoid the label "criminal" and its legal and social consequences. We solemnly declare that the juvenile justice system, which looks much like the criminal system, is civil in nature and that the child has engaged in delinquency, not criminality. We carefully provide for confidentiality of proceedings to protect the child. We protect court and other records from public inspection and, often, destroy or seal them once the process has expended itself and the child has been "rehabilitated."

For children, we believe they will behave as they are labeled by adults— that if we call the child bad, that is the way he or she will view himself or herself and, consequently, behave in the future. Therefore, we attempt to avoid labeling in the juvenile system because we fear that with impressionable children it will have the opposite effect we believe it to have with adults.

If the juvenile system were merged with the criminal, this philosophy of lessened responsibility would, to some extent, have to change. We would have to be willing to call the ten, eleven, and twelve year old who commits a crime a criminal, even though in the criminal system we might treat the child differently from the twenty year old who engages in the same conduct. One might question whether this is a step that we are prepared to take.

There is also the problem of status offenses, such as running away, truancy, and incorrigibility. If we merge the juvenile system into the criminal, we will lose this subsystem. That might be good or bad, depending upon whether one believes the juvenile system to have any business dealing with those problems—a matter of some current controversy. The loss would be almost certain, however, since it is doubtful that a state legislature would be willing to make it a criminal offense for a child to run away from home, or to be truant from school, or to disobey parents' orders. It is, of course, quite another matter to make such conduct a subject of juvenile court jurisdiction, especially when we label it something less serious than delinquency, such as "PINS"[12] or "MINS."[13] The fact that we engage in juvenile sublabeling is strong evidence that we would be unwilling to handle such problems in the criminal system. After all, if we are unwilling to call such conduct delinquent, would we be willing to call it criminal?

To merge the juvenile back into the criminal system is inevitable to abandon all or part of the notion of lessened responsibility of children for their conduct. Childhood would, to be sure, still be taken into account by prosecutors, judges, and juries in the criminal system and would undoubtedly be a major mitigating factor in individual cases. But the labeling would remain that of the adult and many of the legal disabilities of that label would apply to children in the criminal system.

How would the merged system work in those jurisdictions in which judicial sentencing discretion in the criminal system has been replaced by salient factor scores, offense severity scales, and matrices of the two? It might be necessary to reexamine the applicability of various determinate sentence schemes to youthful criminal offenders, since those schemes are premised in part on notions of adult responsibility. But that is a detail that could be worked out. Perhaps a new scale of mitigation could be added to take account of childhood.

B. Greater Rehabilitation Potential of Children

It is now fashionable to doubt the capability of the criminal system to rehabilitate offenders. Too many recidivism studies have been conducted with too many dismal results to permit many knowledgeable observers to maintain the faith. To a lesser extent this agnosticism has even crept into the juvenile system. We now think of "managing" juvenile offenders, rather than "rehabilitating" them. Those who still believe in the rehabilitation of children are likely now to place emphasis upon keeping the juvenile system from interfering with the natural process of maturation into adulthood rather than upon affirmative steps the system can take to rehabilitate an offender: first do no harm, then cure if you can.

It was, of course, one of the prime beliefs of the early juvenile system that children's behavior would respond to the intelligent application of public resources—that we could cure delinquency with the proper effort and with sufficient resources. To some extent, that belief even penetrated the criminal system and spurred the development of probation services, residential treatment facilities, and even treatment programs within the fences of prisons. There are people in both systems who still believe in rehabilitation, but there are proportionally more of them in the juvenile system than in the criminal.

Why is that? Some are merely traditionalists who still hold the beliefs of the pre-1960s. Others acknowledge the obstacles to rehabilitation, but believe that if the juvenile system can shelter a child from the destructive consequences (including legal ones) of his or her conduct until he or she has passed through the difficult years of adolescence, he or she may have a fighting chance of law-abiding adulthood. For them, there are sufficient success stories to cancel the depressing statistics. For them, the goal of the system is to keep the government off the children's backs until they can mature. In any event, many people believe that adolescence is a period of great life change during which anything is possible, and that if public and private resources are likely to be effective, it is during that period.

That belief likely accounts for the undeniable truth that children attract resources. It is easy to be sentimental about children, even those who misbehave in significant ways. They do, after all, have less responsibility for their conduct than do adults. There is always room for the belief that resources applied to children may actually make a difference in adulthood.

Children attract public resources. That is why juvenile probation officers almost always have lower caseloads than their adult counterparts. That is why juvenile institutions are smaller and comparatively better staffed than adult facilities. That is why there are comparatively more public facilities for children than for adults. We are simply willing to put our public monies on children more than on adults.

But the big difference is in private resources. An integral part of any juvenile justice system is a network of private, charitable, or religious institutions, facilities, and programs. These can be used by juvenile courts and their staff for placement or referral. These private ''correctional'' resources are used by the juvenile system thousands of time each year. There really is no adult counterpart to this private segment of the juvenile system, at least not in anything like comparable size.

What would happen to these public and private resources if the juvenile system were merged with the criminal? Would they continue at their current levels, or would they recede because there is no longer an easily identifiable beneficiary—the children of the city, county, state, or nation? Of course, no one really knows what would happen, but there is a risk that these public and, particularly, private resources would gradually recede. Juvenile and adult caseloads on probation, in institutions, and other facilities would gradually equalize at closer to the adult level than the juvenile.

This would likely occur because it would be difficult to maintain that part of the clientele of the criminal system is ripe for rehabilitation, while other parts are not. We would probably have more resources for younger criminals than for older, but the difference would not be as great as it now is. There would be a tendency to blur our devotion to rehabilitation as a consequence of merger, just as there would be a tendency to blur our concepts of responsibility as a consequence of the same merger.

Perhaps these public and private resources could be better spent elsewhere, perhaps not. In any event, one likely consequence of merger would be a net decrease in the resources now devoted to the two systems combined. But, newfound efficiencies might cause a net increase in the effectiveness with which those diminished resources are used.

C. Avoiding Inappropriate Legal Rules

The legal rules of procedure that govern the criminal and juvenile systems are virtually the same as a consequence of the due process decisions by the United States Supreme Court and the round of reform legislation that followed. There is a right to counsel and to provision of counsel at public expense if the accused is unable to afford counsel.[14] There is a privilege against self-incrimination in each system, despite the juvenile system being nominally civil.[15] There is a right to confrontation and cross-examination of witnesses.[16] There is a right to notice of charges[17] and to a requirement that the government prove its charges beyond a reasonable doubt.[18] There is also protection against twice being placed in jeopardy for the same offense.[19] The fourth amendment, with its exclusionary rule, applies in both systems,[20] as do the requirements of *Miranda.*[21]

The only federal constitutional right adults charged with a criminal offense enjoy that a juvenile charged with the same conduct does not is the right to trial by jury. The Supreme Court halted the due process revolution in juvenile justice at that point.[22] A handful of states provide for jury trials as a matter of state law, but most do not.[23]

If the juvenile system were merged into the criminal, there would be no denying children charged with criminal offenses the right to trial by jury.

That would be a healthy development in the law—one the Supreme Court should have taken years ago when it had the opportunity. In any event, it could potentially create a major change in the way we do business in the juvenile system—a change that many a juvenile justice traditionalist would contemplate with horror.

But there is another change that might occur that would be unqualifiedly catastrophic. Children in the criminal system would have the right to bail. Bail is a peculiar constitutional right. It is beneficial to the accused only if he has no other means of being released from pretrial confinement. Otherwise, it is a burdensome and corrupt system. In some communities, bailbondsmen control who is released and who is not before trial; in many, they exert great political influence over the local criminal justice system.

Increasingly, in the criminal system, bailbondsmen are being replaced by public bail systems. A quick investigation is conducted and if the accused shows ties to the community and, therefore, is likely to appear for trial, he or she is released on his or her own recognizance without the necessity of posting security or purchasing a bail bond. In a variation on that practice, he or she may be required to deposit a percentage of the bond amount with the court. Unlike a bail bond premium, however, this amount is returned to the person posting it if the accused makes all of his or her court appearances. Fortunately, in many communities, these public systems have totally displaced the traditional bailbondsman—but not in all.

Where bailbondsmen exist, they are extraordinarily powerful. They are likely to view adolescents as poor risks to appear for trial and are likely to be less willing to post bond for them than for an adult with a proven record of appearing for trial each time he or she is arrested. There could be no denying the applicability of the bail bond system that happens to exist in any community to juveniles now charged in criminal cases.

Bail has been handled in the juvenile system by pretending that it does not exist. The modern juvenile statute does not provide a right to bail and does not deny the right to bail. It simply ignores the subject entirely. Instead of providing by statute for a right to bond in juvenile proceedings, modern statutes typically provide for a prompt judicial detention hearing to be conducted under statutory release criteria.[24] While there are a few appellate opinions holding that such a hearing is an adequate substitute for bail,[25] the matter has not been fully tested, for no one has the heart to risk opening the doors of the juvenile justice center to the bailbondsman.

Yet, if the juvenile system were to be abolished, it would be difficult not to treat adolescents charged with criminal offenses like adults charged with the same offenses. Bail schedules would have to apply to all. Because of the volume of cases, bond would be set without much attention to the individual characteristics of the arrestee. In some communities fortunate enough to have release on recognizance programs, many adolescent offenders would be released. However, in those communities without such programs, release would depend upon the willingness and financial ability of the adolescent's family to post bond and upon the willingness of a bailbondsman to write a bond.

Since most adolescents involved in the juvenile process are totally dependent upon their families for money, whether they would be released on bond would depend not upon their resources, but upon those of parents and other relatives. Usually, that money could be better spent elsewhere, and the parents appreciate that fact. Further, they are very likely feeling quite hostile to their arrested child at that moment and, even if resources are available, may be unwilling to part with them for bail.

In summary, the bail bond system is a major problem in the criminal justice system. It is a problem that has, by common consent, been avoided in the juvenile justice system. Merging the two systems would likely make bail bonds a problem in the juvenile system for the first time. Bail bonds are, further, even less appropriate in the juvenile system than in the criminal because children lack resources of their own.

V. How Would Life Be Different under the Merged System?

The answer to that question depends in part on how different it is under the separate systems. The practical consequences of a merger would be great or small depending upon the legal structures and allocation of resources to the juvenile and criminal systems prior to merger. Here, we shall take a case through the merged system in an effort to detect differences. We shall assume that the now abolished juvenile system was fully implemented both legally and in terms of resources. That will suggest a maximum model of difference as a consequence of merger.

Bill Bob, fifteen years of age, is taken into custody for a felony offense—burglary.

Before merger, he would have been taken from the streets to a special division of the police department, called the Youth Services Division. He would have been processed, but probably not photographed or fingerprinted. His parents would have been contacted by a Youth Services officer. That officer would have screened the paperwork submitted by the arresting officer for factual and legal sufficiency. It is possible that the officer might have questioned Bill Bob in an attempt to clean up several recent unsolved burglaries. In any event, if this were Bill Bob's first felony offense, and if his parents were moderately concerned and stable, chances are that Bill Bob would have been released by Youth Services from its custody to that of the parents on the promise of the parents to bring him to juvenile court when required. The paperwork generated by the taking of Bill Bob into custody would probably have remained at a local law enforcement level, not sent to a central state or federal depository of criminal records.

If Bill Bob had not been released to his parents, he would have been transported by a Youth Services officer to the intake office of the juvenile court, located at the juvenile detention facility. If the arrest had been newsworthy, the local papers would merely report that a juvenile had been taken into custody for burglary, without identifying Bill Bob.

Under the merged system, Bill Bob would be taken from the streets to Central Booking. There he would be photographed and fingerprinted. He might immediately be placed in a cell, probably in a cellblock reserved for youthful criminal offenders, or might be taken to the Burglary Division for questioning, where an effort might be made to clean up recent unsolved burglaries. Someone in the police department might or might not attempt to contact Bill Bob's parents: that would be a matter of local law enforcement policy, since the state law would no longer require it. Once Burglary is through with him, Bill Bob would be returned to his cell to await his first appearance in court. The next morning, his fingerprints and a record of his arrest would be mailed to the central state depository for criminal records and to the F.B.I. If newsworthy, the local paper would fully report the arrest, including Bill Bob's name.

Before merger, Bill Bob, if not released to his parents by police, would have been interviewed by a juvenile court intake worker, who would have attempted to determine how serious the matter was. The worker would have examined, by computer or manually, the available records to determine whether Bill Bob was already on juvenile probation and whether he had any prior referrals to the juvenile court. The worker would have attempted to contact Bill Bob's parents. If they showed an interest in Bill Bob's release, chances are he would be released to them, pending further court processing. If Bill Bob had not been released by intake, he would have been processed into the juvenile detention facility, where he would have been enrolled in academic classes in an effort to prevent a major interruption of his schooling. A detention hearing might shortly have been held, at which Bill Bob would probably have been released if his parents were sufficiently interested in him to show up at the hearing.

After merger, in some communities, Bill Bob would be called from his cell to be interviewed by a personal recognizance program worker in order to determine whether he would be a suitable candidate for release without security. In other communities, bail would be set from an offense schedule and Bill Bob would remain in jail until a bail bond could be purchased by his family or until a lawyer was appointed (or was hired by the family) who could persuade a judge to reduce bond to an amount the family could raise. Bill Bob would be brought before a judge, probably the morning after his arrest. There, he would be warned of his legal rights, informed of the bond amount, and, perhaps, given the opportunity to apply for the appointment of counsel if indigent. If unable to make bond, Bill Bob would remain in the county jail, where he would watch television.

Before merger, Bill Bob's case would have been evaluated by an intake officer and, perhaps, by a prosecuting attorney. A decision would have been made whether to handle the case informally or to file a petition in juvenile court alleging the offense of burglary. The case would likely have been handled informally unless Bill Bob had an extensive record of prior referrals to the court. If a petition had been filed, a date for an adjudication hearing would have been set and Bill Bob, his lawyer, and his parents would be expected to be in court for that hearing. If the evidence against Bill Bob was strong, it would be expected that his attorney would have advised Bill Bob to stipulate to the evidence in the expectation that such a step would guarantee that the judge would give probation in the case.

In the merged system, the complaint filed by the police would be forwarded to the prosecutor's office for review of legal sufficiency. In some jurisdictions, the case would in due course be presented to a grand jury for an almost-certain indictment. In other jurisdictions, Bill Bob might receive a short probable cause hearing in front of a magistrate before the prosecutor filed an information.

Before merger, all of the court proceedings in Bill Bob's case would have been non-public, as would have been all of the court and other legal papers filed in the case. After merger, all of the court proceedings would be open to the public, although, unless the case is extremely newsworthy, at most only a few courthouse regulars might be expected to be present (unless Bill Bob is unfortunate enough to be in court the day Miss Jones brings her eighth grade civics class to observe justice in action). All of the papers in the case that were filed with the clerk of court would also be open to public inspection, although that is not much of a problem because finding the file (even for a court proceeding) often presents some difficulty.

After merger, Bill Bob's lawyer would plea bargain with the prosecutor, seeking a disposition that would permit his or her client to remain on the streets. Whether this materialized would depend mainly upon his prior record, all of which is open and available to the prosecutor and the court. If the record is extensive, Bill Bob, despite his youth, might receive a short prison sentence or perhaps a form of "shock probation," which might even include elements of the boot camp experience for youthful, male offenders.

Before merger, if Bill Bob had been committed to the state training school system, he would have been evaluated and probably assigned to a cottage or dormitory style living arrangement with children approximately his own age and under the supervision of house-parent types. He would have gone to school and perhaps received some vocational training and maybe even some counseling.

After merger, if Bill Bob was sentenced to prison, he would be transported to a large institution for youthful criminal offenders. There he would work and might also receive some vocational training or academic schooling. Forget about counseling. He would live with one or two other inmates approximately his age in a cell in a cellblock under the control of a correctional officer who most definitely is not a house-parent type. If he became a chronic disciplinary problem in the youthful offender institution, he could be transferred administratively to a less desirable facility.

Bill Bob would eventually be released on parole. Before merger, the time as a "resident" would probably be one-third to one-half the time after merger spent as an "inmate." Upon release, before merger, Bill Bob would have a record as a delinquent, although that record would not be public and would be relatively inaccessible from computer terminals. After merger, Bill Bob would have a record as a criminal, and that record would be universally available to any law enforcement officer in the nation with access to a computer terminal and with Bill Bob's full name and date of birth.

Before merger, Bill Bob might be eligible to return to juvenile court, after a respectable time following release from "aftercare," to petition the juvenile court for a sealing or expunction of his juvenile records. After merger, Bill Bob can forget about expunction. He had best spend his time memorizing an explanation for the arrest and subsequent events that he will be required to give for the rest of his life no matter how straight he goes.

VI. On Balance, Don't Abolish It

There are some very good arguments in favor of abolishing the juvenile system by merging it into the criminal. There might be some resource savings through efficiencies and some troublesome frictional costs would be eliminated. The criminal system's inappropriate concept of a fresh start on crime would likely be eliminated or greatly modified by merger.

These are all substantial gains. The losses would, however, be even more substantial. We would lose control over status offenses. While that is controversial, I wonder what a patrol officer is supposed to do when he or she observes a fourteen year old walking the streets at 3:00 A.M. if there is no justice system jurisdiction over running away from home. There are a number of communities that have invested considerable thought and resources into dealing with these status offenders. It is unlikely the legislatures would be willing to make such conduct criminal, and it would be inappropriate to do so. We would simply be withdrawing official authority over such conduct. Of course, status offenses could be made a type of parental neglect and some of the slack taken up in that fashion.

Do we really want to deal with bailbondsmen in our juvenile system? That would be a retrogressive step of giant proportions.

Finally, the undeniable fact is that children attract resources, both public and private. That is why the juvenile system is comparatively better funded and staffed than the criminal system. The juvenile system has a level of resources that officials in the criminal system can envy but not attain. Merger would have a leveling effect. Unfortunately, it would likely be a downward leveling effect. Public and private resources would flee from service to children in trouble with the law because the legislature abandoned all pretense of helping them by abolishing the legal system designed to deal only with them.

Notes

1. F. MILLER, R. DAWSON, G. DIX & R. PARNAS, THE JUVENILE JUSTICE PROCESS 6 (2d ed. 1971).

2. *See, e.g.,* Antieau, *Constitutional Rights in Juvenile Courts,* 46 CORNELL L.Q. 387 (1961).

3. *See In re* Gault, 387 U.S. 1 (1967).

4. 383 U.S. 541 (1966). *See* text accompanying note 10.

5. 387 U.S. 1 (1967). *See* text accompanying notes 14–17.

6. 397 U.S. 358 (1970). *See* text accompanying note 18.

7. *See, e.g.,* INSTITUTE OF JUDICIAL ADMINISTRATION—AMERICAN BAR ASSOCIATION, JUVENILE JUSTICE STANDARDS: STANDARDS RELATING TO DISPOSITIONS 42–56 (1980).

8. For example, in 1987, Texas enacted a determinate sentence statute for violent juvenile offenders that permits a lengthy sentence to be imposed by the juvenile court. The first part of the sentence is served in the juvenile training school. At age 18, there is a second juvenile court hearing to decide whether to release the respondent on juvenile parole or to transfer him or her to the adult prison system for further service of sentence. *See* Dawson, *The Third Justice System: The New Juvenile-Criminal System of Determinate Sentencing for the Youthful Violent Offender in Texas,* 19 ST. MARY'S L.J. 943 (1988).

9. The State of Washington has done so. *See* WASH. REV. CODE ANN. § 13.40.010 (1989).

10. Kent v. United States, 383 U.S. 541 (1966).

11. *See, e.g.,* Dawson, *Responding to Misrepresentations, Nondisclosures and Incorrect Assumptions About the Age of the Accused: The Jurisdictional Boundary Between Juvenile and Criminal Courts in Texas,* 18 ST. MARY'S L.J. 1117 (1987).

12. "Person in Need of Supervision."

13. "Minor in Need of Supervision."

14. *In re* Gault, 387 U.S. 1, 34–42 (1967).

15. *Id.* at 42–57.

16. *Id.*

17. *Id.* at 31–34.

18. *In re* Winship, 397 U.S. 358 (1970).

19. Breed v. Jones, 421 U.S. 519 (1975).

20. New Jersey v. T.L.O., 469 U.S. 325 (1985).

21. Fare v. Michael C., 442 U.S. 707 (1979).

22. McKeiver v. Pennsylvania, 403 U.S. 528 (1971).

23. *See* INSTITUTE OF JUDICIAL ADMINISTRATION—AMERICAN BAR ASSOCIATION, JUVENILE JUSTICE STANDARDS: STANDARDS RELATING TO ADJUDICATION 51–56 (1980).

24. *See, e.g.,* TEX. FAM. CODE ANN. 54.01 (Vernon 1987).

25. *See, e.g.,* L.O.W. v. District Court, 623 P.2d 1253 (Colo. 1981).

DISCUSSION QUESTIONS

1. How does Rubin make his case that protecting the welfare of the child includes providing procedural protections to youths in juvenile court? Do you agree with his logic? Why or why not?

2. What procedural protections did the Supreme Court accord juveniles in *In re Gault*?

3. Why is the Supreme Court reluctant to go beyond *Gault* and grant juveniles the right to a trial?

4. Do you think that providing some procedural protections to juveniles, particularly the right to an attorney, undermines the rehabilitative mission of the juvenile court? Why or why not?

5. What are some of the arguments for the abolition of the juvenile court? Do you agree with them? Why or why not?

SECTION IV

THE CHANGING PHILOSOPHY OF JUVENILE JUSTICE

Introduction

Following the significant changes in procedural justice, reformers focused their attention on the underlying philosophy of the juvenile justice system. There has subsequently been a push for *substantive justice* in juvenile court and corrections.

By the end of the 1970s, lawmakers began to respond to calls for harsher measures against juvenile crime by changing—sometimes substantially—the purposes of the juvenile justice system. In the past decade or so, at least a dozen states have modified the purpose clauses of their juvenile court statutes. Many states are now deemphasizing rehabilitation and stressing punishment, justice, accountability, and public protection.

Law and order groups have proposed more punitive measures for controlling juvenile delinquency. The goal of these proposals is to make the juvenile justice system more like the criminal justice system. These proposals aim to make juvenile sanctions harsher, hold juveniles accountable for their actions, and protect the public.

In some states, policymakers simply added new phrases to the traditional language of "the best interests of the child." Other states have replaced the traditional goals altogether. The new goals more closely approximate the underlying purposes of the criminal justice system—public protection, justice, punishment, deterrence, and incapacitation. Although these theoretical concepts are familiar to the criminal justice system, they remain poorly understood in the juvenile justice system, particularly to the extent that they are merely grafted onto the traditional philosophies of juvenile court law.

Experts have used different terms to describe this shift in juvenile justice philosophy and structure. Scholars speak of new "models" of the juvenile justice system. Among others, these include the "criminal" model, "punitive" model, "penal" model, "justice" model, and "accountability" model. Often these terms or concepts are used interchangeably; insufficient thought has been given to the differences, sometimes subtle, among these models. In addition, the logical corollaries of the models have not been adequately explored.

The meaning of "justice" in juvenile justice has long been confused and the subject of great debate. Some have argued that the concept does not belong in the juvenile justice system to the extent that the system's focus is on the best interests of the child and his or her rehabilitation. Thus, under the rehabilitative model, there is no necessary relationship between the offense committed and the disposition, that is, between the harm done and, for example, the length of stay in an institution.

Others argue, by contrast, that justice is what has long been missing from the juvenile justice system. But this begs the question: What is, or should be, "justice" within the context of the juvenile justice system? Moreover, what is the relationship between justice and punishment? With a justice or just deserts philosophy, it follows that limits must be placed on dispositional alternatives and specifically on the degree of punishment meted out to juvenile offenders. These limits can be, and often are, in direct conflict with the traditional goals and structure of the juvenile justice system.

Justice and punishment seem somehow to be related. To be just, punishment must be proportionate to the seriousness of the offense committed. Seriousness is generally determined by the harmfulness of the act and the degree of culpability of the offender. This notion is summarized in the simple phrase: "Let the punishment fit the crime." This, in turn, implies a gradation of offenses by seriousness. It also implies some corresponding ranking of severity of punishment.

It is easy to envision the conflicts that could arise with differing notions of accountability—that is, instilling a sense of responsibility or inflicting punishment for wrongdoing. Take, for example, a sixteen-year-old armed robber with one prior adjudication for the same offense. Suppose that "justice" (i.e., proportionate punishment as defined by the legislature or a sentencing commission) dictates that the youth spend two years in confinement at a training school. Suppose further that at the end of the two year period the youth does not appreciate or acknowledge the wrongfulness of his or her acts. Should the youth be released at the end of the two year period? If accountability is related to instilling values and fostering responsibility, the answer is no. If accountability is related to just and proportionate punishment, the answer is yes.

These are the issues illustrated by the readings in this section. Martin R. Gardner leads off with some observations on what he calls current trends in juvenile justice. The trend toward punishment has gone by other names or "models," mentioned above. Gardner prefers to use the phrase "punitive juvenile justice."

Gardner points out that if the punitive model replaces the rehabilitative model, or is even an equal partner with it, there will have to be "significant reworking of present juvenile justice systems." He then discusses many of the complicated social and legal issues with the introduction of punishment into the juvenile justice system.

Washington was the first state, in 1977, substantially to revamp its statutory provisions for the juvenile justice system. At the core of the changes in Washington was a basic change in the philosophy of dealing with youths who come within the jurisdiction of the juvenile court.

For example, Washington's revised juvenile code states that delinquent youths "must be held accountable for their offenses" and that the juvenile justice system should "provide for punishment commensurate with the age, crime, and criminal history of the juvenile offender." The notion of proportionality of punishment based on the offense is very different indeed from traditional juvenile justice philosophy.

Washington was not the only state to modify the philosophy and structure of its juvenile justice system. For many states the changes were not as sweeping as they were in Washington. Nevertheless, they were significant departures from the traditional system. For example, in 1984, California inserted the word "punishment" into the purpose clause of its juvenile court law.

The third selection involves a case from the California Court of Appeals addressing the issue of punishment in a juvenile court disposition. *In re Michael D.*, decided in 1987, shows a different tone among the appellate courts regarding the underlying rationale of the juvenile court. The case addresses the "fundamental disagreement over the purposes of the Juvenile Court Law." No longer there simply to "uplift" and "rehabilitate," the juvenile court in California was now authorized, based on the 1984 California statute, to consider punishment and public protection in making its dispositions of delinquents. Interestingly, however, the punishment authorized in California must be used for "rehabilitative purposes." How juvenile correctional officials can punish juveniles for rehabilitative purposes remains unclear.

The final selection, by Stephen Wizner and Mary F. Keller, returns to some of the critical issues in juvenile justice reform. These two legal scholars review the history of the reforms in the juvenile justice system, discuss what they call the new "penal model" of juvenile justice, and review the findings of key commissions that were formed to determine how to reform the juvenile justice system.

Wizner and Keller then get to the heart of the issue and raise a critical question. If the legal procedures of the juvenile justice system are similar to those of the adult system of criminal justice and if philosophy of the juvenile justice system is now like that of the criminal justice system, why have a separate juvenile justice system? This is an issue that will be hotly debated over the next decade.

10

Punitive Juvenile Justice: Some Observations on a Recent Trend

Martin R. Gardner

I. Introduction

From early times, the law has differentiated violations of criminal rules by children and those of their adult counterparts. Until the nineteenth century, most legal systems dealt with youthful offenders through the same criminal justice machinery applicable to adults, but recognized chronological age as the basis for a substantive defense as well as a ground for mitigating punishment.

While juvenile law reform quietly began with New York's House of Refuge in 1825, the creation of the first juvenile court system by the Illinois legislature in 1899 immediately triggered a worldwide movement so extensive that by 1945 every United States jurisdiction, state and federal, as well as most European nations had followed the Illinois lead by creating their own juvenile justice alternatives to the traditional criminal law. These new systems handled the bulk of juvenile crime but, virtually from their inception, provided mechanisms to "waive" juvenile court jurisdiction in certain cases to the criminal courts. The juvenile court movement was founded on a promise to rehabilitate wayward youth by offering individualized and non-punitive dispositions according to the minor's needs without the encumberances of the

Source: *International Journal of Law and Psychiatry*, 10 (1987): 129–151. Reprinted by permission of Pergamon Press Ltd., Oxford, England.

adversarial model familiar to the criminal system. Under the guise of parens patriae, juvenile court functionaries were to promote the welfare of the offender thus rendering unnecessary, indeed counterproductive, the procedural protections of the criminal system.

That the rehabilitative promise of the juvenile system did not materialize for delinquents is now old hat. By the mid–1970s, the United States Supreme Court had constitutionally required juvenile courts to employ most of the criminal system's procedural protections. Moreover, a revolution in substantive theory is presently taking place as one jurisdiction after another expresses disenchantment with the rehabilitative ideal and embraces explicit punitive sanctions as appropriate for youthful offenders. Principles of personal responsibility and accountability, foreign to the earlier premises of juvenile justice, are now routinely coming to the forefront as offending minors are given their "just deserts" through punishment proportionate to the gravity of their offenses. In light of those developments, many commentators argue for the demise of juvenile court jurisdiction in delinquency cases with a return to a single criminal system for adults and minors alike.

This Article argues that the emergence of a punitive theory of juvenile justice ought not result in the system's abolition. Nevertheless, the shift from a model in which punitive considerations replace, or at least share an equal role with, rehabilitative concerns does require significant reworking of present juvenile systems. Before suggesting how some such reworking should occur and arguing against merging juvenile punishment into the criminal system, the Article will account for the emergence of the punitive sanction and its corresponding emphasis on personal responsibility in juvenile justice theory.

II. The Emergence of the Punitive Model of Juvenile Justice

While practitioners of rehabilitation seek to alleviate from the lives of their charges those undesirable states of being thought to contribute to deviate conduct or its propensity, dispensers of punishment purposely inflict suffering upon offenders because of an offense, or perceived offense, committed. Therefore, the move from a rehabilitative to a punitive model constitutes a radical shift of theory. Several converging developments account for the present trend away from rehabilitation in favor of punishment in the juvenile system.

A. Procedural Criminalization: The Demise of Parens Patriae

The seeds of substantive change were initially planted in the 1960s and 70s by the United States Supreme Court cases constitutionally requiring a variety of procedural protections in delinquency adjudications. Beginning with *In re*

Gault[1] and extending through *In re Winship*[2], and *Breed v. Jones*,[3] the Court effectively gutted the notion that the benevolent concept of parens patriae, the supposed justification for the denial of procedural protections, in fact undergirded the exercise of delinquency jurisdiction. The Court discovered when it scrutinized juvenile justice that a de facto system of punishment existed that bore little resemblance to a benign parens patriae scheme.

The *Gault* Court found that, however enlightened the motives of its original founders, the juvenile system had become little more than a mechanism for stigmatizing youths as "delinquents" and restricting their liberty, often in institutions closer akin to adult prisons than to centers of rehabilitation. However, rather than precluding such incarceration altogether, the Court held that it could be administered but only if juveniles were afforded notice of the charges against them, the right to a fair and impartial hearing, the right to assistance of counsel, the opportunity to confront and cross examine witnesses, and the safeguards mandated by the privilege against self-incrimination.

Winship and Breed extended further procedural protections by holding, respectively, that the traditional rule in criminal cases that the government prove the commission of the offense beyond a reasonable doubt was also required in delinquency adjudications and that juveniles enjoy the protections of the double jeopardy clause, which precludes trials of juveniles as adults if they had been subjected previously to a delinquency hearing on the same charge.

While the Court in *McKeiver v. Pennsylvania*[4] refused to completely "criminalize" delinquency adjudications by denying juveniles a right to trial by jury, *Gault, Winship*, and *Breed* significantly call into question the rehabilitative pedigree of juvenile justice. With its parens patriae feet pulled from under it, the juvenile justice system thus stood in need of new theoretical underpinnings which would increasingly be found under the police power, the same foundation supporting the criminal justice system.

B. The Renaissance of Retribution

The decline of the rehabilitative ideal in juvenile justice was paralleled by a similar phenomenon in the criminal justice system. Since the late nineteenth century, the criminal sanction, paradigmatically in the form of incarceration, had been justified primarily in terms of its supposed benefits in reducing crime through incapacitating and rehabilitating offenders. Similar to its juvenile court manifestations, the rehabilitative tradition in the criminal system fostered broad discretion in sentencing and correctional officials in order that dispositions might be tailored to the rehabilitative needs of individual offenders as well as to their perceived threats to public safety. Indeterminate sentencing was the norm with little attention paid to deterrence theory as a basis for dispositional decisions and virtually none to the notion of punishment as desert.

Dramatic change occurred in the 1970s, however, as a spate of scholarly criticism called for a restructuring of the theoretical underpinnings of the criminal sanction. Widespread disillusionment with the rehabilitative ideal resulted from data documenting extensive recidivism of past participants in rehabilitation programs as well as from an increasing awareness of the inability to identify those offenders whose dangerousness required their incapacitation. Moreover, indeterminate sentencing itself came to be viewed as a source of rampant injustice.

The conceptual void left by the demise of rehabilitative theory was filled by a movement towards determinate sentencing which links the sanction and its duration to the offense rather than to the needs of, or the risk posed by, the offender. While the new punishment theory was often unabashedly retributive in its attempt to give offenders their "just deserts," it is also often found utilitarian justification in its perceived ability to deter crime. Where earlier theorists were embarrassed by the fact that punitive sanctions visit suffering upon the offender, the "renaissance of retribution" in the 1970s and 80s marked an era in which many commentators, legislators, and judges, with wide-ranging political views, came to justify punishment largely *because* it results in suffering.

C. Changing Views of Children's Responsibility

As juvenile court procedural innovations and a general rethinking of punishment theory were occurring, a new conceptualization of the nature of childhood itself was emerging which would provide philosophical support for models of punitive juvenile justice. From several directions, influential voices were suddenly calling into question the juvenile court's traditional assumptions of children's incapacity by suggesting that they, at least by adolescence, possess capabilities for rational choice and moral responsibility similar to those of adults.

1. Judicial Doctrine Several United States Supreme Court cases beginning in the late 1960s implied that because children are constitutional "persons" they are thus entitled to the same rights, and possessed of the same capacities to exercise them, as adults. The Court held, for example, that school children are protected in exercising rights of free speech in educational contexts, in making choices to obtain contraceptives and to have abortions. Moreover, by requiring minors to meet the same standard for relinquishing *Miranda* rights as is applicable to adults, the Court implied that little qualitative difference exists in the competence of minors and adults to make important decisions. Such developments suggest to some a judicial commitment to the view that children now possess the status of autonomous persons under the Constitution, notwithstanding a host of seemingly contrary decisions subjecting minors to a variety of restrictions by parents, school authorities, and legislators.

Judicial recognition of minors as competent agents, at least in some circumstances, is also reflected in those decisions recognizing a "mature minor" exception to the general requirement of parental consent for all non-emergency medical care. Several courts have held minors capable of consenting to their own treatment in their own behalf if under the circumstances of the particular case the minor, usually near majority or at least in adolescence, understands the possible consequences of the proposed medical procedure.

Likewise, legislatures in many states have adopted statutes giving minors authority to consent to all treatment after a certain age, or in specifically enumerated instances (usually birth control, pregnancy, or substance abuse) at any age or at some designated point before reaching majority.

2. Social Science Research While judicial doctrine suggested that minors possess greater capacity for decision-making in important matters than had previously been thought, an emerging social science literature, virtually ignored, incidentally, by legal policymakers, was finding that adolescents typically are able to make rational judgments as well as adults. Studies of adolescents' judgments about medical and psychiatric treatment, abortion, and consent to participate in research showed little difference between adult and adolescent decision-making. Moreover, a variety of studies established that most adolescents, unlike most preadolescent children, possess the same moral reasoning skills as adults. Such data led some commentators to urge that "the law should accord the considered choices of competent adolescents the same treatment it accords similar choices of adults." While statements of that kind were often made in the context of extending greater rights to children, the social science data gives credibility to the notion that adolescent youngsters should also be held accountable for their acts of delinquency.

D. Rising Rates of Juvenile Crime

A final factor affecting the trend towards punishment in juvenile justice, the rate of violent youthful crime, deserves brief mention. Between 1960 and 1981, arrests of juveniles for violent crime increased nearly 250 percent, more than double the figure for adults during the same period. Although the juvenile court age group constitutes less than 14 percent of the population, it accounts for nearly one-fourth of those arrested for major violent crime such as homicide, rape, robbery, and felonious assault. Moreover, in the school setting an estimated 282,000 students and 5,200 teachers are physically attacked each month. In light of such statistics and evidence of the ineffectiveness of juvenile court rehabilitation programs, many would naturally question the wisdom of retaining the traditional therapeutic model of juvenile justice.

E. Punitive Juvenile Justice: Justifications

Proponents offer a variety of justifications for a new model of punitive juvenile justice. Most modestly, they sometimes embrace it simply as a last resort given that nothing else appears to work. More ambitious defenses are grounded in punishment's perceived usefulness in preventing youthful crime and its ability to hold youthful offenders accountable for their actions.

While the justifications of punitive juvenile justice are essentially the same as the adult criminal law, it does not follow that the juvenile system should either embrace the same punishment scheme as the adult model, or that the two systems should be merged. However, as discussed in the next section, the move to punitive juvenile justice does necessitate structural innovations, not employed in some punitive systems now in place, which must be employed if the new systems are to be justified.

III. Punitive Juvenile Justice: Addressing Some New Concerns

The recognition that juvenile courts dispense punishment raises several concerns not encountered, at least as directly, by the earlier rehabilitative model. Among the more substantial problems created by the punitive model are: assuring that punishment is just and guaranteeing essential procedural protections at delinquency adjudications. While some punitive systems have anticipated and dealt with such problems, many have yet to recognize their significance.

A. Assuring That Punishment Is Just

To be just, punishment must be proportionate to the seriousness of the offense committed. "Seriousness" is determined by assessing the characteristic harmfulness of the conduct and the degree of culpability of the offender. When related to juvenile crime, these principles of justice require that juvenile offenders be punished less severely than their adult counterparts and that substantive culpability defenses such as infancy and insanity, historically seldom employed if not unavailable altogether, be embraced by the juvenile system.

1. Scaled-Down Punishment The problem of proportioning punishment in juvenile justice must be addressed with the fact in mind that no juvenile system is, or ever was, the exclusive vehicle for dealing with youthful offenders. The adult criminal courts have always asserted jurisdiction over certain juveniles and will surely continue to do so, although perhaps less readily, in jurisdictions adopting punitive juvenile justice models. Therefore, many of the most dangerous and culpable juvenile offenders will continue to be subjected to the adult criminal system leaving the juvenile system to punish the remainder of minors who violate criminal rules.

Assessments of the characteristic harmfulness of juvenile offenses yield no clear conclusions regarding punishment relative to that imposed upon similar adult offenders. While the harm done by juvenile offenders is often the same as that done by adults committing the same offense, such may not always be the case. Because they are often smaller in stature than adults, some crimes against the person committed by minors may be less threatening to their victims, and thus less harmful, than the same offense committed by an adult. On the other hand, because juveniles are often perceived as more impetuous and volatile than adults, the victims of juvenile crimes may actually sense more danger than those similarly exploited by adults. Therefore, considerations of the characteristic harmfulness of given offenses committed by juveniles seemingly do not themselves demand deviations, one way or the other, from punishments imposed upon adults committing the same offense.

Assessments of juvenile culpability do, however, strongly support a system of scaled-down punishments for offenders dealt with through the juvenile system. While the punitive model requires holding juveniles accountable for their offense, the extent of their accountability should not be synonymous with that of similarly situated adults. Developmental differences render youths less culpable or criminally responsible than their adult counterparts. Minority, particularly adolescence, is a period of ''semi-autonomy'' in which youngsters face the ''unfinished business of growing up.'' Because juveniles are in the process of becoming adult, it is unrealistic and unfair to hold them fully accountable for their actions. Therefore, juvenile offenders must be protected from the full burden of adult responsibility but ''pushed along by degrees toward the moral and legal accountability that we consider appropriate to adulthood.''

While justice requires punishing juveniles less severely than adult offenders, considerations of deterrence and social protection are not compromised by less severe penalties. The deterrent effect of punishment is generally thought to be more a function of the certainty, rather than the severity, of punishment. Furthermore, most delinquency is a symptom of adolescence that is generally outgrown and thus demands no lengthy attention in the name of social protection.[5]

2. Culpability Defenses: Infancy and Insanity Because punishment entails the purposeful infliction of suffering and characteristically connotes blameworthiness, it is unjustly applied if the offender lacks responsibility for his offense. Traditional criminal law reflects these considerations by requiring the state to establish that the offender committed the criminal act with the requisite state of mind (*mens rea*) while permitting the defendant a variety of defense mechanisms to excuse or justify the offense.

Historically, no separate juvenile court existed. Recognizing that children lack the adult measure of culpability, the common law embraced a special doctrine for children, the infancy defense, which embodied a series of presumptions reflecting children's incapacity to take responsibility for their actions. Children under the age of seven were conclusively presumed incapable of criminal responsibility while those over the age of fourteen were regarded as adults and presumed capable of committing crimes. Children between the ages of seven and fourteen presumptively lacked criminal capacity and could be punished only if the state showed that the child knew and understood the consequences of his act. Therefore, for youths in this age group the state was required to show not only that they committed the crime with the specific state of mind required by the crime's definition but also that they possessed the general capacity to be responsible. Similarly, mentally abnormal youthful offenders were also afforded the defense of insanity as a means of establishing criminal incapacity.

The advent of the juvenile court movement meant that the overwhelming majority of juvenile offenders were no longer subjected to the criminal courts but instead were dealt with under the auspices of the "civil," rehabilitative juvenile system. The culpability defenses of infancy and insanity had little place within a system premised on assessing the needs rather than the blame of offending youngsters. Therefore, the juvenile courts historically rejected recognition of the infancy defense in delinquency adjudications although they anomalously tended to permit minors to plead insanity. Moreover, several jurisdictions explicitly adopting the punitive sanction for juvenile offenders continue to reject the infancy defense.

The same considerations which generated the common law defenses of infancy and insanity support their recognition in the new juvenile justice. Punishment of the nonresponsible is unjust. Infancy and insanity are the traditional defense vehicles for establishing criminal incapacity and nonresponsibility.

Moreover, the integrity of the various presumptions embodied in the infancy defense is remarkably borne out by social science research. Culpability capacity may be defined as the ability to understand the substantive nature of acts considered right or wrong within a given social order, to generate an internalized set of moral values, and to exercise control over impulses that conflict with such values. Under such a standard, children under seven years of age generally do lack the capacity to be culpable while it is possessed by some in mid-childhood (seven to fourteen years of age) but not others and therefore cannot generally be assumed for youngsters in that age group. On the other hand, adolescents (over age fourteen) generally possess culpability capacity, although often not at the level expected of a mature adult.

If the juvenile system dispenses punishment, it must embrace the substantive principles protecting against unjust punishment. The requirement that punishment be proportionate to the seriousness of the offense demands that juvenile punishments be less severe than those imposed on similarly situated adults and that sanctions be imposed only after carefully determining the culpability of the juvenile offender.

B. Essential Procedural Protections

Apart from substantive doctrinal considerations, use of the punitive sanction within the juvenile system carries procedural consequences, the most significant of which is the sixth amendment requirement that the juvenile offender be afforded a right to trial by jury in delinquency adjudications. While the Supreme Court held in *McKeiver v. Pennsylvania* that the right to trial by jury did not pertain to delinquency adjudications, the Court has also held that the sixth amendment right applies in cases where defendants face potential punitive imprisonment for more than six months. Contrary to its earlier perceptions in *Gault* and *Winship* and later in *Breed*, the *McKeiver* Court uncritically accepted the assumption that delinquency dispositions were rehabilitative rather than punitive. Therefore, the Court could hold that juvenile confinements even in excess of six months would not trigger the jury trial right. On the other hand, punitive incarceration should surely be another matter.

Unfortunately, the lower courts have been reluctant to recognize the procedural implications of the new juvenile justice. For example, in *State v. Lawley*[6] the Washington Supreme Court granted that the presumptive sentencing scheme adopted by the legislature may be punitive but denied the applicability of the sixth amendment right to trial by jury in part because ''punishment [may do] as much to rehabilitate, correct and direct an errant youth as does the prior philosophy of focusing upon the particular characteristics of the individual juvenile.'' Denials of procedural protection by appeals to parens patriae considerations may make some sense within the rehabilitative model, but they cannot be justified when punitive incarceration is imposed as the sanction for given offenses.

Juvenile proceedings are ''criminal'' in nature when punishment is the sanction imposed. Therefore, the full trappings of the criminal process, including trial by jury in hearings open to the public, are constitutionally mandated. Legislatures seeking to avoid such departures from the secrecy and informality of traditional juvenile proceedings can do so only by assuring that punitive sanctions are not visited upon offending youngsters.

IV. Retaining a Separate System of Punitive Juvenile Justice: A Modest Defense

For many, the justification for a separate system of juvenile justice evaporates once the punitive model, complete with the protections of the criminal process, is embraced. If juvenile justice is to be no more than a system of ''kiddie crime and punishment'' why not, in the name of efficiency, employ Occam's

Razor to the whole enterprise and return to a single system of criminal law for adults and children alike? The infancy defense could perform its historic task of deflecting punishment from non-culpable youngsters. A single criminal system could even adopt a "juvenile division" in which minors would receive scaled-down punishments. Separate confinement facilities for adults and minors could be retained and, if avoiding the collateral civil disabilities often attending criminal convictions is desirable for youthful offenders, statutes could be passed exempting persons convicted of crimes under a certain age from such disabilities. The traditional intake and diversion mechanisms of the juvenile system could, if deemed worthy of preservation, either be adopted as components of the criminal system for all offenders or provided solely for youngsters.

Advocates of a separate punitive juvenile system have yet to respond to those calling for a merger into the criminal system. The remainder of this Article suggests some directions such argument could take.

A. A Separate Juvenile Court as Mitigating Stigma

Perhaps the strongest reason for retaining a separate punishment system for juveniles is the possibility that youngsters might, thereby, be spared some of the stigmatic effect flowing from the "criminal" label. Assuming that youthful offenders are less culpable than their adult counterparts, they should no more be saddled with the same stigma imposed upon adult offenders than with the same punishment. While being branded "delinquent" by a punitive juvenile system is surely stigmatic, it may well carry fewer negative connotations, both in the minds of offenders and to the community at large, than flow from being convicted a "criminal" by the adult court.

Labeling theory presumes that those who confront negative reactions from others, such as being found guilty of a criminal offense by a court, come to think of themselves from the vantage point of those others. Moreover, the community tends to perceive stigmatized persons in terms of the stigmatic labels attached by official evaluators.

While empirical support for the contentions of labeling theorists is inconclusive, the plausibility of the theory cannot be ruled out. If negative labels stigmatize, some negative labels may be more stigmatic than others. Many have assumed that the labels "criminal" and "delinquent" are equally stigmatic, but it is at least arguable that the latter is less stigmatic.

"Delinquency" jurisdiction is, by definition, an intervention by juvenile courts in the lives of youthful offenders who have been judged inappropriate subjects for disposition by the criminal system. Assertions of criminal jurisdiction, even in misdemeanor cases, result in dispositions within the same system which treats the most culpable offenders and serious offenses and are, therefore, especially stigmatic. For the same reasons that many call for removing minor offenses from the stigmatic reach of the criminal courts, the offenses of juveniles should not automatically be brought under the umbrella of the criminal system.

Carving out a separate "juvenile division within the criminal system" would likely result in a significant blurring of the distinction between "delinquents" and "criminals." Convictions within the "juvenile division" would still be convictions by "criminal" courts. The distinction between criminal convictions for "misdemeanors" versus "felonies" likely carries little significance for purposes of labeling theory. Similarly, a disposition by the "juvenile division" of the criminal court likely would not be perceived as significantly less stigmatic than a regular criminal disposition, assuming that the distinction between "juvenile division" and "regular criminal courts" is even taken into account in the first place.

It must be noted that virtually no empirical research has been conducted testing the relative stigmatization of the labels "delinquent" attached by juvenile courts and "criminal" imposed by the adult system. Until substantial evidence establishes that the distinction is insignificant, separate juvenile courts should continue to adjudicate, and punish if appropriate, "delinquents" while criminal courts deal with adult offenders and those juveniles deemed proper subjects of criminal jurisdiction.

B. Additional Considerations Against Merging Juvenile and Criminal Courts

A variety of practical considerations argue against merging juvenile and criminal courts. In the first place, the claimed efficiency of the merger is not clear. Removing delinquency jurisdiction to the criminal courts would increase the workload of an already overburdened system. Merger would likely not result in a savings of court time on the "waiver" issue because, unless a system of "legislative waiver" were adopted, judges would still be required to distinguish cases to be tried in the "juvenile division" and those handled in regular criminal courts.

While efficiency might be promoted by abolishing the juvenile court system entirely and merging it into a new, "streamlined," criminal system, complete dismantling of juvenile courts is unlikely given that system's continued need to exercise jurisdiction over neglected children and, more controversially, status offenders. If a separate system of juvenile courts will survive the removal of delinquency jurisdiction to the criminal courts, it is difficult to see how such removal will necessarily result in a more streamlined, efficient system.

Moreover, because of its historic interest in protecting the welfare of youngsters, the juvenile system now in place, while far from perfect, might, in some localities at least, provide sensitive attention to the unique problems of juvenile offenders. Where this is already the case or where it might yet occur within the juvenile model, merger into the criminal system may risk loss of valuable expertise acquired by conscientious juvenile court functionaries in return for the cold indifference towards offenders which often characterizes the criminal courts.

Given these considerations, the burden of persuasion rests on those favoring merger into the criminal system. Until they produce solid evidence establishing their case, the wiser course is to continue to deal with youthful offenders through a system separate from the criminal model, even if punishment is the system's earmark.

V. Conclusion

This article has assessed the reasons for and implications of the recent movement towards punitive juvenile justice. Given the failure of the traditional juvenile system to achieve its therapeutic aims, the emergence of a punitive model is neither surprising nor necessarily unwelcome. However, without the kinds of considerations argued for above aimed at promoting the justice and fair administration of juvenile punishment, its justification is wanting.

Contrary to many, the author's intuitions favor retaining a punitive juvenile system separate from the criminal courts, at least until evidence emerges to support dismantling traditional delinquency jurisdiction. A tired phrase has almost literal application in this context: it appears unwise to throw the "baby" out of the juvenile system simply because the "bathwater" of the rehabilitative ideal is discarded.

Notes

1. 387 U.S. 1 (1967). While Kent v. United States, 383 U.S. 541 (1966) (enumerating procedural rights under the District of Columbia Code in proceedings waiving juvenile court jurisdiction to the adult criminal process) was the Court's first venture into the juvenile justice area, *Gault* marked the first clear attempt to apply constitutional principles. *Kent* is sometimes understood as statutorily, and not constitutionally, grounded. *Cf. Davis, supra* note 11, at 4–6.

2. 397 U.S. 358 (1970).

3. 421 U.S. 519 (1975).

4. 403 U.S. 528 (1971).

5. Serious offenders posing significant danger to society can, of course, be dealt with through the adult system.

6. 91 Wash. 2d 654, 591 P.2d 772 (1979).

11

Excerpts from Washington State Juvenile Justice Act of 1977

13.40.010. Short title—Intent—Purpose

(1) This chapter shall be known and cited as the Juvenile Justice Act of 1977.

(2) It is the intent of the legislature that a system capable of having primary responsibility for, being accountable for, and responding to the needs of youthful offenders, as defined by this chapter, be established. It is the further intent of the legislature that youth, in turn, be held accountable for their offenses and that both communities and the juvenile courts carry out their functions consistent with this intent. To effectuate these policies, the legislature declares the following to be equally important purposes of this chapter:

    (a) Protect the citizenry from criminal behavior;

    (b) Provide for determining whether accused juveniles have committed offenses as defined by this chapter;

    (c) Make the juvenile offender accountable for his or her criminal behavior;

    (d) Provide for punishment commensurate with the age, crime, and criminal history of the juvenile offender;

    (e) Provide due process for juveniles alleged to have committed an offense;

Source: Washington Revised Statutes, Section 13.40.010.

(f) Provide necessary treatment, supervision, and custody for juvenile offenders;

(g) Provide for the handling of juvenile offenders by communities whenever consistent with public safety;

(h) Provide for restitution to victims of crime;

(i) Develop effective standards and goals for the operation, funding, and evaluation of all components of the juvenile justice system and related services at the state and local levels; and

(j) Provide for a clear policy to determine what types of offenders shall receive punishment, treatment, or both, and to determine the jurisdictional limitations of the courts, institutions, and community services.

Enacted by Laws 1977, Ex.Sess., ch. 291, § 55, eff. July 1, 1978. Amended by Laws 1992, ch. 205, § 101.

12

In Re Michael D.

Opinion

LOW, P.J.—(1a) We hold that an order of the juvenile court committing a minor to the California Youth Authority may be validly based on punishment and public safety grounds so long as it will also provide rehabilitative benefit to the minor.

The minor, Michael D., appeals from an order of wardship (Welf. & Inst. Code, § 602)[1] committing him to the California Youth Authority (CYA) after he admitted to one count of sexual battery. (Pen. Code, § 243.4, subd. (a).) The minor contends that the juvenile court judge abused his discretion in committing him to CYA. We affirm.

On January 12, 1986, officers responded to a report that a rape was in progress in the Day Street Park playground. They found a woman being raped by a minor; appellant was observed leaning over the victim near her head and appeared to be holding her down. The minor was leaning over the neck of the victim with his hands out in front, but there was no conclusive evidence he was choking the victim. However, it was clear from the medical evidence that the victim had lacerations and bruises consistent with attempted strangulation. After the incident, the minor showed little remorse for the incident nor any concern for the victim. The minor eventually admitted to one count of sexual battery.

Source: *In re Michael D.*, 188 C.A.2d 1392 (1987).

At the dispositional hearing, the minor introduced letters from various people in support of his request to be placed on probation and assigned to the care and custody of his parents. Dr. Paul Walker, a psychologist retained by the minor, reported that Michael did not have a propensity towards violence or sexual sadism. Paul Gibson, an instructor on adolescent sexuality for the Department of Youth Authority, recommended that the minor be placed with his parents and be given therapy as a condition of probation. Gibson communicated his concern that the minor would only increase his involvement and identification with delinquent groups if placed in CYA. In addition, Hillel Maisel, a counselor at juvenile hall who worked in the unit where the minor was housed, testified that the minor was a "young man [of] tremendous potential" whose placement in CYA "would not be for his benefit" because of his high intelligence level and the level of schooling available from CYA.

However, the court-appointed psychologist, Dr. Korpi, found the minor to possess poor judgment and to be "long . . . beyond the control of a reasonable authority," requiring a program to "slow him down [and] provide firm limits" on his behavior. Further, Dr. Walker expressed doubts about the ability of the minor's parents to place strict limits on the minor's behavior. The minor also admitted that he had a history of alcohol and hallucinogen abuse.

The probation report concluded that "[t]he magnitude and outrageousness of the conduct alone warrants a commitment to the [CYA]." The report concluded that an out-of-home placement (§ 202, subd. (d)(4)) would not be suitable and, "[w]eighing all the factors objectively, . . . in order to afford adaquate [sic] protection of the community and to have this minor atone for his participation in this most 'vicious crime,' " recommended CYA placement.

The juvenile court found the minor "guilty" of a "very brutal, heinous and vicious crime, and the conduct in this matter [was] outrageous." The judge also stated that the minor's history of drug and alcohol abuse was a significant factor, and found him "to be a threat and danger to society. . . . [H]is own interests and the interests of society would be best served by his being at this time in the California Youth Authority." He also stated that the minor would benefit from the reformatory educational discipline provided by the CYA.

I

The minor contends that his commitment to CYA was an abuse of discretion by the juvenile court in that (1) the minor was improperly committed to CYA for purposes of retribution rather than rehabilitation; (2) the juvenile court did not properly consider less restrictive alternatives; and (3) the minor could not be benefited by commitment to CYA.

(2) The decision of the juvenile court may be reversed on appeal only upon a showing that the court abused its discretion in committing a minor to CYA. (*In re Eugene R.* (1980) 107 Cal.App.3d 605, 617 [166 Cal.Rptr. 219]; *In re Todd W.* (1979) 96 Cal.App.3d 408, 416 [157 Cal.Rptr. 802].) An appellate court will not lightly substitute its decision for that rendered by the juvenile court. We must indulge all reasonable inferences to support the decision of the juvenile court and will not disturb its findings when there is substantial evidence to support them. (*In re Eugene R., supra,* at p. 617; *In re Michael R.* (1977) 73 Cal.App.3d 327, 332–333 [140 Cal.Rptr. 716].) In determining whether there was substantial evidence to support the commitment, we must examine the record presented at the disposition hearing in light of the purposes of the Juvenile Court Law. (§ 200 et seq.; *In re Todd W., supra,* at pp. 416–417.)

(1b) At the core of the dispute before us is a fundamental disagreement over the purposes of the Juvenile Court Law. Prior to the amending of section 202, California courts have consistently held that "[j]uvenile commitment proceedings are designed for the purposes of rehabilitation and treatment, not punishment." (*In re Aline D.* (1975) 14 Cal.3d 557, 567 [121 Cal.Rptr. 816, 536 P.2d 65].) The *Aline* court derived its conclusion from the terms of former section 502 (now § 202):[2] "to secure for each minor . . . such care and guidance, preferably in the minor's own home, as will serve the spiritual, emotional, mental, and physical welfare of the minor. . . ." (*Id.,* at p. 562.) Commitment to CYA was treated as the placement of last resort "only in the most serious cases after all else has failed." (*In re Eugene R., supra.* 107 Cal.App.3d at p. 617.) A commitment to CYA had to be supported by a determination based upon substantial evidence in the record of (1) probable benefit to the minor (*In re Aline D., supra,* at p. 566; *In re John H.* (1978) 21 Cal.3d 18, 27 [145 Cal.Rptr. 357, 577 P.2d 177]), and (2) that a less restrictive alternative would have been ineffective or inappropriate. (*In re Ricky H.* (1981) 30 Cal.3d 176, 183 [178 Cal.Rptr. 324, 636 P.2d 13].)

In 1984, the Legislature replaced the provisions of section 202 with new language which emphasized different priorities for the juvenile justice system. (Stats. 1984, ch. 756, §§ 1, 2 pp. 2726–2727.) The new provisions recognized punishment as a rehabilitative tool. (§ 202, subd. (b).) Section 202 also shifted its emphasis from a primarily less restrictive alternative approach oriented towards the benefit of the minor to the express "protection and safety of the public" (§ 202, subd. (a); *In re Lawanda L.* (1986) 178 Cal.App.3d 423, 433 [223 Cal.Rptr. 685], review den.), where care, treatment, and guidance shall conform to the interests of public safety and protection. (§ 202, subd. (b).)

Thus, it is clear that the Legislature intended to place greater emphasis on punishment for rehabilitative purposes and on a restrictive commitment as a means of protecting the public safety. This interpretation by no means loses sight of the "rehabilitative objectives" of the Juvenile Court Law. (§ 202, subd. (b).) Because commitment to CYA cannot be based solely on retribution grounds (§ 202, subd. (e)(5)), there must continue to be evidence demonstrating (1) probable benefit to the minor and (2) that less restrictive alternatives are ineffective or inappropriate. However, these must be taken together with the Legislature's purposes in amending the Juvenile Court Law. Consistent with these new objectives, we turn to the record before us.

II

(3) The crime committed was brutal and violent. The victim had been repeatedly raped with the admitted assistance of the minor. Further, even if we accepted the minor's representations that he merely aided the commission of the crime, by not offering help or aid to the victim exhibits a shocking callousness which requires appropriate treatment and guidance. This conclusion is strengthened when one considers the minor's unrepentant and cavalier attitude following his detention and arrest.

Moreover, the court-appointed psychologist concluded that the minor was "beyond parental control" and the psychologist retained by the minor also seriously questioned whether his parents could place the strict limits on his behavior necessary for rehabilitation. The minor had poor social and moral judgment that required firm guidance. The minor also admitted that he has a problem with drugs and alcohol, which the psychologists agree requires substantial help. From all these facts, the trial court could have inferred (1) that the minor's best interests require an environment providing firm, strict discipline for his "out of control" behavior, evidenced by his participation in a violent crime, (2) without such discipline and realignment of his social and moral structure he poses a demonstrated threat to public safety, and (3) that the minor requires intensive rehabilitative treatment for his substance abuse, and (4) the minor's parents were demonstrably incapable of caring for the minor consistent with the minor's best interests in treatment and guidance and the objective of the protection of the public. The minor may not have been suitable for Log Cabin Ranch placement due to his age, nor suitable for an out-of-home placement. In its discretion, the juvenile court chose commitment to CYA over the obviously unsuitable alternative of release to parental custody. There was substantial evidence supporting the trial court's exercise of discretion.

The order of wardship is affirmed.

Notes

1. All section references are to the Welfare and Institutions Code.
2. Section 502 was repealed and replaced by section 202. (Stats. 1976, ch. 1068, §§ 1.5, 14, pp. 4741, 4781.)

13

The Penal Model of Juvenile Justice: Is Juvenile Court Delinquency Jurisdiction Obsolete?

Stephen Wizner and Mary F. Keller

I

An inability to reconcile society's need for protection from juvenile crime with the use of nonpunitive measures has troubled the juvenile justice system since its inception. Society long ago adopted a paternalistic attitude toward juvenile crime, treating such behavior not as a question of law enforcement, but as a social and psychological problem requiring therapeutic interventions and state assumption of parental rights and duties. The juvenile court was conceived as a kind of social welfare agency rather than as an instrument for the enforcement of the criminal laws. With the mantle of benevolence bestowed and in the name of "individualized treatment," the juvenile courts were given broad jurisdiction over both criminal and noncriminal misbehavior and were vested with virtually unlimited discretion to impose limitations and sanctions on a child's conduct.[1] They were to operate a "no fault" process, geared to providing treatment and rehabilitation to children whose overt misbehavior manifested underlying problems.[2] Juvenile court procedures were to be informal and nonadversarial, and the court was to make dispositions based on the best interests of the child.

Source: *New York University Law Review*, 52 (1977): 1120–1135. Reprinted by permission of New York University Law Review.

The unique features of this system as an approach to deviant behavior are its lack of significant concern with fault or blame; its jurisdiction over noncriminal behavior such as truancy and a failure to obey one's parents; its informality and lack of procedural technicalities; and its approach to rehabilitation, exemplified by a system of indeterminate sentencing in which type and duration of sanction is based on the needs and "best interests" of the offender rather than the seriousness of the offense.

It is now commonly agreed that the juvenile court has failed to achieve its objectives. It has neither provided adequate protection for society from juvenile crime nor succeeded in rehabilitating young offenders. It has compromised important legal values and intervened excessively into the lives of children and their families. And perhaps its principal failure is the lack of proportionality in the sentencing provisions of the juvenile delinquency statutes. Some criminal offenses committed by persons of juvenile court age are so serious that the maximum sentences authorized by these statutes are insufficient to punish the offender, protect the community, and vindicate moral principles inherent in the criminal law. Conversely, intervention in cases involving minor or noncriminal misbehavior often results in the imposition of sanctions related neither to the gravity of the offense nor to the good of the child. The disproportionality problem is exacerbated by the informality of juvenile court procedures and the judge's unfettered discretion which permit widely varying outcomes on similar facts.

In large measure, these failures can be traced to the unrealistic assumptions that underlay the juvenile justice system, such as the belief that the court could act as a substitute for the parent in performing certain child-rearing functions. There is no meaningful similarity between a state's acting to protect society and enforce morality through prosecution and sentencing of offenders, and parents' acting to nurture and socialize children through love, care, discipline, and education. The coercive nature of court-imposed "therapy" inevitably renders it punitive from the child's viewpoint. However benevolently it is intended, involuntary restriction of an individual's liberty because he has engaged in conduct deemed unacceptable *is* punishment. Similarly, the traditional pretense that the problems of juvenile delinquency can be cured with love and understanding is naive and simplistic. The causes of youth crime are so deeply rooted in the poverty and the social disorganization of urban communities, in the family, and in the individual personality, that even the best-intentioned efforts of kindly judges, friendly probation officers, and humane correctional personnel are unavailing in many cases.

Recommendations for reform of the juvenile justice system have generally called for procedural reforms, improved treatment and facilities, and experimentation. These solutions, however, do not affect the unbridled discretion of juvenile courts to intervene in the lives of children and their families and to impose coercive sanctions disproportionate to the behavior that triggered its jurisdiction. Recognizing this, other commentators have gone further and proposed restricting juvenile court jurisdiction—an approach adopted in large measure in the volumes of proposed standards produced by the IJA-ABA Joint Commission on Juvenile Justice Standards (Joint Commission).[3]

The standards contained in the three volumes under review here—*Juvenile Delinquency and Sanctions, Dispositions,* and *Dispositional Procedures*—propose four general principles to meet the problems engendered by the current system of juvenile court jurisdiction. First, the standards provide that juvenile court delinquency jurisdiction should be limited to acts which, if committed by an adult, would constitute a crime, thereby abolishing jurisdiction over so-called "status offenses" such as truancy and incorrigibility. Second, the standards create defenses and mitigations related to fault, degree of culpability, and actual harm, thus rejecting the "no fault" basis of the current juvenile justice system in favor of notions common to the "adult" criminal justice system. Third, the standards restrict dispositional discretion by limiting the type and duration of sanctions and by requiring that the severity of the disposition be proportional to the seriousness of the offense and the offender's prior record. Finally, the standards extend procedural safeguards to the dispositional stage of the delinquency proceedings.

In theory, these standards confront quite successfully the more egregious failings of the current juvenile justice scheme. The limits of both the jurisdiction and the dispositional powers of the juvenile court reduce the potential for overreaching by the state. Juvenile delinquency jurisdiction can be invoked only when the juvenile is charged with specific criminal conduct—that is, conduct causing serious harm to someone other than the juvenile himself or a member of his family—and he intended, knew, or should have known the consequences of his action. The standards that require the judge to impose the least restrictive available disposition and to supply reasons on the record for that disposition mitigate the danger of excessive sanctions—a peril further avoided by the limitation on custodial dispositions to two years (or three for multiple offenders).

In addition, the incorporation into the dispositional proceedings of adversarial procedures required at the adjudicatory stages buttresses procedural fairness. The Joint Commission apparently recognized that dispositional proceedings are often more significant in terms of "grievous loss" than the original adjudication of delinquency. The dispositional inequities so common in the present system, moreover, are met with a grid system of maximum sentences proportional to the seriousness of the offense, thus restricting the enormous discretion currently evidenced by indeterminate sentences putatively based on the "needs" of the juvenile.

One area the Joint Commission does not successfully address is the rehabilitation of juvenile offenders. This failure is perhaps to be expected, for the rehabilitative ideal itself has recently come under attack on both theoretical and pragmatic grounds.[4] Thus it is not surprising that the standards in this area reflect often contradictory and sometimes troublesome principles. For example, in proposing a delinquency jurisdiction based on penal rather than parental considerations—that is, one applicable to the legally guilty, not the merely troubled, youth—the standards reject the concept of therapeutic intervention as the cornerstone for delinquency jurisdiction. One might logically anticipate a concomitant rejection of any "right" existing in the juvenile to rehabilitative services, a right which some courts have argued is a necessary implication of a therapeutically based system. The Joint Commission, however, proposes to retain and indeed enlarge the notion of a juvenile's right to services, suggesting that, although a juvenile should not be forced to accept services, a failure to provide them should justify a reduction in the severity of the disposition or an outright discharge. The fit is an awkward one.[5]

Also puzzling is the standards' almost total failure to acknowledge directly the social interest in protecting society from crime. Perhaps society is thought best protected by achieving a *fairer* system of juvenile justice, one that respects the liberty and privacy interests of young people. Or perhaps the goal has been abandoned altogether because it conflicts with the Joint Commission's overriding concern with limiting state intervention. But surely society has a legitimate interest in identifying and restraining those who demonstrate persistent criminal behavior and thus one might legitimately question whether the maximum sentence lengths allowed under the standards are sufficient. While the standards seek to limit the acts triggering delinquency jurisdiction to "adult" offenses, they do not permit "adult" sanctions: an adult committing murder risks life in prison; a juvenile committing the same act faces two years. Even the most assiduous skeptics of deterrence rationales might find that contrast questionable.

In the final analysis, however, one central thesis can be gleaned from the principles reflected in the standards, namely, that state intervention into the lives of children and their families should be minimized. The standards repudiate the idea that the state, in the form of the juvenile court and under the guise of omniscient benefactor, is best able to effect social goals relating to child development. By drastically curtailing the juvenile court's discretion and imposing procedural safeguards, the standards create a strong presumption against the juvenile court's jurisdiction and in favor of family supervision and treatment of minors. But the more important question is, of course, whether the standards in operation would make any practical difference in the outcome of juvenile delinquency cases.

II

Tested against the principle of limiting state intervention, the practical consequences of the standards may not, in our view, fulfill their theoretical promise.

This conclusion is largely owing to the strong incentives contained in the standards for juveniles to plea bargain, incentives absent in the traditional juvenile justice system and ones likely to increase court intervention in the lives of juveniles.

In the traditional system, a juvenile proceeding results in either an adjudication of delinquency or a dismissal. When the former occurs, the "sentence" imposed is governed by the needs of the juvenile rather than the number or seriousness of the charges brought against him or the frequency with which he has appeared before the court in the past. Because there are no separate classes of offenses, the juvenile cannot reduce his sentence exposure by pleading guilty to a lesser offense. Indeed, even in jurisdictions with separate provisions for status offenders, the prosecutorial procedures and kinds of sanctions that might be imposed on a "person in need of supervision" are quite similar to those applied to juvenile delinquents, and consequently, the juvenile has no incentive to plead guilty to the status offense in the hope of reducing his sentence risk on any more serious charges.

By contrast, if the standards for proportional sentencing are adopted, a juvenile will be able to reduce his sentence risk by offering to plead guilty to a lesser offense. The standards create five classes of offenses, each class defined by the type and duration of the maximum sanction imposed for the same conduct in the criminal law. Thus, for example, a "class one" juvenile offense is any violation which, if committed by an adult, could result in the death sentence or imprisonment from more than twenty years to life. Consider, then, the juvenile charged with a class two offense, which imposes a maximum one-year confinement upon conviction, and a class five offense, which could result in only six months probation without risk of confinement. Given the potential for a material reduction in the maximum sentence exposure, the temptation to bargain is apparent.

Despite its surface appeal, the creation of a plea-bargain environment would probably result in substantially greater judicial intervention into the lives of children and their families. First, crowded dockets and reluctant witnesses often result in dismissals for failure of the state to proceed to trial. A juvenile who pleads guilty, therefore, forfeits the opportunity for such a dismissal. Second, and on a far more important level, bargained pleas under the standards, even when followed by lenient dispositions, nonetheless represent adjudications of delinquency with their attendant stigma and collateral consequences.

The likelihood of increased adjudications of delinquency under the standards can best be seen by applying their provisions to some representative cases. In recent years, the writers have represented a large number of juveniles in delinquency proceedings in New Haven. We have selected four typical cases in the hope that, by comparing the actual outcomes under the present system with the predicted outcomes under the standards, the practical impact of the Joint Commission's proposals can be assessed.

Case One: Bobby D.

At age 14, Bobby D. was charged with criminal trespass. He had no prior record. While walking across the Yale campus with several friends, he was arrested by New Haven police officers responding to a report of an attempted burglary involving several black youths. The case was dismissed when the campus police declined to testify against him on the trespass charge.

Under the proposed standards, the case would be dismissed even if the campus police pursued the charge. The standards only invoke delinquency jurisdiction for acts that would constitute a crime if committed by an adult. Under the applicable adult criminal trespass statute culpability can arise only if "No Trespassing" signs are posted. Because Yale does not post such signs, Bobby's case would be dismissed regardless of the complainants' willingness to testify.

Several months after the trespassing incident, Bobby was charged with attempted robbery, assault, and carrying a dangerous weapon. The police report stated that several youths, Bobby among them, had demanded money from another youth and that Bobby had hit the victim with a blackjack. The case was dismissed because the victim failed to appear in court on the day of the trial.

Although under both the current and the proposed juvenile justice systems the victim's failure to appear at trial would lead to dismissal of the charge, in practice the result under the Joint Commission's scheme would likely be fundamentally different as a consequence of pretrial events. The most serious charge against Bobby was the attempted robbery count, which carries a maximum adult sentence of twenty years. In the proposed juvenile sanctions grid, the crime would thus fall into "class two," with a maximum juvenile sentence of twelve months. Because the traditional juvenile justice system, at the adjudicatory and dispositional stages, does not consider the seriousness or the number of charges involved, Bobby would have nothing to gain by pleading guilty. Under the standards, the number and seriousness of the charges are the chief determinants of disposition. Facing a serious charge and the possibility of a year's confinement, Bobby would have to consider certain factors before trial: with actual harm charged, there would be no chance of the discretionary dismissal permitted in the standards for de minimis infractions; since Bobby claimed to have an alibi, the standards providing for affirmative defenses like consent or lack of mens rea would be inapplicable. In all likelihood, he would opt to plead guilty to a lesser charge—perhaps breach of the peace, with a maximum sanction of six months of conditional freedom. Instead of the dismissal under the current system, there would be an adjudication of delinquency with the attendant state intervention.

In a third encounter with the law, Bobby was charged with robbery. According to the police account, two youths were seen grabbing a nonagenarian woman, taking her purse, and throwing her to the ground. Bobby was arrested with the woman's change purse and keys in his possession. The case was dismissed because the victim was too weak to testify.

In this instance too, the standards would encourage an early plea bargain and thus the application of some sanction in a case in which the traditional system would produce a dismissal. Of course, the outcome under the standards might be perceived by most people as socially preferable—the evidence against Bobby was, after all, very strong, and the dismissal of the case seems uncomfortably fortuitous. But such feelings obscure the underlying issue. If the actual outcome is unpalatable, it should be changed by a straightforward modification of substantive rules, not by means of increased and undue pressure on the juvenile to plea bargain.

Bobby's final contact with the juvenile court system was an arrest for disorderly conduct—shouting obscenities at a passing police car. The case was dismissed after an apology to the police officer. The same result would likely obtain under the standards through invocation of the de minimis discretionary dismissal section.

In sum, then, were Bobby's cases to arise under the standards, the results would be identical in two instances and more severe in two others. Importantly, however, the latter two results would be more severe not because of a direct application of substantive law, but only because of the pressure to plea bargain before trial.

Case Two: Lynn B.

At age 15 and with no prior record, Lynn B. was charged with criminal mischief and attempted burglary. A police officer observed Lynn standing in front of a store at night with a can opener in her hand. Upon investigation, the officer found graffiti on the door and scratches around the door knob. The case was dismissed with Lynn's promise to repaint the door.

Under the standards, the maximum sanction for criminal mischief and attempted burglary would be six months in custody, a class three offense. The most probable disposition would be a plea to the lesser offense, criminal mischief (Lynn admitted responsibility for the graffiti), and a sentence suspended on condition of repainting the door. The standards thus would reach the same result as the traditional system, but with one very important distinction—an adjudication of delinquency.

Case Three: Sean B.

Sean B. had previously been adjudicated delinquent on charges of truancy and running away from home. The juvenile court had committed him to a nonsecure residential facility. He then ran away from the institution and returned home, for which he was charged with escape. The disposition of the case resulted in the revocation of his previous commitment, a new adjudication of delinquency based on the escape, and unsupervised probation.

Under the standards, the escape charge, a class two offense, would carry a maximum sanction of twelve months in custody. The confinement from which Sean escaped, however, had been based on two status offenses, which under the standards would not confer jurisdiction on the juvenile court in the first place and thus Sean's case would be dismissed without even the initial adjudication of delinquency.

Case Four: Danny S.

By the time Danny S.'s case came to trial, he had accumulated nine separate charges against him: two counts of burglary, three counts of criminal mischief, and one count each of disorderly conduct, truancy, possession of marijuana, and being beyond the control of his parent. Most of the misbehavior had occurred at Danny's grandfather's house, where Danny had lived until a year before his trial. Although most of the charges were dismissed, Danny was adjudicated a delinquent based on a finding that he was beyond the control of his mother and he was committed for one year to a nonsecure residential drug treatment facility.

Almost all the charges against Danny involved difficulties with his family and thus would be dismissed outright were the standards in effect: the standards provide for the discretionary dismissal of delinquency proceedings when the persons whose interests are threatened or harmed by the alleged misbehavior are members of the juvenile's family. The standards also remove juvenile court jurisdiction over the marijuana charges and any other "victimless" crimes as well as those noncriminal acts such as truancy believed more appropriately handled by school officials and parents. Accordingly, under the standards, the probability is that no adjudications of delinquency would occur.

If, as we believe, these four cases represent a fairly typical cross-section of juvenile offenders, the application of the standards to them suggests somewhat disturbing possibilities. In two of the cases, the standards would yield less intrusive results, but in the other two cases the standards would have the effect of increasing state intervention by encouraging pretrial plea bargains. Not only does that effect contradict the articulated goal of the Joint Commission, but it also creates an incentive for prosecutors to overcharge juveniles in the hope of securing a "better" bargain, a not uncommon and often criticized practice in the adult criminal justice system. Indeed, overcharging could also be used to circumvent the limits placed on delinquency jurisdiction through the simple device of characterizing otherwise noncriminal conduct as criminal mischief, thereby undermining every premise on which the standards rest. These possibilities intimate that the Joint Commission may have felt itself too tied to the framework of the past, despite its admirable recognition of the basic deficiencies of that framework.

III

The juvenile justice standards contained in the three volumes that we have considered advocate gradualist reforms—procedural safeguards, a right to treatment, and limits on both jurisdiction and the exercise of discretion. The principles guiding these standards, we suggest, point the way to more radical change, namely, the abolition of juvenile court delinquency jurisdiction.

The Joint Commission's rejection of the conventional "no fault" approach and corresponding adoption of mens rea requirements, degrees of offenses, proportional and determinate sentencing, and quasi-criminal affirmative defenses, when coupled with the elimination of jurisdiction over noncriminal behavior and victimless crimes, bespeak the abandonment of paternalism and the acceptance of a criminal law model of juvenile justice. These reforms eliminate the unique features of the juvenile court's approach to deviant behavior and transform the system into one that focuses, as well it should, on questions of crime and punishment, guilt and innocence.

One must admire the courage of the drafters of these standards, for they have relinquished long-accepted therapeutic pretensions and euphemistic terminology in favor of acknowledging the concerns of law enforcement and individual rights in a fresh and forthright manner. Even though the drafters eschewed the final step—abolition of delinquency jurisdiction—the impetus provided by their proposals is apparent and welcome. But if the goal—and limit—of juvenile delinquency proceedings is to be prosecution and sentencing of criminal offenders, if sentencing is to be proportional to the seriousness of the criminal offense and prior record of the offender, and if participation in rehabilitative programs by incarcerated offenders is to be voluntary, then how do juvenile delinquency proceedings differ from criminal proceedings?

The only real differences between these standards and the adult criminal codes are that the former provide for shorter sentences and introduce certain special defenses. That an adult court is capable of dispensing lenient sentences when appropriate, however, is self-evident. And the principles represented by the standards' special defenses are already taken into consideration by adult criminal courts in those instances in which they have dealt with youthful offenders. Criminal court prosecutors and judges, for example, regularly grant youthful offender treatment or "diversion" programs to minors without previous criminal involvement. When no real harm has been done, or mitigating circumstances appear, prosecutors typically "nolle" charges and judges dismiss the cases. Although the regulation of this discretion directly by statutes similar to the standards may be desirable, such regulations could just as easily occur in the context of an adult criminal court.

Perhaps a separate juvenile justice system was justifiable when its rules of adjudication and liability were different from those of its adult counterpart, but if we are to accept the Joint Commission's move to a penal model of juvenile justice, this justification evaporates. Indeed, that procedural safeguards are still in their infancy in juvenile courts suggests that the youthful offender may affirmatively benefit from having his case heard in an adult court where such safeguards are taken for granted. The role strain created for lawyers by the "benevolent" juvenile court, moreover, would not exist and defense counsel would experience no difficulty in assuming their traditional and proper adversary role.

Although it would be unrealistic and unfair to deny that most children— including juvenile delinquents—are more immature, dependent, and irresponsible than most adults, it beggars belief to pretend that we incarcerate a youth who has robbed and beaten an elderly person for the same reason that we place in protective care a child who has been abused by his parents. Whatever rationale is thought to underlie the criminal justice system—deterrence, segregation, retribution, or even rehabilitation—can bear little relationship to the substitute child-rearing model of nondelinquency juvenile court activity. The functions of the jailer and the social worker have little in common and any attempt to combine the two inevitably decreases the effectiveness of each.

Accordingly, while we appreciate the force of Judge Polier's dissent to these standards, in which she characterizes them as an unfortunate retreat from service-oriented and individualized treatment, we believe that rather than going too far, the standards do not go far enough. In our judgment, juvenile court delinquency jurisdiction should be abolished and the jurisdiction of the juvenile court reserved for the protection of abused, neglected, and emotionally disturbed children. The need for a separate delinquency jurisdiction ends where the penal model of juvenile justice begins: surely an adult court is just as competent to weigh factors like diminished responsibility and lack of mens rea as a juvenile court. Thus, while the standards are an excellent attempt at reform of a system that desperately needs reform, they fail to carry through their underlying premises. The drafters may not believe so, but their work is the first step on a path that appears to lead ineluctably to the abolition of juvenile court jurisdiction over criminal acts.

Notes

1. *See* Hazard. *The Jurisprudence of Juvenile Deviance*, in PURSUING JUSTICE FOR THE CHILD 4–6 (M. Rosenheim ed. 1976): Mack, *The Juvenile Court*, 23 HARV. L. REV. 104, 107 (1909).

2. Mack, *supra* note 1, at 109–10.

3. INSTITUTE OF JUDICIAL ADMINISTRATION & AMERICAN BAR ASSOCIATION, JUVENILE JUSTICE STANDARDS PROJECT (Tent. Draft 1977) [hereinafter STANDARDS].

4. *See, e.g.,* E. VAN DEN HAAG, PUNISHING CRIMINALS 188–91 (1975); Martinson, *supra* note 9, at 25–38; Abram, *Social Risk Sentencing*, N.Y.L.J., Oct. 25, 1977, at 1, col. 2.

5. *See* Katz, *The Right to Treatment—An Enchanting Legal Fiction?*, 36 U. CHI. L. REV. 755, 762 (1969) (arguing that the "right to treatment" implies a duty to accept treatment, and thus could result in greater state intervention); *cf.* O'Connor v. Donaldson, 422 U.S. 563, 578–79 (1975) (Burger, C.J., concurring) (patient's refusal to accept psychiatric treatment should be considered in assessing defendant hospital's good faith defense against charge that hospital unconstitutionally confined civilly committed defendant). It could be argued that the standards indirectly impose some obligation to accept treatment, since acceptance of treatment may be made a condition of probation. STANDARDS, *supra* note 22, *Dispositions* 3.2(D). If treatment is made a condition of probation, failure to comply may justify imposition of a more severe sanction. *Id.* 5.4.

DISCUSSION QUESTIONS

---

1. How does the philosophy of the "new" juvenile justice system compare to that of the traditional system?

2. What are some of the critical issues discussed by Gardner in the move toward a "punitive juvenile justice system"?

3. How does the Washington statute compare to the California statute in Section 2?

4. What are the main arguments of the California Court of Appeals in permitting punishment and public protection to be considered in juvenile court dispositions?

5. If the new juvenile court is substantially similar to the criminal court in procedure and substance (punishment), should we continue to have a separate juvenile court? Why or why not?

SECTION V

JUVENILE SENTENCING POLICY

Introduction

The structure of a state's juvenile sentencing system follows logically from its philosophical basis. The traditional model of juvenile justice assumes that a youth's misbehavior is caused by various psychological or social problems. The goal of this model is to solve or "cure" the underlying problems causing the delinquency. But the exact duration of rehabilitation is not easy to predict; it varies significantly from individual to individual. Just as physical therapy following an operation or an accident varies in duration, so too does the psychological or social treatment needed for the rehabilitation of juvenile delinquents.

In order to deal with individual differences among delinquents in terms of the causes and cures of misbehavior, state officials historically have been given broad discretion for the disposition of individual cases. In their decisions, juvenile court judges and state-level correctional officials primarily considered what was best for the child. These officials placed less emphasis on the immediate misbehavior and more emphasis on the youth's general situation, including maladjustments at home, in school, or in the community.

The sentencing system under the traditional model reflected this broad discretion. State juvenile justice systems worked under an indeterminate sentencing structure in which a youth sent to a state correctional institution (often called a training school) would remain incarcerated until he or she was deemed rehabilitated or until the juvenile court's jurisdiction expired. The system was called "indeterminate" primarily because there were no clearly defined standards governing the duration of incarceration.

The unfettered discretion incorporated in this system resulted in a variety of injustices to juvenile offenders. For example, relatively minor offenders were frequently committed to institutional placements where they remained for long periods of time—on the premise that they were being rehabilitated. Civil libertarians came to view the prolonged incarceration of minor offenders as grossly unjust, especially when mounting social science evidence suggested that such incarceration did more harm than good.

Conversely, youths who committed serious offenses could be released from institutional care in relatively short periods and placed back in the community. To some critics, such release practices offended a sense of "justice" in addition to placing society at unwarranted risk of further victimization. There was a call from various groups—law-and-order and victims' rights groups—for greater personal accountability, particularly of youths who committed serious crimes against society.

Juvenile offenders were not the only ones who lacked accountability. Juvenile justice officials, because of their broad mandate to treat and train youths, have not been held properly accountable for the effectiveness or fairness of their decisions. This claim follows from numerous empirical studies of abuses of official discretion. Many studies have shown that discretion too often resulted in discrimination; specifically, that racial minorities are treated more harshly than whites and girls more harshly than boys for comparable offenses.

The changes in philosophical orientation from rehabilitation to punishment or public protection in the state codes have been followed by corresponding changes in sentencing structure. The newer philosophy of "justice," "punishment," or "accountability", generally implies that the severity and duration of the sanction be proportionate to the seriousness of the offense. To the extent that this philosophical orientation focuses on the offense per se, rather than on the offender, the nature and duration of the sentence is made more predictable and uniform because of the direct relationship between the offense and the sanction.

Predetermined standards, whether developed by the legislature, judiciary, parole board, or correctional administrators, have been developed to guide the discretion of juvenile justice officials in choosing the type as well as the duration of sanctions. The trend is for states to develop formal, articulated sentencing standards or criteria designed to do two things. First, the standards are to increase the accountability of juvenile offenders, so that serious delinquents spend longer periods of time in confinement.

Second, the standards are to increase the accountability of juvenile justice officials by restricting their discretion. This newer sentencing structure, called determinate sentencing, is designed to provide greater justice both for juvenile offenders and for society.

Some states have also passed what amount to mandatory sentencing laws for serious delinquents, often referred to as "serious delinquent statutes." These laws mandate that a subset of delinquents (usually labeled as "serious," "violent," "repeat," or "habitual") be adjudicated and committed in a specific manner different from other committed delinquents. These youths are subject to adjudication in juvenile court (as opposed to waiver to adult court), but they receive commitments that may vary significantly from the type given other adjudicated delinquents.

Dissatisfaction with the broad discretion of juvenile officials and the resulting injustices under the indeterminate sentencing structure was so great at the end of the 1970s that several national commissions came to recommend significant changes. One of the most influential was the Joint Commission on Juvenile Justice Standards conducted by the American Bar Association and the Institute for Judicial Administration (ABA/IJA).

The dispositional standards of the Joint Commission on Juvenile Justice Standards would significantly alter the face of juvenile justice. The commission proposed that state legislators adopt a sentencing model similar to that used in the adult criminal justice system, specifically emphasizing retribution, deterrence, and public protection. Additionally, the commission recommended standards for restricting the juvenile court judge's discretion in the sentencing process. The issue, of course, becomes the extent to which the juvenile court judge can or should continue to search for an appropriate treatment program for delinquent youths or give primary consideration to the seriousness of the offense and the protection of the public.

The results of a survey on indeterminate and determinate sentencing policies in all fifty states and the District of Columbia, conducted for the U.S. Department of Justice, is presented in an article by Martin Forst, Bruce Fisher, and Robert Coates. They found that most states continue to subscribe to the indeterminate sentencing approach, but a trend toward determinate sentencing is discernable. The authors discuss some of the issues involved in the construction and implementation of determinate sentencing statutes. One key question, for example, is who or what governmental body will devise the sentencing standards. The legislature, a sentencing commission, the judiciary, a parole board, or a board of correctional administrators are all capable of developing sentencing guidelines. A second issue is who will apply the standards. Sentences could be meted out by juvenile court judges, as they are in Washington state, or a parole board could determine the length of institutional stay, as is done in California. In

Georgia, correctional administrators, using predetermined guidelines, decide how long a youth will remain incarcerated.

Forst, Fisher, and Coates also discuss a new sentencing strategy designed to offer greater public protection from violent juvenile offenders. Called "Serious Delinquent Statutes," these laws provide mandatory minimum sentences in secure confinement for a specified subset of juvenile delinquents. These types of statutes are likely to be adopted by an increasing number of states.

Among the national-level commissions formed to address critical issues in the juvenile justice system was the National Advisory Commission on Criminal Justice Standards and Goals Task Force on Juvenile Justice and Delinquency Prevention. The next section consists of the commission's standard on the duration of disposition and the type of sanction. It appears that the commission recommended at least the rudiments of an offense-based system, as opposed to the traditional offender-based system. The Commentary of the standard illustrates possible juvenile justice sentencing structures following this model. It is important to note that this commission's standards are just that—recommended standards, not law. Each state has the ultimate authority to enact its own juvenile justice sentencing structure.

As mentioned, many states have revised their juvenile codes, particularly to address the problem of serious juvenile criminality. Two such statutory schemes comprise the next selections. New York substantially revised its Juvenile Justice Act in 1976, with subsequent amendments. Section 301.2 of the New York Family Court Act defines a "Designated Felony." And section 353.5 gives the specific provisions of the Designated Felony Act.

Illinois adopted a slightly different strategy. The 1988 version of the Habitual Juvenile Offender Law shows how the legislature structured or checked the discretion of juvenile correctional officials to release serious offenders after only short periods of incarceration.

The case of *People v. J. A.* illustrates the operation of the new Illinois habitual juvenile offender law, another example of a serious delinquent statute. The case shows the structure of the law, how it is applied, and the legal issues on appeal. The court held that the Habitual Offender Law did not violate the due process, equal protection, or cruel and unusual punishment provisions of the Constitution.

The one state that has moved closest to adopting the standards advocated by the Joint Commission on Juvenile Justice Standards is Washington. In 1977, Washington's legislature enacted a radically new Juvenile Justice Act, which is described in the article by Jay Reich. A practicing prosecutor from King County (Seattle) when he wrote the article, Reich suggests how the change in sentencing structure will affect the role of the prosecutor. To the extent that the juvenile sentencing system comes to resemble the adult system, so too will the policies and practices of the prosecutor. Specifically, the prosecutor will be more involved in the charging process, in plea bargaining, and in the ultimate disposition of the case. Thus, under this new system, while the juvenile court judge's discretion is restricted, the prosecutor's discretion—and relative power in the juvenile justice system—appears to be greatly enhanced.

14

Indeterminate and Determinate Sentencing of Juvenile Delinquents: A National Survey of Approaches to Commitment and Release Decision-Making

Martin L. Forst, Bruce A. Fisher, and Robert B. Coates

During the last decade the shape of decision-making in juvenile justice has come under close scrutiny. Of particular interest have been decision-making processes which influence a youth's release from a state correctional institution. Numerous movements have been undertaken to replace indeterminate sentencing and/or release approaches with determinate sentencing.

The purposes of this article are: (1) to identify some of the critical arguments in the debate about sentencing and release policies; (2) to set forth a simple typology for categorizing different approaches within and across the dimensions of determinancy and indeterminancy; and (3) to explore the range and variety of approaches by classifying the existing state approaches across the typology. Findings reported here are from the first phase of a five-year study on indeterminate and determinate institutional release practices in juvenile justice conducted by the URSA Institute and funded by the Office of Juvenile Justice and Delinquency Prevention, U.S. Department of Justice.

The Debate over Sentencing Policy

For most of this century, the indeterminate sentence has been a hallmark of this country's system of criminal justice for adults as well as for juveniles.

Source: *Juvenile and Family Court Journal*, 18(1) (1985): 1–12. Reprinted by permission of Martin L. Forst, Bruce A. Fisher, Robert B. Coates, and the National Council of Juvenile and Family Court Judges.

Within the past decade, however, an assault has been launched against this traditional sentencing model, with calls for change coming from diverse groups throughout the country. Some critics have advocated increasing the certainty and severity of punishment for law-breakers,[1] while others have sought equity and consistency in the sentencing process.[2] As a result, there has been a trend in the adult system toward a "justice" or "punishment" model of sentencing and corrections. Indeterminate sentencing systems are being abolished and replaced with determinate sentencing schemes in which sentencing discretion is severely restricted and the terms of imprisonment are designed to be proportionate to the seriousness of the adult's criminal conduct.[3]

The same criticisms that have been leveled against the adult system of criminal justice are increasingly being directed toward the individualized treatment approach of the juvenile justice system. In addition, a variety of concerns specifically related to the commitment and release of adjudicated delinquents have also emerged in recent years. These criticisms and concerns generally center on three issues. First, some observers object to the institutionalization of status offenders (and other minor offenders) in state training schools. Critics claim that institutionalization, especially for long periods of time, is disproportionate to the seriousness of the youth's conduct, and that the programs such youth must participate in do not rehabilitate.[4]

Second, some critics decry the lack of procedural safeguards for youth in juvenile courts and corrections which occasionally lead, it is asserted, to serious abuses of individual rights. Guggenheim, for example, believes that injustices are perpetuated daily in the juvenile justice system under the guise of "helping youth." He calls this the "myth of beneficence . . . notwithstanding the documented evidence of widespread brutality."[5] Whatever the motives of juvenile justice officials, the ability to do harm to youth in a system based on benevolence has been a central theme in the literature. "In the name of *parens patriae*, our American system of juvenile justice has yearly denied thousands of children due process rights declared essential to preserve the liberty of adults and then confined them to institutions where conditions are intolerable."[6]

Third, "law and order" advocates, concerned about rising crime rates—and particularly about violent crime—contend that juveniles are not held properly accountable for the crimes they commit and that chronic offenders and youth who commit crimes against the person are not incarcerated for long enough periods of time. The rationale for changing current juvenile justice policy is usually one of social protection. As van den Haag states: "The victim of a fifteen-year-old mugger is as much mugged as the victim of a twenty-year-old mugger, the victim of a fourteen-year-old murderer or rapist is as dead or as raped as the victim of an older one. The need for social defense or protection is the same."[7]

Based primarily on these criticisms, there have been calls for change in the juvenile justice system, particularly in the laws and policies governing the commitment and release of adjudicated delinquents. Some reformers seek to eliminate the traditional individualized treatment model of juvenile justice and install a "justice" or "punishment" model of corrections. Specifically, these reformers advocate providing greater procedural protections for youth, holding serious juvenile offenders accountable for their actions, and considering sanctions that bear some reasonable relationship to the seriousness of the youth's criminal conduct.[8] As with the adult system, some critics propose abolishing the indeterminate sentence and substituting a determinate sentencing approach for juveniles.[9]

Calls for change have come from a variety of groups, including academics, legislators, civil libertarians, children's rights groups and law and order advocates. Moreover, a number of juvenile justice standards projects have recommended the abolition of indeterminate commitments for delinquents. The primary standards groups—Institution of Judicial Administration/American Bar Association Joint Commission on Juvenile Justice Standards (IJA/ABA), National Advisory Committee on Criminal Justice Standards and Goals Task Force on Juvenile Justice and Delinquency Prevention (the Task Force), and the National Advisory Committee for Juvenile Justice and Delinquency Prevention (NAC)—agreed that sentences should be legislatively adopted and judicially implemented. They also agreed that sentences for delinquents should be proportionate to offense severity and that maximum length of stay should be established.

Criticism of the traditional approach to juvenile justice, including its emphasis on individualized decision-making, treatment and indeterminate sentences, is not, however, universal. Juvenile court judges, for example, are, for the most part, strong supporters of the basic concepts of the traditional approach. They argue that a response to juvenile offenders based primarily on the youth's specific offense or offense history ignores the fact that such offenders, even though they have been adjudicated for the same crime, vary greatly in their future dangerousness to others, treatment needs, family and peer environments and degree of culpability. Many juvenile court judges oppose "determinate" approaches in juvenile justice because, they suggest, it defeats the very purpose of the juvenile justice system, i.e., a system designed to meet the individual needs of specific youth for rehabilitation and allow greater flexibility in responding to offenders than the adult criminal justice system.

Many juvenile corrections officials also oppose determinate or fixed sentencing based upon the seriousness of the youth's offense. These officials, responsible for managing and staffing juvenile training schools, support indeterminate sentences for a variety of reasons: the importance of developing individualized treatment programs based on a youth's needs; the ability to move youth into community-based and/or family-oriented placements as they become available; the ability to offer institutionalized youth an incentive toward rehabilitation (i.e., early release) while in the correctional program; the ability to maintain a degree of control over the size of the institutional population; and the ability to deter institutional misconduct through threatened or actual deferral of release.

As approaches to juvenile sentencing and corrections are debated, the face of juvenile justice is starting to change. A number of states have already adopted new approaches to commitment and institutional release decision-making. Some states, for example, have adopted a determinate sentencing approach to commitment of adjudicated delinquents based upon the seriousness of the youth's instant offense and prior offense history. In some states (e.g., Washington, New York and Kentucky), statutory reforms were adopted which set forth proportionate sentencing for serious juvenile offenders. In other states, (e.g., Georgia, Arizona and Minnesota), administrative release guidelines designed to make lengths of stay proportional to the seriousness of the youth's delinquent activity have been adopted by the juvenile corrections agency. Other states are giving serious consideration to similar proposals but, in part, await the results from those states that have already adopted determinate sentencing in the juvenile justice system.

The information contained in this article is derived from a national survey of commitment and release decision-making for adjudicated delinquents in the fifty states and District of Columbia, conducted during 1979–1980. The survey methodology consisted of four activities: (1) an analysis of all relevant statutes; (2) an analysis of administrative rules and juvenile corrections policy and procedure manuals, where available; (3) an analysis of secondary sources, such as published and unpublished reports; and (4) a telephone survey of the fifty states and District of Columbia. Five to eight key juvenile justice personnel in each state were interviewed to clarify statutes and administrative rules and, to a more limited extent, shed light on the process by which youth are committed to and released from institutional placement.

It is important to note that the field of juvenile justice generally, and juvenile corrections specifically, is in a constant state of flux. In almost every state, legislative changes have been or are being adopted that revise the legal approach to commitment and release decision-making. Similarly, juvenile corrections agencies themselves have, in the early 1980s, become active in revising their administrative approaches to release decision-making. Any report that attempts to describe "current" approaches in juvenile sentencing policy, therefore, may be partially obsolete on or soon after the date of publication. The information presented in this article may be of limited utility as a reference for the most recent legislation and agency policy. Because the survey materials are up to date, however, they should prove useful to juvenile justice policymakers and correctional practitioners who seek a better understanding of the *range* and *variety* of approaches to commitment and release decision-making existing throughout the country.

A Typology of Approaches to Commitment and Release Decision-Making

It became quite evident during the course of the national survey that statutory and administrative approaches to commitment and release decision-making vary significantly. To conceptualize juvenile justice sentencing policy more clearly, it proved necessary to devise operational definitions for sentencing models, and at the same time to develop a typology of approaches to commitment and release decision-making.

One apparently clear distinction in approaches to commitment and release decision-making is the division between indeterminate and determinate sentencing. The scholarly literature consistently makes reference to these two types of sentencing approaches, as did most interview respondents in the national survey. This fundamental dichotomy of sentencing approaches should, we felt, form the basis for our typology.

The distinction between indeterminate and determinate sentencing was "apparently clear" because utilizing this dichotomy in a typology was not as easy as first anticipated. Despite repeated references to indeterminate and determinate sentencing during the survey, no precise or uniformly accepted definitions of those terms were found to exist, either in the scholarly literature or among juvenile justice personnel. Officials in one state defined the terms one way; officials in another state suggested a different usage. We found it necessary, therefore, to adopt definitions we could apply consistently in the categorization of commitment and release decision-making approaches in all jurisdictions throughout the country. After discussing the definitions of these two basic sentencing approaches at great length, we decided to adopt a slightly modified version of the definitions formulated by von Hirsch and Hanrahan in their classification of sentencing approaches in the criminal justice system for adult offenders.[10]

An indeterminate sentence, for purposes of this article, is defined as consisting of three elements: (1) The period of confinement is relatively open-ended, making the range between the minimum and maximum period of incarceration quite wide. (Because statutorily defined age limitations create jurisdictional restrictions on juvenile courts and corrections agencies, the durational ranges of confinement are normally not as wide as in the adult system.) (2) The decision to release the youth is usually made well into the youth's period of incarceration, and is made after observing the youth's behavior during confinement. (3) The release decision is usually based on factors associated with the offender's progress toward rehabilitation, including his conduct at the institution. As a rule, formal, articulated standards for making the release decision do not exist in states with indeterminate approaches.

A determinate sentence, as defined here, consists of three elements, most of which are in direct contrast to those of the indeterminate sentence: (1) a presumptive sentence or a relatively narrow durational range from which the decision-makers must choose; (2) an early determination of length of institutional stay—that is, one which takes place in court or shortly after the youth is received at the institution; and (3) the presence of formal, articulated sentencing or release standards related specifically to the youth's delinquent activity. That is, the length of stay will be proportionate to the seriousness of the commitment offense, often with the youth's age and/or prior record incorporated into the standards.

These definitions are by design rather broad; they allow significant diversity in the structure and process of each sentencing approach. Although a determinate sentencing system must contain formal, articulated standards, for example, the definition does not dictate which governmental entity is to formulate those standards. In theory, several governmental bodies could develop sentencing standards or standards related to institutional release, including the legislature, judiciary, correctional agencies or sentencing commission. Moreover, no specific governmental agency is required, by definition, to decide the length of institutional stay. One state may call for the trial court judges to determine length of confinement; another system might mandate a parole board to do so; in another state such responsibility may rest with the juvenile corrections agency.

Given the possible variation of approaches within each broad definition, it was necessary further to refine the typology. One of the important variables in indeterminate sentencing states is the governmental entity having authority to make the release decision. We therefore categorized indeterminate sentencing states according to whether legal authority for release lies with a judge, juvenile corrections agency or parole board. These three types of authority represent all of the release decision-making entities currently in use in the United States.

The most important variable in determinate sentencing states, we believe, is which governmental entity has responsibility for devising the sentencing standards. Theoretically, sentencing or release guidelines can be created by any branch of government—i.e., the legislature, judiciary (such as a statewide judicial council) or executive (corrections agency or parole board)—or by a sentencing commission consisting of representatives of each branch of government. The resulting typology, then, reflects these three possible sources of determinate sentencing standards.

The Results of the National Survey

Reflecting the typologies discussed above, the results of the national survey are presented in table 14.1. Each of the fifty states and the District of Columbia has been classified first as having either an indeterminate or determinate approach to commitment and release decision-making for adjudicated delinquents. Determinate sentencing states have further been categorized according to the governmental entity responsible for formulating the sentencing standards, and indeterminate sentencing states have been sub-categorized by the entity having authority to make the release decision.

It is important to reiterate that the classification of states is not based solely on a state's statutory structure. Arizona, for example, is classified as a determinate state because the state juvenile corrections agency sets the standards for release by promulgating administrative length of stay guidelines based on offense variables that can be applied at intake. New Mexico, on the other hand, is classified as an indeterminate state because the New Mexico Parole Board may release a youth at any time based on individual characteristics and progress toward rehabilitation.

At the time this research was conducted, only five states had implemented commitment or release decision-making structures which could be classified as determinate. One state, Washington, has adopted a sentencing statute for committed juveniles.[11] The juvenile court judge determines the length of commitment by referring to legislatively devised standards. The standards, located in the Juvenile Code, are based on the seriousness of the commitment offense and the youth's prior record. (For purposes of this article, Washington is classified a determinate sentencing state even though the judge may specify the length of stay outside the requirements of the statute in those cases where the judge finds that use of the prescribed penalties would result in "manifest injustice" to the youth or to the public.)

Three states classified as determinate—Arizona, Georgia and Minnesota—have developed release guidelines administratively, without being required to do so by the legislature. In each state, the release guidelines are based primarily on the commitment offense, with prior record taken into consideration. In California, the fifth state classified as determinate in the national survey, the state parole board (California Youth Authority) devised durational guidelines based primarily on the youth's commitment offense.

Table 14.1 also indicates that at the time of the survey no determinate sentencing state had yet adopted judicially created commitment or release guidelines. Judges have been experimenting with judicially devised guidelines in *some* segments of certain states. But because these guidelines are not binding on all judges within a state, they were not included in our state-by-state survey. Moreover, table 14.1 shows that no state has adopted commitment or release standards devised by a sentencing commission, as has been the case in some jurisdictions for adult offenders in the criminal justice system.[12]

Forty-five states and the District of Columbia have been classified as indeterminate states. Of these, thirty-two states and D.C. vest the institutional release decision with the juvenile corrections agency, six other indeterminate states give responsibility for release decisions to a parole board and in five

Table 14.1.

State	Determinate (who sets the standards)				Indeterminate (release decision-maker)			Serious Delinquent Statute
	Administrative		Legislative	Judicial				
	Agency	Parole Board	Statute	Judge	Agency	Parole Board	Judge	
Alabama					X			
Alaska					X			
Arizona (1)	X							
Arkansas					X			
California (1)		X				X		
Colorado						(2)	X	X
Connecticut					X			
Delaware					X			X
District of Columbia					X			
Florida					X			
Georgia (1)	X							X
Hawaii					X			
Idaho					X			
Illinois						X		X
Indiana					X			
Iowa							X	
Kansas					X			
Kentucky					X			X
Louisiana							X	
Maine					X			
Maryland							X	
Massachusetts					X			
Michigan						X		X
Minnesota (1)	X							
Mississippi					X			
Missouri					X			
Montana					X			
Nebraska					X			
Nevada					X			
New Hampshire					X			
New Jersey						X		
New Mexico						X		
New York					X			X
North Carolina					X			X
North Dakota					X			
Ohio					X			
Oklahoma					X			
Oregon					X			
Pennsylvania							X	
Rhode Island							X	
South Carolina						X		
South Dakota					X			
Tennessee					X		(3)	
Texas					X			
Utah					X		(4)	
Vermont					X			
Virginia					X			
Washington (1)			X(5)					
West Virginia					X			
Wisconsin					X			
Wyoming					X			

(1) In Arizona, Georgia, Minnesota and Washington, the juvenile corrections agency is responsible for the actual institutional exit decision. In California, the parole board is responsible for the actual exit decision.

(2) Colorado has two statutory provisions, one allowing for a determinate commitment and release by the judge, the other an indeterminate commitment and release by the Juvenile Parole Board.

(3) Tennessee Department of Corrections with the assent of the judge. If disagreement as to the release, the final decision is made by the Tennessee Children Service Commission.

(4) Utah has two types of commitments: regular (agency decides release) and short-term (judge decides release).

(5) Washington has a sentencing commission, but the legislature has final approval of the proposed sentencing standards.

other indeterminate states, the judge has authority for release decision-making. In three states—Colorado, Tennessee and Utah—overlapping or dual statutory provisions provide for two release decision-makers.

Parameters of Indeterminate Commitments

In analyzing indeterminate state commitments, two basic variables are significant: (1) the maximum age at which commitments terminate and (2) where applicable, the maximum period allowed for a commitment. Table 14.2 lists the thirty-four indeterminate states whose statutes allow commitments up to a statutorily fixed age and identifies that age. An indeterminate commitment to a statutorily fixed age is one in which the potential length of time begins with the dispositional order and terminates when the delinquent reaches the statutorily determined age. Because the delinquent can be released from institutional placement (and from the juvenile corrections authority altogether) at any time up to the maximum age, this type of commitment is classified as indeterminate.

A committed delinquent in Idaho, for example, must be released from an institution (and from jurisdiction of the juvenile corrections agency) by age twenty-one if the youth has not been released earlier by the juvenile corrections agency. In New Hampshire an adjudicated delinquent may receive an indeterminate commitment until age eighteen. However, if the youth is between seventeen and eighteen at the time of commitment, he may be committed until age nineteen. In Maine, a committed delinquent may receive an indeterminate commitment until age eighteen. The court may extend the commitment to age twenty-one. In addition, the court may make a limited commitment expressed in terms of either a minimum or maximum length of time. Such commitment may not exceed age eighteen or twenty-one if the court extends the original commitment.

Table 14.3 identifies the twelve states that have been classified indeterminate and in which the maximum period of the commitment is statutorily defined. The maximum period of confinement in these states is a specified number of years (unless the youth first reaches the maximum age for juvenile court commitments). In the District of Columbia, for example, a youth may be committed, initially, for a two-year period. At the expiration of that period, the court may extend the commitment for one year. At the expiration of that year, the court may again extend the commitment for successive one-year periods. However, no commitment period, the original two-year or the successive one-year commitments, may go past the youth's twenty-first birthday. In addition, because the commitment is indeterminate, the youth may be released by the youth corrections agency at any time. In Pennsylvania, an adjudicated delinquent may be committed for one three-year period. That commitment automatically terminates at the expiration of the three-year period or at

Table 14.2.   Indeterminate to Fixed Age

State	Age of Automatic Termination	Statutory Exceptions
Arkansas	18	
Delaware	18	If youth is 17-18 when committed, terminates at 19
Florida	18	
Hawaii*	18	Court may extend to 19
Idaho	21	
Illinois	21	
Indiana	21	
Iowa	18	
Kansas	21	
Kentucky	18	
Maine	18	Court may extend to 21**
Massachusetts	18	
Michigan	19	
Mississippi	18	
Missouri	18	
Montana	21	
Nebraska	19	
Nevada	20	
New Hampshire	18	If youth is 17-18 when committed, terminates at 19
New York	18	Court may extend to 21 with youth's consent
North Carolina	18	
Ohio	21	
Oklahoma	18	
Oregon	18	
Rhode Island	18	
South Carolina	21	
South Dakota	21	
Tennessee	19	
Texas	18	
Utah	21	Youth may be committed for a short term (90-day maximum)
Vermont	18	
Virginia	21	
West Virginia	18	
Wyoming	21	

*Youth may be committed for a short term, determinate commitment (up to one year) as a condition of probation.
**The committing court may make a limited commitment expressed in terms of either a minimum or maximum length of time. However, the indeterminate commitment is the most common type.

the age of twenty-one, whichever occurs first. A juvenile court judge may release a committed youth in Pennsylvania at any time. In Wisconsin, the adjudicated delinquent is committed for a one-year period and, by court extension, for successive one-year periods. However, the youth must be released (by the state agency) upon reaching age eighteen.

Table 14.3.   Indeterminate with a Maximum Period of Time

State	Maximum Period of Time	Court Extensions	Age of Automatic Termination	Statutory Exception
Alabama	2 year	One limited period up to 21	21	
Alaska	2 year	One two-year period	19	One year beyond 19 with youth's consent
Colorado	2 year	Two-year periods	21	
Connecticut	2 year	One two-year period	16	
District of Columbia	2 year	One-year periods	21	
Louisiana	*		18, 21**	
Maryland	3 year	Three-year periods	21	
New Jersey	3 year		21	For homicide—adult sentence for same offense
New Mexico	2 year	One-year periods	21	
North Dakota	2 year	Two-year periods	18, 20***	
Pennsylvania	3 year	One three-year period	21	
Wisconsin	1 year	One-year periods	18	

*The committing court must specify a maximum period of time which may not exceed the maximum sentence provided for an adult convicted of the same offense.

**If a youth is under 13 at the time of commitment, the age of automatic termination is 18; if a youth is between 13 and 17, the age of automatic termination is 21.

***If the youth is committed directly to SIS, the court may extend the commitment to age 20. If the youth is committed to SYA, the age of automatic termination is 18.

Serious Delinquent Statutes

Earlier in this article five states were designated as having a determinate approach to commitment or release decision-making. In each of these states, the determinate sentencing provisions (either by statute or administrative rule) applied to *all* adjudicated delinquents committed to a state-level institution (e.g., a training school). It is important to note that some states have adopted legislation that provides for what might be considered determinate sentencing for a specified segment of adjudicated delinquents. Because this subclass generally consists of the more ''serious'' delinquents, we have labeled these statutes ''serious delinquent statutes.'' These laws mandate that a subset of delinquents (usually statutorily labeled serious, violent, repeat or habitual) be adjudicated and committed in a specific manner different from other committed delinquents. Although the youth subject to serious delinquent statutes are adjudicated by the juvenile or family court, they receive commitments which may vary significantly from the type given other adjudicated delinquents.

Serious delinquent statutes are designed for more serious delinquents and reduce the usual discretion given to the judge at disposition and to the state youth corrections agency at release. Although these laws vary as to their specific mandates, they usually require some sort of institutional placement for a specified period of time for youth subject to the jurisdiction of the act. For example, some statutes require minimum lengths of commitment, others prescribe a fixed range of time for the commitment, while still others mandate a minimum length of stay in a type of placement (e.g., secure institution for a six-month minimum).

Table 14.4 lists the eight states identified as having serious delinquent statutes at the time of the national survey, and briefly describes the subset of delinquents for which the statute applies. In addition, table 14.4 identifies the dispositional alternatives available to the court for these youth. For example, discretion as to release decision-making has been virtually eliminated in Illinois' Habitual Offender Act, at least in theory. Under the Act, if a minor has been adjudicated twice for an offense which would be a felony if committed by an adult, and the instant offense is one of an enumerated list of violent offenses, the youth *shall* be adjudged an habitual juvenile offender and must be committed to the Department of Corrections until his twenty-first birthday, without possibility of parole, furlough, or non-emergency authorized absence from confinement of any sort. Pursuant to the statute, however, the minor is entitled to earn one day of good conduct credit for each day served as a reduction against the period of confinement. Such good conduct credit is determined by the Department of Corrections.

Both Colorado and Delaware have serious delinquent statutes which direct the juvenile court to make a minimum institutional or out-of-home placement upon finding that a youth is a violent juvenile offender according to the criteria specified in the statutes. In Colorado, if youth fifteen years of age or older at the time of the alleged offense are adjudicated delinquent for statutorily defined crimes of violence, *or* if youth have probation revoked for statutorily defined crimes of violence, they are designated violent juvenile offenders. If youth of any age, who previously have been adjudicated delinquent, are adjudicated delinquent for a felony, *or* their probation is revoked for the commission of a felony, they are designated repeat juvenile offenders. Upon adjudicating a youth a violent juvenile offender, the court *shall* commit or place such youth out of the home for not less than one year.

The serious delinquent statutes discussed above provide for a youth who meets specific statutory criteria to be committed to the state youth corrections agency and, in some cases, institutionalized for a minimum period of time. The above statutes do not address the type of institutionalization (e.g., secure or non-secure). Two states, New York and Georgia, have instituted serious delinquent statutes that give the judge wide discretion to find that the youth qualifies, but once that judicial determination is made, the two statutes detail not only the length of commitment but the type and length of residential confinement.

Based on the national survey, a number of other states were considering the adoption of serious delinquent statutes. These statutes also reflect the current "law and order" mood of the public and policymakers toward criminal and juvenile justice issues. They may be seen, however, as an alternative to statutes which mandate or allow juveniles to be tried as adults in the criminal

Table 14.4.   Serious Delinquent Statutes

State	Subset	Dispositional Alternatives
California	Youth between 16 and 18 adjudicated delinquent for any one of a number of designated felonies.	The committing court must order the youth committed to CYA for a 2-year period, although there is no prescribed period of institutional stay.
Colorado	Violent offenders (instant offense is a class A felony), repeat offenders (2 prior adjudications of delinquency), repeat offenders (1 prior adjudication of delinquency).	Violent offenders and repeat offenders **must** be placed outside of the home for a minimum of 1 year. Repeat offenders **may** be placed outside of the home for a minimum of 1 year.
Delaware	Youth with a prior adjudication of delinquency within 12 months from an instant adjudication for either the commission of a felony, or escaping from a Department of Corrections placement.	Commitments may be for a 6-month minimum **and** the juvenile court judge must approve the youth's release.
Georgia	Youth 13 or older adjudicated delinquent for specifically enumerated designated felonies.	Commitment is for 5 years. The judge may order restrictive custody for a 12-month minimum, 18-month maximum (some youth for an 18-month minimum). Such youth must remain in Division of Youth Services custody for a minimum of 3 years. The commitment automatically terminates at 21.
Illinois	Youth having been twice adjudicated delinquent for felonies **and** thereafter adjudicated delinquent for specifically enumerated serious offenses shall be adjudged habitual offenders.	The committing court must commit the youth to age 21 without the possibility of parole. However, the youth's time may be reduced by earning good conduct credit (1 day for each day served).
Kentucky	Youth 16 to 18 adjudicated delinquent for a capital offense, class A or class B felony.	The committing court may order the youth confined in a secure institution for at least 6 months.
New York	Youth between 13 and 16 adjudicated delinquent for any one of a number of designated felonies.	The committing court may order restrictive placement (the youth is committed to OYS for either 5 years or 3 years, with either a minimum of 12 months or 6 months in secure confinement depending on the type of adjudicated felony).
North Carolina	Youth 14 or older with previous adjudications of delinquency for 2 or more felonies **and** previously committed to a facility operated by the Division of Youth Services.	Commitment may be for a specific period of time with 2-year maximum. The Division of Youth Services may reduce the time by 25%. The court may reduce the time an additional 25%.

courts. As such, their adoption in a number of states is a significant aspect of current approaches to commitment and release decision-making for adjudicated delinquents.

Conclusion

The above analysis depicts the range and variety of sentencing and/or release approaches existing in the United States in 1980. In some instances, the fact that a given statute exists does not necessarily mean that it is frequently implemented. For example, observers believe that the Illinois Habitual Offender Law is underused because it is too harsh and constraining. These various approaches, however, have significant implications for how correctional resources will be used and managed, how juvenile offenders will be handled and protection of the public. The varying approaches reflect different underlying philosophies which continue to be debated across the nation. How these philosophies and approaches are actually implemented will be reflected in the larger five-year study of which this work is a part.

Notes

1. For example, see: Ernest van den Haag, *Punishing Criminals*, (New York: Basic Books, Inc., 1975).

2. For example, see: Andrew von Hirsch, *Doing Justice*, (New York: Hill and Wang, 1976); Marvin E. Frankel, *Criminal Sentences: Law Without Order*, (New York: Hill and Wang, 1972); David Fogel, *We Are the Living Proof* (Anderson Publishing Co., 1979); and *Struggle for Justice*, A Report on Crime and Punishment in America, Prepared for the American Friends Service Committee (New York: Hill and Wang, 1971).

3. Andrew von Hirsch and Kathleen Hanrahan, "Determinate Penalty Systems in America: An Overview," *Crime and Delinquency*, 27 (1981): 289–316.

4. See for example: Lamar T. Empey, "Juvenile Justice Reform: Diversion, Due Process, and Deinstitutionalization," in Lloyd Ohlin, *Prisoners in America*, (Englewood Cliffs, N.J.: Prentice-Hall, Inc., 1973); Frances A. Allen, *The Borderland of Criminal Justice*, (Chicago: University of Chicago Press, 1964); and P. Lehman, "The Medical Model of Treatment," *Crime and Delinquency*, 18 (1972): 204–212.

5. M. Guggenheim, "Abolishing the Juvenile Justice System," *Trial*, 15 (1979): 14.

6. W.M. Marticorena, "Take My Child, Please—A Plea for Radical Nonintervention," *Pepperdine Law Review*, 6 (1979): 643.

7. Van den Haag, *Punishing Criminals*, page 174.

8. For example, see: R.E. Sheppard, Jr., "Challenging the Rehabilitative Justification for Indeterminate Sentencing in the Juvenile Justice System: The Right to Punishment," *St. Louis University Law Journal*, 21 (1977): 12–43; and M.J. Rector, "People v. Juvenile Justice: The Jury Is Still Out," *Trial*, 15 (1979): 18–21.

9. *Ibid.*

10. Von Hirsch and Hanrahan, "Penalty Systems."

11. M.K. Becker, "Washington State's New Juvenile Code: An Introduction," *Gonzaga Law Review*, 14 (1979): 289–312.

12. Washington has subsequently created a Sentencing Commission charged with the responsibility of formulating sentencing standards.

15

Standards for the Administration of Juvenile Justice

3.181 Duration of Disposition and Type of Sanction— Delinquency

All conduct subject to the jurisdiction of the family court over delinquency should be classified for the purpose of disposition into categories that reflect substantial differences in the seriousness of the offense. Such categories should be few in number. The maximum term that may be imposed for conduct falling within each category should be specified.

The types of sanctions that may be imposed for conduct subject to the jurisdiction of the family court over delinquency should be grouped into categories that are few in number and reflect differences in the degree of restraint on personal liberty.

Commentary

The degree of dispositional discretion that should be accorded family court judges is one of the major debates in juvenile justice today. Approximately

Source: Standards for the Administration of Juvenile Justice, Report of the National Advisory Committee for Juvenile Justice and Delinquency Prevention, U.S. Department of Justice, July 1980, pp. 337–338.

80 percent of the states permit the juvenile or family court to exercise jurisdiction over a juvenile found delinquent until he/she reaches twenty-one, regardless of the offense. *See* National Task Force to Develop Standards and Goals for Juvenile Justice and Delinquency Prevention, *Comparative Analysis of Standards and State Practices: Juvenile Dispositions and Corrections,* 28 (1975). This dispositional scheme is often based on the view that the "delinquent act is an indication that the youth is in need of "treatment" and that it is in the youth's best interest for such treatment to continue as long as it is necessary. Most of these states leave the decision of when juveniles should be released from custody or supervision to the public or private agency to which they have been committed.

A number of other states provide that the court may commit a juvenile for an indeterminate period up to a statutory maximum, which is the same for most offenses. Many of these also provide for extensions of the dispositional period. *See National Task Force, supra; see also* Wisconsin Council on Criminal Justice Special Study Committee on Criminal Justice Standards and Goals, *Juvenile Justice Standards and Goals,* Standards 14.1(k)–(m) (2d draft, 1975). National Conference of Commissioners on Uniform State Laws, *Uniform Juvenile Court Act,* Section 36(b) (1968); U.S. Department of Health, Education and Welfare, *Model Act for Family Courts,* Section 37 (1975).

On the other hand, some commentators have recently proposed a return to a "just deserts" model of mandatory sentences, at least for adult offenders, although the degree of restraint to be imposed would still be decided by the judge. *See., e.g.,* D. Fogel, *We Are the Living Proof: The Justice Model for Corrections* (1975).

Proponents of indeterminate sentencing suggest that such sentences facilitate rehabilitation by motivating the offender with the reward of early release, place the "treatment" and release decisions in the hands of qualified professionals, protect society from hardcore youthful offenders, deter nondelinquent youth, and reduce unnecessary incarceration. *See* E. B. Prettyman, Jr., "The Indeterminate Sentence and the Right to Treatment," 7 Am. Crim. L. Rev. 15–17 (1972). Opponents of indeterminate sentences cite studies that indicate that release or parole decisions are more often based on institutional classificatory schemes and offender characteristics than on individualized progress toward rehabilitation; that offenders, both juvenile and adult, perceive the release or parole decision as made without valid or consistent criteria; and that the indeterminate sentence is open to abuse both by inmates who can "con" their way into early release and by institutional personnel who may wrongfully or arbitrarily withhold release. *Id.* at 17–21.

This standard, together with Standard 3.182, follows the lead of the National Advisory Committee on Criminal Justice Standards and Goals, *Cor-*

rections, 575 (1973); the IJA/ABA, *Dispositions, supra;* IJA/ABA, *Sanctions, supra;* and the *Report of the Task Force, supra,* by taking a middle course between these conflicting views. These standards recommend that:

a. Delinquent offenses be grouped into categories according to the relative degree of seriousness;
b. Maximum dispositional time periods be set for each category; (e.g., for offenses in category I, the term of disposition shall not exceed X years);
c. The type of sanctions be categorized according to the extent to which they restrain the juvenile's liberty (e.g., category (a) out-of-home custody, category (b) probation); but
d. The responsibility for determining the length of disposition within the statutory maximum, the degree of restraint that should be imposed, and the type of program to which the juvenile should be assigned should be retained by the family court judge. In this way, increased equity and consistency in the disposition of delinquency cases can be achieved without sacrificing the family court's ability to fashion a dispositional plan on the basis of the mitigating and aggravating factors of the particular case and the juvenile's needs and interests. *See* Standard 3.182.

To assure that the equity achieved at the dispositional stage is maintained and the intent of the dispositional determination carried out and to increase the visibility and accountability of dispositional decision making, Standards 3.189, 3.1810, and 4.71–4.73 recommend a greater role for the family court than under many current statutes. Reductions in the duration of disposition must be ordered by the family court. *See* Standard 3.189. The same is true for transferring a juvenile from a nonresidential to a residential program. *See* Standards 3.1810 and 4.33. The supervisory agency may shift juveniles between individual programs of the type specified by the court, but any change in the degree of restraint imposed is subject to court review. *See* Standards, 3.182, 3.189, 4.71, and 4.72. In addition, transfers of juveniles from a facility operated by the juvenile corrections to one maintained by a mental health or drug abuse agency require judicial approval following a court hearing. *See* Standard 4.73.

Unlike the provisions approved by the IJA/ABA Joint Commission and the *Report of the Task Force, supra,* this standard does not recommend any particular set of categories or maximum terms. Although the National Advisory Committee agreed that the length of dispositions in delinquency cases should never exceed those that an adult could receive for the same conduct, it concluded that the current state of knowledge does not provide a basis for determining which of the classifications that have been proposed is the most appropriate. Each state should decide what are the exact dispositional time limits on the basis of its own needs, problems, and priorities. The IJA/ABA Joint Commission

Table 15.1.   IJA/ABA Joint Commission Recommended Maximum Durations for Custodial and Noncustodial Sanctions

Class	Maximum Duration if Custodial Sanction is Imposed	Maximum Duration if Noncustodial Sanction is Imposed
1	24 months	36 months
2	12 months	24 months
3	6 months	18 months
4	3* months	12 months
5	2† months	6 months

*Confinement in a secure facility only if the juvenile has a prior record—i.e., adjudication for a class (1), (2), or (3) offense committed within twenty-four months of the commission of the current offense, or adjudication of three class (4) or (5) offenses, at least one of which was committed within twelve months of the commission of the current offense.

†Confinement only in a nonsecure facility and only if the juvenile has a prior record as defined above.

Source: IJA/ABA, *Sanctions, supra* at Standard 7.2.

and Task Force proposals are summarized as illustrations of the differing approaches that have been taken on these issues.

The IJA/ABA Joint Commission adopted provisions calling for the division of juvenile offenses into five classes based on the maximum sentence that can be imposed on adults following conviction for similar conduct. Specifically, Class (1) juvenile offenses should include criminal offenses for which the maximum authorized sentence is death or imprisonment for more than twenty years. Class (2) juvenile offenses should include criminal offenses with maximum authorized or sentences of imprisonment for more than five years. Class (3) should include criminal offenses with maximum authorized sentences of imprisonment for more than one year. Class (4) juvenile offenses should include criminal offenses with a maximum authorized sentence of imprisonment for more than six months. And, Class (5) juvenile offenses should include criminal offenses with maximum authorized sentences of imprisonment for six months or less. IJA/ABA, *Sanctions, supra* at Standard 5.2 the IJA/ABA Joint Commission recommended maximum durations for each class of juvenile offenses as in table 15.1.

The IJA/ABA standards also suggest that the types of sanctions be divided into three broad categories: nominal, conditional, and custodial. Nominal dispositions include reprimand and release and suspended dispositions. Conditional dispositions include fines, restitution, community service, supervision by a probation officer, day custody programs, and required attendance at educational, vocational, and counseling programs. Custodial dispositions include placement in secure and nonsecure facilities and custody on a continuous or intermittent basis—i.e., only at night, on weekends, or during vacations. IJA/ABA, *Dispositions, supra* at Standard 3.2.

Table 15.2.   Task Force Recommended Maximum Durations for Dispositions

Class	Normal Duration	Possible Extensions*
I	8 months	4 months
II	24 months	6 months
III	36 months	12 months or the juvenile's 21st birthday whichever occurs first
IV	The juvenile's 21st birthday	

*Extensions are permitted only upon a showing of clear and convincing proof that additional community supervision of the juvenile is required for the protection of the public. The juvenile may not be confined during the extension. The total dispositional period should not exceed twelve months for Class I offenses, thirty months for Class II offenses, and forty-eight months or beyond the juvenile's 21st birthday for Class III and Class IV offenses.

Source: *Report of the Task Force, supra* at Standards 14.13 and 14.14.

The *Report of the Task Force, supra,* proposed four classes of delinquent acts: Class I to include conduct that would be a misdemeanor if committed by an adult; Class II to include crimes against property that would be a felony if committed by an adult; Class III to include crimes against persons and Class II offenses if the juvenile has a prior adjudication for a Class II offense; and Class IV to include acts that if committed by an adult would be punishable by death or imprisonment for over twenty years. The maximum duration for dispositions for each class is as shown in table 15.2.

The Task Force categories for the types of sanctions that may be imposed are nearly identical to those proposed by the IJA/ABA Joint Commission. IJA/ABA, *Dispositions, supra.*

16

New York Designated Felony Act

§ 301.2. Definitions

As used in this article, the following terms shall have the following meanings:
1. "Juvenile delinquent" means a person over seven and less than sixteen years of age, who, having committed an act that would constitute a crime if committed by an adult, (a) is not criminally responsible for such conduct by reason of infancy, or (b) is the defendant in an action ordered removed from a criminal court to the family court pursuant to article seven hundred twenty-five of the criminal procedure law.
2. "Respondent" means the person against whom a juvenile delinquency petition is filed pursuant to section 310.1. Provided, however, that any act of the respondent required or authorized under this article may be performed by his attorney or law guardian unless expressly provided otherwise.
3. "Detention" means the temporary care and maintenance away from their own homes of children held pursuant to this article or held pending a hearing for alleged violation of the conditions of release from a school or center of the division for youth, or held pending return to a jurisdiction other than the one in which the child is held, or held pursuant to a securing

Source: New York Family Court Act, Sections 301.2 and 353.5.

order of a criminal court if the person named therein as principal is under sixteen years of age.

4. "Secure detention facility" means a facility characterized by physically restricting construction, hardware and procedures.
5. "Non-secure detention facility" means a facility characterized by the absence of physically restricting construction, hardware and procedures.
6. "Fact-finding hearing" means a hearing to determine whether the respondent or respondents committed the crime or crimes alleged in the petition or petitions.
7. "Dispositional hearing" means a hearing to determine whether the respondent requires supervision, treatment or confinement.
8. "Designated felony act" means an act which, if done by an adult, would be a crime: (i) defined in sections 125.27 (murder in the first degree); 125.25 (murder in the second degree); 135.25 (kidnapping in the first degree); or 150.20 (arson in the first degree) of the penal law committed by a person thirteen, fourteen or fifteen years of age; (ii) defined in sections 120.10 (assault in the first degree); 125.20 (manslaughter in the first degree); 130.35 (rape in the first degree); 130.50 (sodomy in the first degree); 130.70 (aggravated sexual abuse); 135.20 (kidnapping in the second degree) but only where the abduction involved the use or threat of use of deadly physical force; 150.15 (arson in the second degree) or 160.15 (robbery in the first degree) of the penal law committed by a person thirteen, fourteen or fifteen years of age; (iii) defined in the penal law as an attempt to commit murder in the first or second degree or kidnapping in the first degree committed by a person thirteen, fourteen or fifteen years of age; (iv) defined in section 140.30 (burglary in the first degree); subdivision one of section 140.25 (burglary in the second degree); or subdivision two of section 160.10 (robbery in the second degree) of the penal law committed by a person fourteen or fifteen years of age; (v) defined in section 120.05 (assault in the second degree) or 160.10 (robbery in the second degree) of the penal law committed by a person fourteen or fifteen years of age but only where there has been a prior finding by a court that such person has previously committed an act which, if committed by an adult, would be the crime of assault in the second degree, robbery in the second degree or any designated felony act specified in paragraph (i), (ii), or (iii) of this subdivision regardless of the age of such person at the time of the commission of the prior act; or (vi) other than a misdemeanor committed by a person at least seven but less than sixteen years of age, but only where there have been two prior findings by the court that such person has committed a prior felony.
9. "Designated Class A felony act" means a designated felony act defined in paragraph (i) of subdivision eight.

10. ''Secure facility'' means a residential facility in which the respondent may be placed under this article, which is characterized by physically restricting construction, hardware and procedures, and is designated as a secure facility by the division for youth.
11. ''Restrictive placement'' means a placement pursuant to section 353.5.
12. ''Presentment agency'' means the agency or authority which pursuant to section two hundred fifty-four or two hundred fifty-four-a is responsible for presenting a juvenile delinquency petition.

. . . .

§ 353.5. Designated felony acts; restrictive placement

1. Where the respondent is found to have committed a designated felony act, the order of disposition, shall be made within twenty days of the conclusion of the dispositional hearing and shall include a finding based on a preponderance of the evidence as to whether, for the purposes of this article, the respondent does or does not require a restrictive placement under this section, in connection with which the court shall make specific written findings of fact as to each of the elements set forth in paragraphs (a) through (e) in subdivision two as related to the particular respondent. If the court finds that a restrictive placement under this section is not required, the court shall enter any other order of disposition provided in section 352.2. If the court finds that a restrictive placement is required, it shall continue the proceeding and enter an order of disposition for a restrictive placement. Every order under this section shall be a dispositional order, shall be made after a dispositional hearing and shall state the grounds for the order.
2. In determining whether a restrictive placement is required, the court shall consider:
   (a) the needs and best interests of the respondent;
   (b) the record and background of the respondent, including but not limited to information disclosed in the probation investigation and diagnostic assessment;
   (c) the nature and circumstances of the offense, including whether any injury was inflicted by the respondent or another participant;
   (d) the need for protection of the community; and
   (e) the age and physical condition of the victim.
3. Notwithstanding the provisions of subdivision two, the court shall order a restrictive placement in any case where the respondent is found to have committed a designated felony act in which the respondent inflicted serious physical injury, as that term is defined in subdivision ten of section 10.00 of the penal law, upon another person who is sixty-two years of age or more.

4. When the order is for a restrictive placement in the case of a youth found to have committed a designated class A felony act,
   (a) the order shall provide that:
      (i) the respondent shall be placed with the division for youth for an initial period of five years.
      (ii) the respondent shall initially be confined in a secure facility for a period set by the order, to be not less than twelve nor more than eighteen months provided, however, where the order of the court is made in compliance with subdivision five the respondent shall initially be confined in a secure facility for eighteen months.
      (iii) after the period set under clause (ii), the respondent shall be placed in a residential facility for a period of twelve months.
      (iv) the respondent may not be released from a secure facility or transferred to a non-secure facility during the period provided in clause (ii) of this paragraph, nor may the respondent be released from a residential facility during the period provided in clause (iii). No home visits shall be permitted during the period of secure confinement set by the court order or one year, whichever is less, except for emergency visits for medical treatment or severe illness or death in the family. All home visits must be accompanied home visits: (A) while a youth is confined in a secure facility, whether such confinement is pursuant to a court order or otherwise; (B) while a youth is confined in a non-secure residential facility within six months after confinement in a secure facility; and (C) while a youth is confined in a non-secure residential facility in excess of six months after confinement in a secure facility unless two accompanied home visits have already occurred. An "accompanied home visit" shall mean a home visit during which the youth shall be accompanied at all times while outside the secure or residential facility by appropriate personnel of the division for youth designated pursuant to regulations of the director of the division.
   (b) Notwithstanding any other provision of law, during the first twelve months of the respondent's placement, no motion, hearing or order may be made, held or granted pursuant to section 355.1, provided, however, that during such period a motion to vacate the order may be made pursuant to 355.1, but only upon grounds set forth in section 440.10 of the criminal procedure law.
   (c) During the placement or any extension thereof:
      (i) after the expiration of the period provided in clause (iii) of paragraph (a), the respondent shall not be released from a residential facility without the written approval of the director of the division for youth or his designated deputy director.

(ii) the respondent shall be subject to intensive supervision whenever not in a secure or residential facility.

(iii) the respondent shall not be discharged from the custody of the division for youth, unless a motion therefor under section 355.1 is granted by the court, which motion shall not be made prior to the expiration of three years of the placement.

(iv) unless otherwise specified in the order, the division shall report in writing to the court not less than once every six months during the placement on the status, adjustment and progress of the respondent.

(d) Upon the expiration of the initial period of placement, or any extension thereof, the placement may be extended in accordance with section 355.3 on a petition of any party or the division for youth after a dispositional hearing, for an additional period not to exceed twelve months, but no initial placement or extension of placement under this section may continue beyond the respondent's twenty-first birthday.

(e) The court may also make an order pursuant to subdivision two of section 353.4.

5. When the order is for a restrictive placement in the case of a youth found to have committed a designated felony act, other than a designated class A felony act,

(a) the order shall provide that:

(i) the respondent shall be placed with the division for youth for an initial period of three years.

(ii) the respondent shall initially be confined in a secure facility for a period set by the order, to be not less than six nor more than twelve months.

(iii) after the period set under clause (ii), the respondent shall be placed in a residential facility for a period set by the order, to be not less than six nor more than twelve months.

(iv) the respondent may not be released from a secure facility or transferred to a non-secure facility during the period provided by the court pursuant to clause (ii), nor may the respondent be released from a residential facility during the period provided by the court pursuant to clause (iii). No home visits shall be permitted during the period of secure confinement set by the court order or one year, whichever is less, except for emergency visits for medical treatment or severe illness or death in the family. All home visits must be accompanied home visits: (A) while a youth is confined in a secure facility, whether such confinement is pursuant to a court order or otherwise; (B) while a youth is confined in a non-secure residential facility within six months after confinement in a secure facility; and (C) while a youth is confined in a non-secure residential facility in excess of six months after confinement in a secure facility unless two accompanied home visits have already occurred. An "accompanied home visit" shall mean a home visit during which the youth shall be accompanied at all times while outside the secure or residential facility by appropriate personnel of the division for youth designated pursuant to regulations of the director of the division.

(b) Notwithstanding any other provision by law, during the first six months of the respondent's placement, no motion, hearing or order may be made, held or granted pursuant to section 355.1; provided, however, that during such period a motion to vacate the order may be made pursuant to such section, but only upon grounds set forth in section 440.10 of the criminal procedure law.

(c) During the placement or any extension thereof:

(i) after the expiration of the period provided in clause (iii) of paragraph (a), the respondent shall not be released from a residential facility without the written approval of the director of the division for youth or his designated deputy director.

(ii) the respondent shall be subject to intensive supervision whenever not in a secure or residential facility.

(iii) the respondent shall not be discharged from the custody of the division for youth.

(iv) unless otherwise specified in the order, the division shall report in writing to the court not less than once every six months during the placement on the status, adjustment and progress of the respondent.

(d) Upon the expiration of the initial period of placement or any extension thereof, the placement may be extended in accordance with section 355.3 upon petition of any party or the division for youth, after a dispositional hearing, for an additional period not to exceed twelve months, but no initial placement or extension of placement under this section may continue beyond the respondent's twenty-first birthday.

(e) The court may also make an order pursuant to subdivision two of section 353.4.

6. When the order is for a restrictive placement in the case of a youth found to have committed any designated felony act and such youth has been found by a court to have committed a designated felony act on a prior occasion, regardless of the age of such youth at the time of commission of such prior act, the order of the court shall be made pursuant to subdivision four.

7. If the dispositional hearing has been adjourned on a finding of specific circumstances pursuant to subdivision six of section 350.1 while the re-

spondent is in detention, where a restrictive placement is subsequently ordered, time spent by the respondent in detention during such additional adjournment shall be credited and applied against any term of secure confinement ordered by the court pursuant to subdivision four or five.

8. The division for youth shall retain the power to continue the confinement of the youth in a secure or other residential facility beyond the periods specified by the court, within the term of the placement.

Added L.1982, c. 920, § 1; amended L.1983, c. 398, §§ 38 to 42.

17

Illinois Habitual Juvenile Offender Law

805-35. Habitual Juvenile Offender

§ 5-35. Habitual Juvenile Offender. (a) Definition. Any minor having been twice adjudicated a delinquent minor for offenses which, had he been prosecuted as an adult, would have been felonies under the laws of this State, and who is thereafter adjudicated a delinquent minor for a third time shall be adjudged an Habitual Juvenile Offender where:

    1. the third adjudication is for an offense occurring after adjudication on the second; and

    2. the second adjudication was for an offense occurring after adjudication on the first; and

    3. the third offense occurred after January 1, 1980; and

    4. the third offense was based upon the commission of or attempted commission of the following offenses: first degree murder, second degree murder or involuntary manslaughter; criminal sexual assault or aggravated criminal sexual assault; aggravated or heinous battery involving permanent disability or disfigurement or great bodily harm to the victim; burglary of a home or other residence intended for use as a temporary or permanent dwelling place for human beings; home invasion; robbery or armed robbery; or aggravated arson.

Source: Illinois Court Statutes, 37-805-35.

Nothing in this section shall preclude the State's Attorney from seeking to prosecute a minor as an adult as an alternative to prosecution as an habitual juvenile offender.

A continuance under supervision authorized by Section 5-19 of this Act shall not be permitted under this section.

(b) Notice to minor. The State shall serve upon the minor written notice of intention to prosecute under the provisions of this Section within 5 judicial days of the filing of any delinquency petition, adjudication upon which would mandate the minor's disposition as an Habitual Juvenile Offender.

(c) Petition; service. A notice to seek adjudication as an Habitual Juvenile Offender shall be filed only by the State's Attorney.

The petition upon which such Habitual Juvenile Offender notice is based shall contain the information and averments required for all other delinquency petitions filed under this Act and its service shall be according to the provisions of this Act.

No prior adjudication shall be alleged in the petition.

(d) Trial. Trial on such petition shall be by jury unless the minor demands, in open court and with advice of counsel, a trial by the court without jury.

Except as otherwise provided herein, the provisions of this Act concerning delinquency proceedings generally shall be applicable to Habitual Juvenile Offender proceedings.

(e) Proof of prior adjudications. No evidence or other disclosure of prior adjudications shall be presented to the court or jury during any adjudicatory hearing provided for under this Section, unless otherwise permitted by the issues properly raised in such hearing. In the event the minor who is the subject of these proceedings elects to testify on his own behalf, it shall be competent to introduce evidence, for purposes of impeachment, that he has previously been adjudicated a delinquent minor upon facts which, had he been tried as an adult, would have resulted in his conviction of a felony. Introduction of such evidence shall be according to the rules and procedures applicable to the impeachment of an adult defendant by prior conviction.

After an admission of the facts in the petition or adjudication of delinquency, the State's Attorney may file with the court a verified written statement signed by the State's Attorney concerning any prior adjudication of an offense set forth in subsection (a) of this Section which offense would have been a felony had the minor been tried as an adult.

The court shall then cause the minor to be brought before it; shall inform him of the allegations of the statement so filed, and of his right to a hearing before the court on the issue of such prior adjudication and of his right to counsel at such hearing; and unless the minor admits such adjudication, the court shall hear and determine such issue, and shall make a written finding thereon.

A duly authenticated copy of the record of any such alleged prior adjudication shall be prima facie evidence of such prior adjudication.

Any claim that a previous adjudication offered by the State's Attorney is not a former adjudication of an offense which, had the minor been prosecuted as an adult, would have resulted in his conviction of a felony, is waived unless duly raised at the hearing on such adjudication, or unless the State's Attorney's proof shows that such prior adjudication was not based upon proof of what would have been a felony.

(f) Disposition. If the court finds that the prerequisites established in subsection (a) of this Section have been proven, it shall adjudicate the minor an Habitual Juvenile Offender and commit him to the Department of Corrections, Juvenile Division, until his 21st birthday, without possibility of parole, furlough, or non-emergency authorized absence. However, the minor shall be entitled to earn one day of good conduct credit for each day served as reductions against the period of his confinement. Such good conduct credits shall be earned or revoked according to the procedures applicable to the allowance and revocation of good conduct credit for adult prisoners serving determinate sentences for felonies.

For purposes of determining good conduct credit, commitment as an Habitual Juvenile Offender shall be considered a determinate commitment, and the difference between the date of the commitment and the minor's 21st birthday shall be considered the determinate period of his confinement.

P.A. 85–601, Art. V. § 5–35, eff. Jan. 1, 1988.

18

People v. J. A.

**Appellate Court of Illinois, First District, Third Division.
Sept. 28, 1984.**

McNamara, Justice:

A petition for adjudication of wardship charged the minor respondent with robbery in that he took food and $10 from another person. Because respondent had two prior adjudications for robbery, the juvenile court granted the State's motion that he be prosecuted as a habitual juvenile offender under section 5-12 of the Juvenile Court Act. (Ill.Rev.Stat.1983, ch. 37, par. 701-1 *et seq.*) After a hearing respondent was adjudicated a ward of the court. At another hearing he was committed to the Department of Corrections, Juvenile Division, until his 21st birthday. On appeal respondent contends that the juvenile habitual offender statute cannot be construed to include adjudications of delinquency occurring prior to respondent's 13th birthday; that the application of the habitual offender statute here constitutes a denial of due process; that the commitment constitutes cruel and unusual punishment; that the prosecution of respondent under the habitual offender statute constitutes an abuse of prosecutorial discretion; and that the trial court's denial of respondent's request for a continuance constituted reversible error.

Source: *People v. J. A.*, 469 N.E.2d 449 (1984).

Jeffrey Pryor testified that, on August 31, 1982, as he was carrying a bag of chicken, he was accosted by several teenagers, one of whom was respondent. When Pryor refused to give up his food, respondent summoned two more boys and began pushing the victim against a wall. After one assailant struck Pryor in the face and another grabbed him in a headlock, respondent took $10 from Pryor's pocket. The robbers then fled.

Respondent, 13 years old, testified that he knew his friends intended to rob and beat Pryor. Respondent, however, stood 10 feet away and did not participate. Two other boys, charged with the same robbery, corroborated respondent's testimony.

Respondent first maintains that because he was 12 years old at the time of his two prior adjudications of delinquency and at that time could not be prosecuted as an adult under any circumstances, the requirements of section 5–12 were not met. Section 5–12 of the Juvenile Court Act provides in pertinent part:

> (a) Any minor having been twice adjudicated a delinquent minor for *offenses which, had he been prosecuted as an adult, would have been felonies under the laws of this State,* and who is thereafter adjudicated a delinquent minor for a third time shall be adjudged an Habitual Juvenile Offender where:
>
> . . . .
>
> 4. the third offense was based upon the commission of or attempted commission of the following offenses: murder, voluntary or involuntary manslaughter; rape or deviate sexual assault; aggravated or heinous battery involving permanent disability or disfigurement or great bodily harm to the victim; burglary of a home or other residence intended for use as a temporary or permanent dwelling place for human beings; home invasion; robbery or armed robbery; or aggravated arson. (Emphasis added.) Ill.Rev.Stat.1983, ch. 37, par. 705–12.

Respondent interprets the emphasized statutory language as an age classification restricting the statute's applicability, since only minors between the ages of 13 and 17 may be prosecuted as an adult. (Ill.Rev.Stat.1983, ch. 37, par. 702–7.) The State urges that the Act merely defines the type of crime to which the statute will apply and that it is applicable to all delinquency adjudications.

[1–3] The language of a statute must be given its plain and ordinary meaning. (*People v. Moore* (1978), 69 Ill.2d 520, 14 Ill.Dec. 470, 372 N.E.2d 666.) And from our reading, the plain and ordinary meaning of the Act precludes respondent's claim. There is nothing in the language to indicate the legislature intended to create a special class of juvenile offenders under the age of 13 whose adjudications would not subject them to the Habitual Juvenile Offender statute. That the pertinent language describes the type of offense and not the age of the offender is clear from a reading of the entire statute.

The fourth requirement of the statute specifies the felonies which must be committed before a minor is subject to such an adjudication. The legislature intended to deal with the problem of serious crime committed by minors, and it did not draw a distinction for serious offenders under the age of 13. The juvenile court properly considered respondent's prior adjudications in adjudging respondent a habitual juvenile offender.

Respondent next contends that consideration of his prior adjudications of delinquency denies his right to due process and equal protection. He argues that, had his prior offenses occurred after his thirteenth birthday, he could have transferred the cases to the criminal court to be tried as an adult thereby circumventing the Habitual Juvenile Offender statute. Respondent further argues that the statute illogically imposes the harshest and longest penalty on the youngest and least serious offender.

[4] We find the holding of *People ex rel. Carey v. Chrastka* (1980), 83 Ill.2d 67, 46 Ill.Dec. 156, 413 N.E.2d 1269, to be dispositive of the issue. There, our supreme court held that the Habitual Juvenile Offender statute did not violate the due process or equal protection clauses of the constitution. The court stated at p. 81, 46 Ill.Dec. 156, 413 N.E.2d 1269. "[w]e do not believe that the fortuitous disparity of the terms of confinement of habitual juvenile offenders which results from the variance in age of such individuals serves to invalidate the means chosen to effectuate the purpose of the Act." We also reject respondent's position that a younger juvenile, adjudged a habitual juvenile offender for the commission of three robberies, is any less a serious threat to society than an older juvenile committing the same acts.

Respondent next contends that the imposition of an eight year sentence was cruel and unusual punishment for robbing another boy of ten dollars and a bag of chicken. Although the *Chrastka* court specifically rejects this argument, respondent maintains that the decision of the United States Supreme Court in *Solem v. Helm* (1983), 463 U.S. 277, 103 S.Ct. 3001, 77 L.Ed.2d 637, requires a reassessment. In *Solem,* the court considered three factors in evaluating whether a particular sentence constituted cruel and unusual punishment. The court looked at the gravity of the offense compared to the harshness of the penalty; the sentence imposed on other criminals in the same jurisdictions; and the sentences imposed for the same crime in other jurisdictions.

[5] Assuming the *Solem* factors apply to juvenile proceedings, we find that the criteria are met in the present case. Respondent's previous adjudications, in October and December 1981, were for two robberies of a total of $36. Contrary to respondent's assertions, pushing a victim into a wall, holding him in a headlock, striking him in the face, and robbing him of his money on a public street is indeed a serious offense. Respondent's conduct was violent and unprovoked, and the gravity of the offense justified the court's disposition. Moreover, the remaining criteria are also met. Rather than applying the same penalty to offenses of unequal severity, the statute is limited to specific serious,

multiple offenses. The Act is also comparable to juvenile statutes in other jurisdictions. See e.g., Cal.Welf. & Inst. Code § 607(b) (West Supp.1984); N.Y. Family Court Act Law § 353.5 (McKinney 1983).

Respondent also maintains that the prosecutor abused his discretion in proceeding under the Habitual Juvenile Offender statute when respondent was charged with a minor offense. Respondent concedes that his offense technically constituted robbery, but urges that it is not the serious offense intended by the legislature to trigger the application of the statute.

[6, 7] A prosecutor has wide latitude in determining the charges to be brought, after a fair evaluation of the evidence and a fair consideration of what the proper charge should be. (*People v. Rhodes* (1967), 38 Ill.2d 389, 231 N.E.2d 400.) We find no evidence of abuse of discretion or vindictiveness here in charging respondent as a habitual juvenile offender when he was twice adjudged delinquent and was again before the juvenile court charged with robbery. As we have already noted, the robbery was indeed serious.

Respondent finally urges that the juvenile court abused its discretion in denying his request for a continuance to call a material witness.

During the hearing, the State presented the testimony of Officer Caddigan who had questioned Pryor after the robbery. Caddigan stated that Pryor first told him that respondent held him while another boy took the money and later said that respondent took the money. At the hearing, Pryor testified that respondent took his money. Defense counsel requested a continuance to call Officer Keever who had spoken with Caddigan and compiled the police report on the incident. The judge denied the request.

[8, 9] An accused, of course, has the right to summon witnesses in his defense. A motion for continuance may be made when a material witness is unavailable, but the right to a continuance is not absolute. (*People v. McEwen* (1982), 104 Ill.App.3d 410, 60 Ill.Dec. 144, 432 N.E.2d 1043.) In claiming an abuse of discretion the accused must demonstrate that the denial of the continuance impeded him in the preparation of his defense or prejudiced his rights. *People v. Petrovic* (1981), 102 Ill.App.3d 282, 58 Ill.Dec. 64, 430 N.E.2d 6.

[10] The testimony of Caddigan adequately established that Pryor had given him two different versions of who took the money, and McKeever's testimony would have been cumulative on the issue. Consequently, the absence of the witness did not prejudice respondent, and the juvenile court did not abuse its discretion in denying the request for a continuance.

For the reasons stated, the judgment of the circuit court of Cook County is affirmed.

Judgment affirmed.

19

The Juvenile Justice Act of 1977: A Prosecutor's Perspective

Jay A. Reich

I. Introduction

In 1977, the Washington State Legislature redefined juvenile delinquency as a problem of crime rather than a behavioral pattern of adolescence. This radical shift of emphasis from the social development of the child to the criminal accountability of the juvenile offender has transformed the juvenile court and, in turn, catapulted the county prosecutor into a new rule. While enforcing the criminal code has been a traditional task of prosecutors, confronting young burglars whose feet only occasionally touch the courtroom floor has been the function of social workers. The central challenge to prosecutors, and others concerned about juvenile justice, is to help shape a new system that readdresses old imbalances without recreating the failures of our adult system.

II. The Traditional Role of the Prosecutor

Prior juvenile codes in Washington did not mention the prosecutor. These laws, mirrored throughout the country at the turn of the century, created a separate juvenile court that treated juvenile offenders as children in need of

Source: *Gonzaga Law Review*, 14 (1979): 337–358. Reprinted by permission of Gonzaga Law Review.

care, custody, and guardianship. "Delinquency" was a pattern of behavior that symptomized depravity, immaturity, or a lack of a basic socialization. The key actor in this system became the social worker, assisting the court in a determination of what was in the child's best interest. The notion was that if society could isolate the underlying problems that manifested themselves in criminal, or hopefully pre-criminal behavior, then society could humanely and effectively intervene in the child's life.

In this system the prosecutor had little to offer. Crime was but one symptom of social diseases too profound to be susceptible to legal process. Prosecutors were not trained in social diagnosis and were surely ill-equipped to assist in religious salvation. The juvenile system was purposely informal and social workers routinely "prosecuted" crimes. Children had few legal rights, for formality stigmatized the child and delayed treatment. The very dangerous or older offenders, for whom lengthy control and therefore formal process seemed appropriate, could and would be transferred to the adult court.

Case law during much of this century defined the goal of juvenile court as acting in the best interests of the child. The court process was neither adversarial nor criminal. The prosecutor, to the extent that he participated in juvenile court at all, focused on what would be good for the child rather than the more traditional areas of deterrence or public safety. Any charge could be adjusted by a social worker or dismissed by the court. Local rules for King County, adopted as late as 1975, allowed children to admit to any count in a multi-count petition; the remaining counts were automatically adjusted or dismissed, though considered at disposition. After the child was found to be delinquent, every subsequent offense would be treated as a violation of probation to be proven by only a preponderance of the evidence. Sentences were indeterminate and a finding that a child had committed an act which if done by an adult would have been a crime, resulted in the child being sentenced to the Department of Social and Health Services until the age of twenty-one. This was not considered punishment but rather treatment. The criminal charges themselves were often perceived as technicalities that gave rise to a delinquency status; this status, in turn, guaranteed to the child social services provided by the court.

III. Criticisms of the System

Criticisms of this system came from far beyond the few prosecutors who viewed their role as inadequate and ineffectual. On the right side of the political spectrum, police and concerned citizens observed that the juvenile court did not hold children accountable for their criminal acts in any systematic manner. Minor offenders with major social problems were often committed to state institutions, while serious offenders, amenable to social work in the community, were not punished. The almost exclusive emphasis on the child rather than his crimes left victims of crime and law enforcement personnel frustrated and angered. Shrouded in a veil of secrecy to protect the child, the system was viewed with suspicion and cynicism. It appeared to be inconsistent and "soft" and, if it did not foster, it surely had not curtailed what was perceived to be rising juvenile crime.

On the political left, defense attorneys and civil libertarians saw the system as unpredictable and fraught with over-diagnosis and premature social intervention. Each caseworker and judge within a county and each county within the state exhibited different notions of what was in a child's best interest. Due process safeguards were regulated to a position of lesser importance than the "benevolent" attempts by the court to "help" the child. There was the belief that the legal bases for obtaining jurisdiction over a child were conveniently vague which allowed the court to intervene in a child's life whenever it was deemed necessary and proper—for many a misguided reason.

Prosecutors throughout the state were split with respect to these criticisms: some were simply oblivious to juvenile prosecution; some feared a drain on already limited resources if juvenile justice were to be formalized; some enjoyed the extraordinary informality of the system where the ends seemed to justify the means; and others found themselves aligned with this strange coalition of the political left and right, believing that these same juveniles deserved the due process that was afforded adults.

The debate was not local in scope, however. The American Bar Association and the Institute of Judicial Administration had spent several years exploring these problems on the national level; the older consensus of parens patriae was being torn apart. In Washington, eight years of legislative efforts and failures lead to a unique set of circumstances. A combination of political leadership, convenient alliances, lobbying resources, fortuitous timing, and frustration with the repeated legislative debates on juvenile law led to the passage of the new juvenile code.

The new juvenile code has essentially transformed the former "benevolent" juvenile court into a traditional criminal court system. The legislature unabashedly states as its purpose the protection of the public, accountability of the juvenile, and punishment of the offender. The juvenile prosecutor has assumed the same functions he performs in the prosecution of adult crimes, and this new role symbolizes the fundamental change in the juvenile court philosophy.

IV. Statutory Provisions

RCW chapter 13.40 of the new code clearly defines the role of the prosecutor with respect to juvenile offenders, formerly referred to euphemistically as juvenile delinquents. Generally, the prosecutor is party to all offender cases, though the option is available for the prosecutor to allow misdemeanor cases to be prosecuted by the juvenile court probation counselor. This provision was adopted at the request of rural prosecutors who foresaw the added responsibilities of juvenile prosecution as an impossible fiscal burden.

Virtually all prosecutors have chosen to become involved with both felonies and misdemeanors for several reasons. First, the tasks of screening and prosecuting felonies and misdemeanors is legal in nature. It is difficult to distinguish these functions on the basis of the offender's age or the seriousness of his crime. Second, many gross misdemeanors, such as simple assault, are not only serious crimes, but others such as shoplifting are of special interest to certain segments of the public; for example, the business community. Given the code's acknowledged goal of public protection, it is not inappropriate for the public's interest to be more directly represented through the elected prosecutor. Third, as the system becomes formally adversarial, it is less appropriate for the social worker to play the dual roles of prosecutor and counselor. Finally, to the extent that the same work has to be performed by either a prosecutor or a caseworker, it is not illogical for the prosecutor to desire to have these resources within his own budget rather than that of the courts.

While referrals to the court previously were screened by caseworkers, under the new code all cases must go to the prosecutor. The threshold question traditionally asked was whether court intervention was necessary in the child's interest. The threshold question now asked is a legal one: Is there a prosecutable case? The initial decision of whether the case is sufficient or not, and how far it will penetrate into the system is made almost exclusively with reference to the facts and the law, and not the social situation of the child.

The screening function itself is analogous to that done by the adult prosecutor. The law states that the prosecutor is to determine if there is probable cause and whether the court has jurisdiction of the case. The bill is unclear whether this two-pronged standard is exclusive. From a prosecutor's perspective and probably that of the public's interest, such a definition would be too narrow. There are many cases in which there is probable cause to believe the respondent committed a crime and the court has jurisdiction but still should not be filed. Examples include where the state could not possibly prove the charge beyond a reasonable doubt because there is inadequate evidence, evidence would likely be suppressed, the victim does not want to proceed, or even where the state is convinced it has the wrong person. To force filing or even diversion of such a case would be at least a waste of limited resources and at worst an injustice.

The statute suggests that if the prosecutor does not wish to file the case then he must list his reasons and keep that record for one year. This was a legislative attempt to ameliorate the dilemma posed by the two-pronged standard and yet hold the prosecutor accountable. There was a belief by the legislature that, as a matter of public policy, the prosecutor should be held accountable and be prevented from avoiding difficult cases. On the other hand, to force the prosecutor to file every case would probably be an unwise if not an unconstitutional invasion into the independent power of the prosecutor to find a case legally sufficient. The compromise reached was that while the prosecutor did not have to file every case, he had to give his reasons for not filing those cases in which there is jurisdiction and probable cause. The provision, however, was misplaced in the code. Rather than applying to the entire filing and diversion standards, it appears to only affect a relatively small group of cases. Amendments have been proposed, however, to correct this error.

Once a case is determined to be legally sufficient or more aptly, when the prosecutor decides that it has prosecutorial merit, then the decision must be whether the case is to be filed or diverted. Diversion implies a less formal processing of the case in the child's community; filing implies the formality of an adult courtroom. While both routes create a type of criminal history, only formal filing can lead to detention. This decision to file or divert is generally dictated by statutory standards. The more serious crimes and the crimes committed by the most chronic offenders must be filed. However, the filing of an information of an alleged offender accused of a class C felony, regardless of the juvenile's criminal history, is discretionary with the prosecutor. And juveniles accused of less serious crimes and with less serious criminal records will be diverted.

Prosecutors have taken varied positions with respect to the discretion to file class C felonies. Most prosecutors file all class C felonies regardless of the offender's prior history. In King County, however, class C felonies against property where the offender has no history will be diverted. Joyriding is the most obvious example of cases which will be diverted in the first instance in King County but filed elsewhere. The reasons for the differing approaches emanate from the circumstances of the county. The volume of the more serious crimes in King County suggests the need to divert the minor offenses into the less expensive and less stigmatizing community diversion system. In smaller counties, the volume of all crime is significantly lower while the diversion resources are not as extensive. It is, therefore, not so much a depreciation of the crime as much as a different allocation of resources. However, the law was intended to decrease statewide discrepancy and allowing such discretion promotes disparate treatment.

When a case is filed, it progresses through the court system much like an adult case would. The papers filed closely resemble those of the adult system, and all of the rights of an adult, with the exception of the jury trial, are afforded the juvenile. In some counties such as King, the formality of the juvenile process has not changed; in others, however, where attorneys were not regular participants in the system, the process will inevitably be slower and more cumbersome. While the rights of the child are arguably better protected under this system, the question remains whether the child will understand or be impressed by a process which is now dominated by lawyers and legal questions. While to the child the symbolic importance of the proceeding may be enhanced, he may paradoxically be more isolated and unaffected from the outcome due to the omnipresence of his legal counsel.

By its terms, the bill significantly alters the mode of disposition of criminal matters. The perceived emphasis is on accountability, punishment, and restitution rather than social planning. Standard dispositions are calculated by reference to the offender's age, crime and criminal history. However, social history and diagnosis may be utilized to legitimate special probationary terms or exceptions to the set standards. The reasons for the change are the result of the pre-juvenile code experience. For example, some judges were appalled by the fact that children who committed burglaries would not only proceed formally to court but also receive a day or two in detention as a standard punishment. Other judges, however, were equally appalled because one or two days was but a "slap on the wrist" and in their counties ten to fifteen days was the pre-code "standard" range of punishment. These opposing perspectives reflected the pre-code need for a statewide standardized system.

The prosecutor views the new system of diversion and determinate sentencing as a more comprehensible and predictable system. The difference between two and ten days of detention is often less significant than the difference between the informality and social work perspectives of the past and the formalism and accountability of the new system. While there surely will be disagreement among prosecutors with respect to the appropriate degree of sanctions to be applied, there is probably universal acceptance of the notion that punishment is an appropriate and long overdue consideration of the juvenile court.

With respect to public trials, the emphasis on crimes, and the new formality of juvenile justice, the prosecutor is cautiously optimistic. While the system is more complex, expensive, and time consuming, its recognition of juvenile crime as a serious public safety problem is welcomed. Whether the behavior of juveniles will be affected by threats of punishment, incarceration in juvenile institutions, the payment of restitution or hours of community service, remains to be seen. For whatever reasons, and surely there are many, the older system did not deter juvenile crime. The question to be asked may not be how successful is the new system, but how does it compare with the past in terms of equity, candor, and the reinforcement of the fundamental ethical principles of right and wrong.

V. Implications for Prosecutorial Discretion

The specificity of the new law with respect to filing and sentencing standards is misleading. While the decisions as to whether a case is filed or diverted relates directly to the crime charged, the labelling of an act as a particular crime is not as clear-cut. Crimes proscribe general conduct; individuals display particular behavior. Labelling is inevitably arbitrary and yet, in the context of the new code, exceedingly important.

One extreme example may suffice to demonstrate the point. Imagine a fifteen-year-old child without a criminal record who throws a lighted match into a wastebasket in a school restroom. The wastebasket bursts into flames and the child yells ''fire.'' On its face it is difficult to characterize this act. It could be arson in the first degree if the child knowingly and maliciously started the fire; such a fire in a school could be considered manifestly dangerous to human life. If the act were labelled as arson in the first degree, then the case would have to be filed rather than diverted. The child would be considered a serious offender and would be committed to a state institution for sixteen to twenty months. If the act were characterized as arson in the second degree— because there was damage to the building but the fire was not considered manifestly dangerous to life—then the case would still have to be filed. The child, however, would receive the standard range of punishment of sixty to ninety hours of community service but no detention time. If the act were labelled as reckless burning in the first degree then the decision whether to file or divert is left with the prosecutor. If filed, the child would be subject to a standard range of punishment of thirty to forty-five hours of community service. If the act were characterized as reckless burning in the second degree then the case must be diverted and the diversion unit would determine restitution and community service up to one hundred fifty hours. Not only are the consequences significant with respect to the crime charged, but dispositions for future crimes will be influenced by how the criminal act is recorded in the child's criminal history; the more serious the characterization, the more it will increase the penalty for subsequent criminal acts.

It is the prosecutor who has primary responsibility for determining the appropriate label and thus he, to a great extent, controls the consequences of the crime. In the first instance, it is at the screening stage that such decisions are made. Later, in the context of plea negotiation, the prosecutor can alter the characterization of the crime or the number of crimes alleged to effectuate a different result. While the court retains significant discretion, the code structures that discretion in such a way that the court must often overcome presumptions established as a result of the label attached.

The difficulties of characterization and plea negotiation are encountered daily by the prosecutor within the adult system. The new code, however, may make such decisions more difficult in the juvenile context. First, the labels of the adult system—with the exception of those in the firearm, deadly weapon, habitual offender, and rape in the first degree statutes—do not carry the impact of the new juvenile labels. The courts in the adult system retain virtually unlimited discretion to suspend or sentence the offender up to the maximum of the charge which in the adult system is five, ten, or twenty years to life. Second, the Board of Prison Terms and Parole, absent in the juvenile system, retains significant discretion to alter sentences once the adult felon is committed to the Department of Social and Health Services. Third, juvenile crimes may reflect a wider variety of behavior than that normally seen in the adult system. Surely adults commit many kinds of crimes for many reasons; however, juvenile crime is exceedingly difficult to characterize because juveniles change so rapidly during adolescence and their crime motives are often the result of peer pressure and adolescent experimentation. It is not that there is an absence of variety among adults, but rather much more variety among juveniles. Finally, the prosecutors, due to their lack of participation in the traditional juvenile system coupled with their adult orientation, may not be equipped or trained to prosecute juveniles.

This is not to suggest that the legislature was misguided in its attempt to confront juveniles with their criminal acts. It is to suggest, however, that this is a difficult task and a task for which prosecutors may be ill prepared. Furthermore, if the legislative intent of the act to provide consistent, predictable sentencing is to be achieved, it is important that disparity among prosecutors not distort the system. If some prosecutors characterized our juvenile match thrower as an arsonist and others as a reckless burner, then we have merely displaced the roots of disparity from the court and caseworkers to the prosecutor. Moreover, if a single prosecutor decides such acts are sometimes arson and sometimes reckless burnings, then even within the same county and the same office there might be manifest disparity.

Discretion is inherent within any criminal justice system. Attempts to close off discretion at one level of the system will only cause decisions to be made elsewhere, perhaps in a less observable and responsible place. If the law required judges to incarcerate all drug sellers for life terms regardless of the quantity of drugs sold, then it is possible that prosecutors would not charge and the police would not arrest all dealers. For this reason, among many, the courts retain significant discretion under the new juvenile code. To the extent that the judges sentence outside certain standard ranges, they must justify their reasons. Similarly, prosecutors have significant discretion and in some instances, the new law forces them to articulate their reasons for not filing cases. To the extent, however, that the law does not force the articulation of a prosecutor's decisions, prosecutors must exercise discretionary self-control. This can be done by establishing their own standards and justifying their own exceptions in writing. The very act of establishing standards forces their consideration and articulation. It also enables public scrutiny of prosecutorial decision making; the accountability that the legislature sought to achieve. While discretion is an inherent part of any justice system, and while the new code invests with the prosecutor significant discretion, such discretion is not a license. It is a means of doing justice, of resolving the inevitable problems of general statutes and specific acts, and of holding juveniles accountable in a context sensitive to their unique criminality.

VI. Early Experience

It is too early to accurately assess the impact of the new juvenile code. The implementation date was delayed for one year to facilitate planning and analysis. It was anticipated that a special legislative session would be called in 1978 and thus an opportunity would be provided for "clean-up" amendments. The legislature was not called into session, however, and thus, for the first six to eight months at least, the system will labor under the obvious problems that should be changed in 1979. Some of these areas include: jurisdiction over traffic offenses, venue with respect to disposition, placement of the respondent pending an appeal of a manifest injustice finding, and various other ambiguities that will arise in particular cases. Until the various technical problems are resolved and the application of the new code has become routine, it is impossible to discern what the "normal" experience of the code will be.

In King County, the code has dramatically increased the number of criminal referrals to the court and the number of formal filings. Total referrals increased from July 1977 to July 1978 from 813 to 1369, and from August 1977 to August 1978 from 1093 to 1677. Filings of felony charges increased from 192 in July 1977 to 477 in July 1978, and from 233 in August 1977 to 378 in August 1978. These increases have imposed significant burdens on the entire system. It is difficult to isolate the reasons for these increases because the data has not been carefully analyzed, but nonetheless, several explanations do exist. It is quite possible that juvenile crime did dramatically increase in the last year. It is more likely, however, that law enforcement members have more confidence in the new juvenile system and would rather have their cases formally prosecuted and records established than dispose of them informally as was previously the procedure. Or the increased felony filings may have resulted from the new statutory provisions which require mandatory filing in certain cases.

Assuming that these explanations are valid, the question remains whether this extraordinary trend is desirable. From the perspective of accountability, the increased filings of felonies are welcomed by prosecutors. While the punishment for first time offenders is not severe, the formal response of the system is more predictable and certain and thus may create a more effective deterrence factor. The increase of referrals for less serious crimes, however, may pose a problem because their penetration into the system deflects resources from more serious crimes and offenders. While the new law provides that these minor offenders will generally be diverted, the formality of the diversion process, requiring prosecutors to screen and keep records, will undoubtedly be expensive.

When the data can be analzyed, the issues can be more carefully framed. It must be asked whether the community is willing to pay for and participate in juvenile accountability. Should there be finer distinctions made between crimes or even the decriminalization of some acts to limit the number of cases that enter the system? Would certain crimes such as a minor in possession of alcohol, misdemeanor possession of marijuana, boating, and fish and game violations be more efficiently prosecuted in courts of limited jurisdiction? Should law enforcement be encouraged to handle every juvenile crime formally, or is society willing to tolerate the potential for abuse and injustice through increased police discretion? The ultimate question is only now being understood as the code has become implemented: To what extent should the juvenile justice system resemble the adult court?

VII. Conclusion

The new juvenile code has changed the focus of the juvenile court and dramatically changed the role of the prosecutor. This is a role for which the adult prosecutor may be unprepared, not only because he has not dealt extensively with juveniles but because their crimes are often child-like. The juvenile system is not a replica of the adult system; its assumptions, while similar, are different, for juveniles are different. They change more quickly, and may be more amenable to rehabilitation programs. Their punishment need not be as severe, and their risk to the community, with certain limited exceptions, may not be as great. Paradoxically, the prosecutor's new role is at once more central to the juvenile court and yet his experience in adult prosecution is less relevant. Among all of the actors of the new system, the prosecutor's role has changed the most. His greatest responsibility is to balance the polar forces that both attract and repel the juvenile system vis-à-vis its adult counterpart.

Appendix A: Filing/Diversion Decision under RCW 13.40.070

Offense	Criminal History	Decision
Any Crime	(1) A	
	(1) B	
	(2) C	
	(1) C & (1) Gross Mis.	Must File
	(1) C & (1) Mis.	
	(2) Gross Mis.	
	(1) Gross Mis. & (2) Mis.	
	(3) Mis.	

Class A Felony		
Class B Felony &		
Attempt	Any or No History	Must File
Assault in the 3d°		
Rape in the 3d°		

	(1) C	
Class C Felony, except	(1) Gross Mis. & (1) Mis.	Prosecutor's Choice
Assault 3d°	(2) Mis.	
Rape 3d° and Attempted	(1) Gross Mis.	
Class B	(1) Mis.	
	No History	

	(1) C	
	(1) Gross Mis. & (1) Mis.	Must Divert
Gross Misdemeanor	(2) Mis.	
Misdemeanor	(1) Gross Mis.	
	(1) Mis.	
	No History	

Violation of Diversion		
Requests Prosecution	Not Applicable	Must File
Referred by Diversion		*
Unit to P.A.		

Appendix B: Using the D.S.H.S. Sentencing Guidelines

I. Calculating the Sentencing Range for Each Offense
   1. Current Offense
      a) On the worksheet, write in the name of the offense, the class (A+ through M/V), the date of the offense, and the age of the child at the time of the offense.
      b) From this information, and using the "Current Offense" Matrix, write in the points for the offense.
      c) When using the Current Offense Matrix, count "age" as the age at the time of the offense.
   2. Computing the Increase Factor
      a) On the worksheet, write in the name of the offense, the class (A+ through M/V) and the date of the offense.
      b) By comparing the date of each prior offense with the date of the current offense, calculate whether each prior offense was committed within 6 months of the current offense, between 6 and 12 months, or more than 12 months before the current offense.
      c) Using the Criminal History Matrix write in the increase factor (.1 through .9) for each prior offense as it relates to the current offense.
      d) Add the increase factors together, and add 1.0 to find the total increase factor.

Current Offense	Criminal History
Class B felony	*no* criminal history
Class C)	C, C
Class GM)	or
CLass M/V)	C, GM, GM,
	(M) (M)
	or
	GM, GM, GM,
	(M) (M) (M)

NAME _____ DOB _____ CAUSE & J _____

CURRENT OFFENSE						CRIMINAL HISTORY			
CLASS						CLASS	TIME SPAN		
	17	16	15	14	13	12		0-6	6-12	12-

CLASS	17	16	15	14	13	12	CLASS	0-6	6-12	12-
A+	400	350	300	300	250	250	A+	.9	.8	.7
A	300	300	250	250	225	200	A	.9	.8	.6
B+	150	140	120	110	110	110	B+	.9	.7	.4
B	54	52	50	48	46	44	B	.9	.6	.3
C+	42	40	38	36	34	32	C+	.5	.3	.2
C	30	28	26	24	22	20	C	.4	.3	.2
GM+	26	24	22	20	18	16	GM+	.3	.2	.1
GM	24	22	20	18	16	14	GM	.2	.1	.1
M&V	10	8	6	4	4	4	M&V	.1	.1	.1

				POINTS × TOTAL –			RANGE		
CURRENT	DATE OF	AGE AT	FOR	INCREASE	TOTAL	COM.	RANGE	RANGE
OFFENSE(S)	CLASS	OFFENSE	OFFENSE	OFFENSE	FACTOR	POINTS	SERV.	DETENTION	COMMITMENT

___ ___ ___ ___ ___ ___ ___ ___ ___ ___
___ ___ ___ ___ ___ ___ ___ ___ ___ ___

PRIOR   TIME INCREASE
OFFENSE CLASS DATE SPAN FACTOR

_____
_____
_____
_____
_____
_____
_____
_____

LIMITATIONS

SUBTOTAL _____

+1.0   Separate Acts: 300%

TOTAL _____   Same Act: 150%

INCREASE   Minor and First Offender: No

FACTOR _____   detention Time

FINAL
RECOMMENDATION

_____ HRS. C/S
_____ DAYS DETENTION
_____ COMMITMENT
_____ DECLINE
$_____ RESTITUTION

COUNTY _____

Serious Offender minimum: 110 pts.
Community Service Maximum: 150 hrs.
Date from most recent offense: _____
VARIANCE? _____
REASON _____
_____
APPROVED _____

AGE CURRENT OFFENSE(S)							TIME	CRIMINAL HISTORY		
CLASS	17	16	15	14	13	12	CLASS SPAN	0-6	6-12	12+ MORE
A+	400	350	300	300	250	250	A+	.9	.8	.7
A	300	300	250	250	225	200	A	.9	.8	.6
B+	150	140	120	110	110	110	B+	.9	.7	.4
B	54	52	50	48	46	44	B	.9	.6	.3
C+	42	40	38	36	34	32	C+	.5	.3	.2
C	30	28	26	24	22	20	C	.4	.3	.2
GM+	26	24	22	20	18	16	GM+	.3	.2	.1
GM	24	22	20	18	16	14	GM	.2	.1	.1
M&V	10	8	6	4	4	4	M&V	.1	.1	.1

POINTS	COMMUNITY SERVICE HOUSE & SUPERVISION	CONFINEMENT PARTIAL COM.	CONFINEMENT	L.O.S. FOR PAROLE
1-9	5-25 and max. 3 mo.			
10-19	20-35 and max. 3 mo.			
20-29	30-45 and max. 6 mo.			
30-39	40-65 and max. 6 mo.			
40-49	50-75 and max. 6 mo.			
50-59	60-90 and max. 9 mo.	and 1-2*		
60-69	70-100 and max. 9 mo.	and 3-6*		
70-79	80-110 and max. 1 yr.	and 7-14*		
80-89	90-130 and max. 1 yr.	and 10-20*		
90-109	100-150 and max. 1 yr.	and 15-30*		
110-119			60-90 days	max. 4 mo.
120-129			13-16 weeks	max. 4 mo.
130-139			15-20 weeks	max. 6 mo.
140-149			21-28 weeks	max. 6 mo.
150-169			30-40 weeks	max. 8 mo.
170-199			38-52 weeks	max. 8 mo.
200-229			12-15 mo.	max. 12 mo.
230-269			16-20 mo.	max. 12 mo.
270-309			20-25 mo. (2 yr.)	max. 12 mo.
310-349			24-30 mo.	max. 18 mo.
350-399			32-40 mo. (3 yr.)	max. 18 mo.
400 or over			48-50 mo.	max. 18 mo.

*Not included in range for Minor & First Offenders

3. Computing Sentence for Current Offense
   a) Multiply the points for the current offense (from Current Offense Matrix) times the total increase factor to reach the Total Points.
   b) Using the Sentencing Grid, write in the ranges of community service, detention, and institution time which follow from the Total Points for the offense.

II. Deriving the Proper Sentences for Multiple Offenses
   1. Compute the sentencing ranges for *each current offense separately.* Do *not* add points for the offenses.
   2. Use the same Total Increase Factor for each current offense. When computing the Total Increase Factor based on prior offenses, the "time span" of the priors should be dated from the *most recent offense* of the multiple offenses.
   3. The judge will sentence each offense separately, guided by the range for each offense.
   4. All sentences are served *consecutively* subject to the following restraints:
      a) Where the offenses are separate acts, the total time served in detention or an institution may not exceed 300% of the sentence for the most serious charge.
      b) Where the offenses are part of the same act, the total time served in detention or an institution may not exceed 150 percent of the sentence for the most serious charge.
      c) The total community service imposed pursuant to a multi-count petition may not exceed 150 hours.

III. Limitation for Minor and First Offenders
   If a child is a minor or first offender, do *not* include any indicated detention time in the standard sentence. A child is a minor or first offender if his/her instant offense and criminal history can be counted *within* the following chart *and* he/she is *sixteen years old or younger.*

DISCUSSION QUESTIONS

---

1. How do Forst, Fisher, and Coates distinguish between an indeterminate and a determinate sentencing system? How do they define a "serious delinquent statute"?

2. How does the National Commission's standard on type and duration of sanction differ from the traditional model? Do you think it would be possible to retain a rehabilitative ideology within the juvenile justice system under an offense-based sentencing structure? Why or why not?

3. In what ways do New York's Designated Felony Act and Illinois' Habitual Juvenile Offender Law guide the discretion of juvenile court judges and juvenile correctional administrators?

4. Do you agree with the court's ruling in *People v. J. A.*? Why or why not?

5. In what ways is Washington state's new juvenile justice law a drastic departure from the traditional system? Do you agree with the provisions of the law? Why or why not?

SECTION VI

TRANSFER OF
JUVENILES TO
ADULT COURT

Introduction

From the beginning of the juvenile court movement at the start of this century, legal provisions have existed to remove the most serious delinquents and prosecute them as adults in criminal court. This process is generally known as transfer or waiver.

Most of the early court statutes contained some provision for waiving jurisdiction. Certain youths, described as "serious," "violent," "sophisticated," or "persistent," were thought to be beyond the scope of the rehabilitative-oriented juvenile court. Early statutes gave the juvenile court complete discretion to dismiss a delinquency petition and transfer a youth to the criminal courts. Most statutes did not clearly articulate criteria for the waiver process, which allowed waiver decisions to be made in an informal and highly subjective manner.

To address the perceived increase in serious juvenile crime, policymakers have again focused on prosecuting juveniles as adults—that is, removing them from the juvenile justice system altogether. Over the past twenty years, approximately half of the state legislatures have amended their juvenile codes to simplify or expedite the waiver process. State legislatures have redefined criteria for the age limits of juvenile court jurisdiction and changed the court before which certain types of juvenile cases will appear. Removing a youth from juvenile court jurisdiction can be accomplished in one of three primary ways: judicial waiver, legislative waiver, and prosecutorial waiver.

In all but a few states, statutes empower a juvenile court judge to decide, with varying degrees of statutory guidance, whether to transfer juveniles to criminal court for prosecution. The judicial decision to waive a youth to criminal court assumes that for some cases (or types of cases) juvenile justice sanctions may be insufficient to meet the needs of the public and the offender. Waiver statutes assume that some youths are simply nonamenable to treatment in the juvenile justice system.

A newer approach to prosecuting juveniles as adults, and one that circumvents the juvenile court altogether, is legislative waiver, also known as excluded offense provisions. One strategy to accomplish the removal of offenders from the juvenile court is for the legislature simply to lower the age of criminal court jurisdiction. New York's 1978 legislative change is one example. The Juvenile Offender Law provides that, instead of sixteen-year-olds, the criminal court is to have original jurisdiction in cases of thirteen-, fourteen-, and fifteen-year-olds charged with specified offenses.

Prosecutorial transfer (also known as concurrent jurisdiction or direct filing) is another strategy for circumventing juvenile court jurisdiction. This approach authorizes the prosecuting attorney to file either in juvenile court or directly in criminal court. Statutes permitting direct filing often provide some restrictions or guidelines, such as a combination of alleged offense, age of the juvenile, and whether the youth has had prior adjudications in juvenile court. Nebraska is one state that has historically used this method of prosecuting serious juvenile offenders in adult court. Nebraska's law provides that the county attorney (district attorney) has discretion to file in juvenile court or in the municipal or district (criminal) courts in three types of cases: a juvenile of any age alleged to have committed a felony, a juvenile of sixteen or seventeen alleged to have committed a misdemeanor or infraction, or a juvenile of any age alleged to have committed a traffic offense. This statutory scheme, therefore, encompasses all serious juvenile criminality.

The transfer decision raises serious questions of jurisprudential philosophy—that is, the nature of the proceedings and the purpose and severity of the sanctions. Transfer also raises the important issues of when a juvenile is no longer a juvenile and what factors are necessary to thrust some youths into the criminal courts. Revisions in transfer laws are also closely related to youth crime and the political reactions to youth crime.

Barbara Boland, in the first selection, sets the stage for understanding the increased use of transferring juveniles to adult court. She is an ardent supporter of using transfer to crack down on the most serious delinquents. Her's is a social protection rationale. Since career criminals, according to the data she cites, are most active between sixteen and twenty-two years of age, that would be the best time to lock them up and keep them out of circulation. And one of the best tools to use with serious juvenile offenders is transfer or waiver to adult court where, presumably, harsher (and longer) penalties would be imposed.

But how should transfer laws be structured? Specifically, what types of delinquents should be targeted? The National Advisory Commission on Criminal Justice Standards and Goals for Juvenile Justice and Delinquency Prevention, mentioned in the previous section of this book, also provides standards for transfer or waiver, as shown in the second selection. These standards are presumably aimed at older (sixteen and seventeen years of age) and more sophisticated juvenile offenders. But the standards are also general enough to encompass a broad array of juvenile criminality.

The third selection provides the transfer statute from the state of Indiana. This law seems to set forth some specific provisions for guiding the transfer decision. But notice how the specific provisions of this statute compare with the National Advisory Commission Standards.

In *People v. Thorpe,* the Supreme Court of Colorado addresses the transfer law of that state. Colorado is one of the few states that grants the prosecuting attorney lawful authority to directly file a criminal complaint against a juvenile (age fourteen or older) in adult court (as opposed to granting the juvenile court judge discretion to transfer). The Colorado Supreme Court upheld this statutory construction.

In the final selection, Stephen Wizner points out some of the problems with current transfer laws. After describing the various statutory options used throughout the country, he analyzes the problems with discretionary waiver. He concludes that transfer laws should be carefully written so that only those who truly deserve to go to adult court are actually sent there.

20

Fighting Crime: The Problem of Adolescents

Barbara Boland

Crime rates are high not because large numbers of people commit one or two crimes in a lifetime but because a relatively small number of people are habitual offenders. This commonly recognized fact about crime is beginning to provide a major impetus for devoting extra police and prosecutorial resources to apprehending, prosecuting, and incarcerating the "worst" recidivist offenders. In the past five years, one hundred district attorneys have initiated formal programs to deal with adult habitual offenders. Many rely heavily on prior criminal records to designate individuals as career offenders. There is little doubt that in the end such a strategy punishes most severely the most hardened criminals. But this strategy will not result in the incarceration of the most active offenders. Most crime is committed by offenders when they are young, either as juveniles or young adults. Currently, the criminal justice system is not organized to restrain active young offenders.

If the idea of focusing on career criminals is to incapacitate or to deter, as well as to punish, the system may be incarcerating the wrong people. This problem is not unique to specialized career offender programs. The criminal justice system is more likely to punish an older and often wornout offender than a young and very criminally active one. Studies now show that while individual

Source: *Journal of Criminal Law and Criminology*, 71 (2) (1980): 94–97. Reprinted by special permission of Northwestern University School of Law.

crime rates decrease with age, the severity of official sanctions rises. As a consequence, significant punishment does not occur for many offenders until they reach their middle twenties, when they are at or near the end of their criminal careers.

Age and Crime

Joan Petersilia and her colleagues at RAND have made a detailed study of the crime careers of fifty habitual offenders. Their study found that the most active period in those criminal careers occurred roughly between the ages of sixteen and twenty-two. However, the greatest punishment came at considerably later ages. Specifically, the offenders they studied (all of whom were serving a second prison term for armed robbery in a California state prison) committed between eighteen and forty felonies—including drug sales—per year of "street time" between the ages of sixteen and twenty-two. Between the ages of twenty-two and thirty-two, their average offense rates fell to about eight per year of "street time." Conversely, the amount of time these offenders spent in jail increased from 30 percent between the ages of sixteen and twenty-two to 80 percent between the ages of twenty-two and thirty-two. The increasing time in prison occurred, in part, because judges gave increasingly stiffer sentences as the offenders' official records grew longer; however, offenders were also more likely to be arrested and then convicted as they grew older.[1]

James Collins has reported findings very similar to those of the RAND study in a reanalysis of data that Marvin Wolfgang previously collected from a large sample of offenders arrested in Philadelphia.[2] Collins examined the careers of those offenders, termed chronics, who had at least five contacts with the police. The chronics accounted for only 18 percent of all the persons who committed serious crimes, but they committed 52 percent of the offenses. Although most of them had criminal careers that spanned a considerable number of years (at least ten), their rate of committing serious crimes against persons and property peaked at age sixteen. But the greatest chance that the criminal justice system would apprehend, convict, and punish them did not occur until offenders were in their early twenties.

The decline in crime rates exhibited by young men as they grow older is an established criminological fact that practitioners have long acknowledged and scholars have sought to explain. A question that has not been examined systematically is why official sanctions are likely to be more lenient at a time when offenders are young and crime rates at a peak and more severe when offenders are older and their behavior has begun to improve. To understand how this happens, it is first necessary to understand how the court system is organized to handle juvenile and young adult offenders.

How the Two Systems Work

When juveniles commit crimes, their acts fall under the jurisdiction of the juvenile court. Since its beginning at the turn of the century, the juvenile court has not been viewed as, nor was it intended to be, a formal court of law whose duty was to establish guilt and decide punishment. Rather, it has been viewed as a special kind of social service agency whose motive is benevolence and whose goal is to help children, including large numbers who have not committed any crime. Thus, the procedures of the court have been intentionally nonadversarial, the terminology intentionally noncriminal, and its powers intentionally vast.

One radical difference between the juvenile and criminal court system that affects the outcome of many cases is the manner of determining in which cases a prosecution should be initiated. When an adult is arrested, the police bring him to a prosecutor who reviews the facts surrounding the arrest to determine if the legal evidence warrants prosecution and, if so, what the charge should be. When a juvenile is arrested, he is not brought to a prosecutor, or even a lawyer, rather, he is seen by a probation officer, who often works directly for the juvenile court. In making a decision as to how a case should be handled, the probation officer, like the prosecutor, should consider the facts of the particular case. But the probation officer is also authorized to weigh the child's social and family background. Given both the legal and social factors, he may decide to drop or "adjust" the complaint or to file a petition, the juvenile court equivalent of prosecution. The decision to adjust rather than petition a case in juvenile court does not necessarily mean that the facts are insufficient to support a prosecution; it may mean that under the particular circumstances some kind of informal assistance, such as counseling or referral to a social agency, or no intervention at all, is thought to be a more appropriate disposition.

It is a matter of considerable significance that probation officers, charged with a social mission, rather than prosecutors, charged with a legal responsibility, handle the crucial function of screening in the juvenile court. Prosecutors are lawyers whose duty is to enforce the law according to a set of predetermined legal rules. Probation officers are social workers whose primary task is to help people in trouble. They are more concerned with analyzing and dealing with human situations and tend to deemphasize the legal technicalities of assessing guilt and convictability. When questioned about their work, probation officers are likely to assert that decisions concerning individual delinquents cannot be made according to a given set of rules. Proper handling, according to probation personnel, requires intuition or "feel."[3]

Given the organizational structure of the juvenile court, it is not surprising that a large number of cases fall out at probation intake and that little relationship has been found between the way in which the case is handled and the seriousness of the offense. One national study of intake decisions found that roughly the same proportion (approximately two-thirds) of status offenses, misdemeanors, and felonies involving property were either dropped or adjusted at intake. Violent crimes against persons were somewhat less likely to be adjusted, but still only 50 percent resulted in a formal petition.[4] Another recent study in New York City reported that the rate of adjustment for violent crimes (54 percent) was only slightly lower than the rate for property crimes.[5]

Even if a determination is made to file a petition, it does not necessarily mean that a formal sanction will follow. In many jurisdictions a judge may decide, regardless of the legal facts of the case, that a formal finding of delinquency is not in the best interest of the child, and at the judicial hearing, he would then decide that the case should be "adjusted." Even in those cases where a "finding" results from the hearing, the most common disposition is probation with a suspended sentence or release subject to future incarceration. A Vera Institute study of juvenile violence in three counties around New York City illustrates the infrequency with which juveniles actually are incarcerated in a juvenile facility. Fewer than 9 percent of violent juveniles "adjudicated delinquent" by the court eventually were placed in a juvenile facility. This represented only 2 percent of the juveniles arrested for violent crimes.[6]

Graduation to Adult Court

At approximately the age of eighteen,[7] when criminal offenders graduate from the juvenile to the adult system of justice, one might expect to find a greater correspondence between the seriousness of criminal behavior and the seriousness of sanctions. Ultimately, this is the way the adult court system operates. However, offenders are likely to discover that at the outset, as in juvenile court, little happens when they are caught committing serious crimes. Although witness and evidentiary problems are significant factors, they form only part of the explanation. An important influence on the operation of a criminal court is the existence of a prior criminal record for the accused. The defendant's prior record has been found to be an important factor that enhances convictability, although it is not clear exactly how a prior record enters into the prosecutor's decisions.[8] In addition, numerous studies of sentencing have found that a defendant's prior criminal record is one of the most important factors in predicting the severity of his sentence.[9]

While the existence of a prior criminal history is an important factor for a court to consider, the question is why do courts consider only the adult portion of an offender's criminal record? Because of the separation, both in theory and in practice, of the juvenile and the adult court, there are no formal mechanisms for tracking an offender's entire career. The confidential nature of juvenile records follows from one of the central tenets of the juvenile court system: because of juveniles' immaturity, their offenses should not be considered criminal. It is thought that maintaining the secrecy of juvenile records is one way of minimizing the aftereffects of juvenile crime. As a result of this, when an offender turns eighteen (or whatever age adult status is obtained), the adult criminal justice system considers him a first-time offender, even though he may be at the peak of his criminal career.

Table 20.1.   Offense Rates by Prior Record and Age

	Number of Adult Felony Convictions				
	0	**1**	**2**	**3**	**4 or More**
Offenders Age 18-25					
Number of offenders	847	434	139	32	19
Felonies/year/offender	4.5	5.5	10.5	15.0	17.5
Offenders Age 25-30					
Number of offenders	295	242	88	56	43
Felonies/year/offender	1.5	2.5	4.0	7.0	8.5
Offenders Age 30 and Over					
Number of offenders	561	337	210	147	219
Felonies/year/offender	0.5	1.0	2.0	2.5	5.0

Source: Federal Bureau of Investigation's computerized history file. The sample includes all adults arrested in the District of Columbia in 1973 for an index crime (except larceny) with at least one prior arrest. Offenders with at least one prior arrest represent 70% of all adults arrested. An average annual offense rate was computed for each offender by dividing all arrests (index or felony) before 1973 by the number of years between age 18 and age just prior to the 1973 sampling arrest, less time in prison. Each arrest was presumed to represent five crimes. A modified version of this table appeared in Boland & Wilson, *Age, Crime and Punishment*, 51 PUB. INTEREST 22 (1978).

The figures in table 20.1 illustrate the significant consequences this discontinuity has for crime control. The figures show the annual rate at which criminals commit serious crimes—when they are free—by the age of the offender and the number of prior adult convictions. The youngest group of offenders, controlling for prior record, has the highest offense rates. In fact, young offenders with fewer than two convictions have higher offense rates than most of the older offenders with two or more prior convictions. Consequently, offenders with fewer than two adult convictions commit 80 percent of the crimes. In general, most crime is committed by offenders who are young and who have not had time to acquire an extensive record of adult convictions.

The result of this system is that an offender's incarceration rarely will reflect the degree of his current criminal activity. When a criminal begins his career as a juvenile, his first few offenses rarely will result in a penalty. The penalties he does receive frequently are imposed for reasons related to the child's social or family background as opposed to the seriousness of the crime. Later, when the criminal turns eighteen and is theoretically a responsible adult, he can expect leniency the first, and perhaps the second, time he is convicted in an adult court. The fact that he has had considerable criminal experience and is now in the most productive stage of his criminal career either is not known or is considered a matter of little consequence. Ironically, it is only when an offender nears the end of his career and has begun to shift his energies from illegitimate to legitimate pursuits, sometime in his mid-twenties, that courts begin to impose severe prison sentences for crimes that were overlooked in the past.

What the Prosecutor Can Do

To improve the way the criminal justice system handles adolescent offenders, in general, and career criminals, in particular, one must be able to identify, convict, and incarcerate them at the peak, rather than the end, of their careers. To reach this goal, improvements must first be made in the juvenile court system.

Although traditionally the prosecutor has played a minor role or none at all in the juvenile court, district attorneys can be influential in juvenile court reform. This is illustrated by the recent sequence of events in Washington. The former prosecuting attorney in King County (Seattle), Christopher Bayley, believed that the seriousness of the juvenile crime problem dictated the need for vigorous prosecution. Even without formal statutory authority, he found he was able to involve his office in the juvenile court process. With the cooperation of the police, his office was able to establish a system to monitor police referrals to probation case workers. The case workers could, and the prosecuting attorney's office thought they frequently did, adjust cases involving serious crimes. Under the new system, prosecutors were able to spot and act on serious cases about which nothing was being done. Once the position of the office was established firmly in the juvenile court (after about four years), the office was able to institute a juvenile career criminal program. The office even began to act as an advocate at disposition hearings, recommending sentences based on guidelines they developed. In enacting the state's new juvenile code in 1977,[10] the state legislature formalized many of the informal reforms that the King County office initiated.

Prosecutors also can improve the criminal justice system by making greater use of juvenile records in adult court screening. This is especially true for career criminal cases. Although most state statutes prohibit public inspection of juvenile court records, juvenile court judges generally have the discretionary power to make these records available. The RAND Corp. is conducting a study of the role juvenile records play in adult court processing. Preliminary results reported by Peter Greenwood at the Career Criminal Workshop suggest that some form of juvenile record is generally available to the prosecutor, but that prosecutors rarely take advantage of the availability of the records.[11]

An exception to this situation is the career criminal program in Dallas, Texas. Last year District Attorney Henry Wade and the director of the Career Criminal Program, Robert Whaley, switched the program's emphasis to young offenders at the intensive point of their careers. Accordingly, they established routine procedures for obtaining juvenile records from the probation department. As a result, the average age of the offenders in the career criminal program dropped from about twenty-nine to about twenty-two.

Devising better ways to handle young offenders is a complex problem. The current system has been in place for at least three-quarters of a century. But that does not mean that immediate improvements are impossible. The evidence currently available indicates that for short-term improvements the prosecutor, more than any other public official, can have the greatest impact.

Notes

1. J. PETERSILIA, P. GREENWOOD AND M. LAVIN, CRIMINAL CAREERS OF HABITUAL FELONS 34–38 (RAND Corp. R-2144-DOJ 1977).

2. J. COLLINS, OFFENDER CAREERS AND RESTRAINT PROBABILITIES AND POLICY IMPLICATIONS (1977).

3. Office of Children's Services, Probation: Problem Oriented—Problem Plagued (undated unpublished report).

4. Creekmore, *Case Processing: Intake, Adjudication, and Disposition*, in BROUGHT TO JUSTICE? JUVENILES, THE COURT, AND THE LAW (1976).

5. P. STRASBERG, VIOLENT DELINQUENTS 90 (1978).

6. *Id*. at 96–98.

7. The age varies from state to state. In New York state, for example, the age is sixteen. NY. JUD. LAW—FAMILY COURT ACT § 712 (McKinney 1975).

8. Forst & Brosi, *A Theoretical and Empirical Analysis of the Prosecutor*, 6 J. LEGAL STUDIES 177 (1977).

9. *See, e.g.*, VERA INSTITUTE OF JUSTICE, FELONY ARRESTS: THEIR PROSECUTION AND DISPOSITION IN NEW YORK CITY'S COURTS (1977); L. WILKINS, J. KRESS, D. GOTTFREDSON, J. CALPIN & A. GELMAN, SENTENCING GUIDELINES: STRUCTURING JUDICIAL DISCRETION (1977).

10. WASH. REV. CODE ANN. §§ 13.04.005–13.04.278 (Supp. 1978).

11. Greenwood, *Career Criminal Prosecution: Potential Objectives*. 71 J. CRIM. L. & C. 85 (1980).

21

Standards for the Administration of Juvenile Justice

3:116 Transfer to Another Court—Delinquency

The family court should have the authority to transfer a juvenile charged with committing a delinquency offense to a court of general criminal jurisdiction if:

a. The juvenile is at least age sixteen;
b. There is probable cause to believe that the juvenile committed the act alleged in the delinquency petition;
c. There is probable cause to believe that the act alleged in the delinquency petition is of a heinous or aggravated nature, or that the juvenile has committed repeated serious delinquency offenses; and
d. There is clear and convincing evidence that the juvenile is not amenable to treatment by the family court because of the seriousness of the alleged conduct, the juvenile's record of prior adjudicated offenses, and the inefficacy of each of the dispositions available to the family court.

Source: Standards for the Administration of Juvenile Justice, Report of the National Advisory Committee for Juvenile Justice and Delinquency Prevention, U.S. Department of Justice, July 1980, pp. 262–263.

This authority should not be exercised unless there has been a full and fair hearing at which the juvenile has been accorded all essential due process safeguards.

Before ordering transfer, the court should state, on the record, the basis for its finding that the juvenile could not be rehabilitated through any of the dispositions available to the family court.

Commentary

The President's Commission on Law Enforcement and the Administration of Justice, *Task Force Report: Juvenile Delinquency and Youth Crime*, 25 (1967) termed transfer of accused delinquents to adult criminal courts, "a necessary evil, imperfect but not substantially more so than its alternatives." Waiver of jurisdiction in cases involving juveniles for whom the specialized services and programs available to the family court are inappropriate, functions as a safety valve to relieve the pressure to reduce the maximum age of family court jurisdiction and to facilitate the provision of services to those juveniles who appear more likely to respond.

This standard, following the lead of the *Report of the Task Force, supra,* and *United States v. Kent*, 383 U.S. 541 (1966), recommends criteria to regulate the operation of this safety valve to assure that those juveniles for whom treatment as an adult offender is appropriate are transferred and that those for whom stigmatization as a convicted felon is unnecessary remain under family court jurisdiction.

The first criterion is that juveniles under age sixteen should remain under the jurisdiction of the family court. This is in accord with the recommendations of most recent standards and models and is the practice in about a quarter of the states. *See, e.g., Report of the Task Force, supra;* IJA/ABA, *Waiver, supra;* President's Commission, *supra;* U.S. Department of Health, Education and Welfare, *Model Act for Family Courts*, Section 31 (1975); *Uniform Juvenile Court Act*, Section 34 (National Conference of Commissioners on Uniform State Laws, 1968). No matter what age is set, there will always be a few juvenile offenders for whom transfer may be appropriate. Although many serious crimes are committed by juveniles age fifteen and under, it is anticipated that the number of cases in which transfer of such juveniles would be proper under the other criteria listed in the standard will be minimal.

The standard further recommends that no juvenile be transferred unless it has been determined that there is probable cause to believe that a delinquent act has been committed and that the juvenile committed it. *See, e.g., Report of the Task Force, supra;* IJA/ABA, *Waiver, supra; Uniform Juvenile Court Act, supra; but see Model Act for Family courts, supra.* About half the states with statutory provisions on waiver include such a probable cause requirement. A new probable cause determination regarding the juvenile's involvement in the offense is not necessary if such a determination has been made during a detention hearing or on request of the respondent following the filing of a delinquency petition. *See* Standards 3.155 and 3.165.

However, in most cases, there will still need to be a determination regarding the seriousness of the conduct or the juvenile's prior record of serious felonies. The standard endorses the Task Force provision that a delinquent act must be shown to be of a heinous or aggravating nature or part of a pattern of serious offenses committed by the juvenile. The term "felony" is insufficient to convey the degree of seriousness required for transfer and although linking waiver to the classification scheme used for dispositional purposes may be one method of implementing the standard, *see* IJA/ABA, *Waiver, supra;* and Standard 3.181, the mere citation of a particular class of felonies still does not necessarily address the nature and circumstances of the particular act in question. Between a quarter and a third of the states require that the delinquent act be the equivalent of a felony before a juvenile may be transferred. *The Model Act for Family Courts, supra,* recommends consideration of the "nature" of the offense and the juvenile's prior record in determining the "prospects for rehabilitation." *The Uniform Juvenile Court Act, supra,* does not.

The fourth criteria focuses directly on the issue of the juvenile's amenability to treatment. The standard endorses the position adopted by the IJA/ABA Joint Commission that the family court judge must determine that there is clear and convincing evidence that a juvenile, because of the nature of the alleged offense and his/her response to the dispositions imposed for prior offenses, is unlikely to respond to any of the dispositions available to the family court. In making this decision the judge should review each of the available types of dispositional alternatives. The Task Force standard does not specify the level of proof, but otherwise agrees in concept with the IJA/ABA Joint Commission proposal.

Kent instructs that juveniles subject to a transfer proceeding are entitled to a hearing, to counsel, to "access by counsel to the social records and probation or similar reports which presumably are considered by the court, and to a statement of reasons for the juvenile court's decision." *Id.* 383 U.S. at 557. This holding was raised to constitutional proportions by *In re Gault,* 387 U.S. 1 (1967). The reference in the standard to all essential due process safeguards is intended to go beyond *Kent* and to be read in conjunction with Standard 3.171, which recommends that accused delinquents should be entitled to notice, to be present at all proceedings, to compel the attendance of witnesses, to present evidence and cross-examine witnesses, to an impartial decision maker, to the right against self-incrimination, and to have a verbatim record made of the proceeding.

The explicit statement of the facts and reasons underlying the transfer decision, which is called for in the final paragraph, follows *Kent* and is part of the effort throughout these standards to regularize the exercise of discretionary authority. *See, e.g.,* Standards 3.147, 3.155–3.157, and 3.188. Although the transfer decision can probably never be a "scientific evaluation," President's Commission, *supra*, the enumeration of specific criteria and the explanation of the basis for the transfer decision in terms of those criteria should facilitate review and promote understanding of and consistency in the transfer process.

22

Indiana Transfer Law

31-6-2-4 Waiver of jurisdiction

Sec. 4. (a) Waiver of jurisdiction refers to an order of the juvenile court that waives the case to a court that would have jurisdiction had the act been committed by an adult. Waiver is for the offense charged and all included offenses.

   (b) Upon motion of the prosecutor and after full investigation and hearing, the juvenile court may waive jurisdiction if it finds that:

   (1) the child is charged with an act:
      (A) that is heinous or aggravated, with greater weight given to acts against the person than to acts against property; or
      (B) that is a part of a repetitive pattern of delinquent acts, even though less serious;
   (2) the child was fourteen (14) years of age or older when the act charged was allegedly committed;
   (3) there is probable cause to believe that the child committed the act;
   (4) the child is beyond rehabilitation under the juvenile justice system; and
   (5) it is in the best interests of the safety and welfare of the community that he stand trial as an adult.

Source: Indiana Statutes, Family Law, 31-6-2-4.

(c) Upon motion of the prosecutor and after full investigation and hearing, the juvenile court shall waive jurisdiction if it finds that:

    (1) the child is charged with an act that would be murder if committed by an adult;

    (2) there is probable cause to believe that the child has committed the act; and

    (3) the child was ten (10) years of age or older when the act charged was allegedly committed;

unless it would be in the best interests of the child and of the safety and welfare of the community for him to remain within the juvenile justice system.

(d) Upon motion of the prosecutor and after full investigation and hearing, the juvenile court shall waive jurisdiction if it finds that:

    (1) the child is charged with an act that would be murder or a Class A or Class B felony if committed by an adult, except a felony defined by 1C 35-48-4;

    (2) there is probable cause to believe that the child has committed the act; and

    (3) the child was sixteen (16) years of age or older when the act charged was allegedly committed;

unless it would be in the best interests of the child and of the safety and welfare of the community for him to remain within the juvenile justice system.

(e) No motion to waive jurisdiction may be made or granted after:

    (1) the child has admitted the allegations in the petition at the initial hearing; or

    (2) the first witness has been sworn at the fact finding hearing.

(f) If jurisdiction is waived, the juvenile court shall order the child held for proceedings in the court to which he is waived, and may fix a recognizance bond for him to answer the charge in that court.

(g) The finding of probable cause required to waive jurisdiction is sufficient to establish probable cause in the court to which the child is waived.

(h) The waiver order must include specific findings of fact to support the order.

(i) The prosecutor shall file a copy of the waiver order with the court to which the child has been waived when he files the indictment or information.

As added by Acts 1978, P.L. 136, SEC. 1. Amended by Acts 1979, P.L.276, SEC. 6.

23

People v. Thorpe

Supreme Court of Colorado, En Banc. Feb. 8, 1982

LEE, Justice

    The defendant-appellant, Gary Thorpe, was convicted by jury of murder in the first degree, aggravated robbery, and conspiracy to commit aggravated robbery. We affirm the convictions.

    On October 12, 1978, William Sather, proprietor of Sather Jewelry in Denver, was shot to death during an aggravated robbery of his store. An information was filed against the defendant and Richard Banks on November 14, 1978 charging them with first degree murder. The defendant, who was 16 years of age at the time, was charged in the district court pursuant to section 19–1–104(4)(b)(I), C.R.S.1973 (1978 Repl. Vol. 8).[1] Separate trials were granted on motion of the defendant.

    On November 17, 1978, while the defendant was in custody and after he and Banks had been arraigned, he contacted Officer Thomas P. Haney of the Denver Police Department. In response to the call, Haney went to the detention center and spoke with the defendant in the presence of his mother. Haney advised the defendant of his rights and left him alone with his mother to discuss the situation. Thereafter, the defendant indicated that he wished to make a statement and Haney returned and recorded it. In the statement, the

Source: *People v. Thorpe*, 641 P.2d 935 (1982).

defendant described his role in the robbery and claimed that Banks had killed the victim.

At trial the people presented evidence that the defendant's palm prints had been identified on a display case in the jewelry store and that Banks' fingerprints had been found inside a watch case. Two witnesses, Rodney Chavez and Raymond Riggins, identified the defendant as the black man they had seen running in the alley behind the jewelry store, just before the robbery was discovered. The defendant was seen carrying boxes in a white cloth. They also saw a green Cadillac driven by a white man whom they identified as Banks.

Patrice Hill testified that on the morning of October 12, 1978, the defendant and Richard Banks entered the house she shared with Banks, John James, and her sister. The defendant was carrying a white bundle and Hill noticed blood on his clothing. She also identified a green Cadillac that she had seen the defendant drive.

John James testified that Richard Banks had earlier asked him to assist with the robbery, but James declined to do so. He stated that on October 12 the defendant had entered his house wearing bloody clothing and carrying a white bundle out of which some jewelry fell. James stated that he gave the police information regarding the robbery hoping to receive consideration on assault charges Patrice Hill had filed against him. He was released and the charges were dropped after he gave the statement.

The defendant raises the following arguments for reversal of his conviction. First, he contends that section 19-1-104(4)(b)(I) is unconstitutional and its application to him denied him due process and equal protection of the law. Second, the defendant asserts that it was prejudicial error to deny his motion to suppress his statement and to admit the statement into evidence. Third, it was error to admit the identification testimony of witnesses Rodney Chavez and Raymond Riggins. Finally, the defendant argues it was prejudicial error to admit two photographs of the murder victim which he contends were not probative of any issue and served only to inflame the jury. We discuss the issues raised in order.

I

Defendant's constitutional argument is based on his contention that section 19-1-104(4)(b)(I), C.R.S. 1973 (1978 Repl. Vol. 8), is invalid because it allows a district attorney to charge a child fourteen years of age or older alleged to have committed a crime of violence defined as a class 1 felony, with the commission of a felony and to prosecute the child in a criminal proceeding in the district court rather than as a juvenile in the juvenile court. The defendant reasons that the decision of the prosecutor to charge a juvenile as an adult when there are no statutory guidelines and without a prior hearing cannot be constitutionally justified as a valid exercise of prosecutorial discretion. Since there is no hearing prior to the charging process at which the juvenile may be present and heard, and be represented by counsel, the argument goes, he is denied due process. Furthermore, since the prosecutor may choose to prosecute one 14-year-old violent offender as an adult and another 14-year-old violent offender as a juvenile, and since there are no statutory criteria to guide him in making that decision, the statute denies one in the defendant's position equal protection of law.

The defendant recognizes that the proposition he urges us to adopt is contrary to this court's decision in *Myers v. District Court*, 184 Colo. 81, 518 P.2d 836 (1974), which considered a predecessor section of the Juvenile Code, now codified as section 19-1-104(4)(b)(II), C.R.S. 1973 (1978 Repl. Vol. 8).[2] In *Myers* we held:

> Petitioners' final argument is that the broad discretion granted to the district attorney by C.R.S.1963, 22-1-4(b)(iii) denies them due process and equal protection of the laws.
>
> It is well settled that a prosecutor has constitutional power to exercise his discretion in deciding which of several possible charges to press in a prosecution. *See People v. Couch*, 179 Colo. 324, 500 P.2d 967 (1972); *People v. James*, 178 Colo. 401, 497 P.2d 1256 (1972); *People v. McKenzie*, 169 Colo. 521, 458 P.2d 232 (1969). It follows that the district attorney may properly invoke the concurrent jurisdiction of the district court under C.R.S. 1963, 22-1-4(b)(iii) and C.R.S.1963, 22-1-3(17)(b)(iii) in deciding to proceed against a person between the ages of sixteen and eighteen in district rather than juvenile court. (*United States v. Cox*, 473 F.2d 334 (4th Cir. 1973); *United States v. Bland*, 472 F.2d 1329 (D.C. Cir. 1972) (Footnote omitted).

In *People v. District Court*, 191 Colo. 28, 549 P.2d 1317 (1976), we again upheld the exercise of prosecutorial discretion. In a juvenile proceeding the district attorney elected to amend the petition in delinquency to include a more serious felony, thus causing the case to be transferred for trial as a criminal case. We there stated:

> It is clear that the design of the statute is to permit the juvenile court, in case of a less serious felony, to determine in a transfer hearing whether, in the best interests of the accused juvenile, the case should be transferred to the criminal side of the court, section 19-1-104(4)(a); but in those circumstances where a more serious felony is charged, as set forth in subsections (4)(b)(I), (II), and (III), no such discretion lies in the court to retain the case in the juvenile side of the court when the district attorney elects to have the case transferred for trial as a criminal action. (*People v. District Court, supra*).

[1] The prohibition against judicial intervention in or control of the exercise of prosecutorial discretion flows from the doctrine of separation of powers, expressly set out in Article III of the Colorado Constitution and inher-

ent in the enumerated powers of the United States Constitution. The defendant acknowledges this firmly established principle and recognizes our many decisions upholding the exercise of discretion by a prosecutor in determining what charges shall be brought. See, *e.g., People v. District Court*, 186 Colo. 335, 527 P.2d 50 (1974) (prosecutor's election not to consent to deferred prosecution); *People v. Couch*, 179 Colo. 324, 500 P.2d 967 (1972) (election to proceed under a felony statute rather than misdemeanor statute); *People v. James*, 178 Colo. 401, 497 P.2d 1256 (1972) (determination by prosecutor under which statute to prosecute); *People v. McKenzie*, 169 Colo. 521, 458 P.2d 232 (1969) (election to charge defendant as a felonious possessor of marijuana rather than as a misdemeanant user).

The defendant, however, would have us overrule *Myers, supra*, and *People v. District Court, supra*, and adopt an exception to the principle of prosecutorial discretion in juvenile cases. He urges that we adopt the view espoused by the dissent in the case of *United States v. Bland*, 472 F.2d 1329 (D.C.Cir. 1972), that since the consequences to the child from his prosecution in a criminal case vary so significantly from those flowing from a juvenile proceeding, the child should be afforded the same protections as he would have were the case filed in the juvenile court and transfer to the criminal division sought. *See*, sections 19–1–104(4)(a), 19–1–107, and 19–3–108, C.R.S. 1973 (1978 Repl. Vol. 8).

The defendant cites *Kent v. United States*, 383 U.S. 541, 86 S. Ct. 1045, 16 L.Ed.2d 84 (1966), in support of his argument that a hearing with the assistance of counsel is required before the "critically important" decision is made to put the child through the criminal court process. This case, though instructive, lends no support to his position. There, the Federal Juvenile Court Act required a waiver of jurisdiction by the juvenile court before criminal proceedings could be brought by the United States Attorney.[3] The Federal Juvenile Code vested original and exclusive jurisdiction of a child in the juvenile court and contained no provisions for a direct filing in a criminal proceeding, as does our statute, section 19–1–104(4)(b)(I).

[2,3] We decline to require that a quasi-judicial hearing be held by the district attorney as a precondition to his determination that a child fourteen years of age or older alleged to have committed a crime of violence defined as a class 1 felony shall be prosecuted in a criminal proceeding. The majority opinion in *Bland, supra*, which is consistent with our view, holds that, even though a prosecutor is an officer of the court, he is nevertheless a member of the executive department and acting as such when exercising his discretion in choosing what charges to file and in what court they should be filed. Therefore, while there may be circumstances in which courts would be entitled to review the prosecutorial discretion function, "in the absence of such 'suspect' factors as 'race, religion, or other arbitrary classification,' the exercise of discretion by the United States Attorney [in deciding whether a person shall

be charged as a juvenile or an adult] in the case at bar involves no violation of due process or equal protection of the law.''[4] *United States v. Bland, supra*, at 1337. *See also, United States v. Quinones*, 516 F.2d 1309 (1st Cir. 1975); *Cox, Jr. v. United States*, 473 F.2d 334 (4th Cir. 1973); *United States v. Cox*, 342 F.2d 167, 171 (5th Cir. 1965), *cert. denied; Cox v. Hauberg*, 381 U.S. 935, 85 S. Ct. 1767, 14 L.Ed.2d 700 (1965); *State v. Grayer*, 191 Neb. 523, 215 N.W.2d 859 (1974). The statutory scheme prescribed by the legislature is clear and vests that determination solely in the discretion of the district attorney. If change in the procedures is deemed desirable, that is a matter for the judgment of the General Assembly.

[4] Accordingly, we reject the defendant's argument that he was denied equal protection of the law because the district attorney chose to file a criminal action against him whereas another in his same circumstance could be treated as a juvenile and charged with delinquency. We reiterate that the conscious exercise of selectivity in the enforcement of laws is not in itself a constitutional violation of equal protection of the law, absent a showing that a prosecutor has exercised a policy of selectivity based upon an unjustifiable standard such as ''race, religion, or any other arbitrary classification,'' which was not shown here. *People v. MacFarland*, 189 Colo. 363, 540 P.2d 1073 (1975).[5]

[5] We also reject the defendant's challenge to the facial constitutionality of this state. As we stated in *People v. McKenzie, supra*, ''[W]e must recognize that the legislature is free to adopt any classification it deems appropriate to promote the general welfare, so long as the classification bears a reasonable relation to a proper legislative purpose and is neither arbitrary nor discriminatory and operates equally on all persons within the classification.'' It is clear that the General Assembly intended to exclude certain offenders from the juvenile court system by defining certain serious offenses as per se criminal and properly within the constitutional jurisdiction of the district court even if committed by a juvenile over the age of 14. This is not unreasonable in light of the apparent legislative decision that certain repeat offenders, or those who have committed serious offenses, should be separated from those juveniles who perpetrate relatively less serious or less violent crimes and who, in the view of the legislature, are more likely candidates for rehabilitation.

We are not persuaded by defendant's arguments that section 19-1-104(4)(b)(I), C.R.S.1973 (1978 Repl. Vol. 8), is invalid and we hold it to be constitutional on its face and as applied to the defendant.

II

[6] The defendant argues that the trial court erred in admitting his confession into evidence because it was not voluntarily given. He further claims that he did not waive his right to counsel and that he was psychologically coerced into making the statement. However, the totality of the circumstances indicate

to us that the defendant's statement was made knowingly, intelligently, and voluntarily, and therefore it was properly admitted into evidence against him.

It is undisputed that the defendant contacted the police department while he was in detention subsequent to his advisement of the charges against him. Police Detective Haney, who had not previously worked on the case, was summoned to the detention center where he met with the defendant and his mother. The officer testified that he was unaware that the defendant had secured court-appointed counsel at the time of their meeting, and he did not know where the records of counsel were kept at the police department. He made no effort to ascertain whether counsel had been appointed, nor to advise the appointed counsel to attend the meeting with the defendant and his mother.[6]

[7-9] For a statement to be admissible it must be voluntary. *Jackson v. Denno*, 378 U.S. 368, 84 S.Ct. 1774, 12 L.Ed.2d 908 (1964); *People v. Fordyce*, Colo., 612 P.2d 1131 (1980). The prosecution must prove by a preponderance of the evidence that a confession was voluntarily made. *Lego v. Twomey*, 404 U.S. 477, 92 S.Ct. 619, 30 L.Ed.2d 618 (1972). The trial court must look at the totality of the circumstances to determine whether the defendant has effectively relinquished his rights. The court's findings of fact concerning the voluntariness of a confession will be upheld if supported by the record. *People v. Parks*, 195 Colo. 344, 579 P.2d 76 (1978).

[10] The defendant argues that his youth, as well as the psychological coercion applied by his co-defendant, contributed to his giving an involuntary statement. He also claims that he did not voluntarily waive his right to assistance of counsel. Youth has been recognized as a factor in calculating the voluntariness of a juvenile's statement. *See, Haley v. Ohio*, 332 U.S. 596, 68 S.Ct. 302, 92 L.Ed. 224 (1948). However, youth is but one factor to be considered. *See, e.g., Harris v. Riddle*, 551 F.2d 936 (4th Cir. 1977), *cert. denied*, 434 U.S. 849, 98 S.Ct. 160, 54 L.Ed.2d 118. Thorpe had been formally advised of his rights in court and by Detective Haney just prior to the time the statement was given. Thorpe does not assert that Haney engaged in any wrongful conduct which coerced or influenced him to make the statement. Thorpe met privately with his mother to discuss his situation and nothing in the record indicates that either of them at any time asked to confer with counsel.

Under the facts and circumstances presented in this case, we hold that there is sufficient evidence in the record to support the trial court's finding that the confession was voluntary.

[11-15] In addition, the fact that a statement was obtained without notification of counsel and out of the presence of counsel does not by itself amount to an unconstitutional violation of the defendant's rights. *See, Coughlan v. United States*, 391 F.2d 371 (9th Cir. 1968), *cert. denied*, 393 U.S. 870, 89 S.Ct. 159, 21 L.Ed.2d 139 (1968); *Wilson v. United States*, 398 F.2d 331 (5th Cir. 1968), *cert. denied*, 393 U.S. 1069, 89 S.Ct. 727, 21 L.Ed.2d 712. Not all meetings between the police and a defendant must be attended by

counsel. A defendant may waive the right to assistance of counsel as well as his right to remain silent. In addition to being voluntary, the waiver must be knowing and intelligent, *Miranda v. Arizona*, 384 U.S. 436, 86 S.Ct. 1602, 16 L.Ed.2d 694 (1966); however, it need not be express, *North Carolina v. Butler*, 441 U.S. 369, 99 S.Ct. 1755, 60 L.Ed.2d 286 (1979); *People v. Davis*, 194 Colo. 466, 573 P.2d 543 (1978); *Reed v. People*, 171 Colo. 421, 467 P.2d 809 (1970). The existence of a knowing and intelligent waiver is to be determined from "the particular facts and circumstances surrounding [each] case, including the background, experience, and conduct of the accused." *Johnson v. Zerbst*, 304 U.S. 458, 464, 58 S.Ct. 1019, 82 L.Ed. 1461 (1938).

[16] That the defendant did not waive his right to counsel at the time the trial court appointed counsel to represent him does not change our conclusion that he later effectively waived his right to counsel. *See Olguin v. People*, 179 Colo. 26, 497 P.2d 1254 (1972), *Reed v. People, supra*.

We hold that under the circumstances of this case it was not error for the trial court to admit defendant's statement into evidence.

III

The defendant next contends that the trial court erred in admitting in-court identifications by witnesses Rodney Chavez and Raymond Riggins because the identification procedure was suggestive and there was insufficient independent basis for the identification.

[17] Riggins and Chavez were eye witnesses who observed both Banks and Thorpe leaving the scene of the crime, although they were not aware at that time that a crime had been committed. Riggins and Chavez came forward upon learning that Sather had been robbed and murdered, and offered a description of the persons they had seen fleeing. The police prepared a photographic array but they were unable to identify Thorpe's photograph.[7] Chavez later identified Thorpe at a preliminary hearing and Riggins recognized and identified Thorpe when he saw him standing in the hallway near the preliminary hearing courtroom in which Riggins had been called to testify. The witnesses' inability to identify Thorpe from a photographic array goes to the weight of their in-court testimony but not to its admissibility. *See, People v. Watkins*, 191 Colo. 440, 553 P.2d 819 (1976); *Duran v. People*, 162 Colo. 419, 427 P.2d 318 (1967).

[18] The defendant argues that the trial judge should have made factual findings regarding the identifications. *Huguley v. People*,195 Colo. 259, 577 P.2d 746 (1978). The judge ruled that the identifications were admissible because they were not a result of impermissibly suggestive circumstances. *See, e.g., Neil v. Biggers*, 409 U.S. 188, 93 S.Ct. 375, 34 L.Ed.2d 401 (1972); *People v. Jones*, 191 Colo. 385, 553 P.2d 770 (1976); *see also Manson v. Brathwaite*, 432 U.S. 98, 97 S.Ct. 2243, 53 L.Ed.2d 140 (1967); *People v. Mack*, Colo. 638 P.2d 257 (1981); *People v. Smith*, Colo. 620 P.2d 232

(1980). Because there is nothing in the record which would lead us to conclude that the testimony had been tainted by a prior identification under impermissibly suggestive circumstances, we find no merit in the defendant's argument.

Moreover, the confession of the defendant was admitted into evidence and provided substantial evidence of guilt, thus making the eye witness identifications cumulative of facts that were otherwise presented to the jury. We find no error in the admission of this testimony.

IV

The defendant contends that two gory photographs of the victim were erroneously admitted into evidence at his trial. He claims that the photographs were not probative of any material issue in the case and served only to inflame the jury. The evidence consisted of two photographs of the victim, one taken at the morgue and depicting the fatal wound to the head, and the other taken at the scene of the crime showing the victim lying on the floor of his jewelry shop surrounded by scattered jewelry.

[19–21] Admissibility of a photograph is a matter within the discretion of the trial judge. *People v. Sepeda*, 196 Colo. 13, 581 P.2d 723 (1978). Photographs are admissible if they are relevant and probative, and accurately descriptive of matters which would be competent for a witness to describe in words. Therefore, photographs depicting the circumstances surrounding death are generally unobjectionable. *People v. Sepeda, supra; People v. Jones*, 184 Colo. 96, 518 P.2d 819 (1974). Reversal is required where photographs having no probative value, or only slight probative value, yet depicting scenes which are likely to have an inflammatory or prejudicial effect on the jury, are admitted into evidence. *See, People v. Pearson*, 190 Colo. 313, 546 P.2d 1259 (1976); *Archina v. People*, 135 Colo. 8, 307 P.2d 1083 (1957).

[22] We find no abuse of discretion in the admission of the photographs into evidence. They are probative of the circumstances of the death of Mr. Sather. They are not so shocking that their probative value was outweighed by the likelihood that they would inflame the passions of the jury or cause them "to abandon their mental processes and give expression to their emotions." *Archina v. People, supra.*

We find no merit in the defendant's other arguments for reversal.

Accordingly, the judgement of the trial court is affirmed.

Notes

1. Section 19-1-104(4)(b)(I) provides in relevant part:

"(b) A child may be charged with the commission of a felony . . . when the child is: (I) Alleged to have committed a crime of violence defined by section 18-1-105, C.R.S. 1973, as a class 1 felony, and is fourteen years of age or older. . . ."

2. Section 19–1–104(4)(b)(II) provides in relevant part:

"(b) A child may be charged with the commission of a felony . . . when the child is: (II) Alleged to have committed a crime defined by section 18–1–105, C.R.S.1973, as a class 2 or a class 3 felony or a nonclassified felony punishable by a maximum punishment of life imprisonment or death, except those felonies defined by section 18–3–403(1)(e), C.R.S. 1973, and is sixteen years of age or older, and the child has been adjudicated a delinquent child within the previous two years and the act for which the child was adjudicated a delinquent would have constituted a felony if committed by an adult. . . ."

3. "If a child sixteen years of age or older is charged with an offense which would amount to a felony in the case of an adult, or any child charged with an offense which if committed by an adult is punishable by death or life imprisonment, the judge may, after full investigation, waive jurisdiction and order such child held for trial under the regular procedure of the court which would have jurisdiction of such offense if committed by an adult; or such other court may exercise the powers conferred upon the juvenile court in this subchapter in conducting and disposing of such cases." D.C. Code § 11-914 (1961). The decision in *United States v. Bland, supra*, concerned D.C.Code 16–2301(3)(A), which allowed a direct filing in the U.S. District Court by the United States Attorney without juvenile court intervention against persons over 16 charged with certain violent crimes.

4. There is no issue here, and the defendant does not contend that the district attorney constitutionally abused his discretion in this case by considering any suspect factors such as race, religion, or other arbitrary classification in determining that the defendant should be tried in a criminal proceeding rather than a juvenile proceeding.

We also note that even when a district attorney elects to file criminal charges against a juvenile in district court the court retains the power "to make any disposition of the case that any juvenile court would have and shall have the power to remand the case to the juvenile court for disposition at its discretion." Section 19–1–104(4)(c), C.R.S.1973 (1978 Repl. Vol. 8).

5. This is not to say that the district attorney has no guidelines for the exercise of his discretion. The criteria specified in section 19–3–108(2)(b)(I) through (VI), C.R.S.1973 (1978 Repl. Vol. 8), for transfer from the juvenile court, as well as the legislative declaration of the purpose of the Juvenile Code, are available and should guide him in his decision to by-pass the juvenile court and proceed directly in the district court. Additionally, he should be governed by the standards implicit in the constitutional and statutory duties of his office.

6. The transcript of the taped statement indicates that Detective Haney advised Thorpe of his rights before he made his statement, and that Thorpe and his mother signed an advisement form consenting to waiver of his right to remain silent. After Thorpe had made incriminating statements, Haney asked Thorpe whether he had discussed his situation with his attorney or with his mother, and Thorpe stated that he had not. Thorpe admitted, however, that he had been given the opportunity to talk with his mother.

7. The two witnesses had successfully identified Banks from the photo array.

24

Discretionary Waiver of Juvenile Court Jurisdiction: An Invitation to Procedural Arbitrariness

Stephen Wizner

Since the beginning of this century the American criminal justice system has attempted to be two systems—one for adult criminal offenders, and a separate and different one for misbehaving children and adolescents. The primary purposes of the adult criminal system have been the apprehension, prosecution, and punishment of offenders for the protection of society. The goals of the juvenile justice system have been the identification, evaluation, and treatment of maladjusted youngsters for their own benefit.

From the beginning, however, there have been some cases of juveniles who have committed very serious crimes for whom the nonpunitive, treatment-oriented juvenile court approach has been thought to be inappropriate as an official response to the behavior involved and inadequate as community protection from the young offenders. In 1903, only four years after its establishment, the Chicago juvenile court transferred fourteen children to the adult criminal system. By the 1970s every state, the District of Columbia, and the federal government had laws authorizing, or requiring, the criminal prosecution of certain minors in adult courts.

In the landmark case of *Kent v. United States*, the Supreme Court characterized the waiver of a juvenile to adult court as being a decision "of such

Source: *Criminal Justice Ethics*, 3 (1984): 41–50. Reprinted by permission of Stephen Wizner and the Institute for Criminal Justice Ethics.

tremendous consequences'' that it ought not be made without a hearing that provided "the essentials of due process and fair treatment." There is too much at stake for the young person facing waiver to adult court to permit the decision to be made without a careful and fair assessment of known criteria, reasonably related to the legal justifications for denying a particular youngster the benefits of the juvenile justice system.

It is the thesis of this paper that most current legislative provisions for discretionary waiver of juvenile court jurisdiction are "an invitation to procedural arbitrariness," because the vagueness and multiplicity of transfer criteria and the excessively discretionary nature of waiver decisions undermine the adversary process of decision making. If this thesis is correct, then reform of discretionary waiver of juvenile court jurisdiction will require legislative limitation and clarification of transfer criteria to enable lawyers and judges to engage in the reliable and fair fact-finding procedures that are the goal of our legal system.

Juvenile Justice Criticism

Criticism of the juvenile court has focused on the unbridled discretion, rehabilitative pretensions, and punitive realities of the juvenile justice system. This criticism holds that, under the guise of individualized treatment, there has been excessive intervention in the lives of children and their families, with little to show for this intervention in the way of rehabilitation of young offenders or protection of the community from juvenile crime. Proposals for reform of the juvenile justice system have called for improved treatment and facilities, additional procedural safeguards, determinate and proportional sentencing, and restriction of juvenile court jurisdiction.

Complaints about ineffectiveness, overreaching, and lack of fairness have not been the only criticisms leveled at the juvenile court. Nearly sixty years ago the eminent legal scholar John Wigmore denounced juvenile offender legislation under which "murder, arson, burglary, robbery, rape and all the worst offenses are withdrawn from the regular courts of criminal law for that section of the criminal population." In Wigmore's view, "the social workers and psychiatrists . . . [were] virtually on the way to abolish criminal law and undermine social morality. . . ."

Wigmore's opinion was shared by many in society who feared what they perceived to be a significant incidence of serious criminal behavior by incorrigible young offenders. Eventually, Wigmore's view was reflected in legislation which authorized, among other things, the transfer of certain cases to adult criminal courts; the exclusion of certain offenses from juvenile court jurisdiction; the conferral upon juvenile and adult courts of concurrent jurisdiction over certain offenses, thus giving prosecutors discretion to choose in which court to charge the accused; the lowering of the maximum age of juvenile court jurisdiction; or some combination of these measures.

Both of these divergent lines of criticism are substantially correct. The juvenile court has deprived many children and adolescents of their liberty unnecessarily in cases involving minor or no criminal behavior. Thus, for example, so-called "status offenders" represent one-third to one-half of the caseload of America's juvenile courts. A 1974 study reported that of the more than 65,000 juveniles incarcerated in state training schools, half were status offenders.

Neither the protection of society nor the possible benefit to these children justifies this excessive intervention. These are not juveniles who are engaging in violent or other serious criminal behavior. And "not a single shred of evidence exists to indicate that any significant number of [status offenders] have benefited [from juvenile court intervention]. In fact, what evidence does exist points to the contrary."

Only a small fraction of juvenile delinquency cases involves violent acts. Over one million juveniles are arrested each year, of whom more than half are referred for formal court processing. Some 400,000 are confined for varying periods of time in secure pretrial detention (eight times as many are sent to secure facilities after dispositional hearings). Nearly 200,000 are placed on probation, under formal court supervision, and over 45,000 are incarcerated in juvenile correctional institutions. Yet, property offenses by young people outnumber violent crimes by more than ten to one.

Despite all of this intervention, juvenile crime has increased and continues to increase. This is, in part, a reflection of the growth of the youth population and of the fact that most young people violate the law at some point during adolescence—although few are repetitive, serious offenders, and the vast majority outgrow the propensity to commit crime in the transition to adulthood. In recognition of these facts, the President's Commission on Law Enforcement and Administration of Justice recommended reducing juvenile court intervention in cases involving nonviolent juvenile delinquency.

The opposing view—that the juvenile justice system has not intervened enough in the case of dangerous, violent, young recidivists and has been unable to impose sufficiently substantial sanctions to protect society from such youthful criminals—while correct in individual cases, may be misleading. Although the juvenile court age group (ten through seventeen years) constitutes less than 14 percent of the population, it accounts for nearly one-fourth of those arrested for major violent crimes such as homicide, rape, robbery, and felonious assault. Juvenile courts lack statutory authority to impose long enough periods of incarceration to deal with some of these violent offenders. A juvenile court disposition confining a sixteen-year-old previous offender who has committed a homicide or vicious assault to eighteen months—or two years, or even three years—in a juvenile reform school may simply not be enough. Either juvenile courts must be given increased sentencing powers, or some of these juvenile offenders must be transferred to adult courts for criminal prosecution and sentencing.

In light of these points it is important to put the issue in perspective. Although there do exist chronic, violent juvenile offenders, they are not the principal source of criminal violence. The number of juveniles who commit serious, violent crimes is quite small. The measures we take to deal with them should be aimed specifically at them.

Transfer to Adult Courts

Transfer to adult courts is the common legal mechanism for dealing with serious juvenile offenders who are thought to be too violent, sophisticated, or incorrigible to be handled by the juvenile court. A recently published national survey of juveniles referred to adult courts reports that every state, the District of Columbia, and the federal judicial system have statutory provisions authorizing the prosecution of some juveniles in adult courts. The survey collected and analyzed data from every county in the United States, the District of Columbia, and the federal courts on all juveniles under the age of eighteen who were prosecuted in adult courts during 1978. The results provide an interesting measure of how effective each of the transfer mechanisms is in accomplishing the social policy goals that underlie the reference of juvenile offenders for adult prosecution.

The four transfer mechanisms by which juvenile offenders are referred to adult courts are (1) judicial waiver; (2) concurrent jurisdiction; (3) legislative exclusion; and (4) lowered age of jurisdiction.

Discretionary Transfer

1. Judicial Waiver Statutes in forty-six states and the District of Columbia, as well as the Federal Code, grant juvenile court judges discretion to "waive" their jurisdiction over certain juvenile offenders. Typically this discretion is limited by legislative waiver criteria such as age, offense, prior record, amenability to treatment, and dangerousness.

Over 9,000 juveniles were transferred to adult courts by judicial waiver in 1978, of whom 70 percent were seventeen years of age or older, and less than 9 percent were fifteen or younger.

Fewer than one-third of the judicially waived cases involved crimes against persons.

Ninety percent of the juvenile offenders judicially waived to adult courts were found guilty or adjudicated youthful offenders. Of these, fewer than half were incarcerated, the rest receiving fines or probation.

Of those who received sentences of incarceration, in one-fourth of the cases the maximum imposed was one year or less, and in only one-third of the cases more than five years. "Since most sentences are subject to early release for good behavior, it is a reasonable speculation that at least half of the [convicted] defendants served less than eighteen months in jails or adult corrections facilities."

2. Concurrent Jurisdiction Statutes in thirteen states give prosecutors discretion to charge youths either in juvenile or adult courts. In six of these states, concurrent jurisdiction exists only with respect to traffic, boating, and fish and game violations; in two states (Nebraska and Wyoming), juvenile and adult courts exercise concurrent jurisdiction over all offenses; in the other five states, concurrent jurisdiction is limited to specific criminal offenses.

In 1978 more than two thousand juveniles were prosecuted in adult courts under concurrent jurisdiction provisions, approximately 65 percent of whom were seventeen years of age or older. Fewer than half of the cases involved crimes against persons, and less than 40 percent of those convicted received sentences of incarceration. Of those who were incarcerated, more than one-fifth received maximum sentences of one year or less, and at most 10 percent received maximum sentences of more than five years. Since few offenders actually serve their entire sentences—most of them receiving "good time" credit and parole release well before the expiration of the maximum term—it is reasonable to assume that, as in the judicial waiver cases, the majority of these juvenile defendants serving adult sentences were confined for less than eighteen months.

Nondiscretionary Transfer

1. Legislative Exclusion In 1978, thirty states and the District of Columbia had statutory provisions excluding certain offenses from juvenile court jurisdiction. However, of these thirty-one, twenty excluded only traffic, boating, fish and game, or other minor violations. In the other eleven states, excluded offenses were almost without exception crimes against persons.

While there are no reliable national data on judgments and sentences in excluded offense cases, New York statistics covering a period of 1978 are revealing. For serious personal offenses required by statute to be brought initially in the adult criminal courts, 34 percent were dismissed outright (presumably for lack of evidence), and nearly 40 percent were referred to the Family Court for processing as juvenile delinquency cases.

It is interesting to note that this category of cases, involving offenses which legislatures have determined should not be handled in juvenile courts, constitutes the smallest group of juvenile cases heard in adult courts—fewer than fifteen hundred nationwide in 1978.

2. Age of Jurisdiction By far the largest number of young offenders prosecuted in adult courts comes there as a consequence of legislative lowering of the maximum age of juvenile court jurisdiction from eighteen to seventeen (in eight states) or sixteen (in four states). In 1978, more than a quarter of a million sixteen- and seventeen-year-olds were prosecuted in adult courts pursuant to such age-of-jurisdiction legislation, of whom more than three-quarters were seventeen years of age.

The most common crimes for which sixteen- and seventeen-year-olds were prosecuted in adult courts pursuant to nondiscretionary age of jurisdiction statutes were public order offenses involving drugs and alcohol. Only 5 percent of the cases involved violent crimes.

Summary

If the rationale of juvenile waiver provisions is that some young offenders are too dangerous or incorrigible to be controlled and reformed by the juvenile justice system, current practices belie that intention. Most juveniles referred to adult courts for criminal prosecution are not charged with crimes against persons. Violent offenses—homicide, rape, robbery, and aggravated assault—account for less than one-fourth of the judicial and prosecutorial referrals to adult courts, and they account for only one-twentieth of the arrests of sixteen- and seventeen-year-olds in the twelve states which have lowered the maximum age of juvenile court jurisdiction.

Most juveniles tried in adult courts plead guilty or are convicted, but they are more likely to receive fines or probation than sentences of incarceration. Even when they are sentenced to correctional facilities, very few of them receive substantial prison sentences, and even fewer actually serve long sentences.

What's Going On Here?

The national data on transfer of juveniles to adult courts reflect contradictory notions about the proper role of the juvenile court. Some of the apparent reasons for referring juveniles to adult courts have nothing to do with what is thought to be the rationale for waiver of juvenile court jurisdiction—that some kids are just too tough to be handled in an informal, nonpunitive system. For surely this cannot be the reason why juveniles charged with drug and alcohol offenses or with traffic, boating, fish and game, and other minor violations are referred to adult courts. Rather, it must be that these are cases in which the appropriate disposition is normally a fine, a short jail sentence, or some other penalty that is not available or used in the juvenile court. It may also reflect an effort to reduce juvenile court caseloads by excluding minor offenders.

If the purpose of waiving juvenile court jurisdiction over certain juvenile offenders is to provide added protection for the community from youth crime, the referral to adult courts of these cases makes no sense at all. Nor does it make sense not to refer many older juvenile offenders who are charged with extremely violent offenses or who are chronic offenders, the vast majority of whom remain under juvenile court jurisdiction. Each year over eighty thousand juveniles under eighteen years of age are arrested for homicide, rape, robbery, and aggravated assault. Yet fewer than one-fourth of the juveniles charged with those crimes—of whom nearly 90 percent are sixteen or seventeen years of age—are referred to adult courts.

Obviously, there is no consensus among legislators, prosecutors, and judges as to who belongs in the juvenile court. No doubt this is a reflection of deep ambivalence and substantial disagreement about the consideration to be accorded youth status in the effort to control crime.

Recent proposals for reform of the juvenile waiver process have emphasized the necessity for clearer legislative definition of transfer standards, legislative presumption against, or in favor of, retaining juvenile court jurisdiction over specified juvenile offenders, and more highly structured procedures for determining whether individual juveniles should be transferred to adult courts. All of these changes are necessary in order to reduce and restructure the exercise of discretion in the waiver process and to make discretionary waiver of juvenile court jurisdiction more rational and consistent.

Discretionary Waiver and the Adversary Process

There are no easy solutions to the waiver problem. Requiring that all criminal offenders under the age of eighteen be retained in the juvenile justice system—regardless of offense, prior record, age, or individual personality characteristics—without enlarging the sentencing powers of juvenile courts would not provide adequate protection to the community. Limiting juvenile court jurisdiction to youths under the age of sixteen or seventeen would exclude most of the juveniles who currently are transferred to adult courts but would also have the effect of transferring to adult courts a great many sixteen- and seventeen-year-olds charged with minor offenses. Moreover, this limitation would fail to provide for the possibility of transfer of the nearly two hundred youths under the age of fifteen arrested each year for homicide and the many others under the age of sixteen who are charged with robbery, rape, and aggravated assault.

Requiring the exclusion from the juvenile court of those juvenile offenders over a specified age, or charged with certain crimes, or having particular types of prior records would confer unreviewable discretion on prosecutors in many cases to select criminal charges that either would, or would not, result in adult prosecution. Such a requirement would also preclude the possibility of retaining juvenile court jurisdiction over some of the youngsters in the legislatively excluded category who should not be transferred to the adult criminal system because of the presence of mitigating factors or the availability of appropriate treatment programs in the juvenile justice system.

We are not capable of writing or agreeing upon a precise definition of the juvenile offender who should, in every case, be referred to an adult court— a definition which would guarantee that all offenders who should be transferred, and only those offenders, are in fact transferred. However, our inability to provide such a definition does not mean that we are left with only a totally discretionary waiver process in which judges and prosecutors are empowered to make important decisions affecting individual liberty and public safety on the basis of vague and speculative criteria such as "amenability to treatment" and "dangerousness."

In our legal system we rely upon the adversary process of fact-finding to mediate between the imprecision of legislative standards and the arbitrariness and inconsistency of discretionary decision making. At its best, the adversary system limits the exercise of judicial discretion by applying reasonably precise legislative guidelines to factual determinations that control the outcome of the case. In the context of juvenile court jurisdictional waiver decisions, such an adversary process should contain four elements:

1. A statutory definition of the group of juvenile offenders *eligible* for transfer to adult court by virtue of their offense, prior record, and age
2. A statutory list of *factual* criteria to be applied by the court in making its decision, including (a) probable cause that the offense has been committed by the juvenile; (b) aggravating circumstances of the offense— such as extreme brutality in the perpetration of the offense; serious physical injury to the victim; age, physical infirmity, or other special vulnerability of the victim; use of a weapon; or other exceptional circumstances of the offense; (c) factual details of prior offenses; and (d) unsuccessful past efforts of the juvenile justice system to help the offender by providing appropriate services
3. An adversary hearing, commenced by a prosecution (or defense) motion for transfer to the adult court, in which counsel for both sides have a full and fair opportunity to litigate the factual questions to be determined under the statutory waiver criteria, and in which the judge issues a written decision setting forth his or her factual findings and the reasons for the decision
4. Upon request of either party, an expedited review of the waiver decision by a Review Panel consisting of two or more judges from the juvenile or criminal court, or both, who hear argument from counsel, review the factual findings and decision of the trial judge, and affirm or reverse

the waiver decision based upon the waiver statute and prior decisions of the Review Panel.

Experience has shown that judges are not capable of accurate and consistent application of vague and speculative discretionary standards, even when all other elements of due process are present. The single most important reform of the waiver process would be clarification of the standards to be applied in determining which juvenile offenders ought to be transferred to adult courts.

Reducing the Impact of Discretionary Waiver

As long as we continue to maintain two separate judicial systems for criminal offenders—with different philosophies and methods and with jurisdiction apportioned solely on the basis of the age of the accused—we will require a safety valve that permits the transfer of a small but significant number of offenders from the juvenile to the adult system.

The simplest solution to the waiver problem—although one not without serious and, perhaps, unacceptable consequences—would be to abolish juvenile court delinquency jurisdiction altogether. This seems unlikely, at least for the foreseeable future, since few now are prepared to prosecute in adult courts all children, regardless of age, who engage in criminal behavior.

Assuming the survival of the juvenile court as the primary forum for cases involving juvenile offenders, measures should be taken to relax the arbitrary age boundary between the juvenile and adult system. Individuals are not children one day and adults the next simply because they turn sixteen, seventeen, or eighteen or because they commit serious crimes. The transition from childhood to adulthood is a developmental process. Children mature at different rates, in response to hereditary and environmental determinants. Some youngsters are quite mature at fifteen; others are extremely immature at eighteen.

The two separate criminal justice systems, juvenile and adult, operate as if these were not facts of life. A more realistic approach—one which would afford a range of options and more individualized dispositions based upon both the maturity of the offenders and the nature of their criminal acts and histories, without the all-or-nothing character of the present waiver system—would be a unified, three-level court with juvenile, youthful offender, and adult divisions, with overlapping jurisdiction. Under this proposal, the Juvenile Division would have exclusive jurisdiction over offenders under the age of fifteen and concurrent jurisdiction with the Youthful Offender Division over offenders aged fifteen to eighteen. The Adult Division would have exclusive jurisdiction over offenders twenty-one and older and concurrent jurisdiction with the Youthful Offender Division over eighteen- to twenty-one-year-olds.

The intermediate Youthful Offender Division would share jurisdiction with both the Juvenile and Adult divisions in that it would have only concurrent jurisdiction over fifteen- to twenty-one-year-olds.

Transfer from the Juvenile to the Youthful Offender Division of fifteen- to eighteen-year-olds and from the Youthful Offender to the Adult Division of eighteen to twenty-one-year-olds would be judicial waiver, at the initiative of either the prosecution or the defense. All persons accused of criminal offenses, regardless of seriousness, would be charged initially in the lowest division permissible for their age.

The Juvenile Division would operate much like the current juvenile court, emphasizing diversion, confidentiality, community-based programs, and lenient dispositions. Offenders transferred by waiver proceedings to the Youthful Offender Division would face more substantial maximum sentences but would still be assured of confidentiality and of due consideration of their youth and immaturity. Offenders transferred by waiver proceedings to the Adult Division would face the full range of adult criminal sanctions, with some regard given to their age.

A three-tier system with overlapping jurisdiction would reduce the impact of discretionary waiver by providing a range of courts and penalties that would reflect the gradual, developmental nature of the transition from juvenile to adult status.

Conclusion

The juvenile court is not a place for every child or adolescent who engages in rebellious or illegal behavior. Some misbehaving youngsters do not belong in any court. Others, who commit major crimes of violence or are serious, chronic offenders, may be beyond the control of the juvenile court and should be subjected to more severe sanctions than the juvenile court currently is authorized to impose.

Reference, or waiver, of certain juvenile offenders to adult criminal courts is the primary legal response to public demands for greater protection from youthful criminals. The rationale for waiver is that certain dangerous juvenile offenders require—and will receive and serve, in the adult system— longer terms of incarceration than the juvenile justice system can impose. The reality is that most juveniles who are waived to adult courts are not ''young monsters'' who repeatedly commit violent crimes, but rather adolescents charged with property, public order, and miscellaneous minor offenses. In addition, contrary to the general belief that youths tried as adults receive harsher punishments than those tried as juveniles, the majority of youths referred to adult courts receive no prison sentences at all. Only a very small number of juveniles who are transferred to adult courts are actually confined for longer periods of time than they could have received in juvenile court.

Assuming that some juvenile offenders ought to be prosecuted in adult courts—an assumption that not everyone shares—transfer standards and procedures must guarantee, to the extent possible, that only those juveniles who should be transferred are transferred. Such standards and procedures must protect against arbitrary, unfair, and inconsistent waiver decisions.

The present waiver system is chaotic and irrational. Major reforms are necessary to enable both the juvenile and criminal justice systems to perform their proper functions.

DISCUSSION QUESTIONS

1. What are Barbara Boland's arguments in favor of cracking down on specific categories of juvenile crime? What types of youth does she want to target? Do you agree or disagree?

2. Do you think the transfer standards of the National Advisory Commission are adequately written to remove from juvenile court jurisdiction only those youths who should be sent to adult court? How would you modify these standards?

3. How do the specific provisions of the Indiana transfer law compare to the National Advisory Commission standards? How does the statute differ? Do you prefer the construction of the standards of the Indiana statute?

4. Do you support the statutory construction of the Colorado transfer law? Do you favor direct filing by the prosecuting attorney in adult court, or do you think the juvenile court judge should retain that discretion?

5. What are some of the problems of official discretion in the transfer decision, as discussed by Stephen Wizner? What are some of the different strategies that have been proposed to check or structure official discretion?

SECTION VII

REHABILITATION AND CORRECTIONS

Introduction

With the move toward accountability and punishment in the juvenile justice system, there remains a state of confusion in juvenile corrections. Juvenile correctional officials—from top administrators to counselors—have a "schizophrenic" attitude, a split between the dictates of holding youths accountable for their offenses yet continuing to treat or rehabilitate them.

The mixed messages given to correctional officials cause role conflict. Correctional administrators and rank-and-file juvenile correctional officers are confused and frustrated. They want to continue to do what is in the best interests of the juvenile, taking as long as necessary to provide treatment, but feel that their discretion is hampered by new state laws aimed at punishment or accountability.

But it is important to stress that rehabilitation and accountability are not necessarily incompatible. Accountability, punishment, or justice can be a guiding principle to set limits on the nature and duration of the sanction. However, a sanction of a specified length does not necessarily mean that correctional administrators should abandon rehabilitation and treatment. It simply means that correctional administrators would have a more clearly defined time period during which they can help the youth get prepared for release in the community. The challenge for correctional officials and staff, therefore, is continuing to provide effective rehabilitative services within an accountability-based system.

The crackdown on juvenile crime also has serious implications for the youth correctional system. To the extent that the average length of confinement is increasing, because of harsher and determinate sanctions, there is more crowding in juvenile correctional facilities.

Overcrowding is pervasive in juvenile facilities across the country. A 1993 report issued by the U.S. Department of Justice found that nearly half of all youthful offenders are being housed in facilities that are too crowded. The daily average population of juvenile facilities increased by 30 percent to 65,000 between 1979 and 1991. It said that more than 570,000 youths spent at least some time in detention in 1990. In 1987, 36 percent of the confined juveniles were in overcrowded facilities. By 1991, that number had risen to 47 percent. The report concluded that crowded conditions at many juvenile facilities have led to higher rates of violence, more suicide attempts, reduced health care, and declining safety and security.

California presents the extreme example of the impact of the get-tough philosophy on a state's juvenile correctional system. The tougher policies of California's Youthful Offender Parole Board have caused the overall length of stay for California Youth Authority (CYA) wards to climb steadily since 1978. Increased terms of confinement have had a dramatic effect on the size of the institutionalized population, as well as on demands for programs, resources, and staff. In 1979, the Youth Authority had an institutionalized population of 4,955 wards with an average length of stay of 11.6 months. By 1989, that population had increased to 8,500 wards with an average length of stay of 25.4 months. For every month the Youthful Offender Parole Board has increased the average length of stay for CYA wards, there has been an increase in the incarcerated population of nearly five-hundred juveniles.

Moreover, as the length of incarceration increases for juveniles, time served more closely approximates the prison sentences of adults. In some cases, juveniles receive longer terms of confinement for comparable offenses than do adult convicts. California again provides a good example. Statistics on lengths of stay indicate that California Youth Authority wards on average served longer terms of confinement than adults sentenced to prison for the same offense. In a 1988 comparison with inmates of the California Department of Corrections for fourteen categories of serious felony offenses, CYA wards served an average 28.5 months of confinement overall, while California Department of Corrections prisoners served only 23.6 months. Specifically, in eleven out of the fourteen offenses, CYA wards served as much or more time as their adult inmate counterparts. Only in the category of murder was there a notable difference in the direction of longer terms of confinement for adults sentenced to prison.

There has been a lot of talk—as well as action—about doing away with rehabilitation and moving to a punishment or accountability model of juvenile justice. But is there really widespread support for this trend? In the first selection, Francis Cullen, Kathryn Golden, and John Cullen explore whether "child saving" is dead. After reviewing the origin of the child-saving movement in the United States and subsequent criticisms of the traditional juvenile justice system, the authors present empirical data on the attitudes of various groups toward the *parens patriae* philosophy. Included in the survey are lawyers, judges, legislators, prison guards, and prison inmates, as well as the general public. Although there were variations among the groups, the data presented indicate a continued acceptance of the traditional rehabilitative approach to juvenile justice.

The mixed attitudes about the relative importance of rehabilitation and the best interests of the child versus public protection and the best interests of the community are often reflected in state juvenile court statutes. Some statutes try to combine the traditional and the punitive approaches. The 1990 Florida Juvenile Justice Act, portions of which are found in the second selection, illustrates this point. Notice in particular Section 2(d), which provides that the juvenile court should do both what is in the best interests of the child and the best interests of the society.

The National Advisory Commission on Criminal Justice Standards and Goals on Juvenile Justice and Delinquency Prevention, mentioned in Sections V and VI, also developed standards regarding treatment. The standard presented in this section seems to reinforce the traditional treatment or rehabilitative model of juvenile justice. Rehabilitation is implicit in the call for an "individual program plan" (often called an individualized treatment plan). An individual program plan also implies that each person's needs are different, and the juvenile court and correctional establishment must take those individual needs into account. The focus in the standard continues to be on the individual, not the offense. Yet, it is important to stress that the juvenile justice system could, as noted above, continue to provide rehabilitative programs on an individual basis within the confines of an offense-based sentencing system.

The practical legal implications of the conflict between philosophies and sentencing structures are played out in the next selection—the case of *Matter of Felder*, which was decided by the Family Court (Onondaga County) of New York in 1978. New York had enacted its Juvenile Justice Reform Act in 1976, and this Act provided for specific terms of confinement for designated juvenile felons. The decision shows the dichotomy in thinking in New York—one philosophy and sentencing structure for one set of juveniles and another philosophy and sentencing structure for another set of youths.

The final selection attempts to find a "balanced approach" to juvenile justice. In this article, Gordon Bazemore reviews the competing philosophies and objectives of the juvenile justice system. He finds some merit in each, and rather than taking an all-or-nothing approach, he tries to blend or balance all of them.

25

Is Child Saving Dead? Attitudes toward Juvenile Rehabilitation in Illinois

Francis T. Cullen, Kathryn M. Golden, and John B. Cullen

In recent times, juvenile rehabilitation has been attacked both by liberals seeking to insert greater due process rights and protections into the juvenile justice system and by conservatives calling for more stringent handling of serious youthful offenders. The apparent pervasiveness of this attack raises the question, Is the philosophy of child saving dead? Data drawn from a survey conducted in Illinois suggest, however, that juvenile rehabilitation continues to receive support both from the public and from various groups associated with criminal justice practice and policy making. At the same time, there is also support for the notion that young criminals are responsible for their actions and are currently being treated too leniently by our courts. Finally, child saving is embraced most firmly by judges, lawyers, correctional administrators, and prison inmates and least strongly by legislators, prison guards, and the general public.

In the late nineteenth century, a combination of social and political forces gave birth to a separate system for the legal processing of juveniles. This distinct realm of state control embodied the goal of saving children from troubling social and personal circumstances, and its ideological principles soon achieved widespread acceptance and support. The efforts of "child saving"

Source: *Journal of Criminal Justice*, 11 (1983): 1–13. Reprinted by permission of Pergamon Press Ltd., Oxford, UK.

reformers resulted in the establishment of the first juvenile court in Illinois in 1899. Near the end of the "Progressive era" in 1917, all but three states had created similar institutions, and by 1945 all had passed legislation mandating special juvenile courts and justice systems (Platt, 1969; Rothman, 1980).

The emphasis on the rehabilitation and individualized treatment of the "troubled" child (as opposed to punishment) was inherent in the philosophic origins of the juvenile court. The acceptance of state intervention into the child's life as a "kindly parent" (*parens patriae*) shaped the special nature of the juvenile court, justifying its broad area of concern (dependents, pre-delinquents, delinquents) and its flexible and "non-criminal" nature. Young people involved in crime were assumed to be less responsible for their actions, less inclined to benefit from punishment, and more hopeful targets of a thera-peutic approach than their adult counterparts. A basic optimism concerning youth, the malleability of the adolescent, and the possibilities of successfully rehabilitating and changing youthful natures was the foundation on which the original juvenile court was built (Empey, 1978).

Disenchantment with the reality of the juvenile court first became appar-ent in the 1960s with the growing awareness that its ambitious purposes and original goals were far from being realized. The attacks on the juvenile justice system have come from both ends of the political spectrum for differing reasons and diverged in fundamental ways. Nevertheless, they have coalesced to bring about a potent challenge to the basic premise that the state should endeavor to reform wayward youths and, in turn, have served as an important impetus for changes in the procedures and structure of the juvenile justice system.

Underlying the Progressives' child saving agenda was an abiding faith that the state could be trusted to do good for juvenile offenders. Yet for liberals living in the decade beginning in the middle part of the 1960s, such assumptions about the benevolence of the state became increasingly difficult to sustain (Greenberg and Humphries, 1980:209; Friedrichs, 1979; Bayer, 1981). The civil rights movement initiated a period in which the legitimacy of state author-ity was subjected to continued and widespread debate among liberal forces. By itself, the crusade for civil rights illuminated gross disparities in distributive justice and unmasked the government's role in tolerating and at times actively perpetuating pernicious patterns of racism, sexism, and inequality. In the years ahead, numerous other events—Vietnam, Kent State, Attica, and Watergate being the most poignant—combined to remind the political left of the willing-ness of government officials to invoke their power to suppress dissent and to further prevailing interests.

This social context worked to sensitize liberals to the proclivity of the state to exploit or otherwise neglect its deviant and dependent populations. Unable to embrace the more optimistic notion that the state would uniformly seek the betterment of its charges, those on the left felt compelled to propose a new prescription for reform: efforts should be undertaken to limit the ability of the state to intervene in the lives of the welfare poor, the mentally ill, the mentally retarded, the criminal, and the delinquent (Kittrie, 1973; Rothman, 1978).

In the realm of juvenile justice, the earliest and most direct manifestation of this revisionist policy was the campaign to extend due process rights to youths brought before the court (Allen, 1964). Arguing that the unfettered discretion ostensibly granted to effect the individualized treatment of juveniles had resulted only in arbitrary, if not discriminatory, judicial sentencing as well as in the brutalization of youths by corrections personnel, liberals asserted that juveniles needed legal protections against the abusive exercise of discretionary powers by the state's agents. Observing that juveniles faced with court intervention and potential institutionalization too often experienced the "worst of both worlds . . . [receiving] neither the protections accorded to adults nor the solicitous care and regenerative treatment postulated for children," the Supreme Court (*Kent v. U.S.*, 383U.S.541, 1966) agreed with the liberals' reasoning, and by the first years of the 1970s had mandated the infusion of an array of due process rights into the juvenile court. Both while and after these legal battles were fought, those on the left also championed alternative means to minimize the government's involvement in the "rehabilitation" of youthful offenders and to move toward their preferred policy goal of "radical nonintervention" (Schur, 1973). Most prominent in this regard were the partially successful efforts to introduce programs that would divert youths from the legal process at the earliest feasible point, deinstitutionalize incarcerated youths, and remove status offenders and other non-criminal youths from under the auspices of the juvenile justice system (Empey, 1978; Serrill, 1975a).

While liberals popularized the conclusion that state enforced rehabilitation ultimately resulted in the victimization of juveniles, conservatives came to offer a vastly different critique: child-saving contributed to the victimization of the public (Ryerson, 1978:15). From their perspective, the flexibilities and wide discretion inherent in juvenile justice had encouraged the lenient and meaningless treatment of serious and violent offenders. As a consequence, many predatory young criminals refused to take the proceedings seriously and were allowed to pass through the system virtually untouched and certainly "unsaved." For conservatives, the solution to this problem was to "get tough" with the juvenile offender. Mandatory punishments, including incarceration, would teach these lawbreakers that crime does not pay and thus would bolster the deterrent powers of the juvenile justice system. At the very least, this strategy would afford the public greater protection by incapacitating the dangerous (Empey, 1978:584–586). Speaking in 1976, then President Gerald Ford captured the political right's sentiments when he commented, "If they are big enough to commit the crimes they are big enough to go to jail. . . .

Too many violent and street-wise juveniles are using their age as a cloak of immunity. Detention may not help the juvenile, but if will certainly help its potential victims'' (Kelly, 1976).

The conservatives' concern with the suppression of juvenile crime is intimately related to the high value they place on preserving social order (Empey, 1978:584-586; cf. Miller, 1973). During the 1960s and 1970s, they had witnessed repeated challenges—ranging from dramatic moments of political protest to the acceptance of hedonistic life styles—to the legitimacy of existing patterns of authority. These occurrences led them not to question the motives of the state as had liberals, but rather to worry about the decay of the social fabric. In this context, rising crime took on special meaning, signifying in Quinney's (1977:13) words, ''the ultimate crack in the armor of the existing social order.'' As Finckenauer (1978:15, 17) observed, it was an issue that involved a ''backlash, reaction against youth, malaise, and alienation. . . . Crime was not a simple or single issue, but rather included race, lawlessness, civil rights, and other emotional issues.''

To remedy the urgent problem of crime and the deeper ills it symbolized, those on the right called for an assault on the ''permissive society'' that had attenuated the legitimacy of old morals and ways. On its broadest level, this meant reestablishing discipline and respect for authority within traditional institutions, most notably the family, school, and church. While this larger task was being accomplished, however, a more immediate policy change was manifestly needed and was within reach: introduce discipline into the criminal justice system by purging the permissiveness long justified by the rehabilitative ideal. Getting tough, they believed, promised to advance the cause of ''law and order.''

The liberals' noninterventionist strategy for curing the injustices engendered by state enforced juvenile rehabilitation enjoyed its greatest appeal in the initial stages of the 1970s. By the middle part of the decade, however, conservative proposals for more severe state intervention to control youthful crime began to receive favorable reaction, and it was beginning to have impact on juvenile justice policy. For many Americans, the spread of crime now made tranquility in their neighborhoods a more pressing matter than the potential abuse of power by governmental officials. Fear of crime emerged as a salient social issue, and the public's attitudes toward lawlessness hardened (Cullen et al., 1981; Rankin, 1979; Stinchcombe et al, 1980). And while few academics explicitly endorsed the right's notion that harsher sanctions should be invoked against juveniles, there was no shortage of journalists writing in more widely-read forums who were prepared to link leniency to the ''youth crime plague'' and to expose ''how fifteen-year-olds get away with murder'' (*Time*, 1977; Pileggi, 1977).

In this social climate, politicians in an increasing number of states have been receptive to the conservatives' policy agenda. Paralleling alterations in sanctioning policies in the adult court (Kannensohn, 1979; Cullen and Gilbert, 1982), "getting tough" on serious juvenile crime has become a popular theme in recent legislative changes in the juvenile justice law in many states. Determinate sentencing, mandatory institutionalization, and increasing use of the adult criminal court for serious juvenile offenders are indicative of a tendency to reject the benevolence and optimism of the child saving philosophy and embrace a "punishment" approach to the young who engage in crime (Empey, 1979). Juvenile justice "reforms" in New York, Minnesota, Washington state, Illinois, and other states reflect the growing tendency to define and isolate habitual or violent delinquents and punish them accordingly. A central feature of this legislation is the limiting of judicial and correctional discretion in order to encourage, if not compel, the system to crack down on serious juvenile offenders who are perceived as responsible for their actions and therefore punishable under law (Sussman, 1978; Serrill, 1980; Strobel, 1980; Krajick, 1977; Smith et al., 1980; Kiersh, 1981).

In light of both the serious criticisms leveled by liberal as well as conservative commentators and the recent changes in juvenile law and court procedures—changes which reflect a shift away from and an admission of the apparent failures of the *parens patriae* philosophy—it seems appropriate to ask, "Is child saving dead?" That is, has public and professional disillusionment with juvenile rehabilitation become so pronounced that we are now experiencing a radical transformation in the philosophy that has so long formed the underpinnings of American juvenile justice policy? Or, alternatively, would it be misleading to interpret recent events as a fundamental rejection of the belief that wayward youths can be rescued and, moreover, that the state has a social responsibility to forge ahead with this task? Further, does support of a child saving ideology differ by the degree to which people are involved in the criminal justice system and related policy matters? Through a 1979 survey of legislators, lawyers, judges, correctional administrators, adult prison inmates, prison guards, and the general public in Illinois, we attempt to provide beginning insights into these issues.

Method

In the fall of 1979, questionnaires were mailed or distributed to a sample of 1146 people. Of this number, 200 were residents of Springfield (1970 population = 91,622), the capital city of Illinois. The residents' names were drawn indiscriminately from the city's telephone directory; however, no random numbers table was employed. This directory was also used to obtain a sample of 200 lawyers (approximately 450 are listed). Two hundred circuit court judges were selected from a state-wide roster. A sample of 40 correctional administrators was arrived at by sending surveys to the warden and one additional top administrative official at twenty correctional institutions throughout

Table 25.1.   Status Characteristics of Sample by Group

			Education			Income		
Group	Mean Age	Sex (% Male)	Below 12 Years	12 to 15 Years	College Graduate or Beyond	Below $15,000	$15,000 to $30,000	Above $30,000
General Public	44.9	77.5%	15.5%	47.9%	36.6%	47.1%	36.8%	16.1%
Prison Guards	37.7	82.8%	16.7%	70.0%	13.3%	66.7%	33.3%	—
Legislators	47.7	84.4%	3.1%	25.0%	71.9%	—	47.5%	52.5%
Judges	53.9	97.8%	—	—	100.0%	—	3.4%	96.6%
Lawyers	45.5	94.5%	—	—	100.0%	1.3%	33.4%	65.3%
Correctional Administrators	40.8	58.3%	—	41.7%	58.3%	25.0%	50.0%	25.0%
Prison Inmates*	24.4	100.0%	42.4%	50.6%	7.0%	77.1%	16.9%	6.0%
Sample	42.6	89.9%	12.6%	27.8%	59.6%	28.9%	26.7%	44.4%

*Inmates were asked to report their income for the year prior to incarceration.

the state. Further, all 236 members of the legislature (56 senators, 177 representatives) were surveyed. Seventy guards and 200 inmates sampled were located at Sheridan Correctional Center, a minimum-medium security prison of approximately four-hundred inmates. Questionnaires were distributed to all guards present at the roll call of two of the institution's three shifts, while inmates were provided with and returned surveys through institutional mail. To minimize potential nonresponse problems, only inmates with the equivalent of an eighth-grade education or above received the survey. With the exception of the prison guards and inmates, all other respondents were sent a follow-up letter one week after our initial mailing.

Those who responded included 74 Springfield residents (general public), 77 lawyers, 89 judges, 12 correctional administrators (4 wardens, 4 assistant wardens, 3 personnel directors, 1 casework supervisor), 65 legislators, 31 guards, and 86 inmates. This yielded a sample of 434 or 37.9 percent of those contacted. While this percentage is only slightly below that typically secured in studies utilizing similar survey methods (Miller, 1977:79–80), the response rate is nevertheless somewhat low. As such, the results reported here should be interpreted with a degree of caution. However, in light of the dearth of research investigating attitudes of the public and those associated with criminal justice practice or policy toward juvenile rehabilitation, this study has the advantage of providing beginning, empirical insights into an issue of continuing salience.

Information on each respondent's age, sex, education, and income was also obtained. The status characteristics for the entire sample and for each group are reported in table 25.1.

The questionnaire used in this research contained 55 items assessing attitudes toward various aspects of criminal sanctioning. The order in which each item appeared on the questionnaire was determined through random selection. Using a 7-point Likert scale ranging from 1 = very strongly agree to 7 = very strongly disagree, the respondents were asked to "state the extent to which you either agree or disagree with each statement listed below."

A 7-item scale was included in the questionnaire to measure the degree to which respondents supported "child saving" or the philosophy of juvenile rehabilitation vs. punishment. Using Cronbach's alpha, the scale's reliability was computed to be .648. The items composing this measure are listed in table 25.2, with items number 1, 2, and 3 stated in a pro-rehabilitation direction and items 4, 5, 6, and 7 stated in a punitive or anti-rehabilitation direction. Items 8 and 9 are also set forth in table 25.2 (but not contained in the scale) to allow for a comparison of the sample's support for juvenile as opposed to adult rehabilitation.

Findings and Discussion

The degree of support in the total sample for juvenile rehabilitation/punishment can perhaps best be determined by examining the first column of table 25.2, which contains the percentage of respondents who expressed some degree of agreement with the attitude scale items. Items 1, 2, and 3 are statements of support for "child saving," and as indicated the total sample expressed a predominantly favorable attitude towards rehabilitation of juvenile offenders. Particularly noteworthy are the percentages in agreement with items 2 and 3. A high proportion (81.6 percent) of the total sample felt it would be irresponsible to stop trying to rehabilitate delinquents. A similarly high proportion (76.4 percent) indicated that they support the rehabilitation of juveniles, especially as compared to adult offenders. These responses offer some evidence of the probability that "child saving" as an accepted philosophical approach to juvenile crime is not dead, despite shifts away from rehabilitation in recent juvenile court law and procedure.

However, a further examination of the data reveal that while the philosophy of rehabilitation for juvenile offenders has not been abandoned by those sampled, the idea of "punishing" such offenders also receives support. Item 4, a statement reflective of a classical/free will approach to juvenile criminal behavior, received a high level of agreement (67.9 percent). This level persisted for all subgroups within the sample with the interesting exception of prison inmates. Significantly, a similarly high level of group agreement (55.9 percent) exists for the conclusion expressed by Item 6 that juveniles are treated "too leniently" by the courts. A closer examination of Item 1 also lends support to this theme, although not quite as strongly as the other items. While (as indicated above) 47.4 percent of the total sample agreed that the "best way" to stop juvenile crime is to rehabilitate, a full 40.9 percent of our subjects disagreed with that statement (another 11.7 percent expressed no opinion). It should also be noted that only 33.6 percent of the respondents felt that transfer

Table 25.2.   Percentage Agreeing with Juvenile Rehabilitation or Punishment Philosophy, by Item and Group*

Items	Sample Total	Public	Prison Guards	Legislators	Judges	Lawyers	Correctional Administrators	Prison Inmates
1. The best way to stop juveniles from engaging in crime is to rehabilitate them, not punish them.	47.4	45.8	32.3	32.2	41.5	50.0	58.3	66.3
2. It would be irresponsible for us to stop trying to rehabilitate juvenile delinquents and thus save them from a life in crime.	81.6	81.9	67.7	84.4	89.9	86.8	100.0	68.6
3. While I believe that adult criminals know what they are doing and deserve to be punished, I still support the use of rehabilitation with juvenile offenders.	76.4	64.4	66.7	81.7	79.1	81.1	100.0	76.5
4. Most juveniles who commit crimes know fully well what they are doing and thus deserve to be punished for their offenses.	67.9	84.7	83.9	71.0	64.7	71.1	75.0	45.3
5. All juveniles who commit violent crimes should be tried as adults and given adult penalties.	33.6	51.4	51.6	42.9	21.8	16.9	41.7	31.4
6. Juveniles are treated too leniently by our courts.	55.9	78.1	77.4	58.5	42.0	48.7	50.0	48.8
7. The rehabilitation of juveniles just does not work.	10.3	17.8	12.9	7.9	8.0	4.1	16.7	11.6
8. The rehabilitation of adult criminals just does not work.	26.8	38.8	26.6	26.6	34.1	17.1	25.0	18.6
9. The rehabilitation of prisoners has proven to be a failure.	39.0	39.7	29.1	38.2	55.9	37.7	33.3	27.9
Sample Size (N) =	434	74	31	65	89	77	12	86

*The figures reported are the percentage responding either 1 = very strongly agree, 2 = strongly agree, or 3 = agree.

to the adult court and formal criminal penalties would be the best answer to the problem of violent youthful crime.

The mixture of attitudes expressed by the total sample suggests an overall ambivalence towards the most appropriate approach for handling juvenile offenders. In general, there appears to be continued support for rehabilitation as a theme in the juvenile court and a reluctance to abandon the optimism of "child saving" as a philosophy. However, there is also a strong undercurrent of belief that young criminals are both responsible for their actions and deserve to be punished and that a more punitive juvenile court might better curtail the problem of delinquency. These attitudes thus indicate the coexistence of apparently conflicting philosophies in the treatment of juvenile offenders: save the children, but scold them too.

Juvenile versus Adult Rehabilitation

Our data also provide the opportunity to compare attitudes between adult and juvenile criminal rehabilitation. As indicated in items 7, 8, and 9 (table 25.2), the sample showed a noticeably higher level of support and optimism for the rehabilitation of the youthful offender as compared to the adult criminal. Only 10.3 percent stated that juvenile rehabilitation does not work as compared to 26.8 percent who believed the same about the rehabilitation of adult criminals. In a similar item, 39.0 percent of the group felt that the rehabilitation of prisoners has proven to be a failure. These data suggest the existence of attitudes supportive of the "differentness" of the juvenile offender, a differentness, which offers optimistic possibilities for salvation and rehabilitation. The "child saving" belief that juvenile offenders are essentially malleable and good candidates for reform appears supported by these attitudes.

Group Differences in Attitudes toward Child-Saving

The composition of this sample offers the interesting opportunity to compare attitudes of those who are involved in the criminal justice system with those outside the system (the general public). With the control variables for age, sex, education, and income taken into account, the adjusted means were computed for each group surveyed on the "child-saving" rehabilitative scale. The means suggest that group variations do exist: public ($\overline{X} = 3.565$), prison guards ($\overline{X} = 3.531$), legislators ($\overline{X} = 3.682$), judges ($\overline{X} = 3.945$), lawyers ($\overline{X} = 3.984$), correctional administrators ($\overline{X} = 4.092$), prison inmates ($\overline{X} = 4.218$).

To see if there were statistically significant differences between the general public and the other groups sampled, the juvenile rehabilitation-punishment scale was regressed on six dummy variables representing all groups except the public (which served as the comparison category). In addition, four

Table 25.3.   Regression of Rehabilitation-Punishment Scale on Insider-Outsider Groups and Control Variables

Variable	B	Beta	F
Guards	−0.034	−0.010	0.035
Prison Inmates	0.653	0.324	17.145*
Correctional Adminstrators	0.527	0.116	4.517**
Lawyers	0.419	0.200	6.199**
Legislators	0.117	0.049	0.494
Judges	0.380	0.190	4.968**
Education	0.121	0.221	6.748*
Income	−0.018	−0.028	0.106
Age	−0.008	−0.153	5.474**
Sex	0.248	0.089	2.684*
Constant	3.565		

$*p < .01; **p < .05.$
$R^2 = .141;$ Adjusted $R^2 = .117.$

covariates were included in the equation to control for group variations in age, sex, education and income. The F-ratio for the entire equation was significant at $p < .05$ $(F = 5.782; df = 10, 351)$ (see table 25.3). Inmates, correctional administrators, judges and lawyers were found to be significantly different from the public in their greater support for child saving and juvenile rehabilitation.

These results raise the question of why the attitudes of legislators and guards converge with the public while those of the remaining groups do not. One possible explanation is that the occupational experiences and interests of legislators and guards may either reinforce or not be sufficiently potent to transform inclinations originally brought onto the job. In this light, it must be remembered that many legislators initially won election because they reflected community sentiments on a variety of social issues including crime control. Further, there are both objective and perceived pressures that prevent legislators from embracing a more liberal and less punitive orientation (such as in the case of child saving) than that characteristically manifested by the general public. First, there is the objective reality that the public prefers law and order candidates. One survey, for instance, revealed that fully 79 percent of the public said that they were more likely to vote for a candidate who advocated "tougher sentences for law breakers" (Hindelang, 1974). Second, there is evidence to indicate that politicians are likely to overestimate or exaggerate the actual punitiveness of the general public (Riley and Rose, 1981; Berk and Rossi, 1977). Similarly, many prisons, including the one in this study, are the major source of employment in small towns and their custodial staff is made up of people drawn from the local or surrounding communities. Consequently, the guards often continue to maintain close communal bonds that were established prior to their employment. It can be expected that these attachments would mitigate against attitudinal changes that might otherwise be precipitated by work-related experiences.

Alternatively, there may be greater support for juvenile rehabilitation among the members of the legal profession in our sample (cf. Hackler and Brockman, 1979) because educational and work experience furnish them with a distinct legal perspective and set of interests (cf. McCleary et al., 1981). Significantly, the movement to abandon rehabilitation in favor of a punishment philosophy directly challenges the discretion and hence power traditionally exercised by the legal profession. To the extent that the everyday experiences of dealing with troubled youths teach lawyers and judges that flexibility is required to respond justly and pragmatically to complex cases and heavy case-loads, it can be expected that they would resist such a movement (Cressey, 1980). Some support for this contention that a threatened loss of discretion underlies the legal profession's general support of child saving can be gathered from examining Item 5 in table 25.2. Only 21.8 percent of the judges and 16.9 percent of the lawyers, figures far lower than any other group sampled, were in favor of a mandatory policy to try violent juvenile offenders in adult court.

The comparatively high degree of support for child saving among the corrections administrators surveyed (cf. Serrill, 1975b) may in part be an outgrowth of a human services orientation possessed by the latest and more educated generation of corrections leaders. However, it can also be argued that it is in the self-interest of administrators to embrace the rehabilitative ideal. The absence of a treatment ideology would detract from their profes-sion's status (cf. Platt, 1969) by unmasking what has perhaps been their domi-nant function all along: managing a custodial warehouse. More importantly, the decline of rehabilitation and the corresponding loss of the indeterminate sentence could potentially intensify the problem of maintaining institutional order. Administrators would be robbed of the most effective control mecha-nism currently at their disposal: "Behave in here or you don't get out" (New York State Bar Association, 1978:13). Notably, Wheeler's (1978:91) survey of juvenile correctional superintendents discovered that "professional support of the indeterminate sentence appears intense," with only 15 percent of those sampled endorsing the concept of fixed terms for juveniles.

Finally, the strong support expressed by prison inmates toward juvenile rehabilitation is particularly interesting to note. While this finding may be an artifact of the kind of inmates sampled, it is not inconsistent with previous research on inmate attitudes toward adult rehabilitation (Cullen et al., 1981; Mathis and Rayman, 1972; Toch, 1977:243; Hawkins, 1977:77). Although it is a popular conception that society's captives seek to discard the rehabilita-tive ideal due to the coercion inherent in a treatment ideology (cf. Mitford, 1973), it appears that inmates recognize that rehabilitation programs not only may save certain wayward youths but also are one of the few features of prison life that hold the potential to mitigate the boredom and harshness of idleness, create possibilities of self-improvement, and foster hope.

Status Characteristics and Support of Child Saving

As indicated in table 25.3, three of the covariates included in this study exerted a statistically significant impact on attitudes toward juvenile rehabilitation. Education and sex were found to be positively related to the scale. It thus appears that the most educated and females are more favorable to child saving and less punitive in their attitudes. In contrast, age was negatively related to the scale, indicating that support for juvenile rehabilitation decreases as a person's age increases. Higher levels of fear of crime and feelings of vulnerability among older citizens may be responsible for this relationship (Thomas and Hyman, 1976; Garofalo, 1979). Of relevance is that the above findings are generally consistent with previous research on punitiveness (Blumstein and Cohen, 1980; Rose, 1976).

Conclusion

It is important to note once again that the results of this study must be interpreted cautiously. The potential bias introduced by a low response rate as well as the restriction of the survey to Illinois place obvious limitations on the generalizability of the results. With this caveat in mind, the data indicate that child saving as a juvenile court philosophy appears to be very much alive. All groups surveyed supported the rehabilitation of juvenile offenders, including the legislators who create juvenile court policy and the judges and lawyers who are involved in the day-to-day implementation of that policy. Despite shifts in the juvenile law in Illinois and other states towards "punishing" juvenile offenders, it thus does not appear that rehabilitation as a goal in juvenile justice has been abandoned. At the same time, there is widespread support in our sample for the notion that juvenile offenders should be punished as well as "saved." Most noteworthy, the public and legislative groups show a high level of agreement on this matter. This similarity of opinion on the punishment of juvenile offenders raises the greater possibility that public sentiment to "get tough" will find expression in the actions of similarly-minded legislators. Indeed, the more punitive attitudes of these two key groups (public and legislators) may serve to foretell future shifts in the formulation of juvenile law.

In short, our data suggest that rehabilitation or "child saving" will remain a dominant correctional ideology in the area of juvenile justice, but that we are also likely to see punitive measures finding greater acceptance in the disposition of juvenile cases. Previous research investigating attitudes towards adult criminals and the criminal justice system has reached a similar conclusion: the public wants the system to punish *and* rehabilitate adult offenders (Duffee and Rittee, 1977; Market Opinion Research Co., 1978:71–72; Riley and Rose, 1980; Cullen et al. 1981). This study indicates that the future of juvenile justice will likely involve a mixture of these same conflicting philosophies, which creates a special set of complications for those formulating juvenile law and implementing these policies.

References

Allen, F. A. (1964). *The borderland of criminal justice*. Chicago: University of Chicago Press.

Bayer, R. (1981). Crime, punishment, and the decline of liberal optimism. *Crime and Delinq.* 27: 169–190.

Berk, R. A., and Rossi, P. H. (1977). *Prison reform and state elites*. Cambridge, MA: Ballinger.

Blumstein, A., and Cohen, J. (1980). Sentencing of convicted offenders: An analysis of the public's view. *Law & soc. rev.* 14: 223–261.

Cressey, D. R. (1980). Sentencing: legislative rule versus judicial discretion, in *New directions in sentencing*, ed. B. Grossman, pp. 51–69. Toronto: Butterworths.

Cullen, F. T.; Cullen, J. B.; Sims, N. A.; and Hunter, S. G. (1981). The punishment-rehabilitation controversy: insider and outsider perspectives. Paper presented at the annual meeting of the American Society of Criminology.

Cullen, F. T., and Gilbert, K. E. (1982). *Reaffirming rehabilitation*. Cincinnati, OH: Anderson.

Duffee, D., and Ritti, R. R. (1977). Correctional policy and public values. *Criminal.* 14: 449–459.

Empey, L. T. (1978). *American delinquency: Its meaning and construction*. Homewood, IL: Dorsey Press.

——— (1979). Forward—from optimism to despair: New doctrines in juvenile justice, in *Juvenile corrections and the chronic delinquent*, C. A. Murray and L. A. Cox, Jr., pp. 9–26. Beverly Hills, CA: Sage.

Finckenauer, J. O. (1978). Crime as a national political issue: 1976–77—from law and order to domestic tranquility. *Crime and Delinq.* 24: 13–27.

Friedrichs, D. O. (1979). The law and the legitimacy crisis: A critical issue for criminal justice, in *Critical issues in criminal justice*, ed. R. G. Iacovetta and D. H. Chang, pp. 290–311. Durham: Carolina Academic Press.

Garofalo, J. (1979). Victimization and the fear of crime. *J. of Res. in Crime and Delinq.* 16: 80–97.

Greenberg, D. F., and Humphries, D. (1980). The cooptation of fixed sentencing reform. *Crime and Delinq.* 26: 206–225.

Hackler, J. C., and Brockman, J. (1979). Attitudes toward delinquency by court officials: Comparisons between North America and Europe. *Intl. J. of Comp. and Appl. Criminal Justice* 3: 3–25.

Hawkins, G. (1976). *The prison: Policy and practice*. Chicago: University of Chicago Press.

Hindelang, M. J. (1974). Public opinion regarding crime, criminal justice, and related topics. *J. of Res. in Crime and Delinq.* 11: 101–116.

Kannensohn, M. (1979). *A national survey of parole-related legislation enacted during the 1979 legislative session.* Washington, DC: U.S. Department of Justice.

Kelly, H. (1976). Teen criminals deserve adult penalties: Ford. *Chicago Tribune*, September 28:1.

Kiersh, E. (1981). Minnesota cracks down on chronic juvenile offenders. *Corrections* 7: 21–28.

Kittrie, N. N. (1973). *The right to be different: Deviance and enforced therapy.* Baltimore, MD: Penguin Books.

Krajick, K. (1977). A step toward determinancy for juveniles. *Corrections* 3: 37–42.

Market Opinion Research Co. (1978). *Crime in Michigan: A report from residents and employers.* 6th ed. Detroit: Market Opinion Research Co.

McCleary, R.; O'Neil, M. J.; Epperlein, T.; Jones, C.; and Gray, R. H. (1981). Effects of legal education and work experience on perceptions of crime seriousness. *Soc. Prob.* 28: 276–289.

Miller, D. E. (1977). *Handbook of research design and social measurement.* 3rd ed. New York: David McKay.

Miller, W. B. (1973). Ideology and criminal justice policy: Some current issues, in *The Aldine crime and justice annual, 1973*, ed. S. L. Messinger et al. pp. 453–473. Chicago: Aldine.

Mitford, J. (1973). *Kind and usual punishment: The prison business.* New York: Alfred A. Knopf.

New York State Bar Association. (1978). *Report of subcommittee of criminal justice section committee on the correctional system.* New York: New York State Bar Association.

Platt, A. M. (1969). *The child savers: The invention of delinquency.* Chicago: University of Chicago Press.

Pileggi, N. (1977). Inside the juvenile justice system: How fifteen-year-olds get away with murder. *New York Magazine* 10 (June 13): 36–44.

Quinney, R. (1977). *Class, state, and crime: On the theory and practice of criminal justice.* New York: David McKay.

Rankin, J. H. (1979). Changing attitudes toward capital punishment. *Soc. Forces* 58: 194–211.

Riley, P. J., and Rose, V. M. (1981). Public vs. elite opinion on correctional reform: Implications for social policy. *J. of crim. Just.* 8: 345–356.

Rose, V. M. (1976). *A survey of public opinion concerning correctional policies and prison reform.* Ph.D. dissertation, Washington State University.

Rothman, D. J. (1978). The state as parent: social policy in the progressive era, in *Doing good: The limits of benevolence.* W. Gayline; I. Glasser; S. Marcus; and D. Rothman, pp. 67–96. New York: Pantheon Books.

_____ (1980). *Conscience and convenience: The asylum and its alternatives in progressive America.* Boston, MA: Little, Brown.

Ryerson, E. (1978). *The best-laid plans: America's juvenile court experiment.* New York: Hill and Wang.

Schur, E. M. (1973). *Radical non-intervention: Rethinking the delinquency problem.* Englewood Cliffs, NJ: Prentice-Hall.

Serill, M. S. (1975a). Juvenile corrections in Massachusetts. *Corrections* 2: 3–12, 17–20.

———— (1975b). Is rehabilitation dead? *Corrections* 1: 3–12, 21–32.

———— (1980). Washington's new juvenile code. *Corrections* 6: 36–41.

Smith, C. P.; Alexander, P. S.; Kemp, G. L.; and Lemert, E. N. (1980). *A national assessment of serious juvenile crime and the juvenile justice system: The need for a rational response legislation, jurisdiction, program interventions, and confidentiality of juvenile records.* Washington, DC: U.S. Department of Justice.

Stinchcombe, A. L.; Adams, R.; Heimer, C. A.; Scheppele, K. L.; Smith, T. W.; and Taylor, G. A. (1980). *Crime and punishment: Changing attitudes in America.* San Francisco: Jossey-Bass.

Strobel, L. (1980). State court backs youth crimes law. *Chicago Tribune*, December 2: 1.5.

Sussman, A. (1978). Practitioner's guide to changes in juvenile law and procedure. *Crim. Law Bull.* 14: 311–342.

Thomas, C. W., and Hyman, J. M. (1977). Perceptions of crime, fear of victimization, and public perceptions of police performance. *J. of Police Sci. and Admin.* 5: 305–317.

Time Magazine (1977). *The youth crime plague. Time*, July 11: 18-28.

Toch, H. (1977). *Living in prison: The ecology of survival.* New York: Free Press.

Wheeler, G. R. (1978). *Counter-deterrence: A report on juvenile sentencing and effects of prisonization.* Chicago: Nelson-Hall.

26

Florida Juvenile Justice Act

39.001. Short title, purposes, and intent

(1) This chapter may be cited as the "Florida Juvenile Justice Act."
(2) The purposes of this chapter are:
    (a) To provide judicial and other procedures through which children and other interested parties are assured fair hearings and the recognition, protection, and enforcement of their constitutional and other legal rights, while ensuring that public safety interests are adequately protected.
    (b) To provide for the care, safety, and protection of children in an environment that fosters healthy social, emotional, intellectual, and physical development; to ensure secure and safe custody; and to promote the health and well-being of all children under the state's care.
    (c) To assure due process for each child, balanced with the state's interest in the protection of society, by substituting methods of prevention, early intervention, diversion, offender rehabilitation, treatment, community services, and restitution in money or in kind for retributive punishment, whenever possible, and by providing intensive treatment sanctions only when most appropriate, recognizing that sanctions

Source: Florida Annotated Statutes, Section 39.001.

246

which are consistent with the seriousness of the act committed and focus on treatment should be applied in cases where necessary efforts have been made to divert the child from the juvenile justice system.

(d) To assure to all children brought to the attention of the courts, either as a result of their misconduct or because of neglect or mistreatment by those responsible for their care, the care, guidance, and control, preferably in each child's own home, which will best serve the moral, emotional, mental, and physical welfare of the child and the best interests of the state.

(e) To preserve and strengthen the child's family ties whenever possible, removing him from the custody of his parents only when his welfare or the safety and protection of the public cannot be adequately safeguarded without such removal; and, when the child is removed from his own family, to secure for him custody, care, and discipline as nearly as possible equivalent to that which should have been given by his parents; and to assure, in all cases in which a child must be permanently removed from the custody of his parents, that the child be placed in an approved family home and be made a member of the family by adoption.

(f) To assure that the adjudication and disposition of a child alleged or found to have committed a violation of Florida law be exercised with appropriate discretion and in keeping with the seriousness of the offense and the need for treatment services and that all findings made under this chapter be based upon facts presented at a hearing that meets the constitutional standards of fundamental fairness and due process.

(3) The Department of Health and Rehabilitative Services may contract with the Federal Government, other state departments and agencies, county and municipal governments and agencies, public and private agencies, and private individuals and corporations in carrying out the purposes of, and the responsibilities established in, this chapter.

(a) When the department contracts with a provider for any program for children, all personnel, including owners, operators, employees, and volunteers, in the facility must be of good moral character. A volunteer who assists on an intermittent basis for less than 40 hours per month need not be screened if the volunteer is under direct and constant supervision by persons who meet the screening requirements.

(b) The department shall establish minimum standards for good moral character, based on screening, for personnel in programs for children or youths. Such minimum standards shall ensure that no personnel have been found guilty of, regardless of adjudication, or entered a plea of nolo contendere or guilty to, any offense prohibited under any of the following sections of the Florida Statutes or under a similar statute of another jurisdiction:

1. Section 782.04, relating to murder.
2. Section 782.07, relating to manslaughter.
3. Section 782.071, relating to vehicular homicide.
4. Section 782.09, relating to killing an unborn child by injury to the mother.
5. Section 784.011, relating to assault, if the victim of the offense was a minor.
6. Section 784.021, relating to aggravated assault.
7. Section 784.03, relating to battery, if the victim of the offense was a minor.

27

Standards for the
Administration of
Juvenile Justice

4.214 Development and Implementation of an Individual Program Plan

Within fifteen days of a juvenile's admission to a training school, a comprehensive assessment report should be completed. This report should provide an evaluation of the juvenile's specific problems, deficiencies, and resources, and contain the individual's program plan.

An assessment team, composed of a caseworker, a youth-care worker, an educational diagnostician, a psychiatrist and a psychologist, should perform the assessment.

The assessment should include: family history, developmental history, physical examinations, psychological testing, psychiatric interviews, community evaluation, language and educational analyses, and information concerning the nature and circumstances of the conduct on which the adjudication is based. It should be the responsibility of the family court to ensure that any of the above material in its possession is forwarded to the training school.

After all assessment team members have completed their respective tasks, they should meet together to discuss the findings and finalize their

Source: Standards for the Administration of Juvenile Justice, Report of the National Advisory Committee for Juvenile Justice and Delinquency Prevention, U.S. Department of Justice, July 1980, pp. 392–394.

recommendation for the juvenile's program plan. At such meetings, and throughout the assessment process, the juvenile should be given full opportu- nity to participate in the formulation of the program plan and to have a voice in determining his/her program goals.

The juvenile should be given a copy of the program plan; a copy should be maintained in the juvenile's institutional file; and a copy should be forwarded to the placing family court.

The plan should be reviewed monthly by appropriate staff including members of the assessment team and other members of the treatment staff with knowledge of the juvenile's progress under the plan. Any change in the plan should be noted in the juvenile's file and notification of the significant modifications forwarded to the placing family court.

Commentary

The standard urges that a comprehensive assessment of juveniles placed in a training school be conducted immediately upon their admission in order to determine how the programs and resources available through the facility can most effectively meet each juvenile's needs during the period of placement. *See Report of the Task Force, supra* at Standard 23.3; *Morales* 383 F. Supp. at 88, 92–93. If the ideal of an individualized program is to be realized, obtaining information regarding a juvenile's educational, medical, psychologi- cal, and vocational needs and preferences appears essential.

Given the scope of the assessment and the urgency of involving juveniles in constructive programs, the standard urges that the assessment process be completed within fifteen working days of the youth's arrival at the training school. *See Morales Relief Plan, supra* at 12. Unlike the assessment process outlined in the relief plan, the assessment described in the standard is distinct from the predisposition investigation which is a preliminary assessment solely to determine the appropriate disposition for the juvenile. *See* Standard 3.186. This distinction is made in order to confine the scope of the predisposition report to only that information essential for making a dispositional decision. All adjudicated juveniles may not require the mental health and educational evaluations called for in this standard. Those who do should receive them. However, to require such evaluations for all adjudicated juveniles at the predis- positional stage would not only impose a sizable financial burden on the state or community, but also constitute an unnecessary invasion of individual pri- vacy. *See* Standard 3.187.

In order to avoid unnecessary duplication of the predisposition investiga- tion by the assessment team, the placing court should be responsible for promptly forwarding predispositional reports and any other pertinent informa- tion to the training school for use in the assessment.

The assessment should be used in determining the appropriate housing placement and security classification as well as in developing the individual's program plan. It should also serve as a basis for measuring the juvenile's progress in specific areas of concern. The objectives of the program plan should be clearly stated and in keeping with the objective of the dispositional order.

The assessment team which is to conduct the assessment should be composed of representatives from all components of the treatment staff in order to get an overall perspective of the juvenile's needs, to identify problems, and to establish priorities and program options which complement each other. While the standard does not specify whether or not assignment to the assessment team is permanent, rotation of staff would allow counselors and youth-care staff to participate in making program decisions which they may later be responsible for implementing or monitoring.

The assessment procedures should be designed to allow the juvenile a brief period to adjust to the new setting before the more intensive phase of psychological, educational, and vocational testing commences. *See Morales Relief Plan, supra* at 15. During this phase, the juvenile should have an opportunity to meet each member of the assessment team in order to become more familiar with those who are conducting the assessment and aware of the services provided by each team member. The assessment team should encourage the juvenile to begin developing goals and objectives to be attained while at the training school. Physical and dental examinations should be conducted during this phase and any significant findings or recommendations for treatment should be presented by the examining physician or dentist to the assessment team.

The caseworker assigned to the assessment team should be responsible for reviewing any court papers relevant to the dispositional order, including a summary of the incident which resulted in adjudication, and any family or developmental history already compiled in the predisposition report for their completeness. In addition, the caseworker should interview the juvenile regarding these subjects. Based on the juvenile's personal history and his/her informal observations, as well as those of the youth-care worker, the caseworker should make recommendations regarding the juvenile's housing placement, security classification and program options. If a previous assessment has been conducted on a juvenile, the caseworker should update the last study to cover the period since the last assessment including information regarding the current placement.

With the assistance of the associate psychologist, the psychologist should perform a psychological evaluation which should include individually administered tests of verbal and nonverbal intelligence and psychomotor capacity; tests of social maturity and personality; projective tests, as appropriate; and vocational interest and aptitude tests. Tests selected for the psychological evaluation should meet the standards of the American Psychological Association. They should minimize, to the greatest extent possible, any racial, ethnic, or cultural bias which may affect the validity of the results. *See Morales*, 383 F. Supp. at 88. The psychologist should record the results of the tests administered, and whenever appropriate, communicate these results to the educational diagnostician and psychiatrist for incorporation into their assessment work.

On the basis of recommendations of other team members or the specifications of the dispositional orders, the psychiatrist should conduct a psychiatric evaluation in order to determine whether the juvenile is in need of psychiatric treatment. *See Morales Relief Plan, supra* at 28; *Morales*, 383 F. Supp. at 88; and Standard 4.2174. The psychiatrist should make recommendations as to what mental health services should be made available to the juvenile, and explain the services to the juvenile and to his/her parents, guardian, or primary caretaker.

An educational evaluation should be conducted by the educational diag-nostician and should include an assessment of each juvenile's academic and vocational skill achievement level, level of cognitive development, and attitude toward education by means of testing and review of available educational records. *See* 45 C.F.R. §§ 99.31(a)(2) and *Report of the Task Force, supra*, at Standard 24.6. Professionally recognized standard achievement tests should be administered whenever records are not available on the results of tests administered within the previous twelve months. *See Morales Relief Plan, supra* at 27. Like the tests used for psychological evaluation, the educational achievement tests used should be as free of racial, ethnic, and cultural bias as possible. Whenever preliminary test results indicate the juvenile may have serious learning problems, the educational diagnostician should administer the appropriate diagnostic tests. Depending on the suspected dysfunction, the tests should identify specific problems in information processing including visual, auditory, or language processing; speech; and psychiatric or neurological disorders which may affect learning ability. The educational diagnostician should inform the assessment team of the juvenile's special needs as related to his/her educational and social functioning, including both strengths and weaknesses, and of any items which should be included in the short-term and long-term goals for the educational component of the program plan. The plan should contain strategies designed to accomplish each of these goals.

Wherever appropriate, the vocational counselor should assist the educational diagnostician and psychologist in developing recommendations for vocational training programs to complement the juvenile's educational plan. The assessment team should consider the availability of and feasibility of using community resources to provide the full range of services called for in the program plan or to augment the services provided in the training school. *See* Standard 4.213.

The standard recommends that the entire assessment team meet at least once to review and discuss the findings of each member's analysis and to incorporate these into a workable program plan which addresses the needs and preferences of juveniles. One member of the assessment team should be responsible for preparing a final report on the team's findings, recommendations, and final agreement on the individual's program objectives and strategies. The standard urges that the juvenile actively participate in the development of goals and objectives which form the basis of the program plan as well as in the formulation of the plan itself. Hopefully, the result will be a plan which is realistic and to which the youth has some personal commitment. At a minimum, the juvenile should be present at one of the assessment team meetings.

Copies of the program plan should be given to the juvenile and the placing family court. Formalizing the plan has the advantage that all parties have a record of what is expected of each person or program unit involved. Also, if the juvenile feels he/she has been treated unfairly, it will serve as documentation by review by the ombudsman or through the grievance procedures. *See* Standards 4.81 and 4.82. Notification to the placing court is recommended as a means of assuring the judge that the juvenile's placement is in keeping with the conditions of the dispositional order and also of informing him/her of the availability and adequacy of the programs to address the juvenile's needs.

By defining specific objectives to be achieved and timetables for the implementation of the program plan, the training school staff will have some guidelines for reviewing an individual's progress and some measures of performance. A monthly review is recommended in order to keep appropriate staff, including members of the assessment team, appraised of the youth's progress in other program areas and to provide formal feedback to the juvenile on how the staff perceives his/her progress. Based on this periodic review, the plan may be modified and any changes should be noted in the juvenile's institutional file. Only when significant modifications are agreed upon, such as transfer or release, should the court be notified. Proposed modifications in either the duration of confinement or the level of security are within the review of the family court and should be brought to the attention of the placing judge. *See* Standards 3.181, 3.182, 3.189, 3.1810, 4.71, and 4.72. To avoid undue anxiety on the part of the juvenile awaiting the results of judicial review and undue paperwork for the court, a maximum time limit should be set for the family court to respond to any such proposals. Setting such a time limit may require instituting a uniform court policy to ensure compliance or enactment of legislation. This review process should serve to insure both the safety of the community and the protection of juveniles from unduly extended periods of confinement.

28

Matter of Felder

Family Court, Onondaga County. Feb. 8, 1978.

Decision

EDWARD J. McLAUGHLIN, Judge.
This juvenile delinquency proceeding involves a designated felony pursuant to the *Juvenile Justice Reform Act of 1976,* (L. 1976, ch. 878) N.Y. Family Court Act §§ 711-767, 29A *McKinney's Consolidated Laws 1977.* It presents a case of first impression for this court. Respondent, a boy of fifteen, allegedly committed a robbery in the first degree, Penal Law § 160.15, a designated felony. F C A § 712(h). When the case came before the Court, the Respondent moved for a jury trial, asserting that under *Baldwin v. New York,* 399 U.S. 66, 90 S.Ct. 1886, 26 L. Ed.2d 437 (1970), an individual charged with a crime where the penalty could exceed six months imprisonment is entitled to a jury trial. The respondent alleged that since he can be confined in a secure facility for a period of time up to twelve months, pursuant to section 753-a(4)(a)(ii) of the Family Court Act, the *Baldwin* doctrine applied, and he is entitled to a trial by jury.

On the other hand, the petitioner alleged that the United States Supreme Court decision in *McKeiver v. Pennsylvania,* 403 U.S. 528, 91 S.Ct. 1976,

Source: *In the Matter of Felder,* 402 N.Y.S.2d 528 (1978).

29 L.Ed.2d 647 (1971), is controlling. *McKeiver* holds that a juvenile charged with a delinquency, which precludes, by definition, criminal consequences and tried in a civil court, does not have a due process right to a jury trial. Petitioner further alleged that while New York is not constitutionally precluded from granting a jury trial under *McKeiver,* it has determined not to do so, citing *In re Daniel G.,* 27 N.Y.2d 90, 313 N.Y.S.2d 704, 261 N.E.2d 627 (1970) and *Matter of George S.,* 44 A.D.2d 352, 355 N.Y.S.2d 143 (1st Dept., 1974).

[1] The issue before the court, then, is whether the instant proceeding is controlled by *McKeiver* or by *Baldwin.* Specifically, the question turns on whether this is a juvenile proceeding within the meaning of *McKeiver,* or, whether so many of the attributes of a juvenile proceeding have been discarded that the proceeding is in effect "criminal" in nature and thus within the ambit of *Baldwin.*[1]

A. Is a Designated Felony Proceeding a Juvenile Proceeding?

The concept of designated felony was created as a part of the *Juvenile Justice Reform Act of 1976.* (Chapt. 878, Laws of 1976).

[2] The Legislature has chosen to label this new "designated felony concept" as a "juvenile" proceeding. It is axiomatic that this court is not bound by that designation if, in fact, the new proceeding is indeed a criminal proceeding.[2] The Supreme Court recognized this principle in *Trop v. Dulles,* 356 U.S. 86, at 94, 78 S.Ct. 590, at 594, 2 L.Ed.2d 630 (1958), when the Court taught us:

> But the Government contends that this statute does not impose a penalty. . . . We are told this is so because a committee . . . said it "technically is not a penal law." How simple would be the tasks of constitutional adjudication and of law generally if specific problems could be solved by inspection of labels pasted on them. . . .

Further, "[N]either the label which a state places on its own conduct, nor even the legitimacy of its own motivation, can avoid applicability of the Federal Constitution." *Vann v. Scott,* 467 F.2d 1235, at 1240 (7th Cir. 1972) (decision per Judge Stevens, now Mr. Justice Stevens, on an Eighth Amendment challenge to a training school commitment).

B. Background of the Juvenile Justice System

[3] The fundamental substantive distinction between a juvenile proceeding and a criminal proceeding is that a juvenile disposition is limited to treatment, while a criminal proceeding may impose punishment regardless of whether

the punishment results in retribution and, or, deterrence. The view that the difference between criminal and juvenile proceedings is the difference between retribution and deterrence, on the one hand, and treatment, on the other, is confirmed by an examination of the history of the juvenile court system. This examination will also show that a denial of a juvenile's full exercise of his constitutional rights can only be predicated upon the presence of the treatment principle of the juvenile justice system.

At common law there were no juvenile courts or juvenile proceedings. If a child, over the age of seven, committed a criminal act, he was tried in a criminal court, and afforded all of the privileges of an adult charged with the same conduct. Thus, he was arrested, indicted by a grand jury, tried by a petit jury, and, if convicted, sent to prison. Mack, *The Juvenile Court,* 23 Harv. L.R. 104, at 106 (1909).

The reformers of the nineteenth century were appalled by the fact that juveniles could be given long prison sentences to be served with hardened criminals. They recognized that criminal jurisprudence was founded not on ''Reformation of the Criminal, but punishment; punishment as expiation for wrong, punishment as a warning to other possible wrongdoers.'' Mack, *supra,* at 106. To alleviate this situation, special juvenile centers were established which were authorized to admit children convicted of petty criminal offenses. The premise of these juvenile centers was that children were not criminal offenders, and, if properly treated, could be saved from a life of crime. The juvenile reform movement later became concerned not only with the disposition received by the juveniles but with the adjudication of juveniles as well. Thus, separate court proceedings were established.

The juvenile statutes were early challenged on the basis that the statutes were criminal in nature and the procedures employed were, therefore, violative of the constitutional protection applicable to criminal proceedings. In most cases the challenges were rejected on the ground that the disposition was rehabilitative and not grounded on motivations of punishment and deterrence. E. g. *Commonwealth v. Fisher,* 213 Pa. 48, 62 A. 198 (1905). Where the challenge succeeded was in those situations where the proceeding was, in effect, criminal in nature. E. g. *Robison v. Wayne Circuit Judges,* 151 Mich. 315, 115 N.W. 682 (1908).

This historical examination of the origins of the juvenile justice system shows that the informality, flexibility, and, concomitantly, the absence of constitutional safeguards at juvenile proceedings was justified on the ground that the juvenile was to be treated and rehabilitated. Conversely, when the juvenile proceeding was primarily for retributive and deterrent purposes, it was considered criminal in nature, and hence subject to all of the limitations of a regular criminal proceeding. Sometimes referred to as the ''exchange principle of juvenile law'',[3] the trading of the constitutional protections of a criminal proceeding for rehabilitation still remains today the *sine quo non* of juvenile proceedings. Typical is the comment of the court in *Inmates of Boys' Training School v. Affleck,* 346 F.Supp. 1354, at 1364 (D.R.I.1972). The court said:

> (T)he constitutional validity of present procedural safeguards in juvenile adjudi-cations, which do not embrace all of the rigorous safeguards of criminal court adjudications, appears to rest on the adherence of the juvenile justice system to rehabilitative rather than penal goals
>
> ·
>
> Rehabilitation, then, is the interest which the state has defined as being the purpose of confinement of juveniles. Due process in the adjudicative stages of the juvenile justice system has been defined differently from due process in the criminal justice system because the goal of the juvenile system, rehabilitation, differs from the goals of the criminal system, which include punishment, deter-rence and retribution.

[4] It is against this background that *McKeiver v. Pennsylvania, supra,* must be viewed. It is true that *McKeiver* stated that in a juvenile proceeding trial by jury is not a constitutional requirement. The Court specifically refused to abandon the salutary goals of the juvenile system and rejected the jury trial because it could "tend once again to place the juvenile squarely in the routine of the criminal process." 403 U.S., at 547, 91 S.Ct. at 1987. Indeed, the Court acknowledged that when a child is adjudicated as a juvenile, but treated as a criminal, an inconsistency results, for the Court stated: "Of course there have been abuses. . . . We refrain from saying at this point that these abuses are of a constitutional dimension." *Id.*, at 547–48, 91 S.Ct. at 1987. In effect, the Court deferred until a more appropriate occasion the determination of when a juvenile disposition fails to meet the rehabilitative premise of the juvenile system. The determination in *McKeiver* that in a juvenile proceeding a jury trial is not required, is, therefore, necessarily limited to those proceed-ings that are juvenile in nature. Thus, there is no requirement of a jury trial in family court where the disposition is rehabilitative and non-penal. When, however, the protections provided to the juvenile criminal offender have been so eroded away that what is actually a punishment is characterized as a treat-ment, an abuse of constitutional dimension has occurred, and, a jury trial is required before punishment, although appropriate, may be inflicted.

C. Background of the 1976 Act

In response to the reported increase in the frequency and severity of crimes committed by juveniles, the Legislature in the 1976 session enacted the *Juvenile Justice Reform Act* (L.1976, ch. 878). This bill significantly amended Article 7 of the Family Court Act. The express purpose of Article 7 was redefined to include, for the first time, consideration of the needs of the community:

"In any juvenile procedure under this article, the court shall consider the needs and best interests of the respondent as well as the need for protection of the community." F C A § 711. To this end, the Legislature created restrictive placement. Rejecting proposals to transfer seriously violent juveniles to the adult criminal system, the Legislature adopted restrictive placement as a method of dealing with the juveniles within the juvenile system. Gottfried, R. and Barsky, S. *Practice Commentaries,* F C A § 753-a, pp. 217–219, *29A McKinney's Consolidated Laws of New York, 1977.*

The amendments to Article 7 define four new terms—designated felony act,[4] designated Class A felony act,[5] secure facility,[6] and restrictive placement.[7] F C A § 712. Further, the amendments allow the County Attorney to be assisted by members of the District Attorney's staff, F C A § 254(c); provides that the probation service may not attempt to adjust some cases without the prior written approval of a judge, F C A § 734(a)(ii); requires that, with a few exceptions, the judge presiding at the fact finding hearing shall preside at the dispositional hearing, F C A § 742; and, eliminates in designated felony cases the judge's discretionary right to prevent disclosure of portions of the juvenile's reports and histories to either the respondent or the petitioner. F C A § 570.

D. An Analysis of the 1976 Act

A significant change made by the *Juvenile Justice Reform Act* is the requirement that restrictive placement may be ordered for a juvenile found to have committed a designated felony, when the court determines that a juvenile requires such restrictive placement. F C A § 753-a. Once restrictive placement is ordered by the court, the delinquent must remain in the placement for twelve months, if the placement results from an adjudication on a Class A designated felony, or for six months, if the placement results from the adjudication of any designated felony. F C A § 753-a(3)(a)(ii); (4)(a)(ii). Further, during the period of restrictive placement, the right to petition the court to stay the execution, to set aside, modify, or vacate the disposition is suspended. It is this suspension of the provisions of part six, Article 7, of the Family Court Act which distinguishes a restrictive placement disposition from all other dispositions under Article 7. Thus, the Legislature has created a definite sentence of placement nearly indistinguishable from definite sentences imposed upon adults under section 70.20(2) of the Penal Law.

Further, in mandating the minimum period of restrictive placement, when restrictive placement has been found to be needed at all, the Legislature has introduced two other concepts of the criminal justice process previously unknown in the juvenile system. First, the length of the commitment is determined by the act committed rather than by the needs of the child, and second, the sentence is mandatory. In effect, the Legislature has determined that a child who at the time of his dispositional hearing requires restrictive placement will continue to require restrictive placement for the entire period of the minimum sentence. Prior to the enactment of this statute, the court was only required to determine that at the time of the dispositional hearing the needs of the child were for placement in an institution and that at any time during that initial period, if the child was successfully rehabilitated, he was entitled to release. Consistent with this philosophy of treatment was the provision that if at the end of the initial placement the child was not successfully rehabilitated, then, the period of placement could be extended. In effect, once the court makes a finding that restrictive placement is needed at the time of the disposition, the act then mandates a minimum sentence, a result which is more harsh on the juvenile than is the criminal procedure for the adult who is entitled to an indeterminate sentence in nearly all cases. P L § 70.00.

The distinction between indeterminate and determinate sentencing is not semantic, but indicates fundamentally different public policies. Indeterminate sentencing is based upon notions of rehabilitation, while determinate sentencing is based upon a desire for retribution or punishment.

In his vigorous dissent *In re Gault,* 387 U.S. 1, 87 S.Ct. 1428, 18 L.Ed.2d 527 (1967), Mr. Justice Stewart succinctly distinguished the purpose and mission of the juvenile system of justice from the purpose and mission of the criminal system. "The object of the one [juvenile] is correcting a condition. The object of the other [criminal] is conviction and punishment for a criminal act." 387 U.S., at 79, 87 S.Ct., at 1470. By mandating restrictive placement in a secure facility for a minimum of six months, the Legislature has created a disposition that more nearly resembles a punishment than a treatment and, thereby, has blurred the clearly distinct objectives of the juvenile justice system with those of the criminal justice system.

The thinly disguised intent of the Legislature to punish an adjudicated designated felon, based upon the criminal act and upon the characteristics of the victim of the criminal act, as opposed to rehabilitating and treating a juvenile offender is revealed by the 1977 amendment to section 753-a of the Family Court Act which states:

> . . . the court shall order a restrictive placement in any case where the respondent is found to have committed a designated felony act in which the respondent inflicted serious physical injury . . . upon another person who is sixty-two years of age or more. F C A § 753-a(2-a).

This court does not deny that punishment may be appropriate for certain designated felons. This court does insist, however, that deprivation of liberty for purposes of punishment based on the nature of criminal acts committed must be surrounded by constitutional protections not now available in family court proceedings.

The very heart of the rehabilitative nature of the juvenile justice system in New York is the array of remedies provided in part six of Article 7 of the Family Court Act, for it is these remedies that have protected the right of a juvenile to an indeterminate sentence. *Cf. In the Matter of Ilone I.*, 64 Misc.2d 878, 316 N.Y.S.2d 356. (Family Court, Queens County, 1970). It is the indeterminate quality of a juvenile disposition that makes the disposition rehabilitative. To refuse to allow a part six motion (Family Ct. Act §§ 761–768) to modify or to terminate a placement gives the disposition clearly criminal characteristics.

E. Treatment

The *Juvenile Justice Reform Act* requires that treatment be available at restrictive placement facilities. The availability and quality of treatment available to the respondent is not at issue here. What is at issue is the mandatory time period required for treatment. F C A § 753-a.

Analogies may be made between the treatment of persons confined because of mental illness and juveniles confined because of delinquency. Serious consideration has been given recently to the constitutional rights of persons involuntarily committed to mental hospitals following non-criminal dispositions. In identifying treatment as a right for the mentally ill, for instance, a court concluded that at the least an institution must make a *bona fide* effort to cure, since the purpose of the involuntary hospitalization is treatment, not punishment. *Rouse v. Cameron*, 125 U.S.App.D.C. 366, 373 F.2d 451 (1966). Similarly, another federal district court found that non-criminal procedures for commitment which lacked constitutional safeguards were valid only for treatment and not for punishment. *Wyatt v. Stickney*, 325 F.Supp. 781 (M.D. Ala.1971). Cf. *O'Connor v. Donaldson*, 422 U.S. 563, 95 S.Ct. 2486, 45 L.Ed.2d 396 (1975); *Jackson v. Indiana*, 406 U.S. 715, 92 S.Ct. 1845, 32 L.Ed.2d 435 (1972).

Juveniles also have a right to treatment. *Martarella v. Kelley*, 349 F.Supp. 575 (S.D.N.Y.1972); *Inmates of Boys' Training School v. Affleck, supra; M. v. M.*, 71 Misc.2d 396, 336 N.Y.S.2d 304 (Family Court, Bronx County, 1972). Moreover, one court has found that " 'the right to treatment' includes the right to *individualized* care and treatment." *Nelson v. Heyne*, 491 F.2d 352, at 360 (7th Cir.), *cert. den.* 417 U.S. 976, 94 S.Ct. 3183, 41 L.Ed.2d 1146 (1974)(emphasis in the original). The reasoning of the court in *Nelson* is helpful in analyzing time limited restrictive placement:

> Because children differ in their need for rehabilitation, individual need for treatment will differ. . . . Without a program of individual treatment the result may be that the juveniles will not be rehabilitated, but warehoused,

and that at the termination of detention they will likely be incapable of taking their proper places in free society; their interests and those of the state thereby being defeated. *Id.*

Clearly, treatment may result in a cure in six days, or in six weeks, or in six months, or in one year, or never! By setting a mandatory minimum time period for restrictive placement, treatment becomes indistinguishable from punishment.

F. Intake—A Critical Stage in Designated Felony Act Proceedings

Intake proceedings are a unique feature of the juvenile justice system in this state. The intake conference provides for a screening out of cases not suited to court intervention. *In the Matter of Charles C.,* 83 Misc.2d 388, 371 N.Y.S.2d 582 (Family Court, New York County, 1975). It is designed to return the juvenile to the community prior to the formulation of a petition. *In the Matter of Frank H.,* 71 Misc.2d 1042, 337 N.Y.S.2d 118 (Family Court, Richmond County, 1972). The intake procedure of the family court, as it applies to juvenile delinquency, confers authority on the probation service to offer informal, voluntary conferences to settle the differences between the petitioner and the respondent. In fact, in his concurring opinion in *McKeiver, supra,* Mr. Justice White said that "the distinctive intake policies and procedures of the juvenile court system to a great extent obviate [the] important function of the jury." 403 U.S., at 552, 91 S.Ct., at 1990.

Under the 1976 amendments to the Family Court Act, a juvenile accused of a designated felony must obtain the "prior written approval of a judge of the court" before an adjustment may take place. F C A § 734(a)(ii). It had been the rule in New York that "no statement made during a preliminary conference may be admitted into evidence at a fact-finding hearing." F C A § 735; 22 NYCRR 2507.4(a)(6), 1977, (previously NYCRR 2506.3(d), 1976). This rule had been interpreted as a protection for the respondent against self incrimination, and, thus, the intake conference had not been considered a "critical" stage of adjudication and, therefore, the child was not entitled to counsel at the conference. *In re Frank H., supra; In the Matter of Anthony S.,* 73 Misc.2d 187, 341 N.Y.S.2d 11 (Family Court, Richmond County, 1973).

It now appears that the kind of information previously protected during intake proceedings and not admitted as evidence in fact finding hearings must be made available to the court before the court can determine whether the case is, or is not, suitable for adjustment. Thus, the informality, responsiveness, and flexibility of the intake proceeding, a unique tool of the juvenile justice process, is vitiated, and intake becomes a critical stage of the proceedings and the protection of the constitutional rights of the respondent becomes essential. Whether a respondent is entitled to counsel at a designated felony intake conference is now certainly a consideration.[8] See, *Argersinger v. Hamlin,* 407 U.S. 25, 92 S.Ct. 2006, 32 L.Ed.2d 530 (1972).

G. Other Features of the Act

Other features of the *Juvenile Justice Reform Act* are traditionally more associated with criminal proceedings than with civil proceedings. While these procedures are legally less significant than those discussed above, the new procedures do serve to flavor the act with criminal spice.

For instance, in a juvenile proceeding the petitioner's case is presented by the county attorney. F C A § 254-a, but in a designated felony case the district attorney may present the case. F C A § 254-c. This provision, at the least, demonstrates a recognition by the Legislature of the criminal nature of a designated felony proceeding. Further, the court must authorize the fingerprinting and photographing of juveniles adjudicated as designated felons. F C A § 753-b. Then, the assignment of the same judge to both fact finding and dispositional hearings represents a major shift in juvenile justice processes. The *New York Juvenile Justice Act of 1976:* Restrictive Placement—An Answer to the Problem of the Seriously Violent Youth? 45 Fordham L.R. "to ensure that the judge who makes the disposition . . . will have familiarity with all the circumstances surrounding the case." Gottfried, R. & Barsky, S. *Practice Commentary,* F C A § 742, *29A McKinney's Consolidated Laws of N.Y.* 1977 Pocket Part. The presentencing hearing has its parallel in criminal proceedings. Compare CPL §§ 380.30, 390.20, 390.50, 400 and F C A § 753-a(2). The requirement of psychological tests, reports and histories fails to distinguish the designated felony proceeding from a criminal proceeding. Compare CPL § 390.20 and F C A § 750(3).

[5] In a criminal proceeding the court may in its discretion except from disclosure to counsel portions of the pre-sentencing investigation reports "which might seriously disrupt a program of rehabilitation." CPL § 390.50(2). The same discretion is not afforded the court in a juvenile designated felony case. F C A § 750(4). Ironically, the juvenile court judge is faced with restrictions that fly in the face of rehabilitation the very purpose for which there is a system of juvenile justice distinct from the criminal justice system.

H. The Need for a Jury Trial

[6] The revision of the Family Court Act by the *Juvenile Justice Reform Act of 1976* transformed a purely rehabilitative juvenile statute into a statute that mirrors a retributive criminal statute, but fails to reflect the constitutional protections presumed to apply to such statutes. This transformation is most particularly evidenced by the requirement of restrictive placement in a secure

facility for a definite period of time for a person found to have committed a designated felony and to be in need of restrictive placement with no provision for changing the placement if rehabilitation of the juvenile offender is found to have occurred. Other aspects of the revision also indicate that the designated felony proceeding is in its very essence a criminal proceeding, although labeled a juvenile proceeding. Since it is essentially a criminal proceeding, it is required that all the safeguards mandated by the United States Constitution be afforded the accused.

The particular constitutional safeguard now before the court is the Sixth Amendment right to a trial by jury. Since it is the conclusion of this court that the designated felony portions of the *Juvenile Justice Reform Act of 1976* are fundamentally criminal in nature, the respondent is entitled to a trial by jury for a criminal prosecution.

[7] Were it possible to extend this right to the respondent, no serious problem would arise. Unfortunately, it is not possible for this court to have the facts determined by a jury, since the law in this state is clear that no court may conduct a trial by jury unless such proceeding is authorized by statute. *People v. Carroll,* 7 Misc.2d 581, 161 N.Y. S.2d 329 (Kings County, County Court, 1957); *In re Daniel G., supra.*

[8] The quandary thus created for the court is, may it proceed in this case given its inability to extend a right to a trial by jury? And further, if it may so proceed, how does it protect the rights of the respondent and the rights of society?

It is the determination of this court that it is entitled to proceed to the fact finding hearing on this alleged act of delinquency without a jury, provided that prior to the taking of any testimony the court advises the respondent that regardless of the outcome, this court will not order restrictive placement, and this it now does. *Baldwin v. New York, supra.*

If the alleged facts are proven, thereby giving this court jurisdiction to make a disposition, and if at that dispositional hearing it is determined that placement is necessary, such disposition will be ordered and the respondent may be placed for an initial period of eighteen months. If the treatment is not completed at the end of such time, placement will be extended within the provisions of the law and, accordingly, the right of society to be protected from further depredations will be as effectively insured as if a restrictive placement were ordered, and at the same time the right of the respondent to modification of that disposition as soon as he responds to treatment will be preserved.

Accordingly, motion for trial by jury is denied.

Notes

1. Without reaching the conclusion that a proceeding in a designated felony case was a *juvenile* proceeding, the Family Court of King's County recently concluded

that the U.S. Constitution Sixth Amendment right to a trial by jury in a *criminal* prosecution did not apply. *William M. v. Harold B.*, 90 Misc.2d 173, 393 N.Y.S.2d 535 (1977). While *McKeiver* left to the discretion of the states the use of jury trials in *juvenile* proceedings, the right to a jury trial in a *criminal* proceeding applies to the states through the Fourteenth Amendment. *Duncan v. Louisiana*, 391 U.S. 145, 88 S.Ct. 1444, 20 L.Ed.2d 491 (1968).

2. In holding that the Fifth Amendment protection from double jeopardy applied to juvenile recognized proceedings, a constitutional guarantee traditionally associated with criminal prosecutions, the U.S. Supreme Court in *Breed v. Jones*, 421 U.S. 519, 529, 95 S.Ct. 1779, 1785, 44 L.Ed.2d 346 (1974), noted:

> "We believe it is simply too late in the day to conclude . . . that a juvenile is not put in jeopardy at a proceeding whose object is to determine whether he had committed acts that violate a criminal law and whose potential consequences include both the stigma inherent in such a determination and the deprivation of liberty for many years. For it is clear under our cases that determining the relevance of constitutional policies, like determining the applicability of constitutional rights, in juvenile proceedings, requires that courts eschew 'the "civil" label-of-convenience which has been attached to juvenile proceedings,' *In re Gault*, 387 U.S. 1, 87 S.Ct. 1428, 18 L.Ed.2d 527, and that 'the juvenile process . . . be candidly appraised.' 387 U.S. at 21, 87 S.Ct., at 1428. 421 U.S., at 529, 95 S.Ct. at 1785."

Doubtless even a clear legislative classification of a statute as "non-penal" would not alter the fundamental nature of a plainly penal statute.

3. For an extensive analysis of the exchange principle in juvenile law see Katz, *Juveniles Committed to Penal Institutions—Do They Have a Right to a Jury Trial?*, 13 J.Fam.Law 675 (1973).

4. F C A § 712(h) " 'Designated felony act.' An act committed by a person fourteen or fifteen years of age which, if done by an adult, would be a crime (i) defined in sections 125.27 (Murder in the first degree); 125.25 (murder in the second degree); 135.25 (kidnapping in the first degree); or 150.20 (arson in the first degree) of the penal law; (ii) defined in sections 120.10 (assault in the first degree); 125.20 (manslaughter in the first degree); 130.35 (rape in the first degree); 130.50 (sodomy in the first degree); 135.20 (kidnapping in the second degree), but only where the abduction involved the use or threat of use of deadly force; 150.15 (arson in the second degree); or 160.15 (robbery in the first degree) of the penal law; or (iii) defined in the penal law as an attempt to commit murder in the first or second degree or kidnapping in the first degree."

5. F C A § 712(i) "Designated class A felony act." A designated felony act defined in clause (i) paragraph (h) of this section.

6. F C A § 712(j) "Secure facility." A residential facility in which the juvenile delinquent may be placed under this article, which is characterized by physically restricting construction, hardware and procedures, and is designated a secure facility by the division for youth.

7. F C A § 712(k) "Restrictive placement." A placement pursuant to section seven hundred fifty-three-a.

8. The quasi-criminal nature of juvenile proceedings has long been recognized. *In the Matter of Gergory W.*, 19 N.Y.2d 55, 277 N.Y. S.2d 675, 224 N.E.2d 102 (1966). The current recognition of the critical and criminal nature of the early stages

of these proceedings is evidenced by the strict application of the Criminal Procedure Law to these juvenile proceedings. For instance, a court held that the more stringent pretrial discovery procedures of the CPL should apply to such proceedings rather than the more generous disclosure provisions of the CPLR. *Matter of Terry T.,* 90 Misc.2d 1015, 397 N.Y.S.2d 548 (Family Court, New York County, 1977). Another court denied a respondent's motion for an identification hearing, a suppression order and a bill of particulars because the motion was not timely under CPL § 255.20. *In the Matter of Archer,* 89 Misc.2d 526, 392 N.Y. S.2d 362 (Family Court, Queens County, 1977). On the other hand, a court found that in the case of a six-month delay between initial detention and initial appearance that Article 30 of the CPL did not apply and no speedy trial problems resulted. *Matter of Walters,* 91 Misc. 2d 728, 398 N.Y.S.2d 806 (Family Court, Suffolk County, 1977). It would appear that juveniles have *quasi-rights* in *quasi-criminal* proceedings.

29

On Mission Statements and Reform in Juvenile Justice: The Case of the ''Balanced Approach''

Gordon Bazemore

At their best, agency mission statements in criminal justice set internal goals and priorities for staff and create a common standard for evaluating individual and agency effectiveness. For the outside world, a good mission statement should leave little doubt about the fundamental purpose of the agency and should clarify in the public mind what tasks and service outcomes the agency is responsible for. Equally important, a good mission statement places clear limitations on what the public should expect from an agency.

At their worst, mission statements give little guidance to staff and managers, confuse the public about the agency's goals, and create false or unachievable expectations. Often, vaguely worded mission statements (e.g., ''to protect and serve'') may be used to disguise hidden agendas or mask failure to develop clear objectives.

According to many critics, the traditional mission statement of juvenile justice to act ''in the best interests of the child'' has often been used to cover layers of abuse of due process rights of children while offering little in return that could be described as in their best interest (e.g., Feld, 1991). On the other hand, juvenile justice agencies have sometimes been held to unrealistic expectations due to the vagueness of their mission. Asked to fulfill legalistic and social welfare objectives, juvenile justice is often placed in the role of

Source: *Federal Probation*, 56(3) (1992): 64–70.

being "all things to all people." This ambiguity in mission has also made juvenile justice vulnerable to political pendulum swings and fads which probably add to the confusion of staff and the public about priorities and objectives (Maloney, Romig, and Armstrong, 1988: 47–50).

While some might argue that vagueness in mission statements is deliberate and serves to protect the status quo, a number of juvenile justice policymakers and agency managers now view an effective new mission statement as essential to the reform of policies and practices in their agencies. By setting new objectives for the agency, mission statements can guide the way to reform. To do so, however, the mission statement must at a minimum specify:

1. *what* activities, behaviors, and practices must change in order to meet the new objectives;
2. *who* must change (clients, staff, managers) and the role of each system actor in the reform;
3. *how* resources must be reallocated or new resources created based on partnerships with other agencies and community organizations.

While one might choose among several justice agencies in illustrating these points about mission statements, this article will draw on the author's experience with juvenile justice reform. Specifically, I will examine recent efforts to implement the "Balanced Approach" for community supervision of juvenile offenders as a "case study" in how a new mission statement may be adopted only symbolically or may be used to bring about change in an agency.

The Balanced Approach as a New Mission

One of the most promising attempts to state a clear and coherent mission for community supervision in juvenile justice in the past two decades can be found in an article appearing in the *Journal of Juvenile and Family Court Judges* which proposes a "Balanced Approach" for probation (Maloney, Romig, and Armstrong, 1988). As a response to the long-term failure of the juvenile court to fulfill its traditional treatment mission and also to the punitive trends of the past decade, the Balanced Approach specifies a distinctive role and unique objectives for juvenile probation and parole.

As outlined in the journal article and elaborated in a subsequent article (Armstrong, Maloney, and Romig, 1990), the Balanced Approach sets forth three practical objectives as part of a revitalized mission for community supervision of juvenile offenders: accountability, community protection, and competency development.

Simply stated, Accountability in the Balanced Approach refers to the requirement that offenders "make amends" for the harm resulting from their crime by repaying or restoring losses to victims and the community ("when

Figure 29.1.   The Balanced Approach

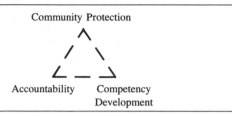

Source: Maloney, Romig, and Armstrong (1988).

an offense occurs, an obligation by the offender incurs''). Competency Development requires that youth who enter the juvenile justice system should exit the system "more capable of being productive and responsible in the community." The Community Protection objective explicitly acknowledges and endorses a long-time public expectation that juvenile justice must place equal emphasis on ensuring public safety at the lowest possible cost using the least restrictive level of supervision possible to protect the community (Maloney, Romig, and Armstrong, 1988:59).

Tying these three objectives together is the concept of "balance," or the idea that no one objective can take precedence over any other without creating a system that is "out of balance." For example, attention to competency needs serves to temper excessive concern with prompt repayment to victims (accountability) if, for example, the latter interferes with a juvenile's educational needs. Balance is achieved in dispositions for each offender through "individualization" which assumes that differences between individual youth require specialized rather than standardized sanctioning, supervision, and treatment responses (Palmer, 1975; Armstrong, Maloney, and Romig, 1990).

Taken together, these objectives provide both a coherent philosophy— symbolized by a triangle (see figure 29.1)—for community supervision and a way of prioritizing activities and organizing resources. Ideally, these outcomes also work together in a balanced system to make juvenile justice more responsive to local needs and concerns while at the same time asking the community to take ownership and participate in solving its own delinquency problem (Maloney, Romig, and Armstrong, 1988: 13–14).

Perhaps the most attractive feature of the Balanced Approach as a juvenile justice mission is its broad appeal to widely shared, traditional values about youth and their role in the community and its potential for changing the image of juvenile justice. Unlike policy and program innovations of recent decades such as diversion and various delinquency prevention initiatives which often failed to win local support and were thus often never properly implemented (Lab, 1982: 127–133), the Balanced Approach appears to be rooted in and responsive to traditional values in many American communities (e.g., making amends to victims and the public; the work ethic). As a result, the model appears to be more easily sold and accepted than other concepts. Since publication of the journal article, the Balanced Approach has been adopted as the official mission for juvenile justice in several states and numerous local community supervision agencies and has been discussed extensively as a model for juvenile corrections by other national advocacy groups (e.g., Barton and Streit, 1991).[1]

Unfortunately, the strong "marketing" value of the Balanced Approach has its negative side for those who view these principles as a new way of doing business in juvenile justice. The temptation is often great for agencies to adopt an approach with such broad public appeal without consideration of the implications of its objectives for new policy and practice. As a trainer and technical assistance consultant working with courts and other juvenile justice agencies wishing to improve restitution practices and initiate youth employment alternatives, I have had the opportunity to observe "up close" implementation of the Balanced Approach in several jurisdictions across the country in the past two or three years.[2] Unfortunately, on numerous occasions I have wondered if some of the practitioners and policymakers who claim to have adopted the Balanced Approach in their agencies are talking about the same set of concepts outlined in the Maloney and Armstrong statements. While the Balanced Approach authors clearly call for fundamental changes in juvenile community supervision, a number of agencies seem to have adopted the symbols of this mission statement without making the substantive modifications in staffing, resource allocation, sanctioning, and supervision policy and practice implied.

Who Is "Unbalanced" and How Are "Balanced" Systems Different?

Even the best researchers would be hard-pressed to find many juvenile justice administrators willing to admit, even in an anonymous survey, that they support "unbalanced" systems and do not believe in community protection, holding offenders accountable to victims, or trying to increase offender competency. One would have to look harder still, however, to find concrete examples of the practices advocated by the Balanced Approach in most community supervision units.

Fortunately, a few probation departments or components of supervision units do provide promising, positive examples of these practices. Combining work experience and restorative justice sanctions for young offenders, programs and supervision units in parts of Oregon and selected jurisdictions of a few other states like Massachusetts, California, and Pennsylvania seem to stand apart from traditional juvenile probation in the priority being given to competency development and accountability outcomes (Bazemore, 1991). Further, by carefully "programming" offenders' free time in the community using close adult supervision, often in group settings, these community-based programs ensure public protection in ways not possible using standard case-work probation approaches and without use of incarceration (Klein, 1991). These agencies are also unique in the way the three Balanced Approach princi-ples are operationalized in new activities for probation.

Observing the probation or community supervision process in these lo-cales, one would typically see youth actively involved with adult supervisors in productive work projects with clear value to the community while earning money to pay back their victims (and some to keep)(Jenkins, 1988; Mosier, 1988). One would be less likely to observe delinquent clients passively receiv-ing counseling or being reprimanded by probation officers for failing to obey rules of supervision. Observing staff in juvenile justice agencies that have adopted the Balanced Approach, one would be less likely to find caseworkers sitting behind desks completing court paperwork or admonishing young offend-ers about curfews missed, office visits missed, or violations of other standard court rules unrelated to the objectives of the Balanced Approach. Rather, one would see these adults working with young offenders on community projects supported by local businesses and other public agencies (Bazemore, 1991), perhaps meeting with an offender and his victim to arrive at a fair restitution settlement, or working with an employer group and civic organization to develop new work experience and educational opportunities for offenders. When a youth in these departments has violated community supervision by committing a new offense or is failing to comply with requirements as agreed (e.g., has been absent from a work crew or failed to make a restitution pay-ment), a "progressive response system" gives staff in these agencies a variety of options for intermediate sanctions without the use of confinement (and also provides for positive incentives for youth doing well).

At their best, these Balanced Approach programs present to the public a new image of offenders and a new image of the juvenile justice system. Most have at least begun to create new roles for community supervision workers and to reallocate resources to support new sanctioning and supervision activities which operationalize the external (community) and internal (agency) message of the mission statement. Generally, one would not have difficulty recognizing differences between these agencies and traditional supervision units in their assumptions about offenders, the role of community supervision, and desirable supervision activities. Further, one would not be likely to hear "accountabil-ity" used to mean punishment rather than restoring victims, "competency" development confused with treatment/services, or community protection used as a codeword for incarceration.[3] The specific sanctions, supervision tech-niques, and services offered by these programs and agencies give concrete meaning to (operationalize) accountability, public safety, and competency ob-jectives and highlight the contrast between the Balanced Approach and current practices of most surveillance and traditional treatment/services-oriented com-munity supervision approaches.

More commonly, however, state and local juvenile justice agencies claiming to have adopted the Balanced Approach often look scarcely different in their approach to sanctioning and supervision practices than any traditional probation department. My first hint of the scope of misunderstanding about the Balanced Approach came in 1989 at a training workshop on restitution and offender employment in which a senior administrator in a large juvenile corrections system announced that her agency had been ''doing the Balanced Approach for the last five years.'' At the time that agency held some 9,500 youths in secure facilities and appeared to be doing little in the way of getting victims of these youths reimbursed for the harm done to them. Could it be that this system was somewhat ''out of balance'' and had become tilted drastically in the direction of community protection to the detriment of accountability and competency development?

Another disappointment came in my own state soon after I began working with a group developing training curricula on the Balanced Approach in delinquency case management (Florida adopted the Balanced Approach in 1989 as the official mission for juvenile community control, now called case management). It was disheartening in one of the first curriculum design meetings to hear one of the better senior supervisors say that in his view the Balanced Approach ''has not been a problem because I just tell my counselors to take all the things they've been doing all along with their cases and group them under some new 'laundry lists' (i.e., competency development, accountability, and public safety).'' Later, I found examples of predispositional reports which listed ''submit to daily urine screen'' as a competency development objective and ''obey curfew'' as an accountability objective. To be fair, juvenile justice staff I have met are in fact dedicated to providing positive alternatives to the youth they supervise and are generally sensitive to victims' needs; most also remain enthusiastic and are committed to the Balanced Approach. And Florida is definitely *not* alone in the problem of pouring old wine into the new Balanced Approach bottles; most states and jurisdictions I have visited have their own ''laundry lists.''

Most probation departments, for example, now endorse the restorative sanctions required for accountability. But while judges have learned to regularly order restitution and service hours (often in inappropriate amounts not linked to the harm caused by the actions of the offender), they have often done little to ensure that youth have the means and supervision to complete these orders. Accountability or restorative justice gets low priority when it comes to resource allocation, and most probation departments still struggle to collect even token restitution and feel burdened with monitoring community service placements (Bazemore, 1992).

Competency development, though envisioned by the Balanced Approach authors as a way to ensure that youth caught up in the juvenile justice system begin to take on positive, productive roles in the community (Maloney, Romig, and Armstrong, 1988, p. 7), seems to have been interpreted by some simply as a call for more treatment or services. While the Balanced Approach certainly presumes that youths will be assessed and receive services as needed for identi-fied problems such as drug abuse and family dysfunction, competency develop-ment must go beyond simply *correcting problems* (as is the mandate of the tradi-tional treatment agenda). Competency development as an outcome must be assessed not by the number of counseling sessions or even remedial classes at-tended by an offender (one sometimes wonders if these activities address the competency needs of the offender or the counselor and remedial teacher) but by measurable gains in social skills, productive contributions to the community, and successful experiences in learning to work with others in meaningful roles.[4] These are clearly problems in conceptualization and operationalization of (or failure to operationalize) the Balanced Approach. If the Balanced Approach is to have any chance of getting community supervision beyond ''business as usual,'' advocates must clarify what outcomes are in fact intended by the three objec-tives, how these outcomes are to be measured, and what activities are most likely to get us there.[5] Otherwise we can expect to continue to see probation officers recommending curfews to help youth be more ''accountable'' and probation officers measuring competency improvement by the number of times a client attended a counseling session. Such clarification is necessary even if it means—and it undoubtedly will—losing the support of some who really do view account-ability as locking up thousands of offenders. Through this process, Balanced Approach advocates will also gain new allies (who may have opposed the ap-proach because they thought accountability meant punishment).

Operationalization of Balanced Approach objectives is an issue that can be addressed through training and dialogue which may lead to refined strategies for implementation and the development of new and creative ways of achieving the three objectives. When its key principles are operationalized well, the Balanced Approach, like any good mission statement, sets forth clear and practical objectives for offenders and signals staff that these objectives should receive priority. Good operationalization, however, does not change priorities, develop resources, or reallocate existing resources.

A common fundamental problem with mission statements as a tool in achieving agency reform is who they target for change. That is, when they go beyond symbols and public relations, mission statements often seem to address *client outcomes* only—and at best are interpreted as applicable primar-ily to the behavior and practice of line staff. Thus, narrowly interpreted, the Balanced Approach states general offender outcomes to be achieved and sets forth new activities as requirements for successful completion of supervision. More broadly viewed however, the Balanced Approach demands changes in the activities and priorities of agency *managers* and the *community*—as well as offenders and staff.

Thus, recommendations for implementing the Balanced Approach which follow below primarily address the responsibilities of juvenile justice adminis-trators. These recommendations assume that the Balanced Approach *is signifi-*

cantly different in the vision it suggests for juvenile justice and implies both internal changes in organizational priorities as well as changes in external relationships between juvenile justice agencies and community institutions. To ensure that this revolutionary conceptualization leads to real change, however, managers must take deliberate steps to direct or redirect resources and alter incentive structures to support the new activities required by the Balanced Approach. They must also proactively engage the community in ways not common in juvenile justice agencies in the past.

Mission Statements and Internal Change

It is easy for chief probation officers and other juvenile justice managers to issue directives. Certain activities presumed to increase competency, for example, may be required of offenders on community supervision, and staff may be directed to develop checklists to ensure that these activities are assigned and monitored. It is more difficult, however, for managers in casework-driven departments to allocate time for staff to develop new competency-building activities and programs for offenders. It is relatively easy for managers to say that restitution will be ordered/recommended for every offender with an identifiable victim. It is more difficult to allow staff time to work with youth and the community to ensure that restitution is paid and even more difficult (and necessary) for managers to persuade employers and other agencies to help develop work options for offenders who do not have a source of income for victim payment. While it is not difficult for managers to encourage staff to take actions necessary to meet Balanced Approach objectives, developing incentives for staff members who demonstrate success in these efforts (e.g., to link staff members' evaluations to number of employers they convince to agree to hire young offenders, number of their cases who completed restitution orders, or creativity in developing new means of supervising more serious offenders in the community) requires more initiative and leadership.

The problem of mission statements as a tool for reform, in other words, is bigger than inappropriate staff "laundry lists" for offenders. Even well-crafted mission statements like the Balanced Approach will not result in real change unless and until agency managers are willing to set internal priorities which support new objectives. If operationalization has been carefully thought through, this should mean reallocation of resources and new reward structures which support new programs and practices.

It should also mean deemphasizing some other traditional activities and practices which do nothing to achieve the new objectives. For example, a wide array of what have become "boilerplate" sanctions and requirements of court orders such as curfews, office visits, and other activities vaguely associated with surveillance, as well as a standard list of traditional treatment activities (e.g., counseling), are often mandated for every youth on community supervision. If such tasks do not clearly relate to Balanced Approach objectives, however, they—as well as purely punitive requirements—should no longer be the responsibility of probation staff (and in fact may need to be discouraged). In place of many of these traditional activities, managers serious about the Balanced Approach should develop new programs, activities, and staff positions more consistent with accountability, competency development, and community protection. Could an employment or work experience project be substituted for new caseworker positions or a counseling program? While ending or deemphasizing traditional practices in probation and justice agencies generally may result in hurt feelings of some staff and disappointed contracting agencies, few major changes have been brought about without some organizational disruption and risk-taking. And generally speaking, managers do not need to adopt a new mission like the Balanced Approach if traditional practices are working so well that they cannot be sacrificed.

Although such choices may not always be necessary, most agency directors will recognize from a workload perspective that they will not get something for nothing from staff. For most probation employees, being asked to develop jobs, begin cultural competency groups, or set up a rational system for collecting restitution is likely to provoke resistance unless there are cutbacks in (or elimination of) requirements for office visits, curfew checks, and various paperwork tasks. Further, even in a climate of unlimited funding, too many services and supervision activities may serve to confuse staff (not to mention youth and the community) about what the real priorities are. The beauty of the Balanced Approach is its simplicity in guiding staff members about how they should prioritize activities in a limited time schedule and reassuring them that their performance will be evaluated on how well they meet the specified objectives. If probation and parole professionals attend to the tasks of getting clients to make measurable advances in competency, assist them in being accountable to their victims, and ensure that they do not engage in behaviors that threaten public safety, they have already accomplished far more than ever occurs in most departments oriented toward the casework model. The Balanced Approach should not be diluted by grafting new objectives and activities onto existing practices.

These limitations do not imply that the Balanced Approach abandons pursuit of rehabilitative outcomes in juvenile justice in favor of narrowly legalistic or technocratic models of justice administration. Rather it assumes, based on some rather sound theory and research in criminology (see note 1), that pursuing activities that foster accountability and competency development should have a higher likelihood of keeping offenders from coming back to the juvenile justice system or becoming involved in adult crime than the surveillance and treatment services activities prescribed in the past (Maloney, Romig, and Armstrong, 1988: 2–11). Further, in the emphasis on community outreach, capacity building, and partnerships, the approach actually may expand the impact of the juvenile justice system in exchange for less emphasis on traditional treatment service tasks.

Mission Statements and External Change

The second set of recommendations for using the Balanced Approach mission statement to bring about reform in community supervision practices concerns the external audience of the statement, the community. Externally, an important message of the Balanced Approach to the public is that juvenile probation (and juvenile justice generally) cannot be "all things to all people"; while juvenile justice is capable of meeting some objectives well (e.g., ensuring that youths pay restitution and make gains in measurable competencies), it cannot do everything (cure the psychological problems of every offender; reduce recidivism). The agency director must take action on this front as well to ensure that this and other messages of the Balanced Approach are delivered to the community. Equally important, managers must ensure that changes occur in the agency's responsiveness to community needs and, likewise, get community institutions to begin to recognize their responsibility for and some ownership of the delinquency problem.

Juvenile justice administrators often complain that they have few options in creatively addressing Balanced Approach outcomes. Managers frequently insist, for example, that competency development is difficult because of limited justice system influence on schools, employers, and most community agencies. Administrators are *right* in insisting that juvenile justice alone can't do much about helping youth develop a legitimate identity when, by virtue of being there, youth under court supervision are defined as "bad kids." Competency development requires creating new roles and opportunities for at-risk and delinquent youth in the world of work, education, and the community (Pearl, Grant, and Wenk, 1978).

Administrators are wrong, however, in assuming that they have no influence with these socializing institutions. Many educators and employers, for example, recognize their own self-interest in finding new ways to engage youth in productive activity that can lead to skill development, increases in learning, and general interest in education and conventional activities. Further, most can identify with the goals of accountability and public protection and will often be able to provide creative input and assistance in achieving these objectives. Those juvenile justice administrators who have been successful in operationalizing the Balanced Approach principles have in fact taken on new leadership and entrepreneurial roles in reaching out to businesses, educators, and directors of a range of agencies—not limited to youth service organizations (e.g., public works agencies, civic and conservation groups). By asking for their participation in new partnerships for youth development and community revitalization (Bazemore, 1991: 35–36), juvenile justice managers begin to play a capacity-building and educative role in local communities (Jenkins, 1992).

While relaying the initial message that juvenile justice cannot be the sole service provider for at-risk youth, managers can also affirm that they should not be *limited* to this role—(nor should youth, who can also be viewed as a community *resource,* be limited to the role of "service recipient"). This is not an appeal for managers to become cold, non-nurturing bureaucrats; rather the intent is to suggest that the Balanced Approach demands involvement of the "socializing institutions" (e.g., schools, work) and that this involvement demands that managers play a proactive role (cf., Radin and Benton, 1988: 29).

What real "clout" do agency managers have beyond the simply educative and collaborative roles suggested above? First, juvenile justice administrators often control large budgets that include contracts for services ranging from construction to drug treatment to food preparation. Through this "power of the purse" managers might, for example, require that treatment service providers adhere to performance-based objectives consistent with competency development or develop ways to engage youth they serve in decisionmaking and/or community service activities. Others have suggested that juvenile department directors could even require (or recommend) that food and maintenance service contractors agree to train and hire certain numbers of young offenders (Jenkins, 1992). Juvenile justice administrators could also negotiate agreements with school officials to support certain of their policies and initiatives in return for agreements to offer academic credit for juveniles on community supervision who successfully complete educative, conservation, service, or civic improvement projects.

Finally, managers need to be aware that operationalization and implementation of the Balanced Approach need not occur in an information and organizational vacuum. Assuming adherence to some basic principles and general clarity about what activities do *not* represent the Balanced Approach, it should be understood that exact implementation of Balanced Approach objectives should be largely a local decision based on the unique resources and needs of individual communities (Maloney, Romig, and Armstrong, 1988: 13–19). Thus, the first guideline is to turn to community leaders for ideas about how they see competency development, accountability, and public protection objectives being actualized given the local environment. Specifically, civic, public agency, and business leaders could be asked what work and service activities in the community might allow for youth involvement (Bazemore, 1991: 36–37).

Second, to develop activities intended to provide youth with a sense of competency and an understanding of accountability, adults need to ask young people themselves. In a real sense, youth are more qualified than we are to tell us what activities they and other young people will be likely to take seriously; simply providing this input to juvenile justice practitioners in planning activities may itself provide the first chance for many youth to demonstrate competency in an activity valued by others.

Finally, agency managers should be aware that delinquency theory and research can often be brought to bear in the sanctioning and supervision activities chosen to operationalize the Balanced Approach. Rather than arbitrarily grouping activities under the heading of competency development, for example, managers might consult control theory (e.g., Hirschi, 1968) and the positive youth development literature (e.g., Polk and Kobrin, 1972; Pearl, Grant, and Wenck, 1978) for guidance in choosing activities that might be expected to strengthen "bonds" to conventional peers and adults. Viewed as more than an academic exercise, application of theory and research can also aid managers in eliminating services and activities that may be expected to have little influence on Balanced Approach objectives and can help in linking each activity to an expected performance outcome.

In summary, the Balanced Approach articulates a clear and distinctive vision and a new mission for community supervision of juvenile offenders and for juvenile justice generally. While some have assumed that this conceptualization is merely a restatement or reaffirmation of the traditional treatment mission of the juvenile court or an attempt to merge this perspective with punitive sentiments of the past decade, I have argued that understanding and consistent operationalization of Balanced Approach objectives will clearly distinguish agencies utilizing this approach from those who continue in the traditional vein. At once comprehensive in scope and also restrictive in the specific objectives implied for juvenile probation, the Balanced Approach as a mission statement can also send a strong internal and external message about what should and should *not* be expected of community supervision. The challenge for managers wishing to use the Balanced Approach as a mission statement for juvenile justice reform is to ensure that adoption of the objectives of this statement are translated into action by rethinking internal priorities and the relationship between juvenile justice and community organizations.

Notes

1. Although the linkage is seldom explicitly stated, most of the ideas in the Balanced Approach are firmly grounded in criminological, criminal justice, and youth development theory. Competency development as a requirement for normal growth has been a major emphasis in the social-psychological literature generally and cuts across several theoretical traditions in criminology including strain, social control, social learning, and labeling theory. Developing a sense of competency is certainly linked, for example, to the "bond" to legitimate society and commitment to conformity posited as essential to avoidance of delinquent behavior in control or containment theory (Hirschi, 1968; Polk and Kobrin, 1972). Accountability, though addressing the needs of victims and restorative justice, demands that offenders make amends and also has strong implications for rehabilitation and reduced recidivism (Galaway and Hudson, 1990; Schneider, 1986). Recent discussions emphasize the need for "healing" between victims, offenders, and the community (Zehr, 1990). Finally, prescriptions for commu-

nity protection in the Balanced Approach are grounded in a body of literature in criminal justice spanning the past two decades which encourages development and use of graduated, intermediate community-based alternatives to use of incarceration which ensure public safety through careful structuring of offenders' time (Klein, 1991; Petersilia and Turner, 1990). Thus, unlike many new juvenile justice interventions of the past two decades—especially popular fad programs such as "Scared Straight" and boot camps—the Balanced Approach has both a theoretical and research basis (see Maloney, Romig, and Armstrong, 1988: 37–46, for a review of some of the research pertinent to the Balanced Approach).

2. This experience occurred over several years as co-director of OJJDP's Restitution Education, Specialized Training and Technical Assistance (RESTTA) program and later as curriculum development specialist with Florida's Department of Health and Rehabilitative Services through Florida Atlantic University.

3. The operational meaning of accountability, for example, is clarified in a number of works on restitution and restorative justice sanctions (Schneider, 1985; Bazemore, 1992), while competency development is distinguished from treatment as an active, productive enterprise in which offenders develop skills through productive meaningful work (Bazemore, 1991). Even a cursory reading of the Balanced Approach authors' discussion of community protection should make clear that their view of public safety envisions a wide variety of creative intermediate sanctions (and positive incentives) with confinement as a last resort (Maloney, Romig, and Armstrong, 1988: 28–35; see also Klein, 1991).

4. While a competency development focus, like the accountability objective, in no way prohibits provision of treatment or services as required, the assumption that all youth need to be "treated" (and failure to identify and build on existing competencies of young offenders) has done much to divert attention and resources away from developing alternative ways for young people to enhance and demonstrate existing competencies. Where traditional treatment models assume an offender whose problems and deficiencies demand only services and guidance, a competency development approach assumes that most offenders are capable of some healthy, productive activity given access to conventional roles and experiences.

5. It should be noted that Armstrong, Maloney, and Romig have made a good start in this direction in the two articles referenced here. Some of their statements need to be further clarified to avoid misunderstanding with additional emphasis placed on distinguishing Balanced Approach sanctioning and supervision practice from traditional community supervision of juvenile offenders.

References

Armstrong, T. L., Maloney, D., and Romig, D. (1990). The Balanced Approach in juvenile probation: Principles, issues and application. *Perspectives, 14*(1).

Barton, W. H., Streit, S., and Schwartz, I. (1991). *A blueprint for youth corrections.* Ann Arbor, MI: Center for the Study of Youth Policy, University of Michigan.

Bazemore, G. (1991). New concepts and alternative practice in community supervision of juvenile offenders: Rediscovering work experience and competency development. *Journal of Crime and Justice, 14*(1).

Bazemore, G. (1992). Beyond punishment, surveillance, and traditional treatment: Themes for a new mission in U.S. juvenile justice. In J. Hackler (Ed.), *Official responses to problem juveniles: Some international reflections.* Onati, Spain: International Institute for the Sociology of Law.

Feld, B. (1991). Transformed but unreformed: Juvenile court and the criminal court alternative. Minneapolis, MN: University of Minnesota Law School.

Galaway, B., and Hudson, J. (1990). *Criminal Justice, restitution and reconciliation.* Monsey, NY: Criminal Justice Press.

Hirschi, T. (1968). *Causes of delinquency.* Berkeley, CA: University of California Press.

Jenkins, R. (1992). *Why collaborate.* Paper presented at the 45th Annual Restitution Education, Specialized Training and Technical Assistance (RESTTA) Conference, Washington, DC.

Klein, A. (1991). Restitution and community work service: Promising core ingredients for effective intensive supervision programming. In T. L. Armstrong (Ed.), *Intensive interventions for high risk youths.* Monsey, NY: Criminal Justice Press.

Lab, S. (1988). *Crime prevention: Approaches, practices, and evaluations.* New York: Anderson.

Maloney, D., Romig, D., and Armstrong, T. L. (1988). Juvenile probation: The Balanced Approach. *Juvenile and Family Court Journal, 39*(3).

Palmer, T. (1975). Martinson revisited. *Journal of Research in Crime and Delinquency, 12.*

Pearl, A., Grant, D., and Wenk, E. (1978). *The value of youth.* Davis, CA: Dialogue Books.

Petersilia, J., and Turner, S. (1990). *Intensive supervision for high risk probationers.* Santa Monica, CA: Rand.

Polk, K., and Kobrin, S. (1972). *Delinquency prevention through youth development.* Washington, DC: U.S. Department of Health, Education, and Welfare.

Radin, B., and Benton, B. E. (1988). Linking policy and management in human services. *Public Administration Quarterly, 12*(1).

Zehr, H. (1990). *Changing lenses: A new focus for crime and justice.* Scottsdale, PA: Herald Press.

DISCUSSION QUESTIONS

1. How would you have answered the survey questions in the study by Cullen, Golden, and Cullen? Why?

2. If you were a judge or a probation officer in Florida, would the Florida statute provide you with sufficient guidance to know what to do in different types of juvenile offender cases? Why or why not?

3. Do you think the Standard for an individual program plan, presented in this section, conflicts with the Standard for offense-based sentencing ranges, as presented in Section V? Why or why not?

4. Do you agree with Bazemore's "balanced approach" to juvenile justice? Why or why not?

5. Do you think the balanced approach is really different from the traditional system? If accountability dictated that a youth spend one year in a training school, what do you think should happen if he or she had not sufficiently gained in competency development after that one year period? Which part of the equation should take precedence?

SECTION VIII

THE DEATH PENALTY FOR JUVENILES

Introduction

Legal provisions for executing juveniles have existed since colonial times. Under common law doctrine, the legal system the colonists brought with them from England, a child under the age of seven was considered incapable of criminal intent and could not be convicted or punished for a crime. But children age seven and older could receive the same punishment inflicted on adults—including death.

Although execution was relatively rare for children, it did occur. Before 1800, seven children were lawfully executed in America. The first execution of a juvenile took place in Massachusetts in 1642. Up to 1900, 95 children were executed. As of the 1990s, approximately 285 juveniles (that is, under the age of eighteen) have been lawfully executed in the United States. The youngest person to be executed in the United States was ten years old; however, the vast majority have been over the age of fourteen.

Until recently, the death penalty remained unchanged on the statute books of many states. Thirty-six states plus the federal government authorize the death penalty for adults. Of these thirty-seven jurisdictions, twenty-four authorized the death penalty for persons under the age of eighteen (thirteen states have the death penalty for adults only). Some states specifically set a minimum age for the imposition of the death penalty—for example, sixteen years of age. Some states simply implied by statute that the death penalty could be applicable to any child charged with a capital offense and transferred to adult court for prosecution. Some states, specifically nine, had no minimum restrictions in either their death penalty statutes or their juvenile transfer statutes.

Executions of juveniles have been extremely rare over the past thirty years. But there has been renewed interest in this sanction for juveniles for a variety of related reasons. First, the death penalty fits well with society's desire to crack down on serious juvenile crime. In part, the death penalty can be considered consistent with the changing philosophy of juvenile justice—to hold youths responsible and accountable for their actions. It is also consistent with transferring juveniles to criminal court for prosecution and punishment as adults.

Yet there is great debate about whether juveniles should be executed at all. Of all other countries of the world that have the death penalty, the majority have set the age of eighteen as the minimum age for execution. The United Nations also adopted this position in 1976. And in the United States, the Model Penal Code recommended that children should not be executed.

Amnesty International, the London-based human rights group, condemned the state of Texas for the July 1, 1993, execution of a person for the murder he had committed when he was seventeen. Amnesty International's official statement said that the "United States stands almost alone in the world in still permitting the execution of juveniles under the age of eighteen at the time of the crime and is flouting international standards." According to the Amnesty International report, within the past decade, only five other countries—Bangladesh, Iran, Iraq, Nigeria, and Pakistan—have executed juvenile offenders.

In the first selection, Sandra Skovron, Joseph Scott, and Francis Cullen add to this debate by polling a sample of the American population. They describe their telephone survey of six hundred adults—three hundred in Cincinnati and three hundred in Columbus, Ohio—which provides empirical evidence of attitudes regarding the use of the death penalty for juvenile murderers.

In this survey, the specific question asked about the respondents' opinions of a death penalty statute for youths over fourteen years of age convicted of murder. The majority of respondents in each site were opposed to such a law. One must wonder, however, what the responses would have been if the respondents were asked their opinions of the death penalty for youths sixteen and above convicted of murder.

Despite strong feelings on both sides, the U.S. Supreme Court avoided the issue of executing juveniles for many years until recently.

Over the past decade or so, the Supreme Court has addressed this complex and controversial issue. Most of the litigation in this area revolves around the question of whether the execution of children violates the Eighth Amendment of the U.S. Constitution, which prohibits the imposition of cruel and unusual punishment.

One of the first important cases was *Eddings v. Oklahoma,* decided by the U.S. Supreme Court in 1982. The Court did not specifically rule in this case whether executing juveniles violated the Eighth Amendment, but it did talk about the nature of juvenile responsibility. The Court stated that children have a "special place" in the law, and this is evidenced by the fact that every state in the country has a separate juvenile court system. The court also expressed in *Eddings* that juveniles possess a lower level of maturity than adults: "Our [American] history is replete with laws and judicial recognitions that minors, especially in their earlier years, generally are less mature and responsible than adults." The Court also stated, "Even the normal sixteen-year-old customarily lacks the maturity of an adult." This language seems to imply that juveniles are inherently different from adults and should not necessarily receive the ultimate penalty.

But things seemed to change for the Supreme Court by 1989. The issue of maturity—and responsibility—of juveniles surfaced again in *Thompson v. Oklahoma,* excerpts of which are provided in the next selection. In January 1983, Charles Keene was murdered in Oklahoma. Four defendants were eventually found guilty and sentenced to death. One of the defendants was William Wayne Thompson, who was fifteen years old at the time. Thompson appealed, claiming that in light of his age, the capital sentence was cruel and unusual punishment. Oklahoma's Court of Criminal Appeals affirmed the conviction and the sentence, citing the Oklahoma transfer law that "once a minor is certified to stand trial as an adult, he may also, without violating the Constitution, be punished as an adult."

Thompson appealed that ruling to the U.S. Supreme Court. And in *Thompson v. Oklahoma,* decided in 1988, the Supreme Court held that the execution of a person who committed a crime at age fifteen violates the Eighth Amendment of the U.S. Constitution, which prohibits "cruel and unusual punishment."

This case is significant because, obviously, it prohibits the execution of persons under the age of sixteen at the time of the commission of the capital crime. But an issue was left unresolved. Would it be constitutionally permissible to execute juveniles sixteen and seventeen years of age? This question was addressed in *Stanford v. Kentucky,* excerpts of which are given in the next selection. In that case, a sixteen-year-old juvenile named Heath Wilkins murdered a twenty-six-year-old woman in a convenience store robbery. He was tried as an adult, convicted, and sentenced to die. He appealed. In 1989, the U.S. Supreme Court decided in *Stanford v. Kentucky* that executing sixteen and seventeen year olds did not violate the Eighth Amendment.

In the final selection, Steven Scott provides a legal analysis of the leading U.S. Supreme Court death penalty decisions for juvenile offenders. He tries to make a case that the Supreme Court was wrong in allowing the execution of sixteen and seventeen year olds. He uses a variety of arguments, from recent legislation, to a statistical analysis of jury decisions, to a comparison with the laws of other nations. He contends that there is a "national consensus opposed to capital punishment for children." And he argues that the United States should no longer use the ultimate penalty on juveniles.

30

The Death Penalty for Juveniles: An Assessment of Public Support

Sandra Evans Skovron, Joseph E. Scott, and Francis T. Cullen

Recently, the issue of the death penalty for juveniles has received considerable media and public attention.[1] The executions of Charles Rumbaugh in September 1985, Terry Roach in January 1986, and J. Kelly Pinkerton in May 1986 focused attention on the issue of executing criminals for murders they committed while under the age of eighteen. Rumbaugh's execution by the state of Texas was the first such execution in over twenty years. More recently, the death sentence imposed by the state of Indiana on Paula Cooper for a murder she committed at the age of fifteen focused international attention and condemnation on the American policy of permitting the death penalty to be applied to juveniles (Hackett, King, and Stanger, 1987).

Several trends are reflected in the re-emergence of executions for offenses committed while the offenders are juveniles. Generally, there has been a resurgence of capital punishment in the United States; executions of youthful offenders reflect this increased reliance on capital punishment and the increase in executions throughout the system. In addition, the trend toward harsher penalties for serious juvenile criminals and the increased tendency to transfer them to adult court where they are subject to adult

Source: *Crime and Delinquency*, 35(4) (1989): 546–561. Reprinted by permission of Sage Publications, Inc.

penalties have created a context conducive to the use of execution as a sanction for juvenile murderers.

Statutes in thirty-seven states provide for capital punishment. Eighteen of these states have established minimum ages for its imposition: Eleven state legislatures have set eighteen as the minimum age, while the remaining seven require the offender to be at least sixteen or seventeen. Nineteen other states have established no minimum age for execution (*Thompson v. Oklahoma*, 1988:2693–2696).[2] In jurisdictions permitting the execution of juvenile offenders, the death penalty may not be imposed by the juvenile courts. A youth must be waived to the jurisdiction of the adult court; then, if convicted, he or she may face the death penalty.

The United States has a long history of executions for crimes committed by persons under the age of eighteen. The first such execution occurred in the Massachusetts Bay Colony in 1642. Since that time, 281 juvenile offenders have been executed in thirty-six jurisdictions throughout the United States (Streib, 1986). As of January 1986, thirty-three inmates were on death row for crimes they committed while under the age of eighteen.

The juvenile death penalty is almost unique to the United States. All European countries and the vast majority of other nations prohibit it (Wilson, 1983:345). Amnesty International reports that this is the case even among totalitarian regimes. In 1976 the United Nations adopted a resolution providing that the minimum age for execution should be eighteen.[3]

A great deal of controversy exists over the juvenile death penalty within the United States. Not only has this penalty been rejected by such organizations as Amnesty International and the United Nations, but at its annual meeting in 1983, the American Bar Association adopted a resolution opposing it (Streib, 1983:614). The juvenile death penalty also was rejected in the Model Penal Code.[4]

Considerable research has been conducted on public support for the death penalty. Since 1966 such support has increased steadily in the United States (Vidmar and Ellsworth, 1974). Recent polls conducted by Gallup and by the National Opinion Research Center found that well over 70 percent of the American public favored capital punishment (*Public Opinion*, 1985:38). These findings were consistent with other recent surveys (Warr and Stafford, 1984:104).

In addition to assessing levels of support for capital punishment, researchers have shown a great deal of interest in understanding this support. They have examined the relationships between personality characteristics, such as conservatism and authoritarianism, and advocacy of the death penalty. Attempts have been made to explain support for the death penalty by examining the demographic, background, and occupational characteristics of individuals.[5] In addition, researchers have tried to explain changes in levels of support as results of changes in social conditions, such as increases in crime rates or in the risk or fear of criminal victimization (Rankin, 1979; Taylor, Scheppele, and Stinchcombe, 1979; Thomas and Foster, 1975; Vidmar, 1974).

The resurgence of the death penalty in this country may reflect the increasingly punitive attitudes of the public and the desire to get tough with serious offenders (Finckenauer, 1988). Indicators show that the public holds punitive attitudes: not only are there high levels of support for capital punishment as noted above, but polls reveal that a substantial majority of the population believes that the "courts are not harsh enough with criminals" (*Public Opinion*, 1982:36). It is risky to assume, however, that citizens embrace uniformly punitive views on crime policy. As Flanagan and Caulfield (1984: 41) observed, "The mood of the public in regard to correctional reform is diverse, multidimensional, and complex."

Further, we cannot assume that because citizens support capital punishment overwhelmingly, they also support its imposition on juvenile offenders. Despite the extensive research on public attitudes toward capital punishment, little effort has been made to examine attitudes toward the juvenile death penalty. The little research that exists seems to indicate that public opinion on the juvenile death penalty differs markedly from opinion on capital punishment in general. A 1965 Gallup Poll revealed that although 45 percent of the respondents favored the death penalty, only 23 percent favored it for those under twenty-one years of age (Vidmar and Ellsworth, 1982: 69). More recent research conducted in Nashville, Tennessee, and in Macon, Georgia, in 1985 indicated overwhelming public opposition to the execution of offenders for crimes they committed while under the age of eighteen. In both cities the juvenile death penalty was opposed by a margin of more than two to one (Southern Coalition on Jails and Prisons, 1986:1).

Obtaining more thorough information on public attitudes toward the juvenile death penalty is particularly important because the courts have evaluated public opinion in deciding death penalty cases.[6] For example, the Maryland Court of Appeals upheld the constitutionality of imposing the death penalty for offenses committed by persons under the age of eighteen (*Trimble v. Maryland*, 1984).[7] The court explicitly considered public opinion in its ruling, inferring the support of contemporary society for the juvenile death penalty from the existence of laws permitting the execution of murderers below the age of eighteen in 60 percent of the states at that time (Klein, 1985).

More recently, the United States Supreme Court held that the Eighth and Fourteenth Amendments prohibited the execution of William Wayne Thompson for a murder committed at the age of fifteen (*Thompson v. Oklahoma*, 1988). A plurality of four justices, relying on a review of legislative statutes and jury behavior, reached the conclusion that "the imposition of the death penalty on a fifteen-year-old offender is now generally abhorrent to the conscience of the community" (*Thompson v. Oklahoma*, p. 2697). As evidence for this conclusion, Justice Stevens stated:

> Most state legislatures have not expressly confronted the question of establishing a minimum age for imposition of the death penalty . . . the 18 states that have expressly established a minimum age in their death penalty statutes all . . . require that the defendant have attained at least the age of 16 at the time of the capital offense. (*Thompson v. Oklahoma*, pp. 2693–94, 2695–96).

Further, the plurality of justices stated that the last execution of an offender for a crime committed while under age sixteen occurred in 1948. Statistics on jury behavior revealed that from 1982 through 1986, only 5 out of 1,393 offenders sentenced to death were less than sixteen years old at the time of the offense (*Thompson v. Oklahoma*, p. 2697).

Justices O'Connor and Scalia questioned the data used by the plurality to reach the conclusion "that the Eighth and Fourteenth Amendments prohibit the execution of a person who was under sixteen years of age at the time of his or her offense" (*Thompson v. Oklahoma*, p. 2700). In a concurring opinion, Justice O'Connor stated that there is "danger in inferring a settled societal consensus from statistics like those relied on in this case" (*Thompson v. Oklahoma*, p. 2709).[8] Justice Scalia's dissent suggested that the plurality "utterly failed in justifying its holding on the basis of 'evolving standards of decency' evidenced by the work product of state legislatures and sentencing juries" (*Thompson v. Oklahoma*, p. 2718).

This article examines and provides a more thorough understanding of public attitudes on the death penalty for juvenile offenders. Rather than inferring citizens' attitudes from statutes and jury behavior, this study assessed public support for the juvenile death penalty through surveys of two communities. The study also examined the demographic and attitudinal characteristics of respondents related to support for this penalty.

Methodology

The data were collected through a telephone survey of adult residents of two major midwestern cities—Cincinnati and Columbus, Ohio—in February and March 1986. Random digit dialing was used; telephone prefixes were weighted as to the number assigned in order to give each household an equal opportunity to be included. Business and government agency numbers were eliminated from the sample. Six hundred adults were surveyed, three hundred in each of the two communities.

The demographic characteristics of the samples appear in table 30.1. The survey respondents from the two communities were comparable with regard to age, education, income, race, and sex. This finding was expected; census data showed that the cities were similar in population size and composition. The Columbus and Cincinnati respondents differed in religious affiliation, however, the Columbus sample had more Protestant respondents and fewer Catholic respondents than the Cincinnati sample. These figures reflected differences in the population compositions of the two cities; comparison of the characteristics of the two samples with data from the U.S. Census showed that the samples were comparable to the larger populations from which they were drawn (Bureau of the Census, 1983a, 1983b).

Table 30.1.   Demographic Characteristics of Respondents

	Cincinnati		Columbus	
	Percent	**Number**	**Percent**	**Number**
Age				
Under 30	28.0	84	35.0	105
30–44	36.3	109	32.3	97
45 and over	35.7	107	32.7	98
Education				
Some High School	14.4	43	9.4	27
High School Graduate	26.4	79	31.5	90
Some College	28.8	86	28.7	82
College Graduate	30.4	91	30.4	87
Income				
Under $20,000	30.4	77	32.2	84
$20,000–29,999	22.1	56	27.7	72
$30,000–49,999	32.8	83	25.4	66
$50,000 or more	14.6	37	14.6	14
Race				
White	85.0	250	87.2	258
Black	14.3	42	10.1	30
Other	0.7	2	2.7	8
Religious Affiliation				
Protestant	42.3	126	50.5	143
Jewish	3.7	11	2.8	8
Catholic	33.9	101	20.8	59
Other	16.1	48	20.8	59
None	4.0	12	4.9	14
Sex				
Male	47.3	142	50.0	150
Female	52.7	158	50.0	150

Respondents were contacted and told that the purpose of the survey was to determine public attitudes toward issues of current interest in their community. They were then asked a number of demographic questions, and questions regarding their attitudes toward a variety of criminal justice issues and policies. Among the latter questions was one assessing attitudes toward the death penalty for juvenile offenders. Information was also obtained on the respondents' support for the death penalty for adults.

Findings

Overall Level of Support for the Juvenile Death Penalty

To assess support for the imposition of the death penalty on juveniles, the following question was asked:

> Ohio presently has the death penalty for adults convicted of murder. Would you favor or oppose the state passing a law to allow the death penalty for juveniles over fourteen years of age convicted of murder?

This research is limited inasmuch as the survey included only one item concerning the juvenile death penalty. This question assessed attitudes toward the execution of offenders for capital offenses committed when they were over fourteen and under eighteen years of age. As the Supreme Court noted, however, in *Thompson v. Oklahoma*, public support may differ regarding the execution of older and younger juvenile murderers. The question excluded the youngest juveniles (under fourteen) from consideration. Even so, had it asked specifically about older youths (e.g., sixteen- or seventeen-year-old juveniles), different levels of support for and opposition to the juvenile death penalty might have been found.

The data reflecting the respondents' attitudes toward the juvenile death penalty appear in table 30.2. Public attitudes in the two cities were very similar. In Cincinnati, 25 percent of respondents favored passage of such legislation and 69 percent opposed it. In Columbus, 30 percent favored the juvenile death penalty and 65.3 percent opposed it. Overall, about two-thirds of the respondents were opposed to the passage of a law allowing the execution of juveniles over the age of fourteen who commit murder. This finding was similar to the results of previous research on public attitudes conducted in Georgia and Tennessee (Southern Coalition on Jails and Prisons, 1986:1).

Notably, the support found for the juvenile death penalty was considerably smaller than that generally found for the adult death penalty: as noted, recent opinion polls have indicated that well over 70 percent of the public favors capital punishment (*Public Opinion*, 1985:38). This research shed additional light on that issue. The survey included the following question:

Table 30.2.   Respondent Attitudes toward the Death Penalty for Juveniles. (Support of a State law allowing the death penalty for juveniles over the age of fourteen convicted of murder)

	Favor	**Oppose**	**Don't know**
Cincinnati	25.0%	69.0%	6.0%
	(75)	(207)	(18)
Columbus	30.0%	65.3%	4.7%
	(90)	(196)	(14)

If you were serving on a jury for a trial of an adult guilty of murder, would it be *extremely difficult, difficult, somewhat difficult,* or *not difficult at all* for you to vote to have the offender put to death?

In contrast to the findings with regard to the death penalty for juveniles, 50.3 percent of the Cincinnati sample and 47.8 percent of the Columbus sample said they would experience little or no difficulty in voting to impose the death penalty on an adult offender convicted of murder. Only 31.8 percent of Cincinnati residents and 28.5 percent of Columbus residents said they would find this task extremely difficult.[9]

Sources of Support for the Juvenile Death Penalty

Probit regression analysis of the relationship between respondents' demographic and attitudinal characteristics and support for the juvenile death penalty was conducted. Probit analysis was chosen because many of the assumptions of ordinary least–squares regression are violated when the dependent variable is dichotomous.[10] The independent variables included in the analysis appear in table 30.3. Two scales, a rehabilitation effectiveness scale and a rehabilitation policy scale, were constructed from the rehabilitation items on the survey and were included as independent variables. A principal component factor analysis with varimax rotation of the rehabilitation items revealed two dimensions of attitudes toward rehabilitation.[11] The rehabilitation effectiveness scale had a coefficient of reliability of alpha equal to .711 for the Cincinnati sample and .773 for the Columbus sample. Scale scores ranged from 4 to 16; higher scores indicated greater belief in the efficacy of rehabilitation. The coefficient of reliability of alpha for the rehabilitation policy scale was .792 for the Cincinnati sample and .751 for the Columbus sample. Scale scores ranged from three to nine; higher scores indicated greater support for rehabilitation as penal policy.

The results of the probit analysis appear in table 30.4. An examination of the "pseudo R^2s" (Aldrich and Nelson, 1984:57) revealed that the probit models, predicting support for the juvenile death penalty, were weak.

Table 30.3. Description of Variables

Variable	Description
Age (in years)	Cincinnati: x = 41.96, sd = 17.00; Columbus: x = 39.20, sd = 16.88
Education	0-8 years = 1; 9-11 years = 2; 12 years = 3; 13-15 years = 4; 16 years = 5; 17+ years = 6. Cincinnati: x = 3.83, sd = 1.33; Columbus: x = 3.85, sd = 1.18
Income	$10,000 = 1; $10,000–19,999 = 2; $20,000–29,999 = 3; $30,000–39,999 = 4; $40,000–49,999 = 5; $50,000 or more = 6. Cincinnati: x = 3.47, sd = 1.54; Columbus: x = 3.34, sd = 1.54
Race	Nonwhite = 0; White = 1. Cincinnati: x = 0.85, sd = 0.35; Columbus: x = 0.87, sd = 0.33
Religiosity	Very religious = 1; Somewhat religious = 2; Not very religious = 3; Not religious at all = 4. Cincinnati: x = 1.91, sd = 0.68; Columbus: x = 2.14, sd = 0.82
Sex	Female = 0; Male = 1. Cincinnati: x = 0.47, sd = 0.50; Columbus: x = 0.50, sd = 0.50
Effectiveness of Rehabilitation	Ranges from 4 to 16; higher scores indicate greater belief in effectiveness. Cincinnati: x = 10.86, sd = 2.00; Columbus: x = 10.65, sd = 2.35
Support of Rehabilitation as Penal Policy	Ranges from 3 to 9; higher scores indicate greater support. Cincinnati: x = 7.53, sd = 1.19; Columbus: x = 7.46, sd = 1.31

Examination of the coefficients and the standard errors for the statistically significant variables revealed no substantial effects. For the Cincinnati sample, only one statistically significant relationship was found—an inverse relationship between belief in the effectiveness of rehabilitation programs and support for the juvenile death penalty. Respondents who expressed greater belief in the effectiveness of rehabilitation programs were less likely to support the juvenile death penalty. The same relationship was found for the Columbus sample, but additional statistically significant relationships also were found for that sample. Citizens who were more supportive of rehabilitation as penal policy and those who rated themselves as less religious were less supportive of the juvenile death penalty. In addition, male respondents in the Columbus sample were more likely than female respondents to support the juvenile death penalty.

Like previous research on attitudes toward criminal justice issues (Langworthy and Whitehead, 1986; Skovron, Scott, and Cullen, 1988), this research found that attitudinal variables were related more significantly and more consistently to public attitudes toward the juvenile death penalty than were demographic variables. Among the demographic characteristics analyzed, only gender was related significantly to attitudes toward the death penalty for juveniles, and this relationship was significant only for the Columbus sample. Attitudes toward the juvenile death penalty were related significantly to respondents' religiosity, philosophies of punishment, and attitudes toward

Table 30.4.   Probit Parameter Estimates for Predictions of Support for the Juvenile Death Penalty

	Cincinnati	Columbus
Constant	−0.365	1.751*
	(.662)[a]	(.638)
Age	0.001	−0.005
	(.005)	(.005)
Education	0.100	−0.109
	(.066)	(.073)
Income	0.015	−0.003
	(.048)	(.050)
Race	0.279	−0.104
	(.194)	(.196)
Sex	0.126	0.623*
	(.168)	(.171)
Religiosity	0.135	−0.231*
	(.123)	(.102)
Effectiveness of Rehabilitation	−0.101*	−0.088*
	(.043)	(.035)
Support of Rehabilitation as Penal Policy	−0.042	−0.071*
	(.032)	(.031)
Pseudo R^{2b}	.075**	.102**

a. The numbers in parentheses are the standard errors of the coefficients.
b. The Pseudo R^2 is calculated according to the formula presented by Aldrich and Nelson (1984, p. 57); Pseudo $R^2 = C + (N + C)$, where C = chi-square and N = sample size.
  *Significant at $p < .05$.
  ** Chi-square significant at $p < .05$.

the effectiveness of rehabilitation programs. Citizens who rated themselves as more religious, who favored more punitive policies, and who thought that rehabilitation programs were ineffective were more likely to support the juvenile death penalty than those who were less religious, who favored rehabilitation programs for offenders, and who believed in the effectiveness of those programs. These findings were consistent with previous death penalty research results (Warr and Stafford, 1984).

Discussion

Consistent with the opinion expressed in *Thompson v. Oklahoma*, the majority of the citizens surveyed disapproved of the execution of young juvenile offenders. Public opposition to the death penalty for young offenders may reflect many of the same beliefs that led to creation of the juvenile justice system. As Empey (1982) has noted, the creation of the juvenile court was linked to the rise of the belief that children possess distinct differences from adults and therefore should be treated differently by the justice system. By the turn of the twentieth century, children were viewed as less responsible, more malleable, and more amenable to rehabilitation than adults (Platt, 1969).

Despite recent trends toward increased punitiveness in the juvenile justice system, it appears that citizens have not totally relinquished these beliefs. When Cullen, Golden, and Cullen (1983) surveyed a sample of the Illinois public and various groups of Illinois criminal justice practitioners and policymakers, they found a high degree of support for juvenile rehabilitation; over 80 percent of those surveyed stated that it would be "irresponsible to stop trying to rehabilitate juveniles." Further, that study revealed higher levels of support and optimism regarding rehabilitation of juvenile offenders than adult offenders. The authors concluded that the research revealed "attitudes supportive of the 'differentness' of the juvenile offender, a differentness which offers optimistic possibilities for salvation and rehabilitation" (Cullen et al., 1983:7).

More recent research, based on the same survey data used in the present study, further corroborated the findings of high levels of public support for rehabilitation of juvenile criminals and greater belief in the effectiveness of rehabilitation programs for juveniles than for adults. The survey of adult residents of Cincinnati and Columbus, Ohio revealed that 85 percent of the Cincinnati sample and 74 percent of the Columbus sample thought that rehabilitation programs were "very helpful" or "helpful" for juvenile offenders. In comparison, only 60 percent of the Cincinnati residents and 57 percent of the Columbus residents thought that rehabilitation programs were similarly helpful for adults (Cullen et al., forthcoming).

Similar views were expressed by the plurality in *Thompson v. Oklahoma* in ruling unconstitutional the imposition of the death penalty on a youth who was fifteen at the time of the crime. Although the Court did not specifically address rehabilitation as a correctional goal, Justice Stevens's comments appeared to support rehabilitation as the focus of corrections for juvenile murderers:

> This Court has already endorsed the proposition that less culpability should attach to a crime committed by a juvenile than to a comparable crime committed by an adult since inexperience, less education, and less intelligence make the teenager less able to evaluate the consequences of his or her conduct while at the same time he or she is much more apt to be motivated by mere emotion or peer pressure than is an adult. Given this lesser culpability, as well as the teenager's capacity for growth and society's fiduciary obligations to its children, the retributive purpose underlying the death penalty is simply inapplicable to the execution of a 15 year old offender. (*Thompson v. Oklahoma*, p. 2688)

Only four justices held that imposition of the death penalty on offenders fifteen years of age and younger is unconstitutional. A fifth justice—O'Connor—held that the imposition of this sanction is unconstitutional if the legislature has not specifically established a minimum age for execution. Three additional justices—Scalia, Rehnquist, and White—dissented from the decision of the Court. Justice Kennedy was appointed to the Court subsequent to the consideration of this case and did not participate in the decision.[12]

The research described above was limited inasmuch as it relied on only one item assessing support for the juvenile death penalty; that item assessed attitudes only toward the execution of persons fourteen years of age and older. More research on public attitudes toward capital punishment for juveniles is needed. Such research is particularly relevant because the Supreme Court relies on an assessment of "evolving standards of decency that mark the progress of a maturing society" in determining whether the Eighth Amendment's prohibition against cruel and unusual punishment applies (*Trop v. Dulles*, 1958:101). As noted above, the Supreme Court reviews relevant state statutes to assess the will of the public. Research demonstrates, however, that legislators and policymakers have overestimated the degree to which citizens favor harsh policies (Gottfredson and Taylor, 1983, Riley and Rose, 1980). Although seven states have established minimum ages for execution below the age of eighteen, this fact may not be a valid measure of public support for the juvenile death penalty in these states.

Future research should be directed toward attaining greater understanding of societal attitudes toward the juvenile death penalty. It seems reasonable to anticipate greater support for executing older juvenile offenders than younger ones. Still, important questions remain: At what point does a majority of the public cease to consider age a mitigating factor in capital cases? To what extent does age weigh against other elements in a capital offense (e.g., victim's race, aggravating conditions) in determining public attitudes? How do citizens view the punishment of defendants who commit murders while juveniles, but are tried and convicted after they pass into adulthood? Direct assessments of public opinion on the execution of juvenile offenders would provide valuable information for assessing societal attitudes toward acceptable sanctions.

Notes

1. Throughout this article, "the juvenile death penalty" refers to the policy of permitting the execution of offenders for murders they committed while under the age of 18. The executions themselves may take place after the offenders turn 18.

2. The Bureau of Justice Statistics (1988) reported that at the end of 1987, 15 states specified minimum ages for executions below 18, and 9 of these states provided for minimum ages below 16. However, the Bureau failed to distinguish between states that specify minimum ages for execution in capital punishment statutes and those that determine minimum age by statutory provisions setting the age at which juveniles may be transferred to criminal court to be tried as adults.

3. International Covenant on Civil and Political Rights, art. 6.5, G.A. Res. 2200A, 21 U.N. GAOR Supp. (No. 16) at 49, 52, U.N. Doc. A/63/6 (1976) (entered into force March 23, 1976).

4. Model Penal Code 210.6(1)(d) (1980).

5. For more extensive reviews, see Finckenauer (1988), Gelles and Straus (1975), Vidmar and Ellsworth (1982), and Vidmar and Miller (1980).

6. See *Furman v. Georgia* (1972) 408 U.S. 238, *Woodson v. North Carolina* (1976) 428 U.S. 280, *Gregg v. Georgia* (1976) 428 U.S. 153, and *Coker v. Georgia* (1977) 433 U.S. 584 for examples of the use of information on public attitudes in death penalty cases.

7. See Klein (1985) for a more thorough discussion of this case.

8. Justice O'Connor concurred in the judgment of the Court, stating that the "petitioner and others who were below the age of 16 at the time of their offense may not be executed under the authority of a capital punishment statute that specifies no minimum age at which the commission of capital crime can lead to the offender's execution" (*Thompson v. Oklahoma*, 1988, p. 2711).

9. It also should be noted that when respondents were asked to rate the difficulty they would experience in recommending the death penalty, substantial percentages (49.3% of Cincinnati residents and 52.2% of Columbus residents) said that they would experience difficulty in recommending that penalty. This finding may indicate that when respondents are asked about behavioral aspects of support for the death penalty, different results are found than when they are asked only whether they favor or oppose a policy.

10. See Aldrich and Nelson (1984) for a discussion of the violated assumptions and their impacts.

11. Attitudes toward the effectiveness of rehabilitation were measured by the following items:

Do you think that rehabilitation programs are very helpful ($=4$), helpful ($=3$), slightly helpful ($=2$), or not helpful at all ($=1$), for violent offenders?

Do you think that rehabilitation programs are very helpful ($=4$), helpful ($=3$), slightly helpful ($=2$), or not helpful at all ($=1$), for nonviolent offenders?

Do you think that rehabilitation programs are very helpful ($=4$), helpful ($=3$), slightly helpful ($=2$), or not helpful at all ($=1$), for juvenile offenders?

Do you think that rehabilitation programs are very helpful ($=4$), helpful ($=3$), slightly helpful ($=2$), or not helpful at all ($=1$), for adult offenders?

Attitudes toward support for rehabilitation as penal policy were assessed by the following items:

Do you favor ($=2$) or oppose ($=1$) expanding the rehabilitation programs now being undertaken in prison?

Which of the following is the best policy for dealing with inmates in your opinion?
• Psychological counseling ($=4$)
• Educational and vocational training ($=3$)
• Keeping inmates locked in their cells ($=2$)
• Hard labor ($=1$)

What do you think should be the main emphasis in most prisons?
• Trying to rehabilitate the individual so that he might return to society as a productive citizen ($=3$)
• Protecting society from future crimes the offender might commit ($=2$)
• Punishing the individual convicted of a crime ($=1$)

The factor loadings for the Columbus sample appear below

Variable	Factor 1	Factor 2
Expand rehabilitation programs	$-.040$	.654
Best policy for prisoners	$-.067$	.683
Main emphasis for prisoners	.108	.615
Effective for violent offenders	.610	$-.023$
Effective for nonviolent offenders	.716	.019
Effective for juvenile offenders	.694	$-.017$
Effective for adult offenders	.750	.021

The inclusion of two scales to measure different aspects of attitudes toward rehabilitation in the probit regression could have led to problems of multicollinearity. Multicollinearity was not a problem, however, because the correlation between the scales was only .381 for the Cincinnati sample and .324 for the Columbus sample.

12. While this article was in press, the Court ruled (June 26, 1989) by 5–4 votes in two separate cases—*Wilkins v. Missouri* and *Stanford v. Kentucky*—that it was constitutional to execute convicted murderers who were 16 or 17 when they committed the crime.

Cases

Cokcr v. Georgia. (1977) 433 U.S. 584
Furman v. Georgia. (1972) 408 U.S. 238
Gregg v. Georgia. (1976) 428 U.S. 153
Thompson v. Oklahoma. (1988) 108 S. Ct. 2687
Trimble v. Maryland. (1984) 300 Md. 387, 478 A.2d 1143
Trop v. Dulles. (1958) 356 U.S. 86
Woodson v. North Carolina. (1976) 428 U.S. 280

References

Aldrich, John H. and Forrest D. Nelson, 1984. *Linear Probability, Logit, and Probit Models*, Beverly Hills: Sage.

Bureau of the Census, 1983a. *1980 Census of Population and Housing: Cincinnati, Ohio-Ky.-Ind. Standard Metropolitan Statistical Area*. Washington, DC: U.S. Government Printing Office.

———— 1983b. *1980 Census of Population and Housing: Columbus, Ohio Standard Metropolitan Area*. Washington, DC: U.S. Government Printing Office.

Bureau of Justice Statistics, 1988. *Capital Punishment 1987*. Washington, DC: U.S. Department of Justice.

Cullen, Francis T., Kathryn M. Golden, and John B. Cullen, 1983. "Is Child Saving Dead? Attitudes Toward Juvenile Rehabilitation in Illinois." *Journal of Criminal Justice* 11: 1–13.

Cullen, Francis T., Sandra Evans Skovron, Joseph E. Scott, and Velmer S. Burton, Forthcoming. "Public Support for Correctional Treatment: The Tenacity of Rehabilitative Ideology." *Criminal Justice and Behavior*.

Empey, LaMar T. 1982. *American Delinquency: Its Meaning and Construction*. Homewood, IL: Dorsey.

Finckenauer, James O. 1988. "Public Support for the Death Penalty: Retribution as Just Desserts or Retribution as Revenge?" *Justice Quarterly* 5: 81–100.

Flanagan, Timothy J. and Susan L. Caulfield, 1984. "Public Opinion and Prison Policy: A Review." *The Prison Journal* 64: 31–46.

Gelles, Richard J. and Murray A. Straus, 1975. "Family Experience and Public Support of the Death Penalty." *American Journal of Orthopsychiatry* 45: 596–613.

Gottfredson, Stephen D. and Ralph B. Taylor, 1983. *The Correctional Crisis: Prison Populations and Public Policy*. Washington, DC: U.S. Department of Justice.

Hackett, George, Patricia King, and Theodore Stanger, 1987. "Indiana Killer, Italian Martyr: A Death Row Cause." *Newsweek*, Sept. 21, 37.

Just, Rona L. 1984. "Executing Youthful Offenders: The Unanswered Question in Eddings v. Oklahoma." *Fordham Urban Law Journal* 13: 471–510.

Klein, Robert Anthony, 1985. "Juvenile Criminals and the Death Penalty: Resurrection of the Question Left Unanswered in Eddings v. Oklahoma." *New England Journal of Criminal and Civil Confinement* 11: 437–87.

Langworthy, Robert H. and John T. Whitehead, 1986. "Liberalism and Fear as Explanations of Punitiveness." *Criminology* 24: 575–91.

Platt, Anthony, 1970. *The Child Savers*. Chicago: University of Chicago Press.

Public Opinion, 1982. "Opinion Roundup: Crime—The Public Gets Tough." *Public Opinion* 5: 36.

_____ 1985. "Opinion Roundup: Death Penalty Considered." *Public Opinion* 8: 38–39.

Rankin, Joseph, 1979. "Changing Attitudes Toward Capital Punishment." *Social Forces* 58: 194–211.

Riley, Pamela Johnson and Vicki McNickle Rose, 1980. "Public and Elite Opinion Concerning Correctional Reform: Implications for Social Policy." *Journal of Criminal Justice* 8: 345–56.

Skovron, Sandra Evans, Joseph E. Scott, and Francis T. Cullen, 1988. "Prison Crowding: Public Attitudes Toward Strategies of Population Control." *Journal of Research in Crime and Delinquency* 25: 150–69.

Southern Coalition on Jails and Prisons, 1986. "SCJP Poll Results: Don't Execute Juveniles." *Southern Coalition Report on Jails & Prisons* 13: 1.

Streib, Victor L., 1983. "Death Penalty for Children: The American Experience with Capital Punishment for Crimes Committed while under Age Eighteen." *Oklahoma Law Review* 36: 613–41.

_____ 1986. "Persons Executed for Crimes Committed while under Age Eighteen." *Augustus* 9: 20–25.

Taylor, Douglas C., Kim Lane Scheppele, and Arthur L. Stinchcombe, 1979. "Salience of Crime and Support for Harsher Criminal Sanctions." *Social Problems* 26: 413–24.

Thomas, Charles W. and Samuel C. Foster, 1975. "A Sociological Perspective on Public Support for Capital Punishment." *American Journal of Orthopsychiatry* 45: 641–57.

Tyler, Tom R. and Renee Weber, 1982. "Support for the Death Penalty: Instrumental Response to Crime, or Symbolic Attitude?" *Law and Society Review* 17: 21–45.

Vidmar, Neil, 1974. "Retributive and Utilitarian Motives and other Correlates of Canadian Attitudes toward the Death Penalty." *Canadian Psychologist* 15: 337–56.

Vidmar, Neil and Phoebe C. Ellsworth, 1974. "Public Opinion and the Death Penalty." *Stanford Law Review* 26: 1245–70.

_____ 1982. "Research on Attitudes toward Capital Punishment." Pp. 68–92 in *The Death Penalty in America*, edited by H.A. Bedau, Oxford: Oxford University Press.

Vidmar, Neil and Dale T. Miller, 1980. "Social Psychological Processes Underlying Attitudes toward Legal Punishment." *Law and Society Review* 14: 565–602.

Warr, Mark and Mark Stafford, 1984. "Public Goals of Punishment and Support for the Death Penalty." *Journal of Research in Crime and Delinquency* 21: 95–111.

Wilson, William, 1983. "Juvenile Offenders and the Electric Chair: Cruel and Unusual Punishment or Firm Discipline for the Hopelessly Delinquent?" *University of Florida Law Review* 35: 344–71.

31

Excerpts from
Thompson v. Oklahoma:
Decided June 29, 1988

Justice STEVENS announced the judgment of the Court and delivered an opinion in which Justice BRENNAN, Justice MARSHALL, and Justice BLACKMUN join.

Petitioner was convicted of first-degree murder and sentenced to death. The principal question presented is whether the execution of that sentence would violate the constitutional prohibition against the infliction of "cruel and unusual punishments" because petitioner was only fifteen years old at the time of his offense.

I

Because there is no claim that the punishment would be excessive if the crime had been committed by an adult, only a brief statement of facts is necessary. In concert with three older persons, petitioner actively participated in the brutal murder of his former brother-in-law in the early morning hours of January 23, 1983. The evidence disclosed that the victim had been shot twice, and that his throat, chest, and abdomen had been cut. He also had multiple bruises and a broken leg. His body had been chained to a concrete block and thrown into a river where it remained for almost four weeks. Each of the four participants was tried separately and each was sentenced to death.

Source: *Thompson v. Oklahoma*, 108 S.CT. 2687 (1988).

Because petitioner was a "child" as a matter of Oklahoma law, the District Attorney filed a statutory petition, see Okla. Stat., Tit. 10, § 1112(b) (1981), seeking an order finding "that said child is competent and had the mental capacity to know and appreciate the wrongfulness of his [conduct]." After a hearing, the trial court concluded "that there are virtually no *reasonable* prospects for rehabilitation of William Wayne Thompson within the juvenile system and that William Wayne Thompson should be held accountable for his acts as if he were an adult and should be certified to stand trial as an adult." *Id.*, at 8 (emphasis in original).

At the guilt phase of petitioner's trial, the prosecutor introduced three color photographs showing the condition of the victim's body when it was removed from the river. Although the Court of Criminal Appeals held that the use of two of those photographs was error, it concluded that the error was harmless because the evidence of petitioner's guilt was so convincing. However, the prosecutor had also used the photographs in his closing argument during the penalty phase. The Court of Criminal Appeals did not consider whether this display was proper.

At the penalty phase of the trial, the prosecutor asked the jury to find two aggravating circumstances: that the murder was especially heinous, atrocious, or cruel; and that there was a probability that the defendant would commit criminal acts of violence that would constitute a continuing threat to society. The jury found the first, but not the second, and fixed petitioner's punishment at death.

The Court of Criminal Appeals affirmed the conviction and sentence, 724 P.2d 780 (1986), citing its earlier opinion in *Eddings v. State*, 616 P.2d 1159 (1980), rev'd on other grounds, 455 U.S. 104, 102 S.Ct. 869, 71 L.Ed.2d 1 (1982), for the proposition that "once a minor is certified to stand trial as an adult, he may also, without violating the Constitution, be punished as an adult." 724 P.2d, at 784. We granted certiorari to consider whether a sentence of death is cruel and unusual punishment for a crime committed by a fifteen-year-old child, as well as whether photographic evidence that a state court deems erroneously admitted but harmless at the guilt phase nevertheless violates a capital defendant's constitutional rights by virtue of its being considered at the penalty phase. 479 U.S. 1084, 107 S.Ct. 1284, 94 L.Ed.2d 143 (1987).

II

The authors of the Eighth Amendment drafted a categorical prohibition against the infliction of cruel and unusual punishments, but they made no attempt to define the contours of that category. They delegated that task to future generations of judges who have been guided by the "evolving standards of decency that mark the progress of a maturing society." *Trop v. Dulles*, 356 U.S. 86, 101, 78 S.CT. 590, 598, 2 L.Ed.2d 630 (1958) (plurality opinion) (Warren,

C.J.). In performing that task the Court has reviewed the work product of state legislatures and sentencing juries, and has carefully considered the reasons why a civilized society may accept or reject the death penalty in certain types of cases. Thus, in confronting the question whether the youth of the defendant— more specifically, the fact that he was less than sixteen years old at the time of his offense—is a sufficient reason for denying the State the power to sentence him to death, we first review relevant legislative enactments, then refer to jury determinations, and finally explain why these indicators of contemporary standards of decency confirm our judgment that such a young person is not capable of acting with the degree of culpability that can justify the ultimate penalty.

III

Justice Powell has repeatedly reminded us of the importance of "the experience of mankind, as well as the long history of our law, recognizing that there *are* differences which must be accommodated in determining the rights and duties of children as compared with those of adults. Examples of this distinction abound in our law: in contracts, in torts, in criminal law and procedure, in criminal sanctions and rehabilitation, and in the right to vote and to hold office." *Goss v. Lopez*, 419 U.S. 565, 590–591, 95 S.Ct. 729, 744, 42 L.Ed.2d 725 (1975) (dissenting opinion). Oklahoma recognizes this basic distinction in a number of its statutes. Thus, a minor is not eligible to vote, to sit on a jury, to marry without parental consent, or to purchase alcohol or cigarettes. Like all other States, Oklahoma has developed a juvenile justice system in which most offenders under the age of eighteen are not held criminally responsible. Its statutes do provide, however, that a sixteen- or seventeen-year-old charged with murder and other serious felonies shall be considered an adult. Other than the special certification procedure that was used to authorize petitioner's trial in this case "as an adult," apparently there are no Oklahoma statutes, either civil or criminal, that treat a person under sixteen years of age as anything but a "child."

The line between childhood and adulthood is drawn in different ways by various States. There is, however, complete or near unanimity among all fifty States and the District of Columbia in treating a person under sixteen as a minor for several important purposes. In no State may a fifteen-year-old vote or serve on a jury. Further, in all but one State a fifteen-year-old may not drive without parental consent, and in all but four States a fifteen-year-old may not marry without parental consent. Additionally, in those States that have legislated on the subject, no one under age sixteen may purchase pornographic materials (fifty States), and in most States that have some form of legalized gambling, minors are not permitted to participate without parental consent (forty-two States). Most relevant, however, is the fact that all States have enacted legislation designating the maximum age for juvenile court jurisdiction at no less than sixteen. All of this legislation is consistent with the experience of mankind, as well as the long history of our law, that the normal fifteen-year-old is not prepared to assume the full responsibilities of an adult.

Most state legislatures have not expressly confronted the question of establishing a minimum age for imposition of the death penalty. In fourteen States, capital punishment is not authorized at all, and in nineteen others capital punishment is authorized but no minimum age is expressly stated in the death penalty statute. One might argue on the basis of this body of legislation that there is no chronological age at which the imposition of the death penalty is unconstitutional and that our current standards of decency would still tolerate the execution of ten-year-old children. We think it self-evident that such an argument is unacceptable; indeed, no such argument has been advanced in this case. If, therefore, we accept the premise that some offenders are simply too young to be put to death, it is reasonable to put this group of statutes to one side because they do not focus on the question of where the chronological age line should be drawn. When we confine our attention to the eighteen States that have expressly established a minimum age in their death-penalty statutes, we find that all of them require that the defendant have attained at least the age of sixteen at the time of the capital offense.

The conclusion that it would offend civilized standards of decency to execute a person who was less than sixteen years old at the time of his or her offense is consistent with the views that have been expressed by respected professional organizations, by other nations that share our Anglo-American heritage, and by the leading members of the Western European community. Thus, the American Bar Association and the American Law Institute have formally expressed their opposition to the death penalty for juveniles. Although the death penalty has not been entirely abolished in the United Kingdom or New Zealand (it has been abolished in Australia, except in the State of New South Wales, where it is available for treason and piracy), in neither of those countries may a juvenile be executed. The death penalty has been abolished in West Germany, France, Portugal, The Netherlands, and all of the Scandinavian countries, and is available only for exceptional crimes such as treason in Canada, Italy, Spain, and Switzerland. Juvenile executions are also prohibited in the Soviet Union.

IV

The second societal factor the Court has examined in determining the acceptability of capital punishment to the American sensibility is the behavior of juries. In fact, the infrequent and haphazard handing out of death sentences by capital juries was a prime factor underlying our judgment in *Furman v. Georgia*, 408 U.S. 238, 92 S.Ct. 2726, 33 L.Ed.2d 346 (1972), that the death penalty, as then administered in unguided fashion, was unconstitutional.

While it is not known precisely how many persons have been executed during the twentieth century for crimes committed under the age of sixteen, a scholar has recently compiled a table revealing this number to be between eighteen and twenty. All of these occurred during the first half of the century, with the last such execution taking place apparently in 1948. In the following year this Court observed that this "whole country has traveled far from the period in which the death sentence was an automatic and commonplace result of convictions. . . ." *Williams v. New York*, 337 U.S. 241, 247, 69 S.Ct. 1079, 1083, 93 L.Ed. 1337 (1949). The road we have traveled during the past four decades—in which thousands of juries have tried murder cases— leads to the unambiguous conclusion that the imposition of the death penalty on a fifteen-year-old offender is now generally abhorrent to the conscience of the community.

Department of Justice statistics indicate that during the years 1982 through 1986 an average of over 16,000 persons were arrested for willful criminal homicide (murder and non-negligent manslaughter) each year. Of that group of 82,094 persons, 1,393 were sentenced to death. Only five of them, including the petitioner in this case, were less than sixteen years old at the time of the offense. Statistics of this kind can, of course, be interpreted in different ways, but they do suggest that these five young offenders have received sentences that are "cruel and unusual in the same way that being struck by lightning is cruel and unusual." *Furman v. Georgia*, 408 U.S., at 309, 92 S.Ct. at 2762 (Stewart, J., concurring).

V

"Although the judgments of legislatures, juries, and prosecutors weigh heavily in the balance, it is for us ultimately to judge whether the Eighth Amendment permits imposition of the death penalty" on one such as petitioner who committed a heinous murder when he was only fifteen years old. *Enmund v. Florida*, 458 U.S. 782, 797, 102 S.Ct. 3368, 3376, 73 L.Ed.2d 1140 (1982). In making that judgment, we first ask whether the juvenile's culpability should be measured by the same standards as that of an adult, and then consider whether the application of the death penalty to this class of offenders "measurably contributes" to the social purposes that are served by the death penalty. *Id.*, at 798, 102 S.Ct., at 3377.

It is generally agreed "that punishment should be directly related to the personal culpability of the criminal defendant." *California v. Brown*, 479 U.S. 538, 545, 107 S.Ct. 837, 841, 93 L.Ed.2d 934 (1987) (O'CONNOR, J., concurring). There is also broad agreement on the proposition that adolescents as a class are less mature and responsible than adults. We stressed this difference in explaining the importance of treating the defendant's youth as a mitigating factor in capital cases:

> But youth is more than a chronological fact. It is a time and condition of life when a person may be most susceptible to influence and to psychological damage. Our history is replete with laws and judicial recognition that minors, especially in their earlier years, generally are less mature and responsible than adults. Particularly 'during the formative years of childhood and adolescence, minors often lack the experience, perspective, and judgment' expected of adults. *Bellotti v. Baird*, 443 U.S. 622, 635 [99 S.Ct. 3035, 3043, 61 L.Ed.2d 797] (1979). *Eddings v. Oklahoma*, 455 U.S. 104, 115–116, 102 S.Ct. 869, 877, 71 L.Ed.2d 1 (1982) (footnotes omitted).

To add further emphasis to the special mitigating force of youth, Justice Powell quoted the following passage from the 1978 Report of the Twentieth Century Fund Task Force on Sentencing Policy Toward Young Offenders:

> [A]dolescents, particularly in the early and middle teen years, are more vulnerable, more impulsive, and less self-disciplined than adults. Crimes committed by youths may be just as harmful to victims as those committed by older persons, but they deserve less punishment because adolescents may have less capacity to control their conduct and to think in long-range terms than adults. Moreover, youth crime as such is not exclusively the offender's fault; offenses by the young also represent a failure of family, school, and the social system, which share responsibility for the development of America's youth. 455 U.S. at 115, n. 11, 102 S.Ct. 877, n. 11.

Thus, the Court has already endorsed the proposition that less culpability should attach to a crime committed by a juvenile than to a comparable crime committed by an adult. The basis for this conclusion is too obvious to require extended explanation. Inexperience, less education, and less intelligence make the teenager less able to evaluate the consequences of his or her conduct while at the same time he or she is much more apt to be motivated by mere emotion or peer pressure than is an adult. The reasons why juveniles are not trusted with the privileges and responsibilities of an adult also explain why their irresponsible conduct is not as morally reprehensible as that of an adult.

"The death penalty is said to serve two principal social purposes: retribution and deterrence of capital crimes by prospective offenders." *Gregg v. Georgia*, 428 U.S. 153, 183, 96 S.Ct. 2909, 2929–30, 49 L.Ed.2d 859 (1976) (joint opinion of Stewart, Powell, and STEVENS, JJ.). In *Gregg* we concluded that as "an expression of society's moral outrage at particularly offensive conduct," retribution was not "inconsistent with our respect for the dignity of men." *Ibid*. Given the lesser culpability of the juvenile offender, the teenager's capacity for growth, and society's fiduciary obligations to its children, this conclusion is simply inapplicable to the execution of a fifteen-year-old offender.

For such a young offender, the deterrence rationale is equally unacceptable. The Department of Justice statistics indicate that about 98 percent of the arrests for willful homicide involved persons who were over sixteen at the time of the offense. Thus, excluding younger persons from the class that is eligible for the death penalty will not diminish the deterrent value of capital punishment for the vast majority of potential offenders. And even with respect to those under sixteen years of age, it is obvious that the potential deterrent value of the death sentence is insignificant for two reasons. The likelihood that the teenage offender has made the kind of cost-benefit analysis that attaches any weight to the possibility of execution is so remote as to be virtually nonexistent. And, even if one posits such a cold-blooded calculation by a fifteen-year-old, it is fanciful to believe that he would be deterred by the knowledge that a small number of persons his age have been executed during the twentieth century. In short, we are not persuaded that the imposition of the death penalty for offenses committed by persons under sixteen years of age has made, or can be expected to make, any measurable contribution to the goals that capital punishment is intended to achieve. It is, therefore, ''nothing more than the purposeless and needless imposition of pain and suffering.'' *Coker v. Georgia*, 433 U.S., at 592, 97 S.Ct., at 2866, and thus an unconstitutional punishment.

VI

Petitioner's counsel and various *amici curiae* have asked us to ''draw a line'' that would prohibit the execution of any person who was under the age of eighteen at the time of the offense. Our task today, however, is to decide the case before us; we do so by concluding that the Eighth and Fourteenth Amendments prohibit the execution of a person who was under sixteen years of age at the time of his or her offense.

The judgment of the Court of Criminal Appeals is vacated, and the case is remanded with instructions to enter an appropriate order vacating petitioner's death sentence.

Is is so ordered.

32

Excerpts from *Stanford v. Kentucky:* Decided June 26, 1989

These two consolidated cases require us to decide whether the imposition of capital punishment on an individual for a crime committed at sixteen or seventeen years of age constitutes cruel and unusual punishment under the Eighth Amendment.

I

The first case, No. 87-5765, involves the shooting death of twenty-year-old Baerbel Poore in Jefferson County, Kentucky. Petitioner Kevin Stanford committed the murder on January 7, 1981, when he was approximately seventeen years and four months of age. Stanford and his accomplice repeatedly raped and sodomized Poore during and after their commission of a robbery at a gas station where she worked as an attendant. They then drove her to a secluded area near the station, where Stanford shot her point-blank in the face and then in the back of her head. The proceeds from the robbery were roughly 300 cartons of cigarettes, two gallons of fuel and a small amount of cash. A corrections officer testified that petitioner explained the murder as follows: " '[H]e said, I had to shoot her, [she] lived next door to me and she would recognize me. . . . I guess we could have tied her up or something or beat

Source: *Stanford v. Kentucky*, 109 S.Ct. 2969 (1989).

[her up] . . . and tell her if she tells, we would kill her. . . . Then after he said that he started laughing.' " 734 S.W.2d 781, 788 (Ky. 1987).

After Stanford's arrest, a Kentucky juvenile court conducted hearings to determine whether he should be transferred for trial as an adult under Ky.Rev.Stat. § 208.170 (Michie 1982). That statute provided that juvenile court jurisdiction could be waived and an offender tried as an adult if he was either charged with a Class A felony or capital crime, or was over sixteen years of age and charged with a felony. Stressing the seriousness of petitioner's offenses and the unsuccessful attempts of the juvenile system to treat him for numerous instances of past delinquency, the juvenile court found certification for trial as an adult to be in the best interest of petitioner and the community.

Stanford was convicted of murder, first-degree sodomy, first-degree robbery, and receiving stolen property, and was sentenced to death and forty-five years in prison. The Kentucky Supreme Court affirmed the death sentence, rejecting Stanford's "deman[d] that he has a constitutional right to treatment" 734 S.W.2d, at 792. Finding that the record clearly demonstrated that "there was no program or treatment appropriate for the appellant in the juvenile justice system," the court held that the juvenile court did not err in certifying petitioner for trial as an adult. The court also stated that petitioner's "age and the possibility that he might be rehabilitated were mitigating factors appropriately left to the consideration of the jury that tried him." *Ibid.*

The second case, No. 87-6026, involves the stabbing death of Nancy Allen, a twenty-six-year-old mother of two who was working behind the sales counter of the convenience store she and David Allen owned and operated in Avondale, Missouri. Petitioner Heath Wilkins committed the murder on July 27, 1985, when he was approximately sixteen years and six months of age. The record reflects that Wilkins' plan was to rob the store and murder "whoever was behind the counter" because "a dead person can't talk." While Wilkins' accomplice, Patrick Stevens, held Allen, Wilkins stabbed her, causing her to fall to the floor. When Stevens had trouble operating the cash register, Allen spoke up to assist him, leading Wilkins to stab her three more times in her chest. Two of these wounds penetrated the victim's heart. When Allen began to beg for her life, Wilkins stabbed her four more times in the neck, opening her carotid artery. After helping themselves to liquor, cigarettes, rolling papers, and approximately $450 in cash and checks, Wilkins and Stevens left Allen to die on the floor.

Because he was roughly six months short of the age of majority for purposes of criminal prosecution, Mo.Rev.Stat. § 211.021(1) (1986), Wilkins could not automatically be tried as an adult under Missouri law. Before that could happen, the juvenile court was required to terminate juvenile-court jurisdiction and certify Wilkins for trial as an adult under § 211.071, which permits individuals between fourteen and seventeen years of age who have committed felonies to be tried as adults. Relying on the "viciousness, force and violence" of the alleged crime, petitioner's maturity, and the failure of the juvenile justice system to rehabilitate him after previous delinquent acts, the juvenile court made the necessary certification.

Wilkins was charged with first-degree murder, armed criminal action, and carrying a concealed weapon. After the court found him competent, petitioner entered guilty pleas to all charges. A punishment hearing was held, at which both the State and petitioner himself urged imposition of the death sentence. Evidence at the hearing revealed that petitioner had been in and out of juvenile facilities since the age of eight for various acts of burglary, theft, and arson, had attempted to kill his mother by putting insecticide into Tylenol capsules, and had killed several animals in his neighborhood. Although psychiatric testimony indicated that Wilkins had "personality disorders," the witnesses agreed that Wilkins was aware of his actions and could distinguish right from wrong.

Determining that the death penalty was appropriate, the trial court entered the following order:

> The court finds beyond reasonable doubt that the following aggravated circumstances exist:
> 1. The murder in the first degree was committed while the defendant was engaged in the perpetration of the felony and robbery, and
> 2. The murder in the first degree involved depravity of mind and that as a result thereof, it was outrageously or wantonly vile, horrible or inhuman. App. in No. 87-6026.

On mandatory review of Wilkins' death sentence, the Supreme Court of Missouri affirmed, rejecting the argument that the punishment violated the Eighth Amendment. 736 S.W.2d 409 (1987).

We granted certiorari in these cases, 488 U.S. __, 109 S.Ct. 217, 102 L.Ed.2d 208 and 487 U.S. __, 108 S.Ct. 2896, 101 L.Ed. 2d 930 (1988), to decide whether the Eighth Amendment precludes the death penalty for individuals who commit crimes at sixteen or seventeen years of age.

II

The thrust of both Wilkins' and Stanford's arguments is that imposition of the death penalty on those who were juveniles when they committed their crimes falls within the Eighth Amendment's prohibition against "cruel and unusual punishments." Wilkins would have us define juveniles as individuals sixteen years of age and under, Stanford would draw the line at seventeen.

[1] Neither petitioner asserts that his sentence constitutes one of "those modes or acts of punishment that had been considered cruel and unusual at the time that the Bill of Rights was adopted." *Ford v. Wainwright,* 477 U.S. 399, 405, 106 S.Ct. 2595, 2600, 91 L.Ed.2d 335 (1986). Nor could they support such a contention. At that time, the common law set the rebuttable presumption

of incapacity to commit any felony at the age of fourteen, and theoretically permitted capital punishment to be imposed on anyone over the age of seven. See 4 Blackstone, Commentaries "23–24; 1 M. Hale, Pleas of the Crown 24–29 (1800 ed.). See also *In re Gault,* 387 U.S. 1, 16, 87 S.Ct. 1428, 1437, 18 L.Ed.2d 527 (1967); Streib, Death Penalty for Children: The American Experience with Capital Punishment for Crimes Committed While Under Age Eighteen, 36 Okla.L.Rev. 613, 614–615 (1983); Kean, The History of the Criminal Liability of Children, 53 L.Q.Rev. 364, 369–370 (1937). In accordance with the standards of this common-law tradition, at least 281 offenders under the age of eighteen have been executed in this country, and at least 126 under the age of seventeen. See V. Streib, Death Penalty for Juveniles 57 (1987).

[2] Thus petitioners are left to argue that their punishment is contrary to the "evolving standards of decency that mark the progress of a maturing society," *Trop v. Dulles,* 356 U.S. 86, 101, 78 S.Ct. 590, 598, 2 L.Ed.2d 630 (1958) (plurality opinion). They are correct in asserting that this Court has "not confined the prohibition embodied in the Eighth Amendment to 'barbarous' methods that were generally outlawed in the eighteenth century," but instead has interpreted the Amendment "in a flexible and dynamic manner." *Gregg v. Georgia,* 428 U.S. 153, 171, 96 S.Ct. 2909, 2924, 49 L.Ed.2d 859 (1976). In determining what standards have "evolved," however, we have looked not to our own conceptions of decency, but to those of modern American society as a whole. As we have said, "Eighth Amendment judgments should not be, or appear to be, merely the subjective views of individual Justices; judgment should be informed by objective factors to the maximum possible extent." *Coker v. Georgia,* 433 U.S. 584, 592, 97 S.Ct. 2861, 2866, 53 L.Ed.2d 982 (1977) (plurality opinion). See also *Penry v. Lynaugh,* __ U.S. at __, 109 S.Ct., at __; *Ford v. Wainwright, supra,* 477 U.S., at 406, 106 S.Ct., at 2600; *Enmund v. Florida,* 458 U.S. 782, 788–789, 102 S.Ct. 3368, 787–788, 73 L.Ed.2d 1140 (1982); *Furman v. Georgia,* 408 U.S. 238, 277–279, 92 S.Ct. 2726, 2746–2747, 33 L.Ed.2d 346 (1972) (BRENNAN, J., concurring). This approach is dictated both by the language of the Amendment—which proscribes only those punishments that are both "cruel and *unusual*"—and by the "deference we owe to the decisions of the state legislatures under our federal system," *Gregg v. Georgia, supra,* 428 U.S., at 176, 96 S.Ct., at 2926.

III

[3] "[F]irst" among the " 'objective indicia that reflect the public attitude toward a given sanction' " are statutes passed by society's selected representatives. *McCleskey v. Kemp,* 481 U.S. 279, 300, 107 S.Ct. 1756, 1770, 95 L.Ed.2d 262 (1987), quoting *Gregg v. Georgia, supra,* 428 U.S., at 173, 96 S.Ct., at 2925. Of the thirty-seven States whose laws permit capital punishment, fifteen decline to impose it upon sixteen-year-old offenders and twelve decline to impose it on seventeen-year-old offenders. This does not establish

the degree of national consensus this Court has previously thought sufficient to label a particular punishment cruel and unusual. In invalidating the death penalty for rape of an adult woman, we stressed that Georgia was the *sole* jurisdiction that authorized such a punishment. See *Coker v. Georgia,* 433 U.S., at 595–596, 97 S.Ct., at 2867-2868. In striking down capital punishment for participation in a robbery in which an accomplice takes a life, we emphasized that only eight jurisdictions authorized similar punishment. *Enmund v. Florida,* 458 U.S., at 792, 102 S.Ct., at 3374. In finding that the Eighth Amendment precludes execution of the insane and thus requires an adequate hearing on the issue of sanity, we relied upon (in addition to the common-law rule) the fact that "no State in the Union" permitted such punishment. *Ford v. Wainwright,* 477 U.S., at 408, 106 S.Ct., at 2601. And in striking down a life sentence without parole under a recidivist statute, we stressed that "[i]t appears that [petitioner] was treated more severely than he would have been in any other State." *Solem v. Helm,* 463 U.S. 277, 300, 103 S.Ct. 3001, 3015, 77 L.Ed.2d 637 (1983).

[4] Since a majority of the States that permit capital punishment authorize it for crimes committed at age sixteen or above, petitioners' cases are more analogous to *Tison v. Arizona,* 481 U.S. 137, 107 S.Ct. 1676, 95 L.Ed.2d 127 (1987) than *Coker, Enmund, Ford,* and *Solem.* In *Tison,* which upheld Arizona's imposition of the death penalty for major participation in a felony with reckless indifference to human life, we noted that only eleven of those jurisdictions imposing capital punishment rejected its use in such circumstances. *Id.,* at 154, 107 S.Ct., at 1686. As we noted earlier, here the number is fifteen for offenders under seventeen, and twelve for offenders under eighteen. We think the same conclusion as in *Tison* is required in this case.

Petitioners make much of the recently enacted federal statute providing capital punishment for certain drug-related offenses, but limiting that punishment to offenders eighteen and over. The Anti-Drug Abuse Act of 1988, Pub.L. 100–690, 102 Stat. 4390, § 7001(b). That reliance is entirely misplaced. To begin with, the statute in question does not embody a judgment by the Federal Legislature that *no* murder is heinous enough to warrant the execution of such a youthful offender, but merely that the narrow class of offense it defines is not. The congressional judgment on the broader question, if apparent at all, is to be found in the law that permits sixteen- and seventeen-year-olds (after appropriate findings) to be tried and punished as adults for *all* federal offenses, including those bearing a capital penalty that is not limited to eighteen-year-olds. See 18 U.S.C. § 5032 (1982 ed., Supp. V). Moreover, even if it were true that no federal statute permitted the execution of persons under eighteen, that would not remotely establish—in the face of a substantial number of state statutes to the contrary—a national consensus that such punishment is inhumane, any more than the absence of a federal lottery establishes a national consensus that lotteries are socially harmful. To be sure, the absence of a

federal death penalty for sixteen- or seventeen-year-olds (if it existed) might
be evidence that there is no national consensus *in favor* of such punishment.
It is not the burden of Kentucky and Missouri, however, to establish a national
consensus approving what their citizens have voted to do; rather, it is the
"heavy burden" of petitioners, *Gregg v. Georgia,* 428 U.S., at 175, 96 S.Ct.,
at 2926, to establish a national consensus *against* it. As far as the primary
and most reliable indication of consensus is concerned—the pattern of enacted
laws—petitioners have failed to carry that burden.

IV

A

[5] Wilkins and Stanford argue, however, that even if the laws themselves
do not establish a settled consensus, the application of the laws does. That
contemporary society views capital punishment of sixteen- and seventeen-year-
old offenders as inappropriate is demonstrated, they say, by the reluctance
of juries to impose, and prosecutors to seek, such sentences. Petitioners are
quite correct that a far smaller number of offenders under eighteen than over
eighteen have been sentenced to death in this country. From 1982 through
1988, for example, out of 2,106 total death sentences, only fifteen were imposed on individuals who were sixteen or under when they committed their
crimes, and only thirty on individuals who were seventeen at the time of
the crime. See Streib, Imposition of Death Sentences For Juvenile Offenses,
January 1, 1982, Through April 1, 1989, p. 2 (paper for Cleveland-Marshall
College of Law, April 5, 1989). And it appears that actual executions for
crimes committed under age eighteen accounted for only about 2 percent of
the total number of executions that occurred between 1642 and 1986. See
Streib, Death Penalty for Juveniles, at 55, 57. As Wilkins points out, the last
execution of a person who committed a crime under seventeen years of age
occurred in 1959. These statistics, however, carry little significance. Given
the undisputed fact that a far smaller percentage of capital crimes is committed
by persons under eighteen than over eighteen, the discrepancy in treatment
is much less than might seem. Granted, however, that a substantial discrepancy
exists, that does not establish the requisite proposition that the death sentence
for offenders under eighteen is categorically unacceptable to prosecutors and
juries. To the contrary, it is not only possible but overwhelmingly probable
that the very considerations which induce petitioners and their supporters to
believe that death should *never* be imposed on offenders under eighteen cause
prosecutors and juries to believe that it should *rarely* be imposed.

B

[6] This last point suggests why there is also no relevance to the laws cited by
petitioners and their *amici* which set eighteen or more as the legal age for engaging

in various activities, ranging from driving to drinking alcoholic beverages to voting. It is, to begin with, absurd to think that one must be mature enough to drive carefully, to drink responsibly, or to vote intelligently, in order to be mature enough to understand that murdering another human being is profoundly wrong, and to conform one's conduct to that most minimal of all civilized standards. But even if the requisite degrees of maturity were comparable, the age-statutes in question would still not be relevant. They do not represent a social judgment that all persons under the designated ages are not responsible enough to drive, to drink, or to vote, but at most a judgment that the vast majority are not. These laws set the appropriate ages for the operation of a system that makes its determinations in gross, and that does not conduct individualized maturity tests for each driver, drinker, or voter. The criminal justice system, however, does provide individualized testing. In the realm of capital punishment in particular, "individualized consideration [is] a constitutional requirement," *Lockett v. Ohio*, 438 U.S. 586, 605, 98 S.Ct. 2954, 2965, 57 L.Ed.2d 973 (1978) (opinion of Burger, C.J.) (footnote omitted); see also *Zant v. Stephens*, 462 U.S. 862, 879, 103 S.Ct. 2733, 2743, 77 L.Ed.2d 235 (1983) (collecting cases), and one of the individualized mitigating factors that sentencers must be permitted to consider is the defendant's age. See *Eddings v. Oklahoma*, 455 U.S. 104, 115–116, 102 S.Ct. 869, 877–878, 71 L.Ed.2d 1 (1982). Twenty-nine States, including both Kentucky and Missouri, have codified this constitutional requirement in laws specifically designating the defendant's age as a mitigating factor in capital cases. Moreover, the determinations required by juvenile transfer statutes to certify a juvenile for trial as an adult ensure individualized consideration of the maturity and moral responsibility of sixteen- and seventeen-year-old offenders before they are even held to stand trial as adults. The application of this particularized system to the petitioners can be declared constitutionally inadequate only if there is a consensus, not that seventeen or eighteen is the age at which most persons, or even almost all persons, achieve sufficient maturity to be held fully responsible for murder; but that seventeen or eighteen is the age before which *no one* can reasonably be held fully responsible. What displays society's views on this latter point are not the ages set forth in the generalized system of driving, drinking, and voting laws cited by petitioners and their *amici*, but the ages at which the States permit their particularized capital punishment systems to be applied.

V

[7] Having failed to establish a consensus against capital punishment for sixteen- and seventeen-year-old offenders through state and federal statutes and the behavior of prosecutors and juries, petitioners seek to demonstrate it through other indicia, including public opinion polls, the views of interest groups and the positions adopted by various professional associations. We decline the invitation to rest constitutional law upon such uncertain foundations. A revised national consensus so broad, so clear and so enduring as to justify a permanent prohibition

upon all units of democratic government must appear in the operative acts (laws and the application of laws) that the people have approved.

[8] We also reject petitioners' argument that we should invalidate capital punishment of sixteen- and seventeen-year-old offenders on the ground that it fails to serve the legitimate goals of penology. According to petitioners, it fails to deter because juveniles, possessing less developed cognitive skills than adults, are less likely to fear death; and it fails to exact just retribution because juveniles, being less mature and responsible, are also less morally blameworthy. In support of these claims, petitioners and their supporting *amici* marshall an array of socioscientific evidence concerning the psychological and emotional development of sixteen- and seventeen-year-olds.

If such evidence could conclusively establish the entire lack of deterrent effect and moral responsibility, resort to the Cruel and Unusual Punishments Clause would be unnecessary; the Equal Protection Clause of the Fourteenth Amendment would invalidate these laws for lack of rational basis. See *Dallas v. Stanglin*, 490 U.S. __, 109 S.Ct. 1591, 104 L.Ed.2d 18 (1989). But as the adjective ''socioscientific'' suggests (and insofar as evaluation of moral responsibility is concerned perhaps the adjective ''ethicoscientific'' would be more apt), it is not demonstrable that no sixteen-year-old is ''adequately responsible'' or significantly deterred. It is rational, even if mistaken, to think the contrary. The battle must be fought, then, on the field of the Eighth Amendment; and in that struggle socioscientific, ethicoscientific, or even purely scientific evidence is not an available weapon. The punishment is either ''cruel *and* unusual'' (*i.e.*, society has set its face against it) or it is not. The audience for these arguments, in other words, is not this Court but the citizenry of the United States. It is they, not we, who must be persuaded. For as we stated earlier, our job is to *identify* the ''evolving standards of decency''; to determine, not what they *should* be, but what they *are*. We have no power under the Eighth Amendment to substitute our belief in the scientific evidence for the society's apparent skepticism. In short, we emphatically reject petitioner's suggestion that the issues in this case permit us to apply our ''own informed judgment,'' Brief for Petitioner in No. 87-6026, p. 23, regarding the desirability of permitting the death penalty for crimes by sixteen- and seventeen-year-olds.

We reject the dissent's contention that our approach, by ''largely return[ing] the task of defining the contours of Eighth Amendment protection to political majorities,'' leaves '' '[c]onstitutional doctrine [to] be formulated by the acts of those institutions which the Constitution is supposed to limit,' '' *post*, at 2986 (citation omitted). When this Court cast loose from the historical moorings consisting of the original application of the Eighth Amendment, it did not embark rudderless upon a wide-open sea. Rather, it limited the Amendment's extension to those practices contrary to the ''evolving *standards of decency that mark the progress of a maturing society.''* *Trop v. Dulles*, 356 U.S. 86, 101, 78 S.Ct. 590, 598, 2 L.Ed.2d 630 (1958) (plurality opinion) (emphasis added). It has never been thought that this was a shorthand reference to the preferences of a majority of this Court. By reaching a decision supported neither by constitutional text nor by the demonstrable current standards of our citizens, the dissent displays a failure to appreciate that "those institutions which the Constitution is supposed to limit" include the Court itself. To say, as the dissent says, that "it is for *us* ultimately to judge whether the Eighth Amendment permits imposition of the death penalty," *post.* at 2986 (emphasis added), quoting *Enmund v. Florida,* 458 U.S. 782, 797, 102 S.Ct. 3368, 3377, 73 L.Ed.2d 1140 (1982)—and to mean that as the dissent means it, *i.e.,* that it is for *us* to judge, not on the basis of what we perceive the Eighth Amendment originally prohibited, or on the basis of what we perceive the society through its democratic processes now overwhelmingly disapproves, but on the basis of what we think "proportionate" and "measurably contributory to acceptable goals of punishment"—to say and mean that, is to replace judges of the law with a committee of philosopher-kings.

While the dissent is correct that several of our cases have engaged in so-called "proportionality" analysis, examining whether "there is a disproportion 'between the punishment imposed and the defendant's blameworthiness,' " and whether a punishment makes any "measurable contribution to acceptable goals of punishment," see *post,* at 2987, we have never invalidated a punishment on this basis alone. All of our cases condemning a punishment under this mode of analysis also found that the objective indicators of state laws or jury determinations evidenced a societal consensus against that penalty. See *Solem v. Helm,* 463 U.S. 277, 299–300, 103 S.Ct. 3001, 3014–3015, 77 L.Ed.2d 637 (1983); *Enmund v. Florida, supra,* 458 U.S., at 789–796, 102 S.Ct., at 3372–3376; *Coker v. Georgia,* 433 U.S. 584, 593–597, 97 S.Ct. 2861, 2866–2869, 53 L.Ed.2d 982 (1977) (plurality opinion). In fact, the two methodologies blend into one another, since "proportionality" analysis itself can only be conducted on the basis of the standards set by our own society; the only alternative, once again, would be our personal preferences.

. . . .

We discern neither a historical nor a modern societal consensus forbidding the imposition of capital punishment on any person who murders at sixteen to seventeen years of age. Accordingly, we conclude that such punishment does not offend the Eighth Amendment's prohibition against cruel and unusual punishment.

The judgments of the Supreme Court of Kentucky and the Supreme Court of Missouri are therefore
    Affirmed.

33

Evolving Standards of Decency and the Death Penalty for Juvenile Offenders: The Contradiction Presented by *Stanford v. Kentucky*

Steven M. Scott

> You may hang these boys; you may hang them by the neck until they are dead. But in doing it you turn your face toward the past. In doing it you are making it harder for every other boy who, in ignorance and darkness, must grope his way through the mazes which only childhood knows. . . . You may save them and make it easier for every child that sometime may stand where these boys stand. You will make it easier for every human being with an aspiration and a vision and a hope and a fate.[1]—Clarence Darrow

Introduction

A sentence of death is a reality for Heath Wilkins as a result of the Supreme Court's June 27, 1989 decision upholding the constitutionality of the death penalty for juvenile offenders. In a five to four plurality decision, the Court held that Wilkins had failed to carry the burden of persuasion and that the death penalty for juvenile offenders did not violate the eighth amendment's prohibition against cruel and unusual punishment. Furthermore, the Court found that there was "neither a historical nor a modern societal consensus forbidding the imposition of capital punishment on any person who murders at sixteen or seventeen years of age." It is the purpose of this note to show

Source: *Capital University Law Review*, 19 (1990): 851–867. Reprinted by permission of Steven M. Scott.

that the Court erred in its decision, and that there is indeed a modern consensus that condemns the imposition of the death penalty for juvenile offenders.

I. Juvenile Executions in America

The United States inherited the bulk of its criminal law, including capital punishment, from the English common law. Under the common law, persons under seven were presumed to be incapable of having the requisite criminal intent to commit a crime, and therefore immune from criminal sanctions. For those defendants between the ages of seven and fourteen, the presumption of the inability to entertain criminal intent was rebuttable, and if rebutted, the child was criminally liable and subject to punishment, including the penalty of death. Anyone over age fourteen was considered capable of forming the requisite criminal intent and was subject to arrest, trial, conviction, and the same punishment as an adult offender. This common law view of a child's criminal liability was formally adopted by the United States Supreme Court in *In re Gault*. It was not until *Thompson v. Oklahoma*, nearly twenty-one years later, that the Court decided that age sixteen was the minimum permissible age at which a juvenile offender could be subject to capital punishment for murder, thus protecting the juvenile offender fifteen years old and younger.

Even though it has always been theoretically possible for a juvenile over the age of seven to be executed for their criminal act, there have only been 281 juveniles executed in the United States since 1642, making the execution of a juvenile offender a relatively rare occurrence. Despite the fact that 210 of those 281 juveniles have been executed in the last one hundred years, juvenile executions account for approximately 2.5 percent of the total 8,544 persons executed during the same period. Furthermore, in the twenty-five years since the execution of James Echols in Texas for a rape he committed at age seventeen in 1963, only three juveniles have been executed. Despite thousands of convictions of juveniles for capital offenses, today there are only thirty-two juveniles on death row out of a total population of some 1,800. This dichotomy between crimes committed and the actual enforcement of the penalty at least suggests that juvenile executions are infrequently imposed; moreover, one could reasonably conclude that there exists a consensus in this country that is contrary to the imposition of death on juvenile offenders.

II. Evolution of the Juvenile Justice System

The dichotomy between crimes and sentencing has its roots in the evolution of the juvenile justice system as a separate means of addressing juvenile criminal activity. Beginning in 1899, the state of Illinois enacted laws which created a separate juvenile justice system, and by 1925, nearly every state had a system distinct from the adult system of criminal justice. The primary function of these newly established juvenile justice systems was to rehabilitate rather than punish the juvenile or young offender.

The practice of treating and rehabilitating juveniles was explicitly recognized as a favorable means of dealing with juveniles in *In Re Gault:* "The idea of crime and punishment was to be abandoned. The child was to be 'treated' and 'rehabilitated' and the procedures, from apprehension to institutionalization, were to be 'clinical' rather than 'punitive.' " The assumption which underlies the existence of a separate juvenile justice system is that the factor of age or youth overcome the previous common law presumption that children are completely responsible for their actions. Reformers who advocated the formation of a separate justice system for juveniles wanted to shield the child from any form of adverse publicity, to protect them from the consequences of adult penalties for convictions of felonies, and to establish a methodology for treating and rehabilitating children within the community. These early reformers focused on preventing juvenile offenses and establishing separate juvenile facilities. As states began developing their juvenile court systems and juvenile facilities, the concept of *parens patriae* developed, heightening the special place children were occupying in the legal system and the treatment they received under the law.

Despite the states' assumption of greater responsibility towards juvenile offenders under *parens patriae* authority and pronounced changes in societal attitudes during these years, some 115 juveniles were executed between 1900 and 1939. Because juvenile courts lacked the authority to impose the death sentence, juvenile offenders had to be transferred from juvenile court jurisdiction to adult criminal court jurisdiction.

The mechanism by which children are transferred to adult criminal courts is waiver.[2] The waiver mechanism allows a juvenile offender to be tried for a crime as an adult. However, children do not have the mental capacity of an adult and therefore, should not be held to an adult standard. If children are held to an adult standard, they are no longer children. Thus, the very concept of trying a child as an adult is a contradiction in terms. On the other hand, crimes committed by children can be just as serious and heinous as felonies committed by adults. Herein lies the crux of the problem that society faces with children who murder. Children who murder are not good people, but allowing the courts to try children as adults via the waiver process presupposes that those children have the maturity and responsible decision-making capabilities of an adult. No state permits a child to vote, to serve on juries, to consume alcohol, or to gamble on the presumption that they lack the maturity to do so. As society has struggled with the issue of where to set the line between adulthood and childhood, the most common point has been the age of eighteen. Even the Supreme Court has noted the difficulty that children pose for the law: "Children have a very special place in life which the law should reflect. Legal theories and their phrasing in other cases readily lead to fallacious reasoning if uncritically transferred to the determination of a State's duty toward children." Children are perceived as more vulnerable, more impulsive, and less disciplined than adults; therefore, trying them as adults makes little sense, since they have so few of the skills of an adult.

III. Recent Developments in United States Supreme Court Decisions

Three times during the 1980s the United States Supreme Court has had the opportunity to answer the question whether the Eighth Amendment's prohibition against cruel and unusual punishment should apply in capital cases involving juvenile offenders. The first of these cases was in 1982. In *Eddings v. Oklahoma,* the defendant was sixteen when he murdered a police officer. He was tried and subsequently sentenced to death. The issue of whether the Eighth Amendment's ban of cruel and unusual punishment as it applied to juvenile offenders sentenced to death was squarely presented. However, the Court avoided answering the issue entirely by deciding in a plurality decision written by Justice Powell that the death sentence must be vacated, and the case remanded for further proceedings, since the state had refused to consider all mitigating circumstances surrounding Eddings' crime. The Court found grounds to remand the case without addressing the constitutionality of imposing the death penalty on juvenile offenders.

The issue, however, did not die. Five years later, the Court was presented with *Thompson v. Oklahoma.* Thompson was only fifteen years old when he murdered his former brother-in-law. The Court in a 4–1–3 plurality, (with Justice O'Connor concurring, and Justice Kennedy not taking part), held that the imposition of the death penalty upon a person who was under the age of sixteen when he committed his offense violated the eighth amendment prohibition against cruel and unusual punishment. Justice Stevens writing for the plurality concluded that, of the eighteen states which had expressly considered the question of a minimum age for imposing the death penalty, all had set sixteen as the minimum age. Justice Stevens declined to "draw a line" at age eighteen, since it was not an issue in the case.

Three days short of one year later the Court announced that the death penalty for juvenile offenders did not violate the eighth amendment's prohibition against cruel and unusual punishment in cases involving sixteen and seventeen year olds. The Court's announcement was made in its decision of *Stanford v. Kentucky.* Heath Wilkins was sixteen years old at the time he murdered Nancy Allen, a twenty-six-year-old mother of two small children. Nancy Allen was killed in the convenience store that she and her husband owned. Wilkins entered the store with an accomplice and proceeded to rob the store. He stabbed Allen eight times while she begged for her life. As Allen lay dying, Wilkins and his accomplice stole liquor, cigarettes, rolling papers, and approximately $450.00.

After a waiver hearing, which certified Wilkins for trial as an adult, Wilkins was charged with first degree murder, armed criminal action, and carrying a concealed weapon. The court found him competent to stand trial. Wilkins then dismissed his court-appointed attorney and pled guilty to all charges. At the sentencing hearing both Wilkins and the state's prosecutor urged the imposition of the death penalty. Wilkins stated that he feared incarceration for life more than he feared death. The Supreme Court of Missouri upheld the imposition of the death penalty, and the U.S. Supreme Court granted certiorari to rule on the issue of the death penalty for juvenile offenders.

IV. Analysis of Stanford v. Kentucky

Justice Scalia, writing for the plurality with Justice O'Connor concurring in part, held that, under the traditional two prong test of whether a punishment violates the prohibition against cruel and unusual punishment, Wilkins had failed to carry the burden of persuasion in proving that there was either a historical or a modern societal consensus "forbidding the imposition of capital punishment on any person who murders at sixteen or seventeen years of age." Thus, the Court held that Heath Wilkins could be sentenced to the death penalty without violating the eighth amendment's ban against cruel and unusual punishment.

The two prong test for constitutionality of this issue is "whether the mode or act of punishment was considered cruel and unusual at the time that the Bill of Rights was adopted," and whether a punishment is contrary to the "evolving standards of decency that mark the progress of a maturing society." The test is to be interpreted in a "flexible and dynamic manner." A judgment rendered on the basis of the second prong should be a "judgment . . . informed by objective factors to the maximum possible extent."

The first tier of analysis in determining the constitutionality of the death penalty for juvenile offenders was obviously satisfied since the common law rebuttable presumption of capacity is set at age fourteen, therefore permitting capital punishment for anyone fifteen and older. There can be no reasonable refutation presented to show that capital punishment of juveniles violates this prong since at least seven children were executed prior to 1800, and ninety-five prior to 1900, the youngest only ten years old. Therefore, the death penalty for juveniles cannot be found to be unconstitutional on this basis.

Since the case before the Court failed to contravene the first prong of the test, the issue came down to whether capital punishment for juvenile offenders was contrary to the "evolving standards of decency that mark the progress of a maturing society." Justice Scalia based his opinion on an evaluation of the "objective indicia that reflect the public attitude" toward the imposition of capital punishment on child offenders. Justice Scalia pointed out that it was only American societal standards that ought to be evaluated, therefore, the practices of other democratic nations were irrelevant.

The "objective indicia" as related by the Justice include only those thirty-six states[3] which permit the death penalty. Of these thirty-six states, only fifteen have determined that a minimum age should exist. Of these fifteen, twelve states have concluded that eighteen is the minimum age for which the death penalty may be sought,[4] and the others have set the age at seventeen.[5] The remaining fourteen states and the District of Columbia were excluded from Justice Scalia's list of "objective indicia" as a matter of judicial convenience since they bar imposition of the death penalty in all cases.[6]

The exclusion of those fifteen jurisdictions which ban the death penalty for anyone, begs the question of whether "objective indicia" is an issue of national consensus, or one of selective consensus. When attempting to ascertain society's view on a controversial matter, it is best to consider both sides of the issue. Obviously, in order to develop a national consensus, the consideration of how an entire population perceives the problem and not simply a selected portion's perception is necessary. Justice Scalia's logic in omitting from consideration those states which ban capital punishment, in determining a national consensus representative of an evolving standard of decency in a maturing society, fails to be convincing in light of his conclusion that of the thirty-six states that permit the death penalty, only fifteen set minimum ages at seventeen or above. He concluded that this number "does not establish the degree of *national* consensus this Court has previously thought sufficient to label a particular punishment cruel and unusual." This sort of judicial double-talk runs contrary to the concept of "fundamental fairness" one expects from our nation's highest Court. It is either a national consensus or it is not. It simply cannot be both. If the most reliable indication of what constitutes a national consensus is "the pattern of enacted laws," then one must, in the pursuit of intellectual honesty, include all laws and not only those that conveniently fit one's personal formula.[7]

Since a truly "national" consensus includes all fifty-one jurisdictions and not a selective consensus of only those states permitting the death penalty, the question becomes whether thirty of fifty-one jurisdictions is sufficient to show a consensus running contrary to the imposition of the death penalty for juvenile offenders. It is probable that even with a near 60 percent majority opposing outright or in favor of limiting the death penalty for children, it would still be insufficient to satisfy the "evolving standard of decency" test.[8] However, a closer examination of the twenty-one states which permit executions of juveniles suggests that, of these twenty-one states, only ten are actively engaged in the execution of children.[9]

As of March 1, 1987, there were thirty-two juvenile offenders on death row out of a total population of death row inmates of some 1,800, thus comprising approximately 1.8 percent of the total population of death row inmates.[10] Of these thirty-two juveniles, five must be discounted since there were fifteen at the time they committed their offense, and two are in states which recently raised their minimum age for imposing the death penalty to age eighteen.[11] Thus, a current recalculation of Streib's figures results in only twenty-five individuals age eighteen or younger on death row. Of these twenty-five, eleven are on death row in those three states which place the minimum age for the death penalty at age seventeen,[12] leaving unaccounted the remaining fourteen minor individuals on death row. These fourteen are presently on death row in nine states[13] out of the twenty-one which permit executions of juvenile offenders. Of the remaining twelve states, only one, South Carolina, has engaged in the execution of a juvenile offender in the last twenty-five years. Thus, it would appear that of the twenty-one states that Justice Scalia counted as "objective indicia" of our national consensus only ten of them are actively pursuing the death penalty for juvenile offenders. Out of fifty-one jurisdictions, forty-one states do not execute juveniles and only ten do. Analysis of the "objective indicia" in this light leads to the conclusion that there is in fact a national consensus, at least in practice, of not executing juvenile offenders even though a majority of states theoretically permit it.

Furthermore, recent trends in state legislative action demonstrate a continuing trend away from imposing the death penalty on juveniles. In 1984, thirty-one states permitted the death penalty for children. Today, statutes in only twenty-five states provide for it.[14] Coincidentally, Vermont banned capital punishment in all cases except for kidnapping, and South Dakota has an unconstitutional death penalty on its books, making it a plausible candidate as the sixteenth state without capital punishment in any case. North Carolina in this same five year period raised its minimum age for imposition of the death penalty to seventeen. Thus, in the past five years, eight states have altered their death penalty statutes as they apply to juvenile offenders, either by raising their minimum age to seventeen (one state), or to eighteen (six states), or by banning capital punishment entirely (one state). One state has refrained from revising its existing pre-*Furman* statute, thus leaving it unconstitutional as written. This shift of eight or nine states constitutes nearly a 26 percent decline in the use of capital punishment for juveniles in only a five year period. Certainly, this represents a perceptible shift in the practice of execution of juveniles, and is evidence of a shifting societal attitude, and a furtherance of the evolution away from the death penalty for children.

Further evidence supporting this contention includes statistics of jury sentencing patterns. At the end of 1983, there were thirty-eight juveniles on death row out of a total population of some 1,289 death row inmates, or approximately 3 percent. By March 1, 1987, however, there were only thirty-two juveniles on death row out of a population of over 1,800 death row inmates, or a percentage of 1.8 percent. This decline of 16 percent must be contrasted with the increase of some 511 death row inmates or a 40 percent increase, showing the point that while imposing the death penalty on adults has risen sharply, imposing it on children has decreased markedly in just a thirty-eight month period. The trend on imposing death sentences on juveniles has also decreased from eleven in 1982 to only seven in 1986, with a low of three in 1985. An objective view of these statistics clearly indicates that juries have become more reluctant to resort to the death penalty to punish children, as state legislatures have also become more reluctant to subject juveniles to the death penalty at all.

On the whole, the combination of the declining number of states actively engaged in executing juveniles, coupled with a shift away from subjecting children to the death penalty, and the downward trend in imposing the death penalty on juveniles more clearly illustrates a national consensus opposed to capital punishment for children. Thus, Justice Scalia's interpretation of state statutes does not completely present the ''objective indicia'' of a national consensus in favor of the death penalty for children. In addition, of increasing importance is the effect executing juveniles will have on the United States' position in the international community.

V. United States Position in the International Community

Despite its position as a world leader in the area of human rights, the United States places itself outside the mainstream of international practice by executing juveniles. Perhaps because world opinion is so overwhelmingly against executing juveniles, Justice Scalia found it necessary to state that ''[w]e emphasize that it is *American* conceptions of decency that are dispositive, rejecting the contention that the sentencing practices of other countries are relevant.'' Scalia thereby dismissed any discussion of whether world practice was a viable objective indicator of the contemporary standard of decency. However, as Justice Brennan in his dissent stated: ''[O]ur cases recognize that objective indicators of contemporary standards of decency in the form of legislation in other countries is also of relevance to Eighth Amendment analysis.''

Just how far outside the stream of world opinion the United States is can be plainly seen in light of the fact that in the last ten years there have been only eight executions of juvenile offenders worldwide, with three executed in the United States. Furthermore, there are only five countries in the world still executing juvenile offenders,[15] and none of them are among those considered to be ''tough on crime.''[16]

The United States government has signed two major international human rights treaties which specifically prohibit the death penalty for children who commit crimes under age eighteen. Even though these treaties were signed, they have never been ratified by the Senate. Nonetheless, they do represent an affirmative stance by our nation's highest officials and diplomats against the death penalty for juveniles. Logic dictates that if the United States wishes to continue to influence and shape world opinion, its laws should reflect the spirit, if not the letter, of the treaties that its leaders have morally committed this country to observe. The United States' position on human rights has been persuasive in righting wrongs in many nations. Therefore, the laws of this nation should reflect its stance on human rights by bringing the country into conformity with other nations that forbid the imposition of the death penalty for juvenile offenders. By doing so the United States can sustain its position in the human rights arena. However, by placing the United States among the very few nations which actively engage in the execution of juveniles, the Court has helped to undercut the United States' effectiveness in improving human rights world-wide.

VI. Fourteenth Amendment Analysis

In a cursory and seemingly off-hand manner, Justice Scalia dismissed any real discussion of the equal protection clause of the Fourteenth Amendment. Stating that there was no demonstrable basis for the proposition that a sixteen-year-old is not "adequately responsible" or significantly deterred from committing a crime, requirements imposed by the fourteenth amendment, he concluded that there was no reason or justification for discussing the issue. This dismissal of any fourteenth amendment analysis cannot be summarily excused in light of the stipulation in *Gregg v. Georgia,* which states that capital punishment must serve a legitimate penological-goal, either retribution or deterrence.

A. Deterrence

Whether capital punishment is a deterrent has been the subject of great debate among both legal scholars and the Supreme Court. Justice Brennan in *Furman v. Georgia,* stated that there is "no verifiable general deterrent effect" to capital punishment. Justice Stewart characterized the lack of discernible deterrent effect by stating:

> We may nevertheless assume safely that there are murderers, such as those who act in passion, for whom the threat of death has little or no deterrent effect. But for many others, the death penalty undoubtedly is a significant deterrent. There are carefully contemplated murders, such as murderers for hire, where the possible penalty of death may well enter into the cold calculus that precedes the decision to act.

Justice Stewart's statement calls into question the general deterrent effect of the death penalty on random passionate acts of violence such as the murder by Heath Wilkins.

Adolescence is marked by the acquisition of formal operational thought. Formal operations permit the young person through an abstract process to make contrary-to-fact propositions and conceptualize their own thoughts, as well as to conceptualize the thoughts of other people. In essence, adolescents are obsessed with thoughts of themselves and the thoughts of others about themselves.

This process often leaves the adolescent confused as to his own thoughts as well as those of others. The situation is further heightened by what he perceives to be other peoples' obsession with his behavior and appearance, as he himself is obsessed.

As a result, adolescent egocentrism causes the youth to have a distorted view of himself and his world. Negative side-effects of this distorted world view include the youth's belief in his own indestructibility, and thus, the inability to appreciate his own destructibility. This adolescent egocentrism results in the direct impairment of judgment and often creates a false sense of power, capable of leading the juvenile to perform outrageous acts of violence.

In general, the juvenile is preoccupied with only himself, his wants, his needs, and his feelings, to the exclusion of others. An egocentristic juvenile generally cannot empathize with a murder victim in the same manner as an adult, not as a result of a particularly damaged mind, but as a manifestation of the natural development of the juvenile thought process. Consequently, children are every bit as capable of committing heinous and inhuman crimes as adults are, but without the fully operational thought process of a normal adult. This lack of adult decision-making capabilities has been clearly recognized by the Supreme Court. The Court has observed that children are generally unable to "make sound judgments concerning major decisions," that childhood is "the period of great instability which the crisis of adolescence produces" and that juveniles "generally are less mature and responsible than adults."

Most social scientists agree that juveniles live only for today and that, as a part of their adolescent egocentrism, death has no relevant meaning in their lives. It is therefore only natural to conclude that the death penalty is no deterrent to the impulsive juvenile offender. A well respected study of sixty subjects involved in murder or attempted murder by juveniles concluded that the death penalty was an inappropriate sanction for children. This conclusion was based on several grounds. First, there is no deterrent effect, since murders by juveniles were random events, and were neither planned nor intended. Second, because of their age, children are more responsive to behavioral change. The problem is generally one of immaturity and the self-fixation of the juvenile. Thus, the death penalty is not a satisfactory response, because the juvenile is more likely to respond to the traditional rehabilitative efforts of the criminal justice system.

The great weight of authority demonstrates that adolescents, particularly in the early to middle teen years, are more vulnerable, more impulsive, and less self-disciplined than adults. Crimes committed by youths are just as harmful to victims as those committed by older persons, but juveniles are deserving of less punishment because adolescents have less capacity to control their conduct and to think in long range terms. Death is not a deterrent to a youth because death is too foreign a concept for them to grasp. Moreover, youth crime is not exclusively the juvenile's fault; offenses by the young also represent a failure on the part of the family, school, church, and social system. All of these institutions share responsibility for the development of the young.

B. Retribution

The second justifiable penological goal supporting the imposition of the death penalty is that of retribution. The question is whether retribution serves a measurable contribution to society as a whole, especially in light of the Court's "evolving standards of decency" test. One scholar in this field has made the following observation: "Even if the execution of an adult for revenge or retribution is constitutionally permissible, this justification lacks its appeal when the object of that righteous vengeance is a child." Society should, therefore, restrict executions to only those who have knowingly and willingly murdered others. Based on contemporary psychological knowledge, it is extremely questionable that adolescents are capable of forming the traditional criminal intent required by law. Knowing the difference between right and wrong is simply not the same as fully understanding the ramifications of one's actions in a cognitive manner.

Beginning with *Lockett v. Ohio* and again in *Eddings v. Oklahoma,* the Court has held that "youth" is an appropriate mitigating factor for imposing a sentence of less than death. Armed with this vital mitigating factor and the knowledge that it is "unrealistic to treat juveniles as if they have fully mature judgment and control," society's retribution goal in executing juveniles makes for a shallow sense of satisfaction. The understanding of experts in the field of sentencing, coupled with the court's characterization of children and the special place in the law reserved for them, leaves open to question the measurable contribution that executing children serves in satisfying societies' demand for revenge. As a society matures and evolves, its need for revenge should lessen, and appropriately, its laws should reflect that progress by limiting the penalties levied on its citizens who are less capable of telling the difference between right and wrong. "A decent society places certain absolute limits on the punishment that it inflicts—no matter how terrible the crime or how great the desire for retribution. And one of those limits is that it does not execute people for crimes committed while they were children."

Justice Scalia's dismissal of any substantive discussion with respect to the justifiable goals of retribution and deterrence leads one to wonder what the execution of Heath Wilkins would indeed accomplish. This is of special concern in light of the facts surrounding Wilkins' life prior to his committing murder and raises many alarming questions. He was raised in a poor socio-economic environment, physically abused by his mother through extensive and long-lasting physical beatings, and introduced to drug use by his uncle at age six. He underwent his first psychiatric treatment at age ten, after attempting to kill his mother and her boyfriend with rat poison. He had attempted suicide at least three times and spent numerous stays in detention homes and state facilities for juveniles. His father was committed to a mental institution in Arkansas and his brother was diagnosed to be suffering from schizophrenia. Plainly, Wilkins' background of obvious mental impairment should heighten concern about executing juveniles, since he was incapable of forming the requisite criminal intent to commit murder.

At Wilkins' competency hearing two psychological reports were presented. Neither of these reports suggested that Wilkins was exceptionally mature for his age. One report concluded that he had normal intellectual and reasoning skills for a sixteen-year-old. The other report found him to have a tenuous and inconsistent capacity to manage and control himself, leaving him subject to impulsive actions. He was intolerant of anxiety, depression, or anger, a factor which interferred with his ability to think clearly. Furthermore, he was vulnerable to sudden infusions of rage which lead to destructive acts. After pleading guilty to all charges against him and presenting no mitigating evidence on his behalf, he informed the court that he preferred the death penalty: "[O]ne I fear, the other I don't." Failing to take any steps to appeal his sentence, Wilkins was again examined and diagnosed as being a "conduct disorder, under-socialized aggressive type" with a borderline personality disorder, and that he had been "exhibiting bizarre behavior, paranoid ideation, and idiosyncratic thinking since 1982."

Heath Wilkins is not a choirboy, and he committed a horrible, vile crime. Yet, no goal is served by allowing his execution; how does the right to execute him further society's evolution towards decency? Heath Wilkins is the damaged product of a poor family life, and a society with too few skills, and still fewer resources. Wilkins' cry for his own death can be read to be a cry for help. The response to his expression of need is that because a few unfortunate juveniles have been executed, or can be executed, that an insufficient national consensus exists in opposition to executing juveniles.

Conclusion

The imposition of the death penalty on juvenile offenders should no longer be permitted for children under the age of eighteen. To continue to do so is most assuredly cruel and unusual punishment. The Court should have made age eighteen the least permissible age that a person may be executed for committing murder, since that is the most common age utilized in determining adulthood. There would be nothing lost by legislatively abolishing imposition of the death penalty for juveniles, since there is so little to be gained otherwise.

Fortunately, *Stanford* is only a plurality decision that invites further review; however, that 5–4 decision may cost Heath Wilkins his life. There are many indications that executing juveniles violates our nation's evolving standards of decency. Many states have disposed of capital punishment entirely, nearly as many refuse to impose it on juveniles, and even among those states which permit the death penalty for juvenile offenders, less than half are actively engaged in executing them. These are the true "objective indicia" that constitute a national consensus, not the narrow view presented by Justice Scalia. Furthermore, the leaders and diplomats of our nation have, by their signatures, committed this country to oppose executing juvenile offenders.

The "objective indicia" standard employed by the Court's analysis must be a national analysis, and not merely a partial evaluation of only those states which permit capital punishment. If it is the responsibility of the Court to arrive at a national consensus, then all statutes and all states must be counted. Furthermore, the laws and practices of other nations should be considered as well, especially those countries with whom we share our common legal heritage.

"Where life itself is what hangs in the balance, a fine precision in the process must be insisted upon." Therefore, Justice Scalia's dismissal of any discussion regarding whether the goals of capital punishment are justifiably served by allowing juvenile offenders to be executed is, at its best, imprecise. At its worst, it is judicial callousness. If law must be made supporting the death penalty for juveniles, then it should be made with the most thorough legal analysis. Perhaps there may be revenge motivating the execution of Heath Wilkins, yet one wonders how our nation can justify executing a young man that it helped create. Wilkins did not come into life as the monster he became, and society must meet head-on its responsibility for who he became. Clearly, as readily apparent from Heath Wilkins' own statement regarding death, the death penalty poses no deterrent effect for him. In fact, one might conclude that in his own tortuous manner he sought death all along. The plain truth, as evidenced by Heath Wilkins' life, is that he needed help. There is no righteous vengeance or deterrent effect in executing him or others like him. Heath Wilkins does not exist alone in our troubled society. There are in fact many other young people who are driven by circumstance or need who also commit senseless crimes. They are in need of our assistance, not our moral anger.

The hallmark of an evolving standard of decency that marks the progress of a maturing society is the change that occurs in that society as it acquires greater knowledge, understanding, and insight to the world around it and those who occupy it. In a word, wisdom marks maturity. As we increase this reservoir of knowledge the adaptation of rehabilitative and deterrent oriented practices should increase, and society's demand for retribution should diminish. As wisdom replaces immaturity, and understanding replaces ignorance, the value society places on preserving life should become reflected in its laws. If we, as a society, pride ourselves as maturing and evolving, then the importance of "youth" should outweigh all other circumstances, and the death penalty no longer should be applicable to children.

Notes

1. ATTORNEY FOR THE DAMNED 86 (A. Weinberg ed. 1957) (This excerpt is drawn from Clarence Darrow's closing argument in *Loeb-Leopold* murder trial).

2. Rouse, *Thompson v. Oklahoma, A Special Place in Society for Juveniles; Does It Include Death Row?* 9 Crim. Just. J. 371, 375 (1986–87). There are three types of waiver mechanisms: the judicial waiver, the legislative waiver, and the prosecutorial waiver. The judicial waiver occurs when a juvenile court judge decides that a juvenile should be tried as an adult. Generally, judges have broad discretion in making this determination. The legislative waiver statutorily excludes certain offenses from the jurisdictions of the juvenile court. If a child is charged with one of these offenses, and is above the statutory age, he is automatically tried as an adult. This form of waiver limits discretion in determining whether the child should appear in adult criminal court. The prosecutorial waiver gives a prosecutor wide discretion in deciding which children should be tried as adults.

3. Justice Scalia and I disagree on the number of states which have the death penalty. He included South Dakota which has a clearly unconstitutional pre-*Furman* statute on the books; furthermore, courts in that state have not sentenced anyone to death in over seventeen years.

4. These states are: California, Colorado, Connecticut, Illinois, Maryland, Nebraska, New Hampshire, New Jersey, New Mexico, Ohio, Oregon and Tennessee.

5. These states are: Georgia, North Carolina and Texas.

6. These states are: Alaska, Iowa, Kansas, Maine, Massachusetts, Michigan, Minnesota, New York, North Dakota, Rhode Island, Vermont, West Virginia and Washington. Plus the District of Columbia.

7. If all 51 jurisdictions are viewed there are at least 31 states which refuse to execute a juvenile, not just the 15 that Justice Scalia considered, supporting the proposition that an evolving standard may exist that runs contrary to the Court's holding.

8. Four examples of cases where the Court has struck down punishments as cruel and unusual, *see* Coker v. Georgia, 433 U.S. 584 (where death penalty for rape of an adult woman was considered cruel and unusual since Georgia was the only state which allowed for death penalty in such cases); and Enmund v. Florida, 458 U.S. 792 (where death penalty for participation in armed robbery when accomplice kills someone was struck down since only eight states permitted capital punishment in such situations).

9. For the purposes of this comment active participation in the execution of juvenile offenders will be defined as those states which presently have juveniles among their death row populations or have executed a juvenile offender within the last 20 years.

10. Streib, *The Eighth Amendment and Capital Punishment of Juveniles,* 34 Clev.St.L.Rev. 363, n. 1 (1986), note 11, at 386, table 4. Subsequent to this publication

several changes have occurred which significantly altered his statistics. *Thompson v. Oklahoma* eliminated all inmates under the age 16, Maryland raised its minimum age to 18, and both North Carolina and Georgia raised their minimum age to 17. Thus, a refiguration of current death row populations which include juveniles shows that Alabama has two, Florida has three, Indiana has one, Kentucky has one, Louisiana has two, Mississippi has two, Missouri has two, Pennsylvania has one. Both South Carolina, which executed James Roach in 1986, and Texas have executed two juveniles in the last ten years. Both Georgia and North Carolina have juveniles on death row; however, those states place their statutory age at 17.

    11. These states are Maryland and New Jersey.

    12. These states are Texas, North Carolina, and Georgia.

    13. These states are: Alabama, Florida, Indiana, Kentucky, Louisiana, Mississippi, Missouri, Oklahoma, and Pennsylvania.

    14. The six states which have changed are Colorado, Tennessee, Oregon, Maryland, and New Jersey: New Hampshire raised its minimum age from 17 to 18.

    15. These countries are Pakistan, Bangladesh, Rwanda, Barbados, and the United States.

    16. For example, China, the [former] U.S.S.R., Libya, and [former] Eastern European communist bloc nations forbid the execution of juvenile offenders.

DISCUSSION QUESTIONS

---

    1. Do you think the percentages of respondents opposing the death penalty in Skovron, Scott, and Cullen's article would have differed if the question asked about the execution of juveniles aged sixteen or seventeen convicted of murder? How would the data look different?

    2. What was the U.S. Supreme Court's reasoning in *Thompson v. Oklahoma*? Do you agree with it? Why or why not?

    3. How does the U.S. Supreme Court's decision in *Stanford v. Kentucky* square with the empirical data presented in the Skovron, Scott, and Cullen article? Do you agree with the *Stanford v. Kentucky* decision? Why or why not?

    4. What evidence does Steven Scott present to argue against the execution of juveniles? Do you agree with his arguments? Why or why not?

SECTION IX

CONCLUSION

The preceding chapters describe a juvenile justice system that is drastically different from the one founded by social reformers at the start of this century. Gone are the informality, the paternalism, and the pretense of benevolence.

For most observers, this transformation is, with a few exceptions, a welcome change. Reformers of all ideological and political persuasions find some satisfaction in the policy changes that promote fairness and equity. Children's rights advocates have found solace in reforms that provide greater procedural protections to juveniles facing a deprivation of liberty. They praise revisions that have reduced the capricious and discriminatory aspects of indeterminate sentencing.

The demise of treatment in favor of accountability and punishment has found few mourners in the conservative ranks. Thus, victims' rights and public protection advocates find comfort in reforms that put more serious offenders behind bars for longer periods of time, whether in a prison or a training school. In fact, it is this curious political coalition of liberal and conservative reformers that enabled the sweeping changes described in this book to take place.

The recent changes chronicled here have profound implications for the continued viability of the juvenile justice system. Given that the procedural safeguards in juvenile court are fundamentally the same as those in criminal court (except for bail and trial), that the espoused goals (justice and public protection) are essentially the same, and that the sanctions meted out are approximately the same as those of the criminal justice system, the central question becomes: Why have a separate juvenile justice system?

Indeed, some scholars have concluded that since the rehabilitative ideal has been dismantled, the juvenile justice system itself should—to a greater or lesser degree—be abolished. Some would simply eliminate juvenile court jurisdiction over a specified subset of delinquent youths based on the offense. Others call for an end to the "two-track system" of justice—one for adults and one for juveniles—at least for serious offenders who should be treated as adults.

Another popular proposal is to lower the age limit of juvenile (and criminal) court jurisdiction. Some policymakers advocate placing all persons sixteen years or older who commit crimes under the jurisdiction of the adult criminal courts, thereby limiting juvenile court to the youngest, and presumably most treatable, offenders.

The ultimate "reform" of the juvenile justice system would simply be to abolish it. The logic behind this drastic proposal is clear. Maintaining two separate systems of justice, one for adults and one for juveniles, is no longer tenable, since the two systems are now so similar, at least in terms of procedural protections. Youth who are alleged to have committed a crime, as defined in the penal code, should be proceeded against in adult criminal court, and if, after being provided with the full panoply of constitutional safeguards, they are found guilty, they should be punished accordingly. The other matters traditionally handled by the juvenile court (e.g., status offenders and dependency) should be dealt with in a family court.

The philosophical underpinnings of the juvenile court have always been problematic. American society has been schizophrenic in its attitudes toward the juvenile offender, as well as toward the juvenile court. Feelings of compassion and humanitarianism for juveniles in trouble (particular those who cause trouble) have been tinged with fear and vengeance. The move to transform the jurisprudence and goals of the juvenile justice system has at least served one useful function—it has brought society's ambivalence into the open for discussion and analysis and has caused a soul-searching evaluation of the nature of the "experiment" launched almost one hundred years ago.

Index

333

DATE DUE

OC 3'95		
NO 30'95		
DE 01 '04		
NO 3'97		
OC 4 '02		
AP 16 '04		
DE 01 '04		

DEMCO 38-297